T0302134

COMPASSION IN DISASTER MANAGEMENT

Should leadership minimise suffering? This book argues yes: offering leaders, especially those in disaster management, a way to improve their ability to lead, serve, and protect others during disasters and crises.

Drawing upon his own experiences as a disaster management specialist as well as high-level interviews with disaster management leaders from the USA, Australia and New Zealand, Crosweller bridges theory and practice to achieve three objectives. Firstly, to establish the political and socio-cultural context in which disaster management leaders find themselves when seeking to protect citizens and minimise their suffering and vulnerability. Secondly, to provide an empirical account of how certain sociocultural influences affect their efficacy as leaders and that of their organisations, when seeking to improve well-being, provide protection, and reduce suffering and vulnerability. Third, to propose a relational leadership framework centred upon an ethic of compassion, and supported by behaviours, characteristics, and practices that can guide leaders when addressing the causes of suffering and vulnerability across the entire disaster management cycle. This framework progressively emerges as the reader navigates their way through each chapter.

An essential text for aspiring and experienced leaders, especially those in the fields of Emergency Medical Service, fire services, law enforcement, and emergency management. It will also appeal to students and researchers in related disciplines.

Mark Crosweller has 40 years of experience providing strategic policy advice on disaster management with local, state and national governments. He is a Distinguished Advisor to the National Security College – Australian National University and Director of Ethical Intelligence Pty Ltd. His ongoing research interest is in relational leadership ethics.

"A powerful and deeply authentic account of what it means to be an ethical and compassionate leader, not only in disaster risk management but in many other professions that experience a seemingly pervasive leadership crisis. This book encourages us to recalibrate our responsibility towards all citizens and denizens of this world who deserve protection, empathy, and dignity. Relational leadership means embracing our own vulnerability as the connective tissue that allows us to navigate these turbulent times with care and humility."

Petra Tschakert, *Professor of Geography and Global Futures, Curtin University*

"More than a textbook, more than a leadership manual, more than a philosophical treatise, this book is practical and profound in equal measure. Mark Crosweller singularly combines insights from a career in disaster management with contemporary scholarship and the insights of a great religious tradition to explain why true leadership is about self-knowledge and service."

Rory Medcalf, *Head of the National Security College, Australian National University*

"This book offers theory, research, and contemplative reflections, building upon Mark's leadership journey. His research and curiosity are driven by a desire to understand what underpins compassionate and relational leadership that clearly places people at the heart of what we do as leaders. Mark recognises the current context, where disaster management is increasingly undertaken in a complex, fast paced environment, where the scale and concurrency of emergencies is increasing, and where the challenges leaders face are dynamic and evolving."

Sarah Stuart-Black, *QSO, Secretary General, New Zealand Red Cross*

COMPASSION IN DISASTER MANAGEMENT

The Essential Ethic of Relational Leadership

Mark Crosweller

Routledge
Taylor & Francis Group

LONDON AND NEW YORK

Designed cover image: © Jorg Greuel / Getty Images

First published 2025
by Routledge
4 Park Square, Milton Park, Abingdon, Oxon, OX14 4RN

and by Routledge
605 Third Avenue, New York, NY 10158

Routledge is an imprint of the Taylor & Francis Group, an informa business

British Library Cataloguing-in-Publication Data
A catalogue record for this book is available from the British Library

ISBN: 978-1-032-81378-3 (hbk)
ISBN: 978-1-032-81377-6 (pbk)
ISBN: 978-1-003-49951-0 (ebk)

DOI: 10.4324/9781003499510

Typeset in Galliard
by KnowledgeWorks Global Ltd.

This book is dedicated to all leaders who commit themselves in myriad ways in a multiplicity of roles to lead, serve and protect others from harm.

CONTENTS

1

INTRODUCTION

A brief career overview

The research for this book has been deeply shaped by my lived experiences, education and personal reflections spanning 40 years in disaster management and national security leadership. At the beginning of this project, I was the Director General of Emergency Management Australia (EMA), having been appointed to that position in December 2012, after a distinguished career in emergency services, commencing as a firefighter in 1985 and achieving the rank of Commissioner in 2009. As Director General of EMA, I had the responsibility for co-ordinating Australia's response to crises, including natural hazard events, and to terrorist and security-related incidents, both domestically and internationally. I was also responsible for briefing Australia's prime minister and the Cabinet of the Australian Government in relation to all aspects of disaster management. In April 2018, I was appointed as the Head of the National Resilience Taskforce for the Australian Government, during which time I led the development of numerous national policies including the National Disaster Risk Reduction Framework.

This career path gave me significant access to disaster management leaders, both domestically (Australia) and internationally, as well as great professional and personal insight into what it meant to be a leader—literally from "the end of the fire hose" to the "office of a prime minister." As such, it positioned me as an "insider" who had access to leaders at the highest political and institutional levels and the ability to shape disaster management policy and strategy at the highest levels of government.

DOI: 10.4324/9781003499510-1

Increasing discomfort

My career path also had its shortcomings. Having spent most of my adult life in disaster management and national security, I was institutionalised by the strategies, policies, politics, and cultures within governments and their agencies. I was also growing increasingly uncomfortable with these same influences. For example, I often expressed my discomfort by saying that "we were trying to make resilient people resilient." In other words, governments were only setting policy and strategy for those citizens and businesses that had agency to meet their "gold standard" demands for resilience.

In my view, there appeared to be a whole cohort of citizens that governments were not accessing or to whose needs they were not responding. I was also increasingly uncomfortable with the invulnerable nature of disaster management leadership and culture that would position itself as being able to cope in all situations but then tended to blame citizens when disasters reached thresholds that were beyond a government or agency's ability to cope. Such insensitivity was also pervading our organisational cultures. We seemed to be becoming desensitised to the impacts that disasters were having on our own people while demanding more and more from them to cope with their effects.

Continuing this thread, following the devastating bushfires in 2011 in the Perth Hills in Western Australia, the Special Inquirer leading the Government's Bushfire Inquiry posed a profound question to the disaster management sector: "While there is no doubt about the priority of the primacy of life, the question arises whether the only measure of success in dealing with a bushfire is by counting the number of lives lost" (Keelty, 2011, p. 136). I was not able to answer the question directly or immediately, but it did set me on a path to try and provide a response.

The greatest measure and the greatest mission

Based on over 30 years of disaster management experience at the time, I formed the view that the greatest measure of success was "the upholding of public trust and confidence" and the greatest mission was "the reduction of human and non-human suffering"—in other words, "to be compassionate." I published several journal articles on these perspectives between 2012 and 2022, as well as undertaking research to provide the epistemological, ontological, and empirical foundation upon which to answer this and other related questions.

During my research, I discovered that many leaders from a range of political, operational and administrative roles and responsibilities from Australia, New Zealand and the United States of America (countries where I had strong professional relationships as Director General of EMA) were very interested in the subject area and willingly offered themselves to be interviewed. I was often deeply moved by the depth and honesty in their answers that clearly demonstrated how much they had suffered in fulfilling their commitments as leaders and how much they cared about the colleagues and citizens they had been asked to lead, serve and protect.

I also became aware of how much invulnerability and insensitivity to the suffering of others had been witnessed by many of these leaders. Their responses have had a deep impact on much of the content of this book. Fortunately, to my great delight, the answers that emerged from their insights and my research have resonated with many leaders in the disaster management sector.

As a practising Buddhist for over 20 years, and someone who has studied Buddhist philosophy intensely for over six years under the instruction of an eminent Buddhist nun, I was and remain increasingly uncomfortable with the level of invulnerability being displayed by leadership and culture. Such invulnerability is leading to further suffering towards the citizens and colleagues we are called upon to lead, serve and protect in our communities and organisations.

The purpose of this book

The purpose of this book is to help leaders improve their ability to lead, serve and protect others during times of disasters and crises. As such, this book aims to achieve the following three objectives:

1 To establish the political and socio-cultural context in which disaster management leaders find themselves when seeking to protect citizens and minimise their suffering and vulnerability.
2 To provide an empirical account of how neoliberal and communitarian influences affect our efficacy as leaders and that of our organisations, when seeking to improve well-being, provide protection and reduce suffering and vulnerability.
3 To propose a relational leadership framework (see Figure 1.1) centred upon an ethic of compassion and supported by behaviours (relatability, commitment, venturousness and accountability), characteristics (trust, integrity, truthfulness and humility), and practices (practical wisdom and mindfulness) that can guide leaders when addressing the causes of suffering and vulnerability across the entire disaster management cycle of prevention, preparedness, response, relief, recovery, reconstruction, risk reduction and resilience. This framework progressively emerges as we navigate our way through Parts 1–4, which are outlined shortly.

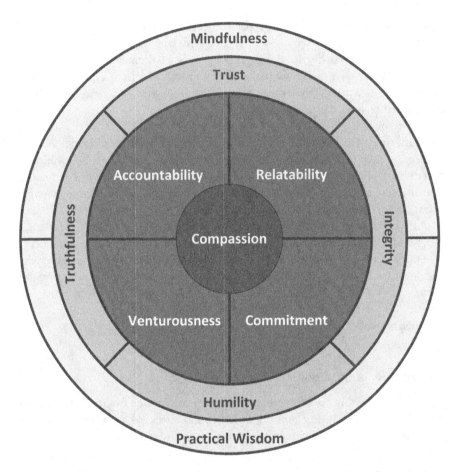

FIGURE 1.1 The relational leadership framework centred on an ethic of compassion.

Why Buddhism?

Readers will notice that I make numerous references to Buddhist philosophy throughout the book, and may rightly ask the question, "why Buddhism?"—especially when there are other "world religions and faiths" such as Christianity, Islam, Judaism and Hinduism (Armstrong, 2011; Dickson, 2004) that could equally help inform the basis of a relational leadership framework. Relatedly, it is important to address a further question, "is Buddhism a religion, a faith, or a moral philosophy?"

Notwithstanding that numerous scholars draw attention to the impossibility of a consistent definition of religion (Hill et al., 1997; Oppy, 2014; Sandberg, 2018), Clarke and Sutherland (1991, p. 7) define religion as a human institution comprising "four important dimensions: the theoretical, including beliefs, myths, and doctrines; the practical, including rites, prayers, and moral codes; the sociological, including churches, leaders, and functionaries; and the experiential, including emotions, visions, and sentiments of all kinds." These dimensions distinguish characteristic objects such as gods or sacred things, as well as goals that include salvation or ultimate good, and functions that provide identity, create meaning and purpose and establish social cohesion (Clarke & Sutherland, 1991).

While faith is often associated with philosophies of religion and their transcendental frameworks, faith is an ontological state, supported by a set of religious or secular beliefs that shape a set of practices. These practices shape patterns of feeling that become embodied and enable us to act or not act in the interests of subjectivities and assemblages, such as appeasing God or another deity, or connecting (or disconnecting) to (or from) community, family, places, values and rituals (Hickey-Moody, 2019).

What differentiates Buddhism?

Such definitions of religion and faith accord with the major world religions of Christianity, Islam, Hinduism, Judaism and Buddhism (Dickson, 2004). However, Buddhism has at least two distinctions that are not found within these other religions and faiths. Firstly, Buddhism does not principally rely upon doctrines of salvation and forms of emotional commitment through systems of faith and belief (Siderits, 2021). Instead, Buddhism distinguishes itself by encouraging the use of our rational faculties along with the combined practices of philosophical reasoning and meditation to address moral questions of "how should I act?," "what should I do?" and "how should I live?" (Gowans, 2015; Keown, 1992). Adherents to Buddhist philosophy are expected to examine the arguments put forwards in the doctrine and determine for themselves whether such claims accord with their understanding of what is true through their intellectual power (Siderits, 2021).

Secondly, Buddhism does not insist that the Four Noble Truths and the Eightfold Path that encapsulate the essence of Buddhist philosophy are the only way to liberation and enlightenment. Instead, revered Buddhist scholars and practitioners such as the Dalai Lama contend that there are many ways in which Buddhist philosophical thought can sit comfortably alongside other religions and secular traditions in the pursuit of answering these moral questions, while at the same time respecting the different tenets of other religions, faiths and traditions (Dalai Lama, 2010, 2012; Keown, 1992).

According to Bhikkhu, the Buddha stated:

[T]he achievement of liberation does not convert one to Buddhism. It is the experience of the person, and not his or her religious identity, which liberates the person into nirvana. One can practice Buddhism without identifying oneself as a Buddhist and still have access to Ultimate Reality. The

Truth is rooted in the pure nature of the mind, which is self-luminous and blissful. In contrast, when the mind is defiled by greed, hatred, and delusion, it gravitates towards suffering and dissatisfaction.

(Bhikkhu, 2000, p. 77)

To quote directly from Buddhist text (Nyanaponika & Bhikkhu, 2010):

One should not be led by report, nor tradition, nor hearsay, nor the authority of the text, nor by logic, nor by philosophical analysis, nor by assumption, nor because it agrees with one's approved theory, nor by possibility, nor by the idea that the speaker is my teacher. [The truth] should be proved through one's own spiritual experience *about* what is good or evil, beneficial or not beneficial, worthy of practice or not worthy of practice.

(Anguttara Nikaya 1, p. 189)

It is for these two reasons that this book draws from Buddhism as a moral philosophy rather than a religion or a faith. A Buddhist-informed relational ethic can assist us as leaders to determine our personal truth through analysis and intellectual power by allowing the philosophical structures of Buddhism to sit alongside and guide, rather than contest, other religious, non-religious and secular traditions. Such an approach opens a space of analytical thought with supportive practices (such as mindfulness) that can assist us in navigating the tensions that often exist between the relational ethics that are most important to our leadership versus the moral/amoral/immoral priorities that may be important to our governments and organisations.

Influence from religion

In developing a relational leadership philosophy, readers will observe that I also reference historical religious figures and religions other than Buddhism. I do this, not to convince you of their doctrinal beliefs, but to honour their contributions to the morality, ethics and rich cultural fabric of our societies that have pervaded for centuries, continue to influence many parts of society today and remain important to many of the leaders I interviewed for my research.

As the British theologian John Bowker writes:

As I put it more than thirty years ago, and long before the invasion of Iraq, the entanglement of religions in virtually all the intransigent problems which confront and threaten us means that we must become more serious in the ways in which we try to understand the power *of* religious belief both for evil and for good... One of the most obvious reasons why we seem to drift from one disastrous ineptitude to another is, ironically, that far too few politicians have read Religious Studies at a University. As a result, they literally do not know what they are talking about on almost any of the major international issues. They simply cannot. It is time we began to educate ourselves, not just in economics, or in politics, or in technology, but also in the dynamics of religious belief and continuity, because whether we like it or not, it is religion which still matters more than anything else to most people alive today.

(Bowker, 2015, pp. 3–4)

As leaders with influence, we do not need to believe in the doctrines of religion, but we do need to understand how significant they have been throughout the course of human history and continue to be in many cultures across the world in shaping moral, ethical, social and political discourse. If we fail to appreciate this (whether we agree with the doctrines or not), then we will fall to an unnecessary ignorance of the human experience.

Influence from philosophers

As well as drawing extensively from Buddhist philosophy, I draw from the early philosophers, such as Socrates, Plato, Aristotle, Confucius and others, some dating back over 3,000 years. I also draw upon enlightenment philosophers (such as Arthur Schopenhauer, Emmanuel Kant and Soren Kierkegaard), contemporary moral philosophers (such as Martha Nussbaum and Alasdair MacIntyre) and feminist philosophers (such as Errin Gilson, Carol Gilligan, Judith Butler and Joan Tronto). Collectively, these and other philosophers have also had a profound impact on the development of cultures and civilisations across the world. They have shaped the way we have lived, worshipped and thought about the big questions that concern all of us.

Although profoundly influential historically and contemporaneously, most of us are not even aware of how much philosophy we have absorbed into our everyday thinking. Thoughts about the nature of the self and our identity, from where and how we derive knowledge, our ethics and morality and how we define the good, the right and the just, how we define beauty and how it both motivates and moves us, how we construct our arguments and how we communicate, are deeply ingrained within us but we are rarely conscious of their presence (Baggani, 2018).

As the French Philosopher Maurice Merleau-Ponty wrote in 1945:

If it were possible to lay bare and unfold all of the presuppositions in what I call my reason or my ideas at each moment, we should always find experiences which have not been made explicit, large-scale contributions from past and present, a whole '*sedimentary history*' which is not only relevant to the genesis of my thought, but which determines its significance.

(Merleau-Ponty, 2002)

Philosophers argue—and my own experiences have taught me—that an awareness of philosophy is fundamental to living a good life, being fulfilled and learning, growing and developing. Philosophy gives us the personal foundation or belief in human and non-human nature, and for living life to the fullest. Through philosophy, we create a system of thought that supports our life-long journey and provides us with the guiding principles to use for action or non-action in the pursuit of our happiness, well-being and flourishing, as well as the happiness, well-being and flourishing of others. Thus, to this extent, we are all philosophers.

According to the British philosopher Bertrand Russell:

> To understand an age or a nation, we must understand its philosophy, and to understand its philosophy, we must ourselves be in some degree philosophers. There is here a reciprocal causation: the circumstances of [people's] lives do much to determine their philosophy, but, conversely, their philosophy does much to determine their circumstances.
>
> *(Russell, 1946, p. 2)*

Influence from research

I also draw extensively from my research and the invaluable insights of 89 leaders that I had the privilege to interview. These leaders came from the USA, New Zealand and Australia. Among them were political leaders, including elected representatives at local/state/national level. There were also operational leaders from uniformed emergency services responsible for preparation and response and administrative leaders responsible for emergency relief and recovery. They either performed their functions at the frontline (directly interfacing with citizens in the delivery of services), at senior institutional levels (indirectly interfacing with citizens but influential in policy development), or as key informants (high-profile leaders with extensive leadership experience). Of the 89 leaders, 61 were men and 28 were women. Collectively, they spanned the entire spectrum of the disaster management cycle—prevention, preparedness, response, relief, recovery, reconstruction, risk reduction and resilience. Without exception, I rate them as extraordinary people doing extraordinary things to assist and protect others while navigating the external limitations of power, wealth and resources, and internal limitations of the human mind—limitations that we all face while trying to make our way in this complex world.

Influence from lived experience

Finally, to be true to one of the premises of this book, I draw from the practical wisdom of my own lived experiences, both professionally and personally. I do so with a great sense of humility, and also as a way of "putting my money where my mouth is"—of demonstrating integrity to my proposition that our lived experiences matter, and the sharing of lived experiences matter even more so.

Questions that help shape a relational leadership philosophy

By bringing these bodies of knowledge together—and using the relational leadership framework centred upon an ethic of compassion (Figure 1.1) as a guide—my aim is to help leaders answer the following questions that can help shape their relational leadership philosophy. Based on my research findings, these are also questions that the people whom we lead and serve will want answered:

- Are we willing and able to relate to the lived experiences of others along with their joys and sorrows? (Chapter 4)
- Are we committed to working with ourselves and others to alleviate suffering and vulnerability wherever possible to be happier, healthier and flourishing? (Chapters 5–7)
- Are we prepared to be venturous with our thoughts, words and actions in this pursuit, and how might we do this? (Chapters 5–7)
- Are we prepared to be accountable for our thoughts, words and actions in this pursuit, and how might we show this? (Chapters 5–7)
- Are we able to identify the ethics that are most important to us in shaping our identities as relational leaders and by which we would like to be known? (Chapters 8–11)
- Are we able to draw from the wisdom of our lived experiences as well as a wisdom that is beyond our own opinions? (Chapter 12)
- Are we clear about what it is we need to be most mindful in our leadership? (Chapter 13)

All these questions are fundamental to relational leadership and deeply philosophical. However, to answer them, we must explore the truth of our ethical premise and the validity of our arguments, draw from our lived experiences, exemplify those ethics most important to us through our thoughts, words and actions and be inspired by others in this pursuit. For it is only then, I argue, that we can claim to be a relational leader.

The structure of this book

Chapter 1 provides an introduction that includes a brief overview of the author's career, the purpose of this book and an outline of the influences that have shaped the manuscript.

The book is then divided into four parts. Part 1 consists of two chapters that set the scene for disaster management leadership. Chapter 2 explores the leadership dilemma in which disaster management leaders find themselves. We begin by providing a guiding conceptual framework to explain the tension between our political and ethical obligations to protect citizens, and the extent to which we are affected by political discourses when providing that protection. The chapter then draws from the literature on critical social theory, political philosophy and resilience theory to describe the confluence of modernity, today's risk society, neoliberalism and governmentality, all of which help shape the disaster management operating environment that we as leaders are asked to navigate.

The chapter then explores the literature from feminist ethics that helps explain why, as leaders, we often feel compelled to deny our own and others' vulnerability while promoting citizen resilience. A heuristic is used to explain this dilemma and to show how we find ourselves in a space of mutual vulnerability with those citizens we are asked to lead, serve and protect.

The chapter concludes by suggesting that this shared space of vulnerability opens new possibilities for how we navigate, manage and ultimately transform from the effects of disasters. It also challenges us to consider that this choice will determine the extent to which otherwise avoidable suffering is either lessened or increased.

Chapter 3 explores the vital role of ethical leadership and decision-making in disaster management. A brief review of ethical leadership in disaster management is presented followed by an analysis of various ethical frameworks that introduce tensions for how ethical standards are determined. The chapter also explores the tension between the law and ethics. The chapter then briefly presents various relational ethics frameworks that can be used to ease these tensions, before concluding by arguing for advancing a relational leadership approach to disaster management as an effective way of contesting the influence of invulnerability identified in Chapter 2.

Part 2 consists of four chapters that address suffering and vulnerability. Chapter 4 explores in some detail our understanding of suffering as a basis of our relationality. The chapter examines western and eastern philosophical perspectives, some of the different ways that suffering is experienced, and how suffering can also be seen as a universal experience through the lens of the First Noble Truth of Buddhist philosophy. The chapter also examines what happens when leaders do not understand suffering.

The chapter concludes by encouraging leaders to become familiar with the ways in which we suffer, rather than choosing to deny, disavow or ignore suffering and further encourages leaders to begin reflecting on how the universally shared notions of suffering can help establish the basis of relationality.

Chapter 5 takes an extensive look at how the social contract for shared responsibility in disaster management addresses responsibility for minimising suffering through the socio-cultural influences of neoliberalism and communitarianism. This is achieved by investigating how either the effectiveness or ineffectiveness of four core elements that capture the relationship between the primary role of governments (governance and leadership), the role of citizens to exercise their resilience (citizen resilience) and the relationship between leaders and citizens (trust) shapes the social contract of shared responsibility. The chapter shows that deficient disaster management governance and leadership, shaped by neoliberalism, biases the expectations for safety and protection towards citizens. It also advocates for the reinstating of a social contract of shared responsibility supported by contested and negotiated policy development that respects citizens' rights and justice.

The chapter concludes by identifying the challenges for disaster management leaders in navigating the tension between individual and social responsibility for the minimisation of suffering. It highlights that, as institutional leaders, we have in our possession to varying degrees the equities of power, wealth and resources. We also have varying degrees of access to senior policy and decision-makers, either directly or indirectly. It argues that by being more conscious of the nature of suffering and its causes, we can help shape policies, decisions and advice in a way that is more aware of and alert to the suffering of others whom we lead, serve and protect.

Chapter 6 begins by recapping our understanding of vulnerability from Chapter 2 as both a positive and negative conception, as well as the potential for leaders to become invulnerable. The influence of institutional habitus is briefly discussed, followed by a brief examination of the effects of vulnerability and invulnerability on organisational culture, as well as a reflection on how leaders can be vulnerable with wisdom.

The chapter concludes by encouraging leaders to expand their understanding of vulnerability from a narrow, negative-only view—often driven by denial, disavowal and ignorance—to a wider view that perceives vulnerability as a universally shared space of affectivity, openness, trust, compassion and community.

Chapter 7 turns its attention to how an invulnerable leadership worldview can render a leader *insensitive* towards the suffering of humans and nonhumans (others); be *insufficient* in our response to alleviate that suffering; be *constrained* by compliance with organisational rules, processes and other factors; and become *defensive* when criticised over inadequate protection and safety of others. The chapter also shows how a relational leadership worldview, premised upon an ethic of compassion, can position disaster management leaders to be *relatable* to the suffering of others; be *committed* to doing something about that suffering using our access to the equities of power, wealth and resources; be *venturous* in that pursuit; and be prepared to be *accountable* for our actions and their outcomes. The chapter demonstrates that, overall, the influence of a relational leadership worldview is dominant, but it is undermined by an insensitivity towards the suffering of others.

The chapter concludes by stressing the importance of bringing greater awareness to how invulnerability increases suffering and vulnerability decreases suffering within our organisational cultures.

Part 3 consists of four chapters that address ethics. Chapter 8 explores how to establish relationality through the ethic of compassion. The chapter begins by defining compassion from numerous eastern and western perspectives. It then explores the ultimate act of compassion—the giving of one's life. It then further explores the tension between the need for compassion and our propensity for blameworthiness of suffering by contrasting the perspectives of Aristotle and the Buddha.

The chapter then reflects on the need for self-compassion and a change of perspective by understanding that (except for involuntary choice) it is often our choices that contribute towards our suffering. The chapter then examines why our ability to show compassion is constrained by the clinical way in which we view citizens as numbers and statistics. It considers how we might move past this constraint by introducing the emotion of affect, moral intuition and narrative. In so doing, it introduces experiential and analytical systems of thought that give rise to the elements of symbolism, sentiment and data to help motivate us towards compassion.

The chapter concludes by encouraging disaster management leaders to be compassionate to self and other in recognition of suffering's universality. It also calls for leaders to be more astute with sentiment, symbolism and data to better understand the suffering of many people.

Chapter 9 turns its attention to political compassion and explores how the negative impacts of compassionate conservatism and neoliberalism can desensitise us to the suffering of those less fortunate. It then examines the complexity of universal compassion and its relationship with love, justice and anger. It also critically analyses the role of anger as a motivator for compassion. Finally, it explores the indigenous concept of Ubuntu as an alternative view of political compassion to contest anger and aggression as evidenced in the liberation of South Africa from the apartheid regime under the leadership of Nelson Mandela.

The chapter concludes by advocating for leaders to be more cognisant of socio-cultural influences that can pull us away from our compassionate dispositions and to be more cognisant of the dangers of anger. It also asks leaders to bracket the question of deservedness of suffering and instead to focus on the causes of suffering and to minimise, manage or negate them wherever possible.

Chapter 10 places the ethic of compassion within the wider context of virtue ethics. The chapter begins by briefly exploring the history of virtue ethics and its focus on character and rightness of action, which leads us to consider the importance of our ethical premise as disaster management leaders. It then discusses the importance of character, the common properties of virtues and the most common virtues across most cultures, doctrines and religions. The chapter then explores one of the key criticisms of virtue ethics from situationists and empirical psychologists that virtue ethics are empirically inadequate. Put simply, we do not act in ways in which we claim we might act when put under pressure in a range of different circumstances. This leads us to examine our human fallibility and moral hypocrisy.

The chapter concludes by stressing that we must become intimately familiar with the virtues that are critical to how we define our moral character and accept that our virtues will need nurturing and development over the course of our lifetime. It also suggests that we must accept that we are all fallible to greater or lesser degrees, that we all suffer from moral hypocrisy and that we would do well to adopt a set of rules to help keep us grounded.

Chapter 11 discusses the Seven Rules of Virtue that can assist us in minimising some of the universal attributes of character (human fallibility and moral hypocrisy) that constrain us. These rules include the need to abandon righteousness, declare our commitment to virtue, be recognised by others for our successes, be wary of virtue signalling, develop moral courage, exemplify our virtues and learn to forgive ourselves and others. The chapter's conclusion urges us to remember the Seven Rules of Virtue as a way of keeping ourselves grounded, relatable and accessible to others.

Part 4 consists of two chapters that consider practices. Chapter 12 examines the practical wisdom of lived experience. The chapter begins by defining practical wisdom from both western and eastern perspectives and examines specifically what Aristotle and the Buddha had to say about it. It then explores how to derive practical wisdom from the meaning and purpose of our lived experiences. This is achieved by reflecting on four brief case studies (informed by existential philosophers and scholars): reflecting upon our youth, looking backwards while living forwards, growing old and leaving legacy. The chapter further explores how to derive practical wisdom from the adversities that we experience in life by briefly examining personal resilience and positive adaptation. It then examines how we might choose to see adversity.

The chapter concludes by reflecting on how we might think about what gifts we brought with us as a child, what life has taught us so far in relation to the development of our virtues, how we have changed as we have grown older and what legacy we wish to leave for others as a way of accessing the practical wisdom of our lived experience. We may also want to think about how we have positively adapted from our experiences of adversity, transformed over time, and how our experiences have redefined our lives towards being more relational, compassionate and virtuous.

Chapter 13 turns its attention to mindfulness, defining it in general terms followed by eastern and western perspectives. It examines how mindfulness can reduce suffering for us and others and briefly discusses the importance of making time for mindfulness by reflecting on the advice of comparative mythologist Joseph Campbell on the need to create a sacred space.

The chapter concludes by emphasising how the cultivation of eastern and western perspectives of mindfulness affords us the opportunity to generate cognitive insights into the nature and causes of suffering in ourselves and others. This includes the social, cultural and political environments in which they exist. It also affords us the opportunity to deepen our cognitive capacity to solve complex problems, make better decisions, develop greater compassion towards others and minimise suffering.

The Conclusion brings together all the various challenges for leaders captured at the end of each chapter. It then provides a summary of insights that can help readers answer the seven questions that help shape a relational leadership philosophy identified in the introduction.

References

Armstrong, K. (2011). *Twelve steps to a compassionate life*. The Random House Group.

Baggani, J. (2018). *How the world thinks: A global history of philosophy*. Granta Books.

Bhikkhu, M. (2000). Buddhism and interfaith dialogue. *Global Dialogue (Nicosia, Cyprus)*, 2(1), 74–81. https://bcu.idm.oclc.org/login?url=https://www.proquest.com/docview/211515979?pq-origsite=primo

Bowker, J. W. (2015). *Why religions matter*. Cambridge University Press.

Clarke, P. B., & Sutherland, S. R. (1991). *The world's religions: The study of religion, traditional and new religions*. Routledge.

Dalai Lama. (2005). *The essence of the heart sutra: The Dalai Lama's heart of wisdom teachings*. In T. Jinpa (Ed.). Simon and Schuster.

Dalai Lama. (2010). *Toward a true kinship of faiths: How the world's religions can come together*. Harmony.

Dalai Lama. (2012). *Beyond religion: Ethics for a whole world*. Rider.

Dickson, J. (2004). *A spectator's guide to world religions: An introduction to the big five*. Blue Bottle Books.

Gowans, C. W. (2015). *Buddhist moral philosophy: An introduction*. Taylor & Francis.

Hickey-Moody, A. (2019). Faith. *Philosophy Today*, 63(4), 927–941. https://doi.org/10.5840/philtoday202019302

Hill, B., Knitter, P. F., & Madges, W. (1997). *Faith, religion & theology: A contemporary introduction*. Twenty-Third Publications.

Keelty, M. (2011). *A shared responsibility—The report of the Perth Hills Bushfire 2011 review*. Government of Western Australia. https://www.wa.gov.au/government/document-collections/perth-hills-bushfire-inquiry

Keown, D. (1992). *The nature of Buddhist ethics*. Palgrave Macmillan.

Merleau-Ponty, M. (2002). *Phenomenology of perception* (2nd ed.). Routledge. (Original work published 1945)

Nyanaponika, T., & Bhikkhu, B. (2010). *Anguttara nikaya: Discourses of the Buddha: An anthology*. Buddhist Publication Society.

Oppy, G. (2014). *Reinventing philosophy of religion: An opinionated introduction*. Palgrave Pivot.

Russell, B. (1946). *History of western philosophy*. George Allen & Unwin.

Sandberg, R. (2018). Clarifying the definition of religion under English law: The need for a universal definition. *Ecclesiastical Law Journal*, 20, 132–157. https://doi.org/10.1017/S0956618X18000030

Siderits, M. (2021). *Buddhism as philosophy*. Hackett Publishing Company.

PART 1
Setting the Scene

2

THE LEADERSHIP DILEMMA

We cannot change the way the world is, but by opening to the world as it is we may discover a shared space of vulnerability between ourselves and those we are called to lead, serve, and protect. In so doing, we open up new possibilities for how we navigate, manage, and ultimately transform from the effects of disasters.

There are numerous interrelated socio-cultural influences that shape how disaster management leaders give advice and make decisions that can significantly affect the extent to which communities strengthen their adaptive capacities and enhance resilience or become vulnerable to the effects of existential threats such as climate change. Relatedly, these influences also contribute towards determining whether or not we as leaders deny our own vulnerability, while at the same time seeking to master the effects of disasters and protect citizens. This tension sits at the heart of disaster management leadership.

In this chapter, to better understand this tension, we begin by briefly highlighting the contemporary existential risk of climate change that we are being asked to lead through and manage, noting that it is constantly evolving, changing and intensifying even as the manuscript for this book was being written. We then journey through a brief history of disaster management to help us understand how it has evolved over time in response to this and other risks. We then explore four interrelated socio-cultural factors that have influenced the evolution of risk and our response to it, as well as how they have shaped our understanding of vulnerability and resilience. Finally, we contemplate the implications of these influences on disaster management leadership.

DOI: 10.4324/9781003499510-3

Disasters influenced by a rapidly changing climate

Australia

In Australia, the 2019–2020 bushfires started in the middle of winter, during the country's hottest and driest year on record. Over the next eight months, 33 people would lose their lives, over 2000 structures would be destroyed, 18 million hectares of vegetated and populated land erased, and billions of animals killed (Binskin et al., 2020). It is estimated that over 450 people lost their lives due to smoke impact (BBC News, 2020b). Between 25 February and 2 March 2022, a series of severe rain and flooding events impacted the east coast of Australia, stretching from the Sunshine Coast in Southeast Queensland to the South Coast of New South Wales. At least 20 people died, over 14,000 homes and businesses were inundated and destroyed, and damages were estimated at $4.3 billion (Fuller & O'Kane, 2022). According to the Insurance Council of Australia, this disaster event was the fourth most expensive disaster in Australia's history behind the 1999 eastern Sydney hailstorm ($5.57 billion), Cyclone Tracey in 1974 ($5.04 billion) and Cyclone Dinah in 1967 ($4.69 billion) (Trajkovich, 2022). Many scientists and researchers linked these tragic events to the effects of the climate emergency (Bureau of Meteorology 2022; Steffen et al., 2019).

USA

In September 2020, parts of California, Oregon, and Washington State in the USA experienced severe to catastrophic wildfires that burned almost 5 million acres of land and killed at least 35 people. Some fires spread with such speed and intensity that, at one point, every 24 hours, an area the size of Washington DC was being burned. During the summer of 2020, five of the six largest blazes in the history of the state of California were recorded. Researchers estimated that hundreds of additional deaths resulted from poor air quality produced by the smoke. Meanwhile, two years earlier, in November 2018, the Camp Fire became the deadliest and most destructive wildfire in California's history. It burned over 150,000 acres, destroyed nearly 19,000 homes, and killed at least 85 people. Many scientists and researchers attributed such events to the climate crisis (Earth.Org, 2022).

Europe

In July 2021, numerous European countries were impacted by severe to catastrophic flooding affecting several river basins across northern and central Europe, including Austria, Belgium, Croatia, Germany, Luxembourg, the Netherlands, Switzerland, and Italy. At least 221 people were reported to have died, including 177 in Germany and 41 in Belgium. The cost of the flooding was estimated to be in the order of €2.55 billion in insured losses, with total damage costs being much higher. In the aftermath, scientists, activists, and reporters highlighted the connection to global trends in extreme weather, especially more frequent heavy rainfall caused by climate change (ABC News, 2021; Cohn & Sims, 2021).

Pakistan

In June 2022, unusual monsoon rains and melting glaciers preceded by a severe heatwave caused the worst floods in Pakistan's history, with over one-third of the country's land mass covered in flood water affecting over 33 million people. Over 1700 people died and damage estimates exceed US$40 billion (Daily Times, 2022; Sarkar, 2022). Average rainfall for the period was exceeded by up to 784% and once again, scientists and reporters attributed the most likely causes to climate change (Clarke et al., 2022).

The IPCC Report

These contemporary disasters are but a small sample of extreme events that have recently occurred across the world with many unprecedented effects and impacts. It is now accepted that, due to the influence of human-caused climate change, similar disasters will continue to occur with increasing intensity and frequency, along with significant increases in loss, damage, other impacts, and the suffering that ensues (Intergovernmental Panel on Climate Change [IPCC], 2014a, 2018; Mechler & Bouwer, 2015).

In its most recent report (AR6), the IPCC (IPCC, 2021, 2022) notes that it is unequivocal that human influence has warmed the atmosphere, ocean and land, and that human-induced climate change is affecting many weather and climate extremes in every region across the planet; much of this change is unprecedented over many centuries to many thousands of years. More recently, evidence of observable changes in extremes such as heatwaves, heavy precipitation, droughts, fire weather, and tropical cyclones has strengthened since 2014 (IPCC, 2021).

The IPCC also reports that between 2011 and 2020, temperatures have exceeded those of the most recent multi-century warm period that occurred around 6500 years ago, and it is virtually certain that hot extremes (including heatwaves) have become more frequent and intense across most land regions since the 1950s. Simultaneously, cold extremes (including cold waves) have become less frequent and less severe, while increases in agricultural and ecological droughts have been observed in some regions due to increased land evapotranspiration (IPCC, 2021).

In addition, the frequency and intensity of heavy precipitation events have increased since the 1950s over most land areas. At the same time, the global proportion of major (Category 3–5) tropical cyclone occurrences has increased over the last four decades, along with associated increases in heavy precipitation. Human influence has also likely increased the chance of compound extreme events since the 1950s, including worldwide increases in the frequency of concurrent heatwaves and droughts, increases in fire weather in some regions of all inhabited continents, and compound flooding in some locations (IPCC, 2021).

The leadership challenge

These changes and their effects, known as the "climate emergency" (Harvey, 2021; Ripple et al., 2019), are unprecedented in the history of human civilisation and threaten the stability and prosperity of all societies. This "climate emergency" poses an enormous challenge for those of us in leadership positions in disaster management. As leaders within (mainly government) organisations, we have ethical, legal and political obligations and responsibilities for providing protection. Also, most of us, to varying degrees, either directly or indirectly play an influential role in advising, formulating, and implementing policies and programs of governments to preserve or improve the well-being of citizens and minimise their suffering from the effects of disasters (Crosweller & Tschakert, 2019, 2021; Okereke et al., 2011).[1] Importantly, these responsibilities are not new, but rather have progressively evolved over time.

A brief history of disaster management

The concept of disaster management finds its roots in the aftermath of World War I when Anglo-Australian, European and American governments began to understand that threats to numerous vulnerable systems deemed vital to collective life (such as electricity, transportation, water, communications and industrial production) were also threats to a nation's economic and social prosperity and therefore required protection (Collier & Lakoff, 2008). Such system-vulnerability thinking began in 1918 with the concept of total war and strategic bombing. Air warfare was developed as a military capability in its own right (separate from Army and Navy capabilities). Air warfare was aimed at destroying vital targets and industrial webs (vulnerable systems) that contributed towards the economic and social vitality and military strength of modern nation-states. The destruction of these systems could effectively end an entire enemy war effort. However, military and civilian strategists also realised that these vulnerable systems existed within their own nation-states and required protection (Collier & Lakoff, 2008).

In the aftermath of World War II, the Cold War between the USA and the Union of Soviet Socialist Republics (USSR) emerged and with it, the possibility of nuclear attack. The USA became increasingly concerned with the

USSR's capacity to attack selected critical targets deemed vital to America's ongoing social and economic prosperity. In response, organisationally dispersed systemic vulnerability mapping was undertaken across the nation to assess the potential impact of a Soviet nuclear attack, and emergency response capabilities (civil defence) were developed to mitigate the vulnerabilities of domestic vital systems to this threat (Collier & Lakoff, 2015).

In the early 1960s, such thinking and the knowledge used to support vulnerability mapping and civil defence capabilities were extended to include a range of additional threats such as natural hazards and pandemics that led to the concept of total preparedness and all-hazards planning (Roberts, 2006). In the 1970s, institutional knowledge of non-deterrable threats such as terrorism, technological failures, natural hazards, and a global oil crisis that threatened America's energy systems prompted broader considerations of critical systems vulnerability and total preparedness beyond the nuclear threats posed by the Soviet Union. Such thinking led to considering these issues as a national security problem in their own right (Collier & Lakoff, 2008).

By the mid-1980s, institutional knowledge extended to understanding that countries such as the USA, the UK and Australia had become cognisant of their economic, technological and psychological dependency on numerous highly complex service networks that contributed towards the daily well-being of citizens. Institutions had also become aware of the fragility, interdependency and interconnectedness of these systems and their potential to threaten national security interests. This led to the development of emergency response and defence mobilisation programs that included improving system resilience and redundancy, undertaking risk analyses to determine resource allocations, conducting scenario exercises, and establishing responsibilities in the event of an emergency (Woolsey et al., 1984).

Such vital systems security has become a central problem for governments in modern western democracies (such as the USA, Australia and New Zealand) that have responsibility for reducing the vulnerability of these systems that are critical to economic and social life, as well as ensuring their ongoing operation in the wake of catastrophes that disrupt them (Collier & Lakoff, 2015). Importantly, national security problems have only increased as we moved into the 21st century.

Emerging threats other than the climate emergency

For example, in 2018, the US Director of National Intelligence, Daniel Coats, reported to a Senate Select Committee that:

> The risk of interstate conflict is higher than any time since the end of the Cold War—all the more alarming because of the growing development and use of weapons of mass destruction by state and nonstate actors. Our

adversaries, as well as the other malign actors, are using cyber and other instruments of power to shape societies and markets, international rules and institutions, and international hotspots to their advantage.

(Garamone, 2018)

On 1 April 2020, the United Nations Secretary General, Antonio Guterres, expressed concern that the global pandemic that would become known as COVID-19 had the potential to create the greatest risk to humanity since World War II (BBC News, 2020a). At the same time, *The Guardian* was reporting that the mental health of as many as 10 million British people, including 1.5 million children, was being affected as a result of the disease, its social consequences and the economic fallout, to the extent that mental health support was warranted in the majority of cases (The Guardian, 2020). According to the World Health Organisation (WHO, 2022), as of December 2022, over 6.5 million people had died and over 620 million people had been infected.

The (USA) Federal Reserve Bank of St. Louis (2021) reported in August 2021 that excess mortality as a result of COVID-19 reached 34% in low-income countries, 14% in middle-income countries, and 10% in high-income countries, indicating that factors such as poverty, under-privilege, and political instability have also played a major role in the suffering of nations. In addition, Gross Domestic Product (GDP) fell by an average of 7.3% across the range of country classifications. As of December 2022, 68.7% of the world's population had received at least one dose of a COVID-19 vaccine, equating to a total of 13.08 billion doses or 2.43 million doses per day. High-income countries have recorded vaccination rates above 70% while the rate sat at approximately 25% for low-income countries (OurWorldInData.org, 2022).

In September 2022, the Australian Cyber Security Centre (ACSC) within the Australian Signals Directorate (ASD) of the Australian Government released its Annual Cyber Threat Report for July 2021–June 2022 (ACSC, 2022). In its report, it noted that the ACSC had received a 13% increase in reported cyber-related crimes totalling over 76,000 reports and equating to one report every seven minutes. It also reported major trends that included an acknowledgement that cyberspace has now become a battleground within the domain of warfare. This is not only in the current Russian–Ukrainian War, but from state actors such as China and Iran, who are actively using cyber warfare to advance state interests as well as undermining the sovereignty of others.

In addition, trends in cybercrime, ransomware attacks, worldwide targeting of critical infrastructure networks, and the rapid exploitation of critical public vulnerabilities became the norm. The Australian Government has taken this rise in threat so seriously that is has increased the budget of the ASD to a $9.9 billion investment over ten years (2022–2032) including employing over 1900 new staff (Slay, 2022).

The central theme running through this genealogy of disaster management has been the "securing of life." Such security has always been geo-historically contingent upon prevailing conditions that are valued and deemed worthy of protection through specific types of state practice. This has included understanding of life as interconnected flows of people, resources, information, and capital sustained by critical infrastructure. In this context, the susceptibility of critical infrastructure to attack renders life as always vulnerable (Grove, 2014), a subject we will explore in more depth throughout this book.

Four socio-cultural influences that have shaped disaster management

From this genealogy of disaster management emerged the development of techniques for vulnerability reduction, resilience, and adaptation through calculated programs of governmental intervention and improvement (Grove, 2014). Along with the development of these techniques, numerous interrelated socio-cultural influences have shaped how disaster management leaders give advice and make decisions that can significantly affect the extent to which communities strengthen their adaptive capacities and enhance resilience or become vulnerable to the effects of existential threats such as climate change. These influences also contribute towards determining whether or not we deny our own vulnerability while at the same time seeking to master the effects of disasters and protect citizens (Crosweller & Tschakert, 2019; Kelman et al., 2016; O'Connell et al., 2018) that results in otherwise avoidable suffering.

This tension sits at the heart of disaster management leadership. To try and understand what might be driving this tension, my colleague, Professor Petra Tschakert, and I proposed a conceptual framework drawing upon the literature of critical social theory, political philosophy, resilience theory and security studies. We theorised that there were four prominent and interrelated socio-cultural influences that pervaded disaster management over the course of its genealogy—modernity, the risk society, neoliberalism, and governmentality—and they have shaped much of the precarious conditions that disaster management leaders are asked to navigate.

We further theorised that these four interrelated factors were influencing the way in which disaster management leaders were perceiving their own and a citizen's vulnerability while promoting so-called resilient subjects. We then suggested that the effect of this double pressure ("squeeze") is that the leader and the citizen are propelled in opposite directions (arrows in Figure 2.1) and that this disjunction denies the opportunity for a relational framing of leadership that could reduce the loss and suffering of both the leader and the citizen (Crosweller & Tschakert, 2019).

To understand this confluence, we begin by examining the four core elements in the conceptual framework (the segments in Figure 2.1) to illustrate

FIGURE 2.1 Conceptual representation of the leadership dilemma. The leadership ("squeeze") emerging at the confluence of modernity, today's risk society, neoliberalism, and the governmentality of risk management (Crosweller & Tschakert, 2019).

how existential risks such as climate change and extreme events are understood in modern societies. This includes the globalised production and uncontrollability of risk, shifting responsibilities from institutions to individual actors, and decreasing levels of trust and confidence by citizens in the expertise and capacity of institutions and their leaders to accurately communicate and effectively manage risk. We then review the growing unease in critical literature on "the governmentality of disaster resilience" that connects late modernity's influence of neoliberalism and governmentality with the problematic expectations imposed upon citizens to be resilient and responsible for their own misfortunes.

Modernity

Modernity is a concept used throughout the social sciences and humanities. It refers to a historical period (17th to late 20th century) associated with a set of norms and practices that includes a division between human society and nature, driven by the promotion of free markets, individualism, and democratic ideals embedded in a constantly moving, anticipated future (Giddens, 1990; Giddens & Pierson, 1998; Latour, 1993). According to American philosopher and Distinguished Professor Marshall Berman, the term "modernity" refers to a body of experience that promises adventure, power, joy, growth, and transformation of ourselves and the world. At the same time, modernity carries the potential to destroy everything we have, know and are, cutting across all boundaries of geography, ethnicity, class, nationality, religion, and ideology—on one hand seeming to unite us, but then paradoxically disuniting us (Berman, 2010).

These modes of life brought into being by modernity have swept society away from all traditional types of social order in quite unprecedented fashion. The transformations involved have emerged more profound than most sorts of change characteristic of prior periods, and while there are continuities between the traditional and the modern, the changes occurring over the past three or four centuries have been so dramatic and so comprehensive in their impact that we get only limited assistance from our knowledge of prior periods of transition in trying to interpret them (Giddens, 1990). It is within this dynamic that disaster management leaders are tasked with managing disasters and reducing harmful effects as part of an interconnected and complex world. A world that is ambiguous, uncertain and in constant flux (Matthewman, 2017).

However, prior to modernity, our experiences of risk and disasters were very different. The work of Anthony Giddens and other sociologists is relevant here, as it explains how the concept of risk has emerged throughout the period of modernity. Specifically, we look at how modernity disrupted local communities and introduced risk in a way never before experienced in our human history. We also explore how expert systems—systems of technical accomplishment and professional expertise—and individuals' trust in them to feel safe emerged and changed throughout modernity. We then briefly explore how the manufactured uncertainty of risks has brought into question those very same expert systems such that they can no longer be relied upon that has resulted in the obligation for safety being placed at the feet of individuals.

Early modernity

During the period generally regarded as *early modernity* (early 17th century through to the mid-20th century), the maelstrom of modern life became shaped by many significant events that changed our images of the universe and our place within it through great discoveries in the physical sciences. Early modernity created the industrialisation of production that transformed scientific knowledge into technology. This transformation resulted in new human environments, as well as the destruction of old ones, increasing the tempo of life, and generating new forms of corporate power and class struggle. It created immense demographic upheavals, severing millions of people from their traditional place of habitat, relocating them far and wide across the world into new societies that experienced rapid and often cataclysmic urban growth (Berman, 2010; Lasch, 1978).

Bureaucratically structured and operated powerful nation-states were created that constantly sought to expand their powers, as well as create mass social movements of peoples. These nation-states challenged the traditional political rulers of other societies while striving to gain control over the lives of their citizens. Dynamic systems of mass communication that enveloped and bound together the most diverse people and societies arose to help facilitate this control. In addition, bearing and driving all of the people and institutions along was, and remains, an ever-expanding and drastically fluctuating capitalist world market that seeks to shape, design, control, and have knowledge of the future (Berman, 2010; Lasch, 1978).

Prior to the age of modernity, societies responded to the challenge of an unknown future by developing knowledge practices (rites, rituals and ceremonies) that attempted to reduce or contain this uncertainty to render the future more manageable. Impending threats or disasters (hazards) such as war, famine and disease were generally considered and accepted as divinely ordained, and setting up a regime of preventive measures against future damage would have appeared futile if not sinful in seeking to oppose the will of God. The dominance of diverse religious thought and influence over most societies and cultures in the pre-modern era, as well as its dominance over the future as pre-ordained but also mysterious, meant that even the individual's prospect of salvation was uncertain. The possible futures in store for them beyond death were unambiguously impressed upon people's minds.

Likewise, the body of rules whose observance or breach were thought to be directly responsible for one's prospects in the afterlife were equally impressed upon them. In this context, religion established the body of knowledge about the future or the unknown and it was only when this knowledge and its fundamental certainties were contested with the rise of modernity that the future became problematic. The idea of risk became bound up with the aspiration to control and particularly to control the future (Beck, 2009b; Giddens, 1999a). The genealogy of disaster management provides useful insight about how institutions responded to risk during this period.

Late modernity

By the latter part of the 20th century, during the period known as *late modernity*, individualism deepened its hold on the western imagination. People became better educated and the technological-information revolutions no longer required unskilled and uneducated work forces. This resulted in the emergence of a highly educated information society which displaced the older manual worker society of the previous period. Instead of a high value on long-term loyalty to the corporate institutions and structures of the 20th century, these new classes of people in the information society reflected on their relationships with these institutions, concluding that they no longer needed to make them the primary focus of their lives to maximise their own individual self-development and biographies. As a result, what began to emerge in the late 20th century was a radical shift in the locus of meaning in western societies. This locus shifted from a culture where meaning and identity were grounded in loyalty to institutions and structures to one grounded in the "Self" or "I" as the primary agent of meaning. Institutions and structures quickly entered a place where their legitimacy was questioned and most loyalty to them was removed as were factors such as meaning, safety and trust (Roxburgh, 2005).

The separation of time and space, disembedding mechanisms, and reflexive modernity

According to sociologist Anthony Giddens (1990), the key difference between pre-modernity and modernity is the *dynamism* of modern social life and its future orientation in which risk inherently arises. Through significant advances in our sciences, technologies and philosophies, we have the opportunity to anticipate, design and control a large part of our futures. However, the ability to anticipate, design and control has also introduced risks into our societies that were not possible prior to modernity. This dynamism can be defined by the following three distinctions: *separation of time and space, disembedding mechanisms*, and *reflexive modernity*.

Separation of time and space

Separation of time and space can be broadly understood as the condition for the creation of social relations across wide spans of time-space, up to and including global systems (Giddens, 1991). At the beginning of human history, the dimension of time itself was understood as something mythic. The only way to make mundane existence meaningful was to integrate it with sacred time through a festive or ritual re-enactment of the events that were presumed to have occurred in primordial time (Gross, 1985). All pre-modern cultures possessed often considerably varied and imprecise modes of the calculation of time. For most of the population, time was always linked with place. No one could tell the time of day (the "when") without connecting it either with the "where" (space and place) or by identified regular natural occurrences. This remained so until the uniformity of time measurement with the invention of the mechanical clock in the late 18th century and its diffusion to almost all members of the population.

When time was connected to the standardisation of calendars, which occurred in the early part of the 20th century, time was "*emptied*" of any local influence (Giddens, 1990).

This "*emptying of time*" was, in a large part, the precondition for the "*emptying of space*": the separation of *space* from *place* where "*space*" was the physical or geographical dimensions of an area and "*place*," or locale, were the physical settings of social activity as situated geographically. In pre-modern societies, space and place largely coincided, since the spatial dimensions of social life were, for most of the population, and in most respects, dominated by localised activities. The effects of modernity increasingly tore space away from place by fostering relations between "absent others": by people, events, and social influences quite distant from these localised activities (Giddens, 1990, 1991).

Finally, with the advent of exploration and charting of the globe and its regions, it was only a matter of time before the world was universally mapped and once it was, "space" was truly emptied of predominantly localised social and cultural influence (Giddens, 1990, 1991). In short, the clock, the calendar, and the map (atlas) connected the world and opened spheres of influence (such as technological, scientific, political, religious and philosophical influences) on individuals and their locales in an unprecedented manner. These influences had never previously been experienced throughout the course of human history.

Disembedding mechanisms: expert systems and symbolic tokens

Following the separation of time and space emerged the process of *disembedding*. Disembedding means the "lifting out" of social relations from local contexts of interaction and then restructuring them across indefinite spans of time and space (Wiley, 2012). The two types of disembedding mechanisms intrinsically involved in the development of modern social institutions are the creation of *symbolic tokens* and *expert systems*. Brought together, both *symbolic tokens* and *expert systems* constitute *abstract systems* (Giddens, 1990).

Symbolic tokens are a means of interchange that can be passed around without regard to specific individuals or groups that handle them at any juncture. Money is a key example. In its developed form, money is defined above all in terms of credit and debt that allows for a wide variety of interchanges between close and distant peoples. Money can be related to time as it is a mode of deferral—it provides the means of connecting credit and liability where the immediate exchange of products and services is impossible (Giddens, 1990; Lea & Webley, 2006).

Expert systems are systems of technical accomplishment or professional expertise that organise large areas of the material and social environments in which we live day to day. The education system is one example. Another example is the banking system. In a disaster management context, it could be state-controlled systems of risk management. These expert systems are disembedding mechanisms because, in common with symbolic tokens, they remove social relations from the immediacies of context—they provide "guarantees" of expectations across time and space without the influence of specific individuals or groups. The notion of an expert system also acknowledges that we as individuals will have no direct knowledge or expertise in these systems, but rather we will need to develop "faith," not so much in other individuals who have designed them (although there will need to be a level of trust in their competence), but rather "faith" in the authenticity of the expert knowledge which they apply—something which we cannot exhaustively check ourselves (Giddens, 1990; Lyng, 2016).

The knowledge of climate and disaster risks held by disaster management organisations and their governments is a key example. For the layperson, trust in expert systems depends neither upon a full initiation into these processes nor upon mastery of the knowledge they yield. Trust is inevitably in part an article of "faith" where there is a pragmatic element in that "faith" based upon the experience that such systems generally work as they are supposed to do (Giddens, 1991). None of this, however, alters the observation that all disembedding mechanisms imply an attitude of trust that, in leadership, becomes the fundamental basis of relationship between the leader and the led (Barnes, 2002).

Reflexive modernity

Inherent in the idea of modernity is a contrast with tradition known as *reflexivity*. There is a fundamental sense in which reflexivity is a defining characteristic of all human condition. We all routinely "keep in touch" with the grounds of what we do as an integral element of doing it—a "reflexive monitoring of action" that is influenced by a constant monitoring of our behaviour and its contexts. Traditionally, we honoured the past and valued its symbols because they contained and perpetuated the experience of past generations, albeit they were both influenced and constrained by religious and cultural dogmas. Our traditions were a means of handling time and space. We inserted certain activities or experiences within our communities of past, present and future. We then sought to structure and stabilise those experiences through our recurrent social practices and dogma as a way of feeling safe and secure. However, our traditions were not entirely static, as they needed to be reinvented by each new generation that inherited their practices, customs and stories. Although our traditions did not so much resist change, they did provide very limited temporal and spatial markers in terms of which change could have any meaningful form that could unsettle us or make us feel unsafe or insecure (Giddens, 1990).

With the advent of modernity, reflexivity takes on a different character known as *reflexive modernity* (Giddens, 1990). The reflexivity of modern life consists of the fact that social practices are now constantly examined and re-formed in the light of incoming technical, scientific, and other information about those very practices, essentially altering their character. Compared with traditional reflexivity, modern reflexivity is deeply unsettling to many. The main reason is that when the claims of reason replace those of tradition, they appear to offer a sense of certitude greater than that provided by traditional practices and dogma.

However, this idea only appears persuasive so long as we do not see that the reflexivity of modernity subverts reason where reason is understood as the gaining of certain knowledge. In other words, when our systems of applied knowledge are subjected to reflexive practices of modernity, that same knowledge is subject to continual change, meaning that we can never be sure that any given element of that knowledge will not be revised through the reflexive process (Giddens, 1990, 1991). As a result, we cannot be certain to have total confidence in our knowledge if the knowledge base itself is being constantly challenged and updated through reflexive thought mixed with new knowledge.

Ontological security

The separation of time and space, the introduction of disembedding mechanisms of abstract systems, and the contingent nature of reflexive knowledge have resulted in most people looking towards experts to give guidance about many aspects of our day-to-day life. We tend to do this even as our doubt about such guidance and expert knowledge increases, as we learn to live with a calculative attitude, and as we continue to choose among various possible courses of action (Lupton, 2013). Importantly, part of our self-identity requires us to consider what risks we might face as a result of coming into contact with and the extent to which we trust this expert knowledge (Giddens, 1991).

Trust is a fundamental means of how we deal psychologically with risks, the absence of which could paralyse our ability to act in our best interests or lead us to feel dread and anxiety. We need to feel secure in who we are in our identities and our sense of self, and some deep forms of uncertainty can threaten this identity security. The reason is that our sense of agency requires a stable cognitive environment—a phenomenon known as *ontological security*. Where we have no idea what to expect, we cannot systematically relate ends to means, and it becomes unclear how to pursue our ends (such as things that contribute towards happiness, well-being, and flourishing). Since ends are essential in shaping our identity (e.g., where we live and what we do for work), in turn, deep uncertainty renders our identity insecure. As a result, we are motivated to create cognitive and behavioural certainty, which we do by establishing routines and placing trust in abstract systems (Mitzen, 2006).

Our reliance on abstract systems allows us to get on with our lives without the need to constantly reflect upon all the risks that could potentially bring us harm. Notwithstanding, there are still "fateful moments" where we are called on to make decisions that are highly consequential for our future. These moments include traumatic events which disrupt our sense of safety by highlighting the risks we are forced to face, as well as questioning our established routines (Giddens, 1991). They emerge when we face low-probability, high-consequence risks over which we have no control (Lupton, 2013) and where we must either trust *abstract systems* or allow fate to take its course.

However, the myriad risks facing many of our western democratic societies have resulted in greater impact in time and space. In so doing, they have significantly altered our identities as individuals, as well as the identities of our organisations and institutions. These risks have also been politicised in everyday life. In addition, the rapid rate of institutional reflexivity of late modernity has resulted in an increasing existential uncertainty, as we can no longer know anything for sure. As a result, our *"ontological security"*—the condition for the creation of a coherent self, capable of coping with the complexity of late modernity—is threatened (Rasborg, 2012).

With the advent of modern communications technology, combined with the dissemination of lay knowledge of modern risk environments through channels such as social media platforms, many of us have become aware of the limits of institutional expertise. In turn, this has created a "public relations" problem that must be faced by "the experts" who seek to sustain lay trust in their expert systems. Research suggests that the more we develop knowledge about risks, the less likely we need to rely upon and trust the advice of experts (Wachinger et al., 2013).

In addition, the limitations of knowledge, which also confront the experts themselves as individual practitioners, also tend to weaken or undermine the trust that we place in their advice. Concerningly, experts often take risks on our "behalf" while either concealing or adjusting the true nature of those risks or, depending on perception and motivation, deciding whether they are risks at all. Even more concerning is the circumstance where the full extent of a particular set of dangers and the risks associated with them are not even realised by the experts. In this case, what is in question is not only the limits of, or the gaps in, expert knowledge, but an inadequacy which compromises the very idea of expertise (Giddens, 1990).

Manufactured uncertainty

This leads us to confront the reality of what Anthony Giddens referred to as *"manufactured uncertainty"*—an existential uncertainty found in societies where traditional certainties are eroded as a consequence of the "end" of tradition and nature. Manufactured uncertainty arises because we cannot fully understand the total effect that science and technology have had on society. While science and technology (by manufacturing outcomes) have solved many problems in society, they have also created further unforeseen problems that remain, as yet, unsolvable. Moreover, we are confronted with "high-consequence risks" that refer to global threats to the environment caused by human intervention in nature, such as holes in the ozone layer and global warming (Giddens, 1994, 1999a).

These manufactured uncertainties are expanding in most dimensions of human life. They are associated with a side of science and technology which the early theorists of industrial society by and large did not foresee and were not experienced at all prior to modernity. The progress of science and technology has created and continues to create as many uncertainties as they dispel—and these uncertainties cannot be "solved" in any simple way by yet further scientific advance (Giddens, 1999a).

Some within the science and technology community, or promoted by media interests, originally laid claim to the establishment of truth—that is, only science could find truth. But progress over time has proven that this is not the case. Scientific discoveries have indeed progressed society in myriad ways that could be claimed as beneficial. But in so doing, science has also produced harm through "unintended consequences," either not foreseen or ignored in the name of scientific progress. Reflexivity in modernity now requires that science investigates science, and this has been driven not by science, but by social factors demanding science is held to account for the "bads" that is has produced, and in this context climate change is an exemplar (Beck, 1992, 2009b).

Manufactured uncertainty also intrudes directly into our personal and social life—it is not confined to more collective settings of risk. In a world where we can no longer simply rely on tradition to establish what to do in a given range of contexts, people have to take a more active and risk-infused orientation to their relationships and involvements (Giddens, 1999a).

The risk society

The *separation of time and space, disembedding, reflexive modernity*, and *manufactured uncertainty* as distinguishing features of early and late modernity are associated with the emergence and embedding of risk throughout contemporary society and in this context, the work of Ulrich Beck and other sociologists is relevant. It explains how risk is an anticipatory process, global in reach, and shaped by knowledge, social definition, and construction that in turn shapes individual perception. It also explains how risk can be amplified or attenuated by relations of power and how, ultimately, it is we as individuals who must shoulder much of the responsibility for risk management.

Risk in general

As a generalisation, all concepts of risk (pre-modernity and modernity) establish the distinction between reality and possibility. If the future is either predetermined (such as in the religious context of fate, predestination, karma, or the will of Allah), or independent of present human activities (such as a bushfire that has no impact on humans or their environment), the term "risk" makes no sense. Therefore, the term "risk" denotes the possibility that an undesirable state of reality (adverse effects) may occur as a result of natural events or human activities sometime in the future. This implies that, as humans, we can and will make causal connections between actions (or events) and their effects, and that undesirable effects can be avoided or mitigated if the causal events or actions are avoided or modified (Krimsky & Golding, 1992).

Risk, then, does not mean disaster or catastrophe, but rather the anticipation of disaster or catastrophe, which exists in a permanent state of virtuality, only becoming "topical" to the extent that it is anticipated. Or put another way, risks are not "real," they are "becoming real." At the moment in which risks become real—for example, in the shape of a natural hazard event—they cease to be risks and become disasters or catastrophes. At this point, their consequences dictate that risk has already moved elsewhere—to the anticipation of further events such as inflation, supply chain interruptions, or the restriction of civil liberties. Risks are always events that are not yet real. Without techniques of visualisation, symbolic forms, or mass media, risks are nothing at all (Beck, 2009b; Beck et al., 2013).

Risk in early modernity

Whilst the term "risk" is generally pertinent to the modern age, its deeper meaning has evolved over time, seeping into European languages in the last 400 years, where there remains a distinct lack of consensus about the etymology of "risk." Some historians believe that the term derives from the Arabic word "*risq*," which refers to the acquisition of wealth and good fortune (Skeat, 1910). Others have claimed that "risk" finds its origins in the Latin word "*risco*" and was first used as a navigational term by sailors entering uncharted waters (Strydom, 2003).

Still others have claimed that these two derivations of risk were soldered together in the 17th century initially through the principle of maritime insurance and then extended into banking, finance and health between the 18th and 20th centuries (Hubbard, 2020). In this context, risk came to relate to the balance between acquisitive opportunities and potential dangers (Wilkinson, 2002). In other words, early modernity was dominated by "external risks"—risks that could somehow be perceived as independent of the actions of the individuals, could be reasonably well calculated, and could be subjected to actuarial tables.

Calculating the risks associated with unemployment and sickness on institutional profitability is but one example (Giddens, 1999b).

Risk in late modernity

However, as also argued by Anthony Giddens (1990) and Giddens and Pierson (1998), for the first time in the course of human history late modernity has created the environment to evolve risk to the global level. This includes radioactivity, which completely evades human perceptive abilities, and toxins and pollutants in the air, the water and foodstuffs, together with the accompanying short and long-term effects on plants, animals and people (Beck, 1992). Climate change and its deleterious effects on humanity, such as mass migration and monumental shifts in food production and water supply, have also become a truly "global risk" (Baldwin, 2017).

Not only are these risks dangerous, but they are also generally not easily perceived or understood. They are complex risks which include patterned processes of increased danger, such as background radiation, ozone depletion, global warming and global dimming. They are permanent rather than temporary, global rather than local, and manufactured by us in practical and ideological ways. Also, while some people are more affected than others, for the distribution and growth of the more traditional risks—such as poverty (due to inequalities such as class, race, gender and social strata positions)—risks of late modernity sooner or later also strike those who produce or profit from them. The ecological disaster that these risks create as future consequences (such as climate change and nuclear radiation) ignore the borders of nations and the rich/poor differentials, threatening not only the health of humans and the environment but also property and profit. Simultaneously, they undermine the order of national jurisdictions, producing new international inequalities, not only between the Third World and the industrial states but also among the industrial states themselves (Beck, 1992).

Hence, these risks are abstract processes in the sense that we cannot necessarily directly see or feel them, but they are material in the sense that they involve the changing form of nature itself or of our societies and their patterns of production and reproduction (Handmer & James, 2007). They are future-oriented and based on *causal interpretations*, and therefore initially only exist in terms of the (scientific or anti-scientific) *knowledge* about them rather than through experience.

Also, while this knowledge shapes us, paradoxically, so does our denial and/or ignorance of it. Therefore, risks can be changed, magnified, dramatised, or minimised within knowledge, and to that extent, they are particularly open to *social definition and construction*. As a result, institutions such as governments, the mass media, and the scientific and legal professions in charge of defining risks become key influencers in determining what is or is not "at risk" or "risky" (Beck, 1992, 2009b).

Risk perception

The social definition and construction of risks can be viewed as a simultaneous process of the experience of potential risks intersecting with the way institutions and individuals perceive them. These perceptions are informed by social systems and value structures which influence the extent in which risks are either amplified or attenuated (Kasperson & Kasperson, 1996). Social amplification and attenuation of risk occurs through information processes, institutional structures, social group behaviour and individual responses. These intensify or weaken signals that individuals and social groups receive. They also filter the multitude of signals regarding the attributes of the risk and their importance (Kasperson & Kasperson, 1996; Kasperson et al., 1988).

This information and filtering are shaped and influenced by scientists, risk management institutions, media, social activists and opinion leaders, personal networks, and public agencies, as well as by us as individuals. It is done through filtering (only processing a fraction of the information coming through), decoding and processing (interpreting). It is also done by attaching values, interacting with social and cultural peers, formulating behavioural intentions, and finally, engaging in individual or group actions to either accept, ignore, tolerate or change the risk (Kasperson et al., 1988).

Often, through the process of amplification and attenuation, our "reality" can be dramatised or minimised, transformed, or simply denied, according to the norms which decide what is known and what is not. Our realities can become the products of struggles and conflicts over definitions of risk within the context of specific relations of definitional power (Beck, 2009a). Put simply, in most cases, it is those who are in power who ultimately decide what is "risky" and what is not.

Risk individualisation

To manage the perception of risk, governments, institutions and organisations develop and implement risk management frameworks. These frameworks generally include the identification, assessment, and prioritisation of risk (defined in ISO 31000 as *the effect of uncertainty on objectives*) followed by co-ordinated and economical application of resources to minimise, monitor, and control the probability and/or impact of unfortunate events (Hubbard, 2020). This process is influenced by the ability to reasonably prevent, mitigate or ameliorate their effects—economically, socially, politically, technologically, legally and environmentally. It is eminently sensible to balance what is reasonably likely to occur, how much society is prepared to invest—money, time, resources, effort—and what level of residual consequence society is prepared to accept, *provided that* residual risks are fully known, understood and negotiated in relation to their potential impacts on what communities and individuals value most.

Unfortunately, as a result of being influenced by modernity's individualisation, most of us tend to produce our own biographies in the absence of cultural traditions and associated forms of knowledge about risk. In so doing, we must choose among risks, conform to our own internalised standards, and be responsible for ourselves while being dependent on conditions outside our control to maintain a sense of safety and identity (Lupton, 2013). This includes a reliance upon the institutional interpretation of risk as well as the expert systems and expertise of institutions tasked with our protection (Esposito, 2008; Foucault, 1991).

In so doing, we must turn to ourselves to cope with the anxiety and insecurity of an unknown future. In these circumstances, our self-choices require intense and continual negotiation with others, and this process also carries and creates new risks (Lupton, 2013). That is to say, our choices may or may not accord with the risk perceptions and, therefore, with risk responses imposed by the state on our behalf. This suggests that notions such as safe and hazardous are consensually determined meanings, not formalised phenomena (Douglas, 1990). Moreover, it glosses over the fact that those in power are typically not accountable from the perspective of those who are affected by the risks, and those who are affected have no real way of participating in the decision-making process (Barnes, 2002; Beck, 2015).[2]

Neoliberalism

A key feature of modernity, its corresponding risk society, and its insistence on individuals taking responsibility for our own risk management is the related socio-cultural influence of neoliberalism. Neoliberalism is a social practice, political approach, and critique of government intervention that advocates that all, or virtually all, economic and social problems have a capitalist market-based solution (Chandler, 2014; Grove, 2017). It also perceives that state failure is typically worse than market failure, suggesting that risk should be transferred away from governments and towards the market wherever and whenever possible (Howard & King, 2004). Neoliberalism extends economic liberalisation policies such as privatisation, fiscal austerity, deregulation, free trade, low taxation, and reductions in government spending to increase the role of the private sector into most aspects of the economy and society (Brassett & Vaughan-Williams, 2015; Dean, 1999).

In this context, the main distinction between market capitalism and Neoliberal capitalism is the role of the market. In market capitalism, the role of the market is limited to the production and distribution of goods and services. In Neoliberal capitalism, the role of the market is extended beyond production and distribution of goods and services to almost all human actions (Harvey, 2005; Williamson, 1990).

From a leadership perspective, liberalism (neoliberalism's precursor) inferred a top-down approach by maintaining obligations upon governments and their institutions to lead in achieving outcomes such as security and safety. Under neoliberalism, at least in theory, leadership moves to a bottom-up approach, imposing obligations upon us as individuals or our communities to lead in areas traditionally led by the same governments and their institutions. The exception is that power, justice and equity remain the prerogative of the state (Chandler, 2014).

This collectively constitutes a paradigm shift away from the post-war liberalism (early modernity), which lasted from 1945 to 1980, towards increasing de-socialisation, privatisation and individualisation of the collective risk management of the state's obligation to facilitate welfare for citizens in need. In late modernity, society is witnessing the emergence of new types of risk management, with neoliberalism influencing the way governments negate their traditional institutional responsibilities for social goods and obligations that address social ills. These include addressing poverty, environmental degradation, unemployment, homelessness, racism, and sexism (Hamman, 2009), as well as affording protection from climate and other disaster risks (Grove, 2017; Lupton, 1999). This shifting of the obligation for citizen safety from public institutions to the functioning of the market (Hamman, 2009; Harvey, 2005) in concert with increased personal responsibility is so pervasive on leadership and culture that neoliberalism "has managed to make itself invisible by becoming common sense" (Sugarman, 2015, p. 103).

Such increased personal responsibility for safety within the context of a functioning market reframes the citizen from a political subject with certain (albeit limited) rights to an economic agent driven by individual optimisation (Collier, 2009; O'Brien et al., 2009). Here, individualism (including self-interest and self-importance), the free market, and the emphasis on economic growth become the higher order principle when governments define social goods (Gregson, 2021; Raco, 2015; Wilson & Swyngedouw, 2015). This type of risk management works through our freedom of choice to transform us into "morally responsible subjects" that embrace competition and entrepreneurship (Read, 2009) and bear the responsibility for our own life planning and reflexive risk management (Brassett & Vaughan-Williams, 2015; Dean, 1999; Kemshall, 2003). Yet, at the same time, it has also triggered institutional voids where leadership responsibilities for the protection of individuals (citizens) remain uncertain (Becker & Kretsch, 2019).

Governmentality

The concept of governmentality, introduced by social theorist and philosopher Michel Foucault (1991), explains how the essential role of responsible citizens that neoliberalism promotes is ensured in disaster risk management. Governmentality proposes a modern approach to social regulation and control where governments view the population as requiring management. This is achieved through the application of technologies, expertise and disciplinary power to monitor and measure populations through mass surveillance. Its purpose is to generate wealth and social welfare and to establish a normal "status" for the population.

As citizens, our desire for safety and security from harm is established by placing faith and trust in a dense assemblage of institutions, knowledge, bodies, and practices (the state) that structure social life around the imperative of self-preservation. The state then requires our compliance with its laws, rules and social norms (controls such as risk management). These controls subsequently negate the qualified life that we seek to preserve by limiting our power for freedom and choice (Campbell, 2006; Esposito, 2011).

Risk management then becomes a strategy which uses regulatory power to manage people while pursuing goals of neoliberalism through government agents (departments and agencies such as emergency services organisations). These agents gather and analyse information about risks and render them calculable and governable (controllable). They then identify those groups or individuals who are susceptible—and therefore amenable to knowledge and interventions—and apply coercive strategies and voluntary compliance to manage risk (Lupton, 1999). The various national and jurisdictional resilience strategies of many western democracies are an exemplar for this type of control.

Further, these agents assert that, as citizens, we should be autonomous, self-regulating individuals who actively control ourselves in our own best interests. We should also maximise our own human capital and seek advice from government institutions and experts to develop skills and knowledge to protect ourselves. In so doing, a failure to protect oneself is seen as a lack of skill, form of irrationality, or moral failure (Gephart et al., 2008; Lupton, 2013).

The neoliberal reconceptualisation of the individual as being responsible for their own risk management and resilience rationalises the radical split between those of us who have a chance of making it in the system and those of us who do not and cannot. The awareness of mutual independence between governments and their citizens is disavowed as social divisions become understood as "failures of individual choice and responsibility" that lead to attitudes of blameworthiness and deservedness for the suffering that ensues (Hamman, 2009).

How these four socio-cultural influences shape vulnerability and resilience

It is in this environment that we, as disaster management leaders, find ourselves squeezed between the logic of modernity, the modern-day risk society, and neoliberal governmentality. Paradoxically, at the same time, we also find ourselves on the side of the citizen being subjected to the influence of these socio-cultural factors.

When events such as fires, floods, heatwaves, pandemics, or other natural or human-caused security related events materialise, citizens have a rightful expectation that disaster management leaders will reduce vulnerability and risk, particularly among the most exposed and disadvantaged populations and sectors. They also expect that governments will offer support in assisting them to strengthen their individual and collective capacities to better prepare for and overcome harmful impacts, loss and suffering.

Yet, what seems straightforward on the surface is complicated by the ways Neoliberal governmentality distorts understandings of vulnerability and resilience by understating one and overstating the other. This distortion occurs in two ways. Firstly, it entails a pervasive denial of vulnerability—not only by governments but also by disaster management leaders—that perpetuates an attitude that vulnerability is self-caused. Secondly, it also promotes an increasingly problematic creation of "resilient agents"—citizens who are expected to take responsibility for their own welfare in all circumstances. Here, we review relevant literature on vulnerability as weakness and strength, influenced to a large extent by insights from feminist philosophy, as well as the critique of making resilient subjects, shaped by advances in security studies and political science.

Vulnerability

Vulnerability, as understood by the authoritative IPCC (IPCC, 2014a), is the propensity or predisposition to be adversely affected that includes the sensitivity or susceptibility to harm, as well as an insufficient capacity to cope or adapt. Together with hazards and exposure, vulnerability shapes the risks for people and systems to be harmed. Vulnerability can also be associated with the disruption of our relationship to the things that we value. These values include people, places, communities, various objects, and systems such as critical services that we rely upon for a sense of continuity and safety.

This particular definition of vulnerability was borne out of the extensive work I undertook with colleagues while leading the National Resilience Taskforce (NRT, 2019). Also, while many processes of risk assessment have tended to focus upon hazards (and this is particularly true for emergency services), such as flooding and fires, other processes focus more on systemic and differential vulnerabilities that pervade all societies (Otto et al., 2017; Ribot, 2014; Wisner et al., 2004), including persistent poverty and intersecting dimensions of inequality, typically along the axes of gender, age, race, class, ethnicity, indigeneity, and disability (Godfrey & Torres, 2016; IPCC, 2014b; Kaijser & Kronsell, 2014; Sultana, 2013).

These definitions, in general terms, support a predominant view of vulnerability that it exists "out there" and therefore can or should be minimised. However, there are alternative readings and definitions of vulnerability that can assist in helping disaster management leaders reshape and recontextualise our relationship with the citizens we seek to protect.

Insights from feminist philosophy

Insights from feminist philosophy allow us to comprehend vulnerability as a pervasive and universal feature of the human condition, experience, and identity, rather than only a property of particular marginalised or disadvantaged groups (Beckett, 2006). Irrespective of who we are or the circumstances in which we find ourselves during the course of our lives, we can be susceptible to harm and suffering without the ability to cope and adapt. Of course, the causes, extent, duration, intensity, frequency, and specific circumstances in which we become vulnerable are highly variable and often driven by the extent to which we are exposed to (unfavourable) biophysical, economic, and social circumstances (Li, 2017). This notwithstanding, because of its universality, we all have ethical obligations towards each other for protection or to prevent, minimise, or manage vulnerability such that we and others are no longer susceptible to harmfulness and suffering (Gilson, 2014; Goodin, 1985a, 1985b). This is particularly important when we hold power and influence over others. However, rather than only seeing vulnerability as something associated with weakness, it can also be viewed as a strength. Its pervasiveness in humans creates the opportunity to experience vulnerability as an openness to being affected both positively within the context of compassion and negatively within the context of weakness, depending upon diverse social situations (Gilson, 2011; McLeod, 2012).

Vulnerability is neither inherently positive nor negative in the form it takes or the way it is experienced. It encompasses conceptions of passivity, affectivity, openness to change, dispossession, and exposure, which make possible other conditions, such as suffering and falling prey to violence and harm. These conceptions can also make possible other conditions, such as falling in love, learning, taking pleasure, and finding comfort in others. Vulnerability provides us with the capacity to imagine, sense, feel and see the suffering of others that includes both humans and non-humans—all of which points to the compassionate dispositions of our humanity. Often, these negative and positive conceptions can occur simultaneously. Therefore, vulnerability not only limits, but it enables the ability of being affected and affecting in return, and, while being common to humanity, it is subjectively experienced individually in different ways, depending upon influencing social and cultural conditions (Gilson, 2011, 2014; McLeod, 2012).

The problem of viewing vulnerability only as weakness

Nevertheless, only viewing vulnerability as weakness is pervasive in disaster management leadership, both in the minds of the leaders and in the risk management systems leaders use to manage risk, and this is deeply problematic for two main reasons. Firstly, equating vulnerability only with risk rather than as the basis of relational autonomy tends to give legitimacy to paternalistic and coercive interventions as advocated by Neoliberal governmentality. These interventions include legislation, regulation, and government policy that, while meant to protect the vulnerable, also perpetuate rather than reduce vulnerability by failing to recognise (and then support) a vulnerable person's ability to exercise their agency (Mackenzie, 2014). Although recognising the relational autonomy of vulnerable others can help to overcome this misplaced binary, it requires democratic societies and their leading decision-makers to comply with the principles of social justice. However, if they fail to do so, they risk perpetuating demands for self-sufficient and independent individuals ("resilient agents") rather than supporting those most disenfranchised (Mackenzie, 2014).

Secondly, the unwillingness to acknowledge individual and collective vulnerability within this wider context results in its transference onto others who are perceived as less fortunate. This allows leaders who deny their own vulnerability to continue the myth of their own autonomy (Tronto, 1998). Of concern is that a denial of vulnerability is not just a lack of knowledge, but an example of what Nancy Tuana (2004) has described as the "epistemology of ignorance," which is actively produced and maintained through social practice, discourse and exercise of power. Feminist philosopher Errin Gilson labels this form of denial "invulnerability" (Gilson, 2011, p. 312).

When we view vulnerability in this way, we genuinely risk severing ourselves from the people that we are called upon to protect, love, and/or be in relationship with, whether that relationship be intimate, transactional, professional, platonic, communal, or familial. Instead, we can devalue or dismiss the agency, knowledge, and resilience of disempowered others who—under more favourable personal, social or economic circumstances—would be capable of exercising their agency while pursuing individual and collective priorities and capacities to achieve genuine happiness, well-being, and flourishing (Applebaum, 2017; Cuomo, 2011). In so doing, we accentuate the leadership dilemma by calling upon citizens to exercise their resilience.

Resilience

The term "resilience" was first introduced in global environmental change literature by C.S. Holling (1973), who defined (ecological) resilience as "determining the persistence of relationships within a system and is a measure of the stability of these systems to absorb changes of state variables, driving variables, and parameters, and still persist" (p. 17). However, as Manyena et al. (2019) highlight in their recent analysis, there have been at least 83 definitions of resilience within the academic literature over the past 50 years, since Holling's definition was first introduced. Some scholars suggest that resilience is often regarded as a "boundary object" encompassing various viewpoints of meaning to differing audiences across different time scales (Brand & Jax, 2007; Frailing et al., 2015). Nonetheless, while it is impossible to give resilience a singular definition, the sharing of obligations to achieve resilience between governments and citizens is common across most definitions, though these obligations are often ambiguous (Lukasiewicz et al., 2017; Singh-Peterson et al., 2015).

Notwithstanding myriad definitions, the sharing of obligations to achieve resilience has been increasingly used by many governments as a strategy that favours individualised adaptive capacity over state responsibility (Garrett, 2015). It also promotes self-reliant, autonomous, and entrepreneurial citizens who should be responsible for their own safety and protection (Evans & Reid, 2013; Hill & Larner, 2017; Joseph, 2016; Taşkale & Sima, 2019). This preferred form of resilience, influenced by neoliberalism, limits direct forms of governance by appealing to citizens to govern themselves, typically through an economy of fear, hope and confidence (Joseph, 2016).

This expectation informs normative assumptions about individual conduct, responsible behaviour, self-reliance, agency, self-efficacy, and adaptive capacity. Governments then exercise these assumptions to design and implement strategies of learning, self-reflexivity, awareness and adaptability regarding crises, disasters, and other insecurities. The citizen's own vulnerability is often downplayed or even denied (promoting invulnerability), coupled with claims that little could be done about the bigger picture, without obligating the state (Bourbeau, 2015; Chandler, 2014; Evans, 2014; Grove, 2014; Joseph, 2016).

In contrast, communitarian approaches to resilience include core features such as collaborative governance and leadership, diverse and innovative economies, sustainable community infrastructure, and cohesive social networks, which give support to an individual's capacity to self-organise and exercise agency (Berkes & Ross, 2013). Communitarian approaches to resilience are recognised as inherently political processes that involve deliberation and negotiation to situate resilience in specific places and across scales with a distinct set of actors and their respective agendas (Harris et al., 2017).

Viewing resilience in this context requires citizen rights to be taken as an object to be made resilient to help address and overcome everyday risk and injustice (Ziervogel et al., 2017). It also requires "communities to have the capacity to engage in genuinely deliberative democratic dialogue to develop contestable alternative agendas and work in ways to meaningfully challenge existing power relations" (MacKinnon & Derrickson, 2013, p. 263) to counteract top-down, state and expert-driven framings of governmental resilience. It can also open up opportunities to contest the leadership dilemma.

Implications for disaster management leadership

The convergence of modernity, the modern risk society, and neoliberal forms of governmentality and their effects on vulnerability and resilience have significant ramifications for disaster management. Firstly, they reshape the ways citizens look up to their leaders in the hope of effective and just decision-making. Secondly, they influence how we, as disaster management leaders, give advice and make decisions that can significantly affect the extent to which communities strengthen their adaptive capacities and enhance resilience, or become vulnerable to the effects of existential risks such as climate change. Thirdly, they also influence the way that we, as disaster management leaders, either deny our own and others' vulnerability while at the same time promoting citizen resilience or seek to relate to others through shared understandings of vulnerability and to whom we have moral obligations to protect.

The following heuristic (Figure 2.2) helps to explain the effects of this convergence in more detail. It exemplifies the inadequacy of the current leadership space to effectively treat risk with increasing intensity and consequences of events to minimise harmful outcomes, including suffering and loss. While the more recent disasters cited in the beginning of this chapter provide fertile ground for demonstrating these inadequacies, in the following chapters I will make specific reference to three specific catastrophic disasters influenced by climate change that are also represented by this heuristic: the 2005 Hurricane Katrina in the USA, the 2009 Victorian Bushfires in Australia, and the 2011 Queensland Floods, also in Australia.

The heuristic draws together insights from the aforementioned convergence, as well as the insights from leaders within the Australian Emergency Management Sector (the Sector) (Australian Institute of Disaster Resilience, 2014) and their experiences over the last ten years with numerous severe to catastrophic natural hazards influenced by climate change. It suggests as the intensities of climate-influenced natural hazards increase, both potential and actual consequences increase. Potential consequences are those that would occur if risk treatments were not present, whereas actual consequences are those that still occur despite the presence of risk treatments. At the same time, leadership's effectiveness at reducing or preventing these consequences through risk treatments reaches a limit. Beyond this point, risk treatments remain constrained and begin to decline, while the consequences, along with resultant loss and suffering, rise substantially.

The thresholds depicted in the heuristic are illustrative and have been derived from the anecdotes, observations, experiences, and insights gained by Australia's Fire and Emergency Services Commissioners, Chief Officers, and other senior emergency management personnel (Crosweller, 2016) through official fora from post-events to formal inquiry findings (Teague et al., 2010). They have also been derived from future projections of extreme events as a

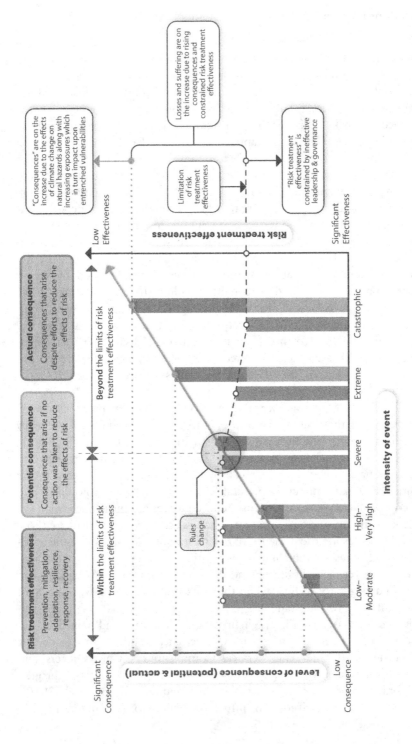

FIGURE 2.2 The relationship between consequence, intensity, and the limitation of risk treatment effectiveness. The result closes down spaces for effective leadership and decision-making (Crosweller & Tschakert, 2019).

result of climate change.[3] Although based on the Australian context using climate change as an example, these thresholds are applicable to various other settings. These include disasters such as the COVID-19 pandemic, and the potential for disasters arising from other potential existential risks, such as those that could be caused by the Ukraine–Russian War (e.g., the potential for nuclear warfare and radiation fallout).

Within the limits of risk treatment effectiveness

The section denoted in the heuristic as "within the limits of risk treatment effectiveness" indicates that the Sector has developed substantial capabilities to mitigate the negative impacts of hazards and threats up to *severe* intensity. These capabilities would include things like fire appliances, helicopters, flood boats and the like, but also legislation, policy, construction standards, various forms of knowledge and intelligence, and so forth. It is within this section of low to severe-intensity events that the Sector often claims success (Eburn & Dovers, 2014). However, damages and losses occur even though risk treatment effectiveness surpasses both potential and actual consequences at *low/moderate* intensity. This is due, in part, to unknown unknowns—circumstances that cannot be foreshadowed and are sometimes referred to as "Black Swan" events (Taleb, 2010). It is also due to entrenched inequalities and uneven vulnerabilities within society being exposed to low-intensity hazard events, producing unacceptable consequences.

For example, in Australia, 66% of all insurable losses for riverine flooding occur during 1:20 return-period events where 58,000 properties are exposed (minor flooding of low/moderate intensity) per annum. In contrast, catastrophic level floods only account for 5% of insurable losses where 280,000 properties are exposed (Andrews et al., 2008). This suggests many people are exposed to risk by living in high-risk areas prone to regular flooding. For those individuals exposed to minor flooding and who experience various dimensions of vulnerability on a daily basis, loss and suffering that could otherwise be largely avoided will occur and trust will be eroded. In contrast, individuals who are distinctly better off will continue to rely on well-established knowledge and capabilities within the *Low* to *Very High* intensities. This reliance establishes a reasonable basis for their individual ontological security and largely upholds trust.

Beyond the limits of risk treatment effectiveness

While the situation appears to be largely unproblematic within the limits of risk treatment effectiveness, the situation is dramatically different for "beyond risk treatment effectiveness." In these circumstances, the Sector's capability to effectively treat risk is far exceeded by the impact of a *Severe* to *Catastrophic* event and its effectiveness rapidly declines in contrast to less intense but more frequent events (DOTARS, 2004). At the junction between "within" and "beyond" risk treatment effectiveness, a critical threshold is crossed and "the rules change." Here, the intensity of the event and its consequences surpass not only the maximum risk treatment effectiveness but also the capacity of even the most ardent "resilient subject." Worse, trust between citizens and governments is breached, the ontological security of the citizen is severely compromised, and substantial loss and suffering occurs across all tiers of society.

Importantly, the illusion of "invulnerable" leadership and governance perpetuated by modernity—the modern-day risk society and Neoliberal governmentality—is shattered. Instead, leadership also becomes vulnerable and experiences loss and suffering, not only in the form of material value but also in reputation and credibility. This compounded challenge of a vulnerable citizen in concert with vulnerable leadership and governance accentuates the pressure on the ethics of disaster management leadership and is at the heart of the leadership dilemma. Yet, conventional approaches to lead through such crises based upon previous experience become increasingly inadequate (Eburn & Dovers, 2015). The distinctive features of the two types of operating environment (within and beyond the limits of risk treatment effectiveness) are summarised in Table 2.1.

TABLE 2.1 Distinct features of the two types of operating environment in risk treatment effectiveness.

Within the limits of risk treatment effectiveness	*Beyond the limits of risk treatment effectiveness*
✓ Relatively high frequency but low consequence events	✓ Rare frequency but severe/extreme consequence events forecast to increase in frequency and intensity
✓ Relatively predictable, known, frequent and trustworthy	✓ Highly unpredictable, virtually unknown, and generationally unprecedented
✓ Scientific and industry-based knowledge and skills are well-equipped to manage causes and effects	✓ Scientific and industry-based knowledge is limited about the more complex causes and effects
✓ Most industry personnel have experienced at least one such event	✓ Most industry personnel have never experienced such an event
✓ Effects are fairly evident and foreseeable with limited, if any, downstream consequences for those who have been afforded risk treatments	✓ Extreme consequences occur, particularly downstream, that may not be evident at the lower scale and appear very difficult to foresee
✓ Effects do not impinge upon the values of individuals or communities that have been afforded appropriate risk treatments	✓ Consequences have a profound effect on society's values system. No effective compensation for the loss of highly valued material and non-material phenomena because they are incompatible with any possible substitutes

Source: Adapted from Crosweller and Tschakert (2019).

The challenge for leaders

The shared space of vulnerability between disaster management leaders and those we are called upon to lead, serve and protect opens up new possibilities for how we navigate, manage, and ultimately transform from the effects of disasters. When we hit the limits of our collective ability to treat risk, when our individual and collective capacity for resilience is exceeded, and when the capacity of our governments to protect its citizens is no longer effective, we are left with a stark choice—we can either seek to blame others (including citizens) and/or become defensive, or we can come together in the spirit of relationality and forge a better world for all.

This choice will be largely shaped either by the extent in which we deny, disavow, or ignore our own vulnerability and that of others, or, alternatively, by the extent to which we understand and accept our shared vulnerability and seek to execute our moral duty to prevent, minimise and manage it collectively. This choice will also determine the extent to which otherwise avoidable suffering is either lessened or increased.

However, before we make this choice, we need to gain a greater appreciation of the ethical challenges that we will face and how those ethical challenges will guide us towards understanding relational leadership ethics.

Notes

1 Providing protection, preserving or improving well-being, and reducing suffering accords with popular expectations of citizens and communities (e.g., see Boin & D'Hart, 2003), as well as with disaster management leaders (e.g., see Caro, 2016a, 2016b). These expectations were also derived from the author's professional experience over 38 years in disaster management.
2 The distance between the decision-maker and the citizen also creates new ways of seeing citizens as subjects of responsibility, autonomy, and choice through perceptions of freedom. This has the potential to all too easily transfer responsibility and accountability for risk to citizens along with notions of blame when risks manifest as consequences (Butler & Pidgeon, 2011; Kuhlicke, et al., 2016). Similarly, senior decision-makers may participate in risk-averse and blame avoidance behaviour in order to protect reputation and in so doing, transfer blame to others (Rickards et al., 2014).
3 Increased frequency and intensity of flood damage to settlements and infrastructure due to the atmosphere's ability to hold more water (Whetton et al., 2015; IPCC 2014); an increase in the number of days of extreme to catastrophic fire weather by 15–65% relative to 1990 and by 100–300% by 2050, coinciding with a lengthening of the fire season into spring and autumn (National Climate Change Adaptation Research Facility (NCCARF), 2016); a greater frequency and intensity of droughts (IPCC, 2014a); and increasing intensity of cyclones (with a decreasing frequency) and the ability to track further south by 2100 with increasing wave heights, storm surge, and rainfall increasing flooding and overland flow (NCCARF, 2016). Australia is also likely to see geographical shifts in the distribution of natural hazard events, resulting in communities experiencing disasters not previously experienced, and a change in catchment hydrology resulting in a change in the severity and frequency of riverine flooding risks across the country (Deloitte, 2016).

References

ABC News. (2021, July 17). Death toll from catastrophic floods in Germany and Belgium exceeds 150. *ABC News*. Retrieved September 29, 2023, from https://www.abc.net.au/news/2021-07-17/germany-belgium-flooding-death-toll-exceeds-150/100302046

Applebaum, B. (2017). Comforting discomfort as complicity: White fragility and the pursuit of invulnerability. *Hypatia, 32*(4), 86–875. https://doi.org/10.1111/hypa.12352

Andrews, T., Billen, G., Kim, H., Lui, A., Pollack, C., Simpson, L., & Whittle, D. (2008, 9–12 November 2008). *The Insurance of Flood Risks*. Paper presented at the Institute of Actuaries of Australia: 16th General Insurance Seminar, Coolum, Australia.

Australian Cyber Security Centre. (2022). *Annual cyber threat report: July 2021– June 2022*. Australian Signals Directorate, Australian Government. https://www.cyber.gov.au/about-us/reports-and-statistics/acsc-annual-cyber-threat-report-july-2021-june-2022

Australian Institute for Disaster Resilience. (2014). *Australian emergency management arrangements*. Australian Government Attorney-General's Department. https://knowledge.aidr.org.au/resources/handbook-australian-emergency-management-arrangements

Baldwin, A. (2017). *Climate change, migration, and the crisis of humanism*. Wiley & Sons, Inc.

Barnes, P. H. (2002). Approaches to community safety: Risk perception and social meaning. *The Australian Journal of Emergency Management, 17*(1), 15–23.

BBC News. (2020a, April 1). Coronavirus: Greatest test since World War Two, says UN chief. *BBC News*. https://www.bbc.com/news/world-52114829

BBC News (2020b, May 26). Australia bushfires: Hundreds of deaths linked to smoke, inquiry hears. *BBC News*. https://www.bbc.com/news/world-australia-52804348

Beck, U. (1992). *Risk society: Towards a new modernity*. Sage Publications.

Beck, U. (2009a). *World at risk*. Polity Press.

Beck, U. (2009b). World at risk society and manufactured uncertainties. *Iris. European Journal of Philosophy and Public Debate, 1*(2), 291–299. https://doi.org/10.1400/181900

Beck, U. (2015). Emancipatory catastrophism: What does it mean to climate change and risk society? *Current Sociology, 63*(1), 75–88. https://doi.org/10.1177/0011392114559951

Beck, U., Blok, A., Tyfield, D., & Zhang, J. Y. (2013). Cosmopolitan communities of climate risk: Conceptual and empirical suggestions for a new research agenda. *Global Networks, 13*(1), 1–21. https://doi.org/10.1111/glob.12001

Becker, A., & Kretsch, E. (2019). The leadership void for climate adaptation planning: Case study of the port of providence (Rhode Island, United States). *Frontiers in Earth Science, 7*(29), 1–13. https://doi.org/10.3389/feart.2019.00029

Beckett, A. E. (2006). *Citizenship and vulnerability: Disability and issues of social engagement*. Palgrave Macmillan.

Berkes, F., & Ross, H. (2013). Community resilience: Toward an integrated approach. *Society & Natural Resources, 26*(1), 5–20. https://doi.org/10.1080/08941920.2012.736605

Berman, M. (2010). *All that is solid melts into air: The experience of modernity*. Verso.

Binskin, M., Bennett, A., & Mcintosh, A. (2020). *Royal commission into national natural disaster arrangements report*. The Royal Commission into National Natural Disaster Arrangements. https://naturaldisaster.royalcommission.gov.au/publications/royal-commission-national-natural-disaster-arrangements-report

Bureau of Meteorology. (2022, May 25). *Special climate statement 76—Extreme rainfall and flooding in south-eastern Queensland and eastern New South Wales* [Media Release]. https://media.bom.gov.au/releases/1014/special-climate-statement-76-extreme-rainfall-and-flooding-in-south-east-queensland-and-eastern-new-south-wales-february-march-2022/

Boin, A., & T'Hart, P. (2003). Public leadership in times of crisis: Mission impossible? *Public Administration Review, 63*(5), 544–553. https://doi.org/10.1111/1540-6210.00318

Bourbeau, P. (2015). Resilience and international politics: Premises, debates, agenda. *International Studies Review, 17*(3), 374–395. https://doi.org/10.1111/misr.12226

Brand, F. S., & Jax, K. (2007). Focusing the meaning(s) of resilience: Resilience as a descriptive concept and a boundary object. *Ecology and Society, 12*(1), 23. https://doi.org/10.5751/ES-02029-120123

Brassett, J., & Vaughan-Williams, N. (2015). Security and the performative politics of resilience: Critical infrastructure protection and humanitarian emergency preparedness. *Security Dialogue, 46*(1), 32–50. https://journals.sagepub.com/doi/10.1177/0967010614555943

Butler, C., & Pidgeon, N. (2011). From 'flood defence' to 'flood risk management': Exploring governance, responsibility, and blame. *Environment and Planning C: Politics and Space, 29*(3), 533–547. https://doi.org/10.1068/c09181j

Campbell, T. (2006). Bios, immunity, life: The thought of Roberto Esposito. *Diacritics, 36*(2), 2–22. https://doi.org/10.1353/dia.2008.0009

Caro, D. H. (2016a). The nexus of transformational leadership of emergency services systems: Beyond the Wu-Shi-Ren (WSR)-Li paradigm. *International Journal of Emergency Services, 5*(1), 18–33. https://doi.org/10.1108/IJES-11-2015-0024

Caro, D. H. (2016b). Towards transformational leadership: The nexus of emergency management systems in Canada. *International Journal of Emergency Management, 12*(2), 113–135. http://dx.doi.org/10.20381/ruor-870

Chandler, D. (2014). Beyond neoliberalism: Resilience, the new art of governing complexity. *Resilience: International Policies, Practices and Discourses, 2*(1), 47–63. https://doi.org/10.1080/21693293.2013.878544

Clarke, B., Otto, F., & Harrington, L. (2022, September 3). Pakistan floods: What role did climate change play? *The Conversation.* https://theconversation.com/pakistan-floods-what-role-did-climate-change-play-189833

Cohn, C., & Sims, T. (2021, July 20). *Berenberg sees $2-3 bln reinsurance losses from European floods, overall losses higher.* Reuters. Retrieved October 7, 2023, from https://www.reuters.com/business/environment/berenberg-sees-2-3-bln-reinsurance-losses-european-floods-2021-07-19

Collier, S. J. (2009). Topologies of power: Foucault's analysis of political government beyond 'governmentality'. *Theory, Culture & Society, 26*(6), 78–108. https://doi.org/10.1177/0263276409347694

Collier, S. J., & Lakoff, A. (Eds.). (2008). *The vulnerability of vital systems: How "critical infrastructure" became a security problem.* Routledge.

Collier, S. J., & Lakoff, A. (2015). Vital systems security: Reflexive biopolitics and the government of emergency. *Theory, Culture & Society, 32*(2), 19–51. https://doi.org/10.1177/0263276413510050

Crosweller, M. (2016). Thinking differently, leading differently: Lessons from the Canberra fires, 2003. In S. Ellis & K. McCarter (Eds.), *Lessons learnt from emergency responses.* CSIRO Publishing.

Crosweller, M., & Tschakert, P. (2019). Climate change and disasters: The ethics of leadership. *WIREs Climate Change, 11*(2), 1–18. https://doi.org/10.1002/wcc.624

Crosweller, M., & Tschakert, P. (2021). Disaster management and the need for a reinstated social contract of shared responsibility, *International Journal of Disaster Risk Reduction, 63*, 1–13, https://doi.org/10.1016/j.ijdrr.2021.102440

Cuomo, C. J. (2011). Climate change, vulnerability, and responsibility. *Hypatia*, 26(4), 690–714. https://doi.org/10.1111/j.1527-2001.2011.01220.x

Daily Times (2022, September 18). Flood death toll reaches 1,545. *Daily Times.* https://dailytimes.com.pk/998913/flood-death-toll-reaches-1545/

Dean, M. (1999). *Governmentality: Power and rule in modern society* (2nd ed.). Sage Publications.

Deloitte Australia. (2016). *The economic cost of the social impact of disasters.* https://www.preventionweb.net/publication/economic-cost-social-impact-natural-disasters

Douglas, M. (1990). Risk as a forensic resource. *Daedalus*, 119(4), 1–16. https://www.amacad.org/publication/risk-forensic-resource

DOTARS. (2004). *Natural disasters in Australia: Reforming mitigation, relief and recovery arrangements.* Commonwealth of Australia.

Earth.Org. (2022, September 15). *Largest wildfires in US history.* Retrieved October 3, 2023, from https://earth.org/worst-wildfires-in-us-history/#

Eburn, M., & Dovers, S. (2014). How chief officers view success in fire policy and management. *Australian Journal of Emergency Management*, 29(3), 16–21.

Eburn, M., & Dovers, S. (2015). Learning lessons from disasters: Alternatives to royal commissions and other quasi-judicial inquiries. *Australian Journal of Public Administration*, 74(4), 495–508. https://doi.org/10.1111/1467-8500.12115

Esposito, R. (2008). *Bíos: Biopolitics and philosophy.* University of Minnesota Press.

Esposito, R., (2011). *Immunitas: The protection and negations of life* (Z. Hanafi, Trans.). Polity Press.

Evans, B. (2014). *Resilient life: The art of living dangerously* (1st ed. ed.). Polity Press.

Evans, B., & Reid, J. (2013). Dangerously exposed: The life and death of the resilient subject. *Resilience: International Policies, Practices, and Discourses*, 1(2), 83–98. https://doi.org/10.1080/21693293.2013.770703

Federal Reserve Bank of St. Louis. (2021). *COVID-19's economic impact around the world.* https://www.stlouisfed.org/publications/regional-economist/third-quarter-2021/covid19s-economic-impact-world

Foucault, M. (1991). *Discipline and punish: The birth of the prison.* Penguin Books.

Frailing, K., Harper, D. W., & Tierney, K. (2015). Resilience and the neoliberal project. *American Behavioral Scientist*, 59(10), 1327–1342. https://doi.org/10.1177/0002764215591187

Fuller, M., & O'Kane, M. (2022). *2022 Flood inquiry—Volume one: Summary report. NSW Government.* https://www.nsw.gov.au/sites/default/files/noindex/2022-08/VOLUME_ONE_Summary.pdf

Garamone, J. (2018, February 13). Cyber tops list of threats to U.S., Director of Intelligence says. *DOD News.* Retrieved October 4, 2023, from https://www.defense.gov/News/News-Stories/Article/Article/1440838/cyber-tops-list-of-threats-to-us-director-of-national-intelligence-says/

Garrett, P. M. (2015). Questioning tales of 'ordinary magic': 'resilience' and neoliberal reasoning. *British Journal of Social Work*, 46(7), 1909–1925. https://doi.org/10.1093/bjsw/bcv017

Gephart, R. P., Van Maanen, J., & Oberlechner, T. (2008). Organizations and risk in late modernity. *Organization Studies*, 30(2–3), 141–155. https://doi.org/10.1177/0170840608101474

Giddens, A. (1990). *The consequences of modernity.* Polity Press.

Giddens, A. (1991). *Modernity and self-identity: Self and society in the late modern age.* Polity Press.

Giddens, A. (1994). *Beyond left and right: The future of radical politics.* Polity Press.

Giddens, A. (1999a). Risk and responsibility. *The Modern Law Review*, 62(1), 1–10. https://doi.org/10.1111/1468-2230.00188

Giddens, A. (1999b). *Runaway world: How globalization is reshaping our lives* (1st ed.). Routledge.

Giddens, A., & Pierson, C. (1998). *Conversations with Anthony Giddens: Making sense of modernity*. Stanford University Press.

Gilson, E. (2011). Vulnerability, ignorance, and oppression. *Hypatia, 26*(2), 308–322. https://doi.org/10.1111/j.1527-2001.2010.01158.x

Gilson, E. C. (2014). *The ethics of vulnerability: A feminist analysis of social life and practice*. Routledge. https://doi.org/10.4324/9780203078136

Godfrey, P., & Torres, D. (Eds.). (2016). *Systemic crises of global climate change: Intersections of race, class and gender* (1st ed.). Routledge.

Goodin, R. E. (1985a). *Protecting the vulnerable: A re-analysis of our social responsibilities*. The University of Chicago Press.

Goodin, R. E. (1985). Vulnerabilities and responsibilities: An ethical defense of the welfare state. *The American Political Science Review, 79*(3), 775–787. https://doi.org/10.2307/1956843

Gregson, J. (2021). The consequences of liberal modernity: Explaining and resisting neoliberalism through Alasdair MacIntyre, *Contemporary Political Theory, 20*, 591–613. https://doi.org/10.1057/s41296-020-00434-0

Gross, D. (1985). Temporality and the modern state. *Theory and Society, 14*(1), 53–82. https://doi.org/10.1007/bf00160928

Grove, K. (2014). Agency, affect, and the immunological politics of disaster resilience. *Environmental and Planning D Society and Space, 32*(2), 240–256. https://doi.org/10.1068/d4813

Grove, K. (2017). Disaster biopolitics and the crisis economy. In J. Lawrence & S.M. Wiebe (Eds.), *Biopolitical disaster* (p. 3046). https://doi.org/10.4324/9781315620213-4

Guardian, T. (2020). Australian bushfire smoke affecting South America, UN reports. *The Guardian*. https://www.theguardian.com/australia-news/2020/jan/07/australian-bushfire-smoke-drifts-to-south-america-un-reports

Hamann, T. H. (2009). Neoliberalism, governmentality, and ethics. *Foucault Studies*. https://doi.org/10.22439/fs.v0i0.2471

Handmer, J., & James, P. (2007). Trust us and be scared: The changing nature of contemporary risk, *Global Society, 21*(1), 119–130. https://doi.org/10.1080/13600820601116609

Harris, L. M., Chu, E. K., & Ziervogel, G. (2017). Negotiated resilience. *Resilience: International Policies, Practices, and Discourses, 6*(3), 1–19. https://doi.org/10.1080/21693293.2017.1353196

Harvey, D. (2005). *A brief history of neoliberalism*. Oxford University Press. https://doi.org/10.1093/oso/9780199283262.001.0001

Harvey, M. (2021). *Climate emergency: How societies create the crisis*. Emerald Publishing Limited.

Hill, L. J., & Larner, W. (2017). The resilient subject. In L. J. Hill & W. Larner (Eds.), *Assembling neoliberalism* (pp. 263–281). Palgrave Macmillan. https://doi.org/10.1057/978-1-137-58204-1_13

Holling, C. S. (1973). Resilience and stability of ecological systems. *Annual Review of Ecology and Systematics, 4*(1), 1–23. https://doi.org/10.1146/annurev.es.04.110173.000245

Howard, M. C., & King, J. E. (2004). The rise of neo-liberalism in advanced capitalist economies: Towards a materialist explanation. In P. Aretsis & M. Sawyer (Eds.), *The rise of the market*. Edward Elgar Publishing. https://doi.org/10.4337/9781845423315.00008

Hubbard, D. W. (2020). *The failure of risk management: Why it's broken and how to fix it* (2nd ed.). Wiley.

Intergovernmental Panel on Climate Change (IPCC). (2014a). *Summary for policy makers. Climate change 2014: Impacts, adaptation and vulnerability*. United Nations. https://www.ipcc.ch/report/ar5/wg2/

Intergovernmental Panel on Climate Change (IPCC). (2018). *Global warming of 1.5°C.* United Nations. https://www.ipcc.ch/report/ar5/wg2/

Intergovernmental Panel on Climate Change (IPCC). (2021). *Summary for policy makers. Climate change 2021: The physical science basis, contribution of working group 1 to the sixth assessment report of the intergovernmental panel on climate change.* United Nations. https://www.ipcc.ch/sr15/

Intergovernmental Panel on Climate Change (IPCC). (2022). *Summary for policy makers. Climate change 2022: Impacts, adaptation, and vulnerability. Contribution of working group ii to the sixth assessment report of the intergovernmental panel on climate change.* United Nations. https://www.ipcc.ch/report/ar6/wg2/

Joseph, J. M. (2016). Governing through failure and denial: The new resilience agenda. *Millennium Journal of International Studies, 44*(3), 370–390. https://doi.org/10.1177/0305829816638166

Kaijser, A., & Kronsell, A. (2014). Climate change through the lens of intersectionality. *Environmental Politics, 23*(3), 417–433. https://doi.org/10.1080/09644016.2013.835203

Kasperson, R. E., & Kasperson, J. X. (1996). The social amplification and attenuation of risk. *The ANNALS of the American Academy of Political and Social Science, 545*(1), 95–105. https://doi.org/10.1177/0002716296545001010

Kasperson, R. E., Renn, O., Slovic, P., Brown, H. S., Emel, J., Gobel, R., Kasperson, J. X., & Ratick, S. (1988). The social amplification of risk: A conceptual framework. *Risk Analysis, 8*(2), 177–187. https://doi.org/10.1111/j.1539-6924.1988.tb01168.x

Kelman, I., Gaillard, J. C., & Lewis, J. (2016). Learning from the history of disaster vulnerability and resilience research and practice for climate change. *Natural Hazards, 82*(Suppl 1), 129–143. https://doi.org/10.1007/s11069-016-2294-0

Kemshall, H. (Ed.). (2003). *Social policy and risk.* McGraw-Hill Education.

Krimsky, S., & Golding, D. (Eds.). (1992). *Social theories of risk.* Praeger.

Kuhlicke, A., Callsen, I., & Begg, C. (2016). Reputational risks and participation in flood risk management and the public debate about the 2013 flood in Germany. *The Chinese Journal of International Politics, 55*(P2), 318–325. https://doi.org/10.1016/j.envsci.2015.06.011

Lasch, C. (1978). *The culture of narcissism: American life in an age of diminishing expectations.* W.W. Norton.

Latour, B. (1993). *We have never been modern* (C. Porter, Trans.). Harvard University Press.

Lea, S. E. G., & Webley, P. (2006). Money as tool, money as drug: The biological psychology of a strong incentive. *Behavioral and Brain Sciences, 29*(2), 161–209. https://doi.org/10.1017/s0140525x06009046

Li, H. L. (2017). Rethinking vulnerability in the age of Anthropocene: Toward ecologizing education. *Educational Theory, 67*(4), 435–451. https://doi.org/10.1111/edth.12264

Lukasiewicz, A., Dovers, S., & Eburn, M. (2017). Shared responsibility: The who, what and how. *Environmental Hazards, 16*(4), 291–313. https://doi.org/10.1080/17477891.2017.1298510

Lupton, D. (1999). *Risk and sociocultural theory.* Cambridge University Press.

Lupton, D. (2013). *Risk.* Routledge.

Lyng, S. (2016). Goffman, action, and risk society: Aesthetic reflexivity in late modernity. *UNLV Gaming Research & Review Journal, 20*(1), 61–77. https://digitalscholarship.unlv.edu/grrj/vol20/iss1/4

Mackenzie, C. (2014). The importance of relational autonomy and capabilities for an ethics of vulnerability. In C. Mackenzie, W. Rogers, & S. Dodds (Eds.), *Vulnerability: New essays in ethics and feminist philosophy* (pp. 33–59). Oxford University Press. https://doi.org/10.1093/acprof:oso/9780199316649.003.0002

MacKinnon, D., & Derickson, K. D. (2013). From resilience to resourcefulness. *Progress in Human Geography, 37*(2), 253–270. https://doi.org/10.1177/0309132512454775

Manyena, B., Machingura, F., & O'Keefe, P. (2019). Disaster resilience integrated framework for transformation (drift): A new approach to theorising and operationalising resilience, *World Development, 123*, 104587. https://doi.org/10.1016/j.worlddev.2019.06.011

Matthewman, S. (2017). Mobile disasters: Catastrophes in the age of manufactured uncertainty. *Transfers, 7*(3), 6–22. http://dx.doi.org/10.3167/TRANS.2017.070303

McLeod, J. (2012). Vulnerability and the neo-liberal youth citizen: A view from Australia. *Comparative Education, 48*(1), 11–26. https://doi.org/10.1080/03050068.2011.637760

Mechler, R., & Bouwer, L. (2015). Understanding trends and projections of disaster losses and climate change: Is vulnerability the missing link? *Climatic Change, 133*, 23–35. https://doi.org/10.1007/s10584-014-1141-0

Mitzen, J. (2006). Ontological security in world politics: State identity and the security dilemma. *European Journal of International Relations, 12*(3), 341–370. https://doi.org/10.1177/1354066106067346

National Resilience Taskforce (NRT). (2019). *Profiling Australia's vulnerability: The interconnected causes and cascading effects of systemic disaster risk.* Australian Government, Department of Home Affairs. https://knowledge.aidr.org.au/resources/profiling-australias-vulnerability/

National Climate Change Adaptation Research Facility (NCCARF). (2016). *Climate adaptation: Synthesis 1–5.* National Climate Change Adaptation Research Facility. https://nccarf.edu.au/synthesis-summary-1-heat-and-heatwaves/

O'Brien, K., Hayward, B., & Berkes, F. (2009). Rethinking social contracts: Building resilience in a changing climate. *Ecology and Society, 14*(2), 12–28. http://dx.doi.org/10.5751/ES-03027-140212

O'Connell, D., Wise, R. M., Doerr, V., Grigg, V., Williams, N., Meharg, R., Dunlop, S., Meyers, J., Edwards, J., Osuchowski, M., & Crosweller, M. (2018). Approach, methods and results for co-producing a systems understanding of disaster: Technical report supporting the development of the Australian vulnerability profile. *CSIRO.* http://dx.doi.org/10.25919/5bc778a6a4d34

Okereke, C., Wittneben, B., & Bowen, F. (2011). Climate change: Challenging business, transforming politics. *Business & Society, 51*(1), 7–30. https://doi.org/10.1177/0007650311427659

Otto, I., Reckien, D., Reyer, C., Marcus, R., Masson, V., Jones, L., Norton, A., & Serdeczny, O. (2017). Social vulnerability to climate change: A review of concepts and evidence, *Regional Environmental Change, 17*(1), 1651–1662. https://doi.org/10.1007/s10113-017-1105-9

OurWorldInData.org (2022). *What share of the population has received at least one dose, and completed the initial vaccination protocol?* Our World in Data. Retrieved December 23, 2022, from https://ourworldindata.org/covid-vaccinations#what-share-of-the-population-has-received-at-least-one-dose-of-vaccine

Raco, M. (2015). Conflict management, democratic demands, and the post politics of privatization. In J. Metzger, P. Allmendinger, & S. Oosterlynck (Eds.), *Planning against the political: Democratic deficits in European territorial governance* (1st ed.). Routledge.

Rasborg, K. (2012). '(World) risk society' or 'new rationalities of risk'? A critical discussion of Ulrich Beck's theory of reflexive modernity. *Thesis Eleven, 108*(1), 3–25. https://doi.org/10.1177/0725513611421479

Read, J. (2009). A genealogy of homo-economicus: Neoliberalism and the production of subjectivity. *Foucault Studies,* 25–36. https://dx.doi.org/10.22439/fs.v0i0.2465

Ribot, J. (2014). Cause and response: Vulnerability and climate in the Anthropocene. *Journal of Peasant Studies*, *41*(5), 667–705. https://doi.org/10.1080/03066150. 2014.894911

Rickards, L., Wiseman, J., & Kashima, Y. (2014). Barriers to effective climate change mitigation: The case of senior government and business decision makers: Barriers to effective mitigation actions on climate change. *Wiley Interdisciplinary Reviews: Climate Change*, *5*(6), 753–773. https://doi.org/10.1002/ wcc.305

Ripple, W. J., Wolf, C., Newsome, T. M., Barnard, P., Moomaw, W. R., & Grandcolas, P. (2019). World scientists' warning of a climate emergency. *Bioscience*, *70*(1), 8–12. https://doi.org/10.1093/biosci/biz088

Roberts, P. S. (2006). FEMA and the prospects for reputation-based autonomy. *Studies in American Political Development*, *20*(1), 57–87. http://dx.doi.org/10.1017/ S0898588X06000010

Roxburgh, A. (2005). *A summary of Ulrich Beck—Risk society: Towards a new modernity.* https://www.academia.edu/4664071/A_Summary_of_Ulrich_Beck_Risk_ Society_Towards_a_New_Modernity

Sarkar, S. (2022). Pakistan floods pose serious health challenges, *BMJ*, *378*, o2141. https://doi.org/10.1136/bmj.o2141

Singh-Peterson, L., Salmon, P., Baldwin, C., & Goode, N. (2015). Deconstructing the concept of shared responsibility for disaster resilience: A sunshine coast case study, Australia, *Natural Hazards*, *79*, 755–774. https://doi.org/10.1007/ s11069-015-1871-y

Skeat, W. W. (1910). *An etymological dictionary of the English language*. Clarendon Press.

Slay, J. (2022, August 4). *Enhancing Australia's national security through ASD's REDSPICE*. International Affairs. Retrieved October 11, 2023, from https:// www.internationalaffairs.org.au/australianoutlook/enhancing-australias- national-security-through-asds-redspice/

Steffen, W., Hughes, L., Mullins, G., Bambrick, H., Dean, A., & Rice, M. (2019). *Dangerous summer: Escalating bushfire, heat and drought risk*. Climate Council. https://www.climatecouncil.org.au/resources/dangerous-summer-escalating- bushfire-heat-drought-risk/

Strydom, P. (2003). *Risk, environment and society: Ongoing debates current issues and future prospects*. Open University Press.

Sugarman, J. (2015). Neoliberalism and psychological ethics. *Journal of Theoretical and Philosophical Psychology*, *35*(2), 103–116. https://doi.org/10.1037/ a0038960

Sultana, F. (2013). Gendering climate change: Geographical insights. *The Professional Geographer*, *66*(3), 1–10. https://doi.org/10.1080/00330124.2013.821730

Taleb, N. N. (2010). *The black swan: The impact of the highly improbable*. Random House.

Taşkale, A. R., & Sima, E. H. (2019). In pursuit of the neoliberal subject. *New Political Science*, *41*(1), 149–152. https://doi.org/10.1080/07393148.2019.1559130

Teague, B., McLeod, R., & Pascoe, S. (2010). *Final report of the 2009 Victorian bushfires royal commission*. The 2009 Victorian Bushfires Royal Commission. http:// royalcommission.vic.gov.au/Commission-Reports/Final-Report.html

Trajkovich, M. (2022, September 11). *February flood disaster fourth most destructive in Australia's history*. 9 News. Retrieved September 29, 2023, from https:// www.9news.com.au/national/february-flood-disaster-fourth-most-destructive-in- australias-history/5206d2eb-2393-46b3-95db-7fbb67728b09

Tronto, J. C. (1998). *An ethic of care. Generations: Journal of the American Society on Aging*, *22*(3), 15–20.

Tuana, N. (2004). Coming to understand: Orgasm and the epistemology of ignorance. *Hypatia*, *19*(1), 194–232. https://doi.org/10.1111/j.1527-2001.2004. tb01275.x

Wachinger, G., Renn, O., Begg, C., & Kuhlicke, C. (2013). The risk perception paradox— Implications for governance and communication of natural hazards. *Risk Analysis*, *33*(6), 1049–1065. https://doi.org/10.1111/j.1539-6924.2012.01942.x

Whetton, P., Holper, P., Clarke, J., Webb, L., Hennessy, K., Colman, R., Moise, A., Power, S., Braganza, K., Watterson, I., Murphy, B., Timbal, B., Hope, P., Dowdy, A., Bhend, J., Kirono, D., Wilson, L., Grose, M., Ekstrom, M., Rafter, T., Heady, C., Narsey, S., Bathols, J., McInnes, K., Monselesan, D., Church, J., Lenton, A., O'Grady, J., Bedin, T., Erwin, T., & Li, Y. (2015). *Climate change in Australia: Projections for Australia's natural resource management regions*. Commonwealth Scientific and Industrial Research Organisation. https://publications.csiro.au/publications/publication/PIcsiro:EP154327

WHO. (2022). *WHO Coronavirus (COVID-19) dashboard*. Retrieved October 18, 2022, from https://covid19.who.int/

Wiley (2012). *The Wiley-Blackwell encyclopedia of globalization*. John Wiley & Sons, Ltd.

Wilkinson, I. (2002). Anxiety in a 'risk' society. *Contemporary Sociology: A Journal of Reviews*, *31*(4), 483. http://dx.doi.org/10.2307/3089130

Williamson, J. (1990). What Washington means by policy reform. In J. Williamson (Ed.), *Latin American adjustment: How much has happened?* Peterson Institute for International Economics.

Wilson, J., & Swyngedouw, E. (2015). *The post-political and its discontents: Spaces of depoliticisation, spectres of radical politics*. Edinburgh University Press. https://doi. org/10.3366/edinburgh/9780748682973.001.0001

Wisner, B., Blaikie, P., Cannon, T., & Davis, I. (2004). *At risk: Natural hazards, people's vulnerability and disasters*. Routledge.

Woolsey, R. J., Wilcox, R. H., & Garrity, P. J. (1984). *America's hidden vulnerabilities: crisis management in a society of networks: A report of the panel on crisis management of the CSIS science and technology committee. CSIS science and technology committee*. Center for Strategic and International Studies, Georgetown University.

World Health Organisation. (2022). *WHO coronavirus (COVID-19) dashboard*. https://covid19.who.int/

Ziervogel, G., Pelling, M., Cartwright, A., Chu, E., Deshpande, T., Harris, L., Hyams, K., Kaunda, J., Klaus, B., Michael, K., Pasquini, L., Pharoah, R., Rodina, L., Scott, D., & Zweig, P. (2017). Inserting rights and justice into urban resilience: A focus on everyday risk. *Environment & Urbanization*, *29*(9), 123–138. http://dx.doi. org/10.1177/0956247816686905

3
INTRODUCING RELATIONAL LEADERSHIP

> Relationships are at the heart of leadership. If you can't connect, you can't lead.

In Chapter 2 we explored how the confluence of neoliberal governmentality and increasing risks such as climate change pose unprecedented challenges for individuals and entities in leadership positions to simultaneously reduce hazards and protect their most vulnerable citizens while denying their own vulnerability. With the increasing likelihood of having to experience events that exceed our capacity to effectively treat risk, I argue a different type of leadership is needed.

In this chapter, we explore the growing scholarship that points towards the vital role of ethical leadership and decision-making in disaster management. What now follows is a brief overview of this literature while foreshadowing their potential limitations as the increasing frequency and intensity of hazards-turned-disasters will stretch leaders to and beyond their limits (see Figure 2.2). These increasingly dire circumstances will most likely require leaders, and all of us, to deepen our relatedness to others and our understanding of loss and suffering. This will require addressing leadership challenges associated with the longer-term temporal dimensions of disaster causation (Wisner et al., 2012), as well as ways to extend relational framings of leadership into these dimensions.

In the last part of this chapter, we briefly explore the literature on relational leadership ethics including insights from environmental philosophy, Asian moral philosophies, virtue theory, feminist philosophy and ethics, and relational leadership theories. I see these as vital elements for advancing knowledge towards a novel approach to the ethics of disaster management leadership.

DOI: 10.4324/9781003499510-4

Ethics in disaster management leadership

Importantly, ethics establishes the principles whereby we mediate our interactions and learn to live together. Without ethics, there is no social coherence and no community resilience (Jordan & Kristjánsson, 2017; Wheatley, 2017). Ethical leadership calls for a leader to embrace positive (ethical) characteristics, such as trust, compassion and care. It also calls for engaging in conduct that makes leaders stand out as ethical agents against an ethically neutral ground while shaping the behaviours of followers through communication, reinforcement and decision-making (Brown et al., 2005; Trevino et al., 2003). Ethical framings of leadership also emphasise the protection of institutional diversity in tandem with better management of the global common pool resources (Ostrom, 1999) that are increasingly threatened by existential risks such as climate change.

There is a growing body of literature that examines the role of ethics in emergent crisis leadership and disaster management structures for novel crises. For instance, in 2012, the Council of Europe published a set of ethical principles on disaster risk reduction and people's resilience prior to, during, and after disasters (Prieur, 2012), which included the following general principles: solidarity, joint responsibility, non-discrimination, humanity, impartiality, neutrality, cooperation, and territorial sovereignty. Geale (2012) identifies the cardinal virtues of prudence, courage, justice, stewardship, vigilance, resilience, self-effacing charity, and communication as critical to disaster response and to ensure that the rights and privileges of all those impacted are respected and maintained. Parkash (2012) stresses the importance of truth-telling and the need to improve institutional capacity for accurate, reliable and timely information to help inform decision-making of communities and governments. Levy and Pandey (2019) advocate the importance of values and ethical considerations being made explicit during the disaster planning process so that, under conditions of pressure and urgency, they can be made consistent with the ethical judgments that underlie disaster management decision processes.

Pine (2018) proposes a leadership framing around six critical skills, namely: sense-making, decision-making, coordination, communicating to community, terminating/ending special measures, and planning for the novel deployment of capabilities and resources. Leadership in disaster management, according to Swoyer (2017), emphasises leading by example, inspiring a shared vision, encouraging the heart, empowering subordinates, accepting input, and speaking with conviction of a higher purpose related to the common good. Caro (2016a) proposes eight attributes of disaster management leadership, including strategic cognition, environmental perception, and social value engagement. He further proposes a set of 12 capabilities that entail ethical leadership attributes of care, compassion, authenticity, courage, equanimity, and decisiveness (Caro, 2016b).

Proctor-Thomson (2019) advocates for a leadership framing that recognises the innate leadership potential and integrity of everyone involved, including community leaders, as critical to disaster leadership. Such a framing appreciates diverse values, as well as mutual obligation and reciprocity arising from daily operational conversations. These attributes extend to the relationships between leaders and followers and their respective roles, rights and responsibilities, ensuring that mutual agency is respected while addressing and removing structural and organisational inequalities (Wilson et al., 2018). In this context, community involvement in the planning stages of crisis becomes essential to the ethical decision-making processes (Rios et al., 2015). Similarly, Voegtlin (2016) advocates for environmental relatedness, critical evaluation of prevailing social norms, shared responsibility, and forward-looking thinking beyond organisational goals. Finally, Jurkiewicz (2017) reflects upon the ethical and unethical behaviour exhibited by leaders during Hurricane Katrina in 2005 and asserts that the ethics of leaders are critical in establishing cultures that are ethical in all aspects of their behaviour, duties and responsibilities.

Ethical egoism, relativism, absolutism and pluralism

Despite the literature advocating for the establishment of ethical cultures within all aspects of leadership, critics have identified constraints for ethical leadership. Some argue that ethical leadership risks propagating a strong leader-centric view (Fairhurst & Connaughton, 2014) and advocating organisational goals that may not take into account wider-reaching outcomes (Austin, 2006), implying an unreasonable level of self-interest (egoism). Other critics argue that the normative basis of ethical leadership may be vague and highly context-dependent (Brown et al., 2005; Eisenbeiss, 2012), implying subjective relativity. Still others see ethical leadership as devoid of critical evaluation against acceptable standards, thus failing to promote positive social change (Bies et al., 2007) and implying a lack of universality. These criticisms are instructive as they lead us to consider four ethical theories for determining ethical standards that leaders will need to consider when executing their obligations to lead, serve and protect others: ethical egoism, ethical relativism, ethical absolutism, and ethical pluralism.

Ethical egoism

Ethical egoism asserts that individuals ought to act in their own self-interest and that an action is morally right if it promotes the self-interest of the individual performing the action. Only when self-interest needs are satisfied can the ethical agent consider other areas of ethical behaviour that benefit others in society (Smith, 2006). This approach can apply firstly as an individual standard and secondly as a universal standard. An individual standard holds that individuals should act in their own self-interest without any moral obligations to others. This suggests that individuals are morally justified in pursuing their own well-being and happiness, even if it comes at the expense of others (Fang & Slavin, 2018).

Adam Smith (1976) put forward in his book *The theory of moral sentiments* that an individual "is first and principally recommended to his own care" and that, "Every man feels his own pleasures and his own pains more sensibly than those of other people" (p. 359). Smith (1937) went on to say in his book *Wealth of nations* that, "By pursuing his own interest he frequently promotes that of the society more effectually than when he really intends to promote it. I have never known much good done by those who affected trade for the public good" (p. 423).

A universal standard holds that everyone should act in their own self-interest, promoting the idea that, if everyone pursues their self-interest, overall societal well-being will be maximised (Tilley, 2023). This approach was influential in the work of Milton Friedman, who was an avid proponent of neoliberalism and who strongly influenced both Margaret Thatcher's and Ronald Reagan's economic policies. In his book *Capitalism of freedom,* he wrote:

> Few trends could so thoroughly undermine the very foundations of our free society as the acceptance by corporate officials of a social responsibility other than to make as much money for their stockholders as possible. This is a fundamentally subversive doctrine. If businessmen do have a social responsibility other than making maximum profits for stockholders, how are they to know what it is?
>
> *(Friedman, 1962, p. 133)*

Critics of ethical egoism argue that it may lead to morally questionable behaviour, as individuals may prioritise their own interests without regard for the well-being of others. They also contend that ethical egoism doesn't provide a satisfactory basis for moral rules that can guide individuals in resolving conflicts of interest or in making decisions that involve competing interests (Burgess-Jackson, 2012). Importantly, ethical egoism is distinct from psychological egoism, which is a descriptive theory asserting that individuals always act in their self-interest, whether they are consciously aware of it or not. Ethical egoism, on the other hand, prescribes that individuals ought to act in their self-interest as a matter of moral principle (Tilley, 2023). Taking care of oneself is a necessary function of being human and being part of a greater collective, including developing resilience to the effects of disasters. But it also runs the risk of taking care of oneself to the neglect of others which, as we shall see in later chapters, is deeply problematic.

Ethical relativism

Ethical relativism gives rise to a core question: "Do moral principles apply universally, or are all values and ethical judgements relative to their context, particularly time and cultural contexts?" Ethical relativism asserts that moral standards differ between groups, within a single culture, between cultures, across time, and that the ethical systems of belief supporting those moral standards of behaviour will differ according to the time and circumstance (McDonald, 2010).

As a result, a moral standard could only apply to one particular culture, society or community, rather than across multiple cultures, societies or communities (Freeman & Gilbert, 1988). In addition, it would not be possible to undertake comparative judgments, as there would be no commonality between them. To do so would be to attempt to derive an "ought" from an "is" (Schmidt, 1955). Finally, ethical relativism would require the continual search for new moral principles, as we would only need to obey the local customs, laws and codes of the culture, society or community in which they operate. However, who decides upon the prevailing norms is usually determined by those in power and therefore not necessarily agreed to by the majority within that culture, society or community (McDonald, 2010).

Ethical relativism, therefore, leaves us with a dilemma. How can we decide or judge on matters of right and wrong, or just and unjust, if morality is always relative to a cultural, societal or community standard? Relatedly, how does a state or national government or disaster management agency adequately respond to such circumstances when setting policies and procedures and allocating resources against the disaster management cycle?

Ethical absolutism

At the other end of the spectrum from ethical relativism sits ethical absolutism (universalism). Ethical absolutism advocates for a set of moral standards that can apply universally in all places at all times, even though adherence to them may vary across individuals, cultures and societies (Frederick, 1999). For example, ethics such as honesty, integrity and compassion are perceived as basic moral standards for most civilisations, even though adherence to them varies widely (Tsalikis & Fritzsche, 1989). Various cross-cultural studies (Abratt et al., 1992; Izraeli, 1988; Tsalikis & Nwachukwu, 1988) have shown that—despite social, cultural and political differences—moral standards varied little between cultures.

Critics of ethical absolutism suggest that those who advocate for such an approach become high-handed in determining what is actually right, good or just and that no one entity or country can claim to provide the dominant moral standard(s). However, this criticism ignores the subtlety of ethical absolutism, which recognises that what is considered right or good does vary across time and culture, while at the same time being everywhere and always the same. The moral standard is independent but concurrently determined by all parties. Ethical absolutists also argue that variations in ethical actions could still be founded upon common universal moral standards influenced by our necessity for long-term survival (McDonald, 2010), such as not killing another human being.

As previously mentioned, universal standards run the risk of being determined by those in power or in self-interest. How, then, does a disaster management leader balance the needs of a culture, society or community against a set of universal moral standards or expectations that may or may not align?

Ethical pluralism

An alternative to ethical egoism, ethical relativism and ethical absolutism is ethical pluralism. Ethical pluralism is an ethical framework that acknowledges the existence of multiple, potentially conflicting, ethical principles (including universal principles) that may be valid and applicable in different contexts. In other words, it recognises that there isn't a single, universally applicable moral theory or set of principles that can guide ethical decision-making in all situations (Liu, 2018). Ethical pluralists argue that different ethical principles may be relevant in different circumstances, and there may be cases where two or more principles are equally valid or where they conflict. This perspective contrasts with ethical monism, which asserts that there is only one fundamental ethical principle or set of rules that should be followed in all situations (Hampshire, 1983; Raz, 2005).

Ethical pluralism allows for a more flexible and context-dependent approach to moral decision-making. It recognises the complexity of ethical issues and the diversity of values that people hold. Adherents of ethical pluralism often emphasise the importance of careful consideration of the specific details and context of a situation when making ethical judgments, rather than relying on a rigid, one-size-fits-all moral framework (Robinson, 2011). It is important to note that ethical pluralism does not imply moral relativism, which suggests that all moral perspectives are equally valid. Instead, ethical pluralism acknowledges the existence of objective moral principles (including universal principles) but recognises the need for flexibility and openness to multiple perspectives in ethical reasoning (Madsen & Strong, 2003).

The challenge for disaster management leaders is to navigate the tensions between ethical egoism, ethical relativism, ethical absolutism, and ethical pluralism. To lead, serve and protect others, we are obliged to honour our own ethical standards as well as the universal ethical standards established by our international, national and state institutions, the ethical standards of our communities and organisations, and our own ethical standards.

The law and ethics

As well as having to navigate the tensions that exist between different ethical frameworks, we also need to navigate the tension between the law and ethics. Law and ethics are related concepts but refer to distinct systems of principles and guidelines governing human behaviour which we will now briefly examine.

Law is a system of codified rules and regulations created by a government or other authoritative body that can be enforced through formal legal processes, including legal sanctions, such as fines, imprisonment or other legal penalties. The authority for laws comes from government bodies, legislatures, and the legal systems that create them, are generally broad in scope, and apply to all members of a society within a specific jurisdiction, irrespective of a person's wealth, social status or family position. They are intended to regulate various aspects of human conduct, including interactions between individuals and the state. They also tend to be relatively rigid and may take time to change through formal legal processes, amendments and revisions typically involving legislative or judicial procedures (Black et al., 1979; Foster, 1981). In modern western democratic societies, law is the result of the social contract obligation from governments to citizens "in exchange for which every individual has resigned a part of [their] natural liberty" (Blackstone, 1818, p. 34).

Ethics, on the other hand, refers to a set of moral principles or values that guide individual or collective behaviour. Ethics may be influenced by cultural, religious, philosophical, or personal beliefs, and are not necessarily enforceable by legal means. Ethics, being a set of moral principles, relies on internalised values, societal expectations, and personal conscience. Therefore, violating ethical principles may not result in legal consequences but it can lead to social disapproval or professional consequences which may or may not be legally based. Because the authority for ethics generally comes from religious beliefs, cultural norms, philosophical principles, or individual conscience, ethical guidelines are often more subjective and may vary among different individuals, groups or cultures within their specific contexts. Ethical principles can be more flexible and adaptable to changing societal norms and may evolve over time through informal means, such as discussions, debates, and changes in cultural attitudes (Lilla, 1981; Martinez, 1998).

While law and ethics are distinct, they often intersect, and ethical principles can influence the creation and interpretation of laws. Ideally, individuals and organisations are encouraged to comply with both legal requirements and ethical standards to promote a just and moral society (Martinez, 1998). However, the tension between legal requirements and ethical standards may create circumstances that are difficult to navigate.

Nomos versus physis

Circumstances such these are well understood in ethical theory, and particularly in the theory of virtue ethics, defined as the tension between "*nomos*" and "*physis*."

Nomos is often translated as "law" or "convention" and refers to human-made laws, social norms, and conventions that are created by societies to regulate human behaviour. *Nomos* is associated with the idea that order and structure in human societies are products of human agreement and convention (Ostwald, 1990).

Conversely, *physis* is often translated as "nature" or "natural order" and represents the intrinsic, underlying order or principle that governs the natural world. *Physis* is associated with the idea that there is an inherent, objective order or structure to the universe that exists independently of human conventions or laws. That is, *physis* is something determined by nature, embracing all those qualities which are psychologically and genetically ingrained in all humans (Ostwald, 1990).

The dichotomy between *nomos* and *physis* reflects the tension between natural order and human-made conventions in ancient Greek philosophy. While *physis* represents the inherent order of the natural world, *nomos* refers to the laws and conventions created by human societies to organise and regulate their collective life. The relationship between these concepts has been a topic of philosophical inquiry and debate throughout the history of Western thought (Morrell & Dahlmann, 2022). Whilst an ancient distinction, the tension is very familiar to contemporary legal-versus-ethical conundrums, as the case study demonstrates. As Morrell and Dahlmann (2022) highlight, *nomos* versus *physis* can also play out beyond individual tensions to those found in societies, such as reconciliation commissions or restorative justice approaches that seek to discover and discuss past wrongdoings and develop shared understandings of how future problems can be collectively addressed and resolved (pp. 624–625).

These tensions can incentivise changes, not only in human-made laws but also by motivating changes in human habits and customs to achieve greater good. For example, in the context of the existential risks associated with climate change, there is a need for individual and collective behaviours and decisions to adhere with existing laws that attempt to moderate these risks. At the same time, there is also a pressing need to be mindful of the wider context of the planetary boundaries and complexities of global socio-ecological systems that require us to apply scrutiny to our taken-for-granted behaviours (Bennett et al., 2021; Folke et al., 2021; Rockström et al., 2021). The experiences of many of the disaster management leaders I interviewed, along with my own experiences, would suggest that, before, during, and after crises, human-made laws will often reveal a limitation that potentially constrains decision-making (see Figure 2.2 in Chapter 2, the point in which the "rules change"). When this happens, ethics become the dominant consideration for making decisions and determining actions.

Relational leadership ethics

The tensions between ethical egoism, ethical relativism, ethical absolutism and ethical pluralism, as well as the tension between the law and ethics, help us to understand how complex the environment is wherein disaster management leaders are asked to make decisions and undertake actions to lead, serve and protect others. Implicit in these tensions is the need for a negotiated process between the leader and those they seek to lead, serve and protect, to determine the most appropriate actions that are good, right, and just. To achieve this, I contend we need to advance our understanding of relational leadership ethics as a way of navigating this tension.

Relational leadership as a social construct means recognising the entwined nature of our relationships with others, whether leading or being led (Cunliffe & Eriksen, 2011): we shape and are shaped by our social experiences in everyday interactions and conversations (Berger & Luckmann, 1966; Gergen, 1999). Cunliffe and Eriksen (2011) identify four main threads of relational leadership: leading as a way of being in the world; understanding, dialogically, what is meaningful with others; working through differences as a moral responsibility; and being guided by practical wisdom. A relational perspective considers leadership in the context of social reality that is emergent and inseparable from leadership itself (Dachler & Hosking, 1995; Hosking, 1988). Therefore, a relational leadership ethic must recognise the interdependencies of relational values, knowledge, and rules that operate within uncertain, ambiguous, and complex societal systems that both create and limit permissible and practical decisions that affect those who are led (Gorddard et al., 2016).

Relational ethics "conceives of moral status, right action, or good character as constituted by beneficent ties or other bonds of sharing" and is "sometimes characterised as 'communitarian'" (Metz & Clark Miller, 2016, pp. 1–2). Relational ethics recognises embodied selves that are interdependent and interconnected with others and from which ethical commitment, agency and responsibility for self and others emerge out of situations that involve and affect two or more beings in relationship (Pollard, 2015). Scholarship from environmental philosophy and related epistemologies extend "others" and "beings" to include both humans and non-humans (Larios, 2019; Tschakert, 2020). Relational ethics has prominence in Asian moral philosophies, such as Confucianism (Li, 1994) and Buddhism (Chu & Vu, 2021; Verchery, 2021), as well as western virtue theory (MacIntyre, 2007; Putman, 1991). Relational ethics is also becoming increasingly influential in environmental ethics (Behrens, 2014; Celermajer et al., 2020; Ray, 2018), feminist philosophy and ethics (Gilligan, 1982; Noddings, 2013), and relational leadership theories (Cunliffe, 2009; Cunliffe & Eriksen, 2011; Fairhurst & Uhl-Bien, 2012).

Buddhist ethics of compassion

For example, out of all the global religions, Buddhism has been given the greatest prominence in the psychological literature about compassion. In Buddhism, compassion is seen not only as an emotional response but as a response founded on reason and wisdom embedded within an ethical framework concerned with the selfless intention of freeing others from suffering (Strauss et al., 2016). For example, there are numerous schools of Buddhist philosophy and ethics, including environmental and engaged Buddhism, that identify human self-importance, separateness, and exploitation of human and non-human others as the main causes of anthropogenic climate change (Humphreys, 2014; Kopnina et al., 2018).

These attributes—along with human greed, fear, anger, and ignorance—are identified as the *causes* of universal suffering. They also recognise that these *causes* are common only to humans, whereas the capacity to experience the *effects* is common to humans and non-humans (Jenkins et al., 2018; Kaza, 2014). In response, Buddhist ethics seeks to achieve universal compassion by recognising that humans are interdependent with all other humans and non-humans and cannot remain indifferent to their suffering (Harris, 1995; Harvey, 2017; Lim, 2019). Buddhist ethics also recognises that when we bring suffering to other humans and non-humans, we also suffer, and this interdependence contributes towards the basis of our relatedness (Lim, 2019; Thich, 1992, 1999).

Unlike western perspectives of compassion that suggest the only people who deserved compassion were those who did not deserve their suffering—and that some suffering was deserved through intentional, thoughtless, or careless acts (Nussbaum, 1996)—Buddhist philosophy rejects any notion of deservedness of suffering. Instead, it advocates that, while all beings, consciously or unconsciously, contribute to the causes of their own and others' suffering, they nonetheless all deserve compassion (Gyatso, 2003; Tsering, 2005).

Virtue ethics

Alasdair MacIntyre (2007) places virtue as a central premise of an unfolding narrative where one's whole life is considered as a character in a story-in-progress. Throughout this lifelong process, the individual, in relationship with others, seeks to profoundly realise a more perfected understanding and practical embodiment of the good for human life. Thus, when virtuous people act, they do so for the good of themselves and others, their communities, their country, and society (MacIntyre, 2007). Substantively, acting with virtue opens the possibility of modifying and transforming public knowledge of existential risks such as climate change through discourse and deliberation and, instrumentally, it can inspire and deliver the changes required to mitigate the effects of their impacts (Hulme, 2014).

Multispecies justice ethics

Multispecies justice ethics concerns itself with ethical relationships between human and non-human others through understandings of shared vulnerability and joint suffering, as well as how "goods" and "bads" are created and distributed (Celermajer et al., 2020). It also includes commitments not to harm others, as well as imposing a duty of assistance. A multispecies justice ethic seeks to mitigate harm; emphasise respect and dignity; and establish trusted, consensual, reciprocal, accountable, fair, and cooperative relationships with vulnerable others (Treves et al., 2019; Whyte, 2020). It is also concerned with creating inclusive, functioning and flourishing environments (Tschakert et al., 2021).

Feminist ethics of care

A feminist ethics of care exemplifies how caring webs of relations function. It was first proposed as an alternative to the more masculine ethical discourses based around power, influence and rights (Gilligan, 1977, 1982, 1995). Care is "a species activity that includes everything that we do to maintain, continue, and repair our 'world' so that we can live in it as well as possible... [it] includes our bodies, ourselves, and our environment" (Fisher & Tronto, 1990, p. 40). Thus, a caring attitude establishes our fundamental human orientation towards others and the basis of our relationships with others and the larger society (Eisler, 2007; Gilligan, 1982; Noddings, 2013).

An ethics of care suggests we are all embedded in a web of relationships that define who we are and what identities we embrace (Hawk, 2011; Held, 2006). It recognises the value of lived realities when engaging in moral deliberation, rather than just identifying abstract and universal principles such as peace, freedom, and human dignity. It also seeks to acknowledge the well-being of all those who will be impacted by our respective actions (Hawk, 2011; Noddings, 2013). Such dynamics establish humility, growth, and mutual trust in learning about the other and oneself, shifting the focus from only self to the appreciation of and active engagement with others (Ciulla, 2009; Hawk & Lyons, 2008; Mayeroff, 1971).

Feminist ethics of vulnerability

A feminist ethics of vulnerability allows us to comprehend vulnerability as a universal dimension of the human experience (Beckett, 2006), as well as a context-specific ontological condition of our embodied humanity (Fineman, 2010) and corporeality (Butler, 2004). Vulnerability also establishes ethical obligations for certain agents (such as disaster management leaders) to be accountable for providing protection and assistance, refraining from harming others, and condemning the myriad ways vulnerability is exploited (Gilson, 2014). Our shared vulnerability allows us "to think beyond human exceptionalism, theorise the multiple entanglements of humans and non-humans" (Hoppe, 2020, p. 126), and establish our relationality with them (Latour, 2017).

Relational leadership theory

Relational leadership theory recognises the entwined nature of our relationships with others (Cunliffe & Eriksen, 2011) and that we shape and are shaped by our social experiences in everyday interactions and conversations (Berger & Luckmann, 1966; Gergen, 1999). What constitutes "ethical" is negotiated between individuals, groups, organisations, industries, and sociohistorical contexts (Fairhurst & Uhl-Bien, 2012; Grint, 2005; Liden & Antonakis, 2009). Furthermore, understanding self, seen in relation to others, and social reality as always in-the-making between people (Stivers, 2008) allows leaders (and others) to think and act ethically. This is achieved through one's accountability and responsibility to others and is borne out of our vulnerable exposures to another, along with our drive to maintain relationships (Butler, 2005; Levinas, 1998).

While relational leadership ethics, such as those described above, do not resolve the tension between ethical egoism, ethical relativism, ethical absolutism and ethical pluralism or the tension between the law and ethics, they do help to ease these tensions by recognising universal experiences of suffering and vulnerability and the need for universal compassion. In addition, they open up opportunities for discourse and deliberation to contest traditional notions of power, influence and rights, and call for accountability in the provision of protection and assistance to vulnerable others. They also seek to condemn exploitation and advocate for justice for both humans and non-humans. Finally, they explicitly recognise our relationship with others and the larger society, including the global society, to which so many existential risks have and will continue to bring harm and suffering.

As philosopher Byron Williston (2019, p. 1) argues when reflecting upon the impacts of climate change risk, "…the crises we are bringing upon ourselves through our profligate carbon emissions… shows that our chief failing so far is an ethical one, and that the solution to the problem—if there is one—must also be ethical." If we are to have any chance of minimising the effects of the impacts of human-caused climate change, let alone surviving these impacts, a shift in our thinking about our place in the earth system is required (Steffen et al., 2011; Williston, 2019). Hence, our relationships with each other and between us and the earth system are of significant ethical concern, and one in which relational ethics offers a response.

Advancing relational leadership

In Chapters 2 and 3, we have seen how there exist scholarly openings for advancing relational ethics to overcome the current leadership dilemma against the backdrop of today's increasingly complex, ambiguous and uncertain disaster management environment. Such a relational ethics would bring us as leaders closer to those that we are called upon to lead, rather than pushing them away (as shown in Figure 2.1) while helping to prepare for future crises. These scholarly advances make it possible to rise above the rationale of Neoliberal governmentality that keeps leaders entrapped in a state of paralysis, and often ignorance, unable or unwilling to reflect on our own vulnerability (O'Neill, 2005). In order to overcome pervasive notions of "invulnerability" (Gilson, 2011, p. 312), influential leaders and ordinary citizens alike will need to recognise that we are all influenced by and ultimately find truth through our vulnerability to life's experiences, and it is this recognition of vulnerability that effects positive changes, in ourselves and our societies (Gilson, 2011; McHugh, 2007; Skeggs, 2005). A relational leadership ethics proposed in this book is predicated upon this recognition.

We have also identified the urgency to abandon the treacherous archetype of resilient and self-reliant citizens that further entrenches, not remedies, inequalities and systematic disenfranchisement. In Chapter 5, we will delineate how, to move away from top-down and expert-driven framings of resilience and instead support community resilience and resourcefulness, committing to rather than shying away from the politics of resilience building is required. The latter involves the ability to engage in deliberations and tolerate contestations, to appreciate what citizens value and wish to protect (Tschakert et al., 2017).

Finally, we have recognised the critical need for a leadership framing that allows leaders to accept and act upon our mutual vulnerability by nurturing relational leadership skills. Such tangible and desirable characteristics allow us to take as a starting point our relatedness with those we lead, serve and protect, which we will explore further in Chapter 7.

These characteristics can provide us with the opportunity to genuinely understand what is of value to others and grasp, at an embodied and affective level, how and why others suffer. Such an approach would seem to be a significant advantage as nations continue with their commitments to the Sendai Framework of Action 2015–2030 (United Nations Office for Disaster Risk Reduction UNISDR, 2015) and the United Nations Sustainable Development Goals (United Nations, 2017).

Such a leadership ethos differs fundamentally from the deep-seated, problematic notion of deservedness that denies such understandings by proliferating individual self-blame, lack of self-worth, and personal failure or inadequacy. Most importantly, relational ethics allows leaders to overcome elitist framings reinforced through Neoliberal discourse that perpetuate and solidify psychological and emotional distress (Feldman & Kuyken, 2011; Gilson, 2011) that consequently inhibit our ability to be caring and compassionate leaders.

In our daily reality, such ethical leaders seem in short supply. The heuristic presented for the emergency sector in Australia (Figure 2.2) illustrates the shrinking space for effective and ethical manoeuvring once a crucial threshold—resulting from the increasing intensity of events and growing levels of adverse consequences—is crossed. However, it *is* possible to enact successful leadership and shake off the shackles of modernity's detachment, disciplining displays of power, and complicity in the performance of invulnerability. The world looked up at the exemplary leadership—full of empathy, integrity, care, and love—that Jacinda Ardern, the Prime Minister of New Zealand, displayed after the horrendous shooting in Christchurch in March 2019 (Moore, 2019; Roy, 2019; Urquhart, 2019). What prevents other leaders, in key governmental positions and in disaster management, from displaying a similar relational ethos and demonstrate unwavering leadership in the context of similar crises?

The challenge for leaders

To advance relational ethics in disaster management leadership, the following chapters investigate the extent to which we, as disaster management leaders are, consciously or unconsciously, entangled in harmful conceptualisations of Neoliberal resilience that tend to institutionalise the very conditions of vulnerability. These chapters reveal the extent to which such influences impede our ability to think, speak and act caringly and compassionately whilst discharging our moral, political and legislative duties to those whom we lead, serve and protect.

Such leadership also needs to be viewed not only through a lens of disaster, but through our capacity to shape and influence the development of law, policy, systems, and procedures that establish the conditions for more caring and compassionate communities.

We will also explore how such leadership can envision communities as spaces in which everyone is genuinely supported—through a more equitable distribution of power, wealth, resources, and knowledge (including indigenous and vernacular knowledge)—to achieve self and community affirmation and mobilisation in the face of disasters, whether they arise from climate-influenced hazards or from the making of our flawed humanity.

References

Abratt, R., Nel, D., & Higgs, N. S. (1992). An examination of the ethical beliefs of managers using selected scenarios in a cross-cultural environment. *Journal of Business Ethics, 11,* 29–35.

Austin, J. E. (2006). Leadership through social purpose partnering. In T. Maak & N. Pless (Eds.), *Responsible leadership* (pp. 202–212). Routledge.

Beckett, A. E. (2006). *Citizenship and vulnerability: Disability and issues of social engagement.* Palgrave Macmillan.

Behrens, K. G. (2014). An African relational environmentalism and moral considerability. *Environmental Ethics: An Interdisciplinary Journal Dedicated to the Philosophical Aspects of Environmental Problems, 36*(1), 63–82. https://doi.org/10.5840/enviroethics20143615

Bennett, E. M., Biggs, R., & Peterson, G. D. (2021, January 13). Patchwork earth: Navigating pathways to just, thriving, and sustainable futures. *One Earth, 4*(2), 172–176. http://dx.doi.org/10.1016/j.oneear.2021.01.004

Berger, P. L., & Luckmann, T. (1966). *The social construction of reality: A treatise in the sociology of knowledge*. Penguin Books.

Bies, R., Bartunek, J., Fort, T., & Zald, M. (2007). Introduction to special forum topic: Corporations as social change agents: Individual, interpersonal, institutional, and environmental dynamics. *The Academy of Management Review*, 32(3), 788–793. https://doi.org/10.5465/amr.2007.25275515

Black, H. C., Connolly, M. J., & Nolan, J. R. (1979). *Black's law dictionary: Definitions of the terms and phrases of American and English jurisprudence, ancient and modern* (5th ed.). West Publishing Company.

Blackstone, W. (1818). *Commentaries on the laws of England*. T. B. Wait & Sons.

Brown, M. E., Treviño, L. K., & Harrison, D. A. (2005). Ethical leadership: A social learning perspective for construct development and testing. *Organizational Behavior and Human Decision Processes*, 97(2), 117–134. https://doi.org/10.1016/j.obhdp.2005.03.002

Burgess-Jackson, K. (2012). Taking egoism seriously, *Ethical Theory and Moral Practice*, 16, 1–14. https://doi.org/10.1007/s10677-012-9372-5

Butler, J. (2004). *Precarious life: The powers of mourning and violence*. Verso.

Butler, J. (2005). *Giving an account of oneself*. Fordham University Press.

Caro, D. H. (2016a). The nexus of transformational leadership of emergency services systems: Beyond the Wu-Shi-Ren (WSR)-Li paradigm. *International Journal of Emergency Services*, 5(1), 18–33. https://doi.org/10.1108/IJES-11-2015-0024

Caro, D. H. (2016b). Towards transformational leadership: The nexus of emergency management systems in Canada. *International Journal of Emergency Management*, 12(2), 113–135. https://doi.org/http://dx.doi.org/10.20381/ruor-870

Celermajer, D., Chatterjee, S., Cochrane, A., Fishel, S., Neimanis, A., O'brien, A., Reid, S., Srinivasan, K., Schlosberg, D., & Waldow, A. (2020). Justice through a multispecies lens. *Contemporary Political Theory*, 19(3), 475–512. https://doi.org/10.1057/s41296-020-00386-5

Chu, I., & Vu, M. C. (2021). The nature of the self, self-regulation and moral action: Implications from the Confucian relational self and Buddhist non-self. *Journal of Business Ethics*, 180, 245–262. https://doi.org/10.1007/s10551-021-04826-z

Ciulla, J. (2009). Leadership and the ethics of care, *Journal of Business Ethics*, 88(1), 3–4. https://doi.org/10.1007/s10551-009-0105-1

Cunliffe, A. L. (2009). The philosopher leader: On relationalism, ethics and reflexivity—A critical perspective to teaching leadership. *Management Learning*, 40(1), 87–101. http://dx.doi.org/10.1177/1350507608099315

Cunliffe, A. L., & Eriksen, M. (2011). Relational leadership. *Human Relations*, 64(11), 1425–1449. https://doi.org/10.1177/0018726711418388

Dachler, H. P., & Hosking, D. M. (1995). The primacy of relations in socially constructing organizational realities. In D. M. Hosking, H. P. Dachler, & K. J. Gergen (Eds.), *Management and organization: Relational alternatives to individualism* (pp. 1–28). Avebury/Ashgate Publishing Co. https://psycnet.apa.org/record/1996-97352-001

Eisenbeiss, S. A. (2012). Re-thinking ethical leadership: An interdisciplinary integrative approach. *The Leadership Quarterly*, 23(5), 791–808. https://doi.org/10.1016/j.leaqua.2012.03.001

Eisler, R. T. (2007). *The real wealth of nations: Creating a caring economics*. Berrett Koehler Publishers.

Fairhurst, G. T., & Connaughton, S. L. (2014). Leadership: A communicative perspective. *Leadership*, 10(1), 7–35. https://doi.org/10.1177/1742715013509396

Fairhurst, G. T., & Uhl-Bien, M. (2012). Organisational discourse analysis (ODA): Examining leadership as a relational process. *The Leadership Quarterly*, 23(6), 1043–1062. https://doi.org/10.1016/j.leaqua.2012.10.005

Fang, J., & Slavin, N. (2018). Ethics–Comparing ethical egoism with Confucius's golden rule. *The Journal of Business and Economic Studies, 22*(1), 17–31. http://dx.doi.org/10.53462/UCAE3552

Feldman, C., & Kuyken, W. (2011). Compassion in the landscape of suffering. *Contemporary Buddhism, 12*(1), 143–155. https://doi.org/10.1080/14639947.2011.564831

Fineman, M. A. (2010). The vulnerable subject and the responsive state. *Emory Law Journal, 60*(2), 251–275.

Fisher, B., & Tronto, J. (1990). Towards a feminist theory of caring. In E. K. Abel & M. K. Nelson (Eds.), *Work and identity in women's lives* (pp. 35–62). Psychology Press.

Folke, C., Polasky, S., Rockström, J., Galaz, V., Westley, F., Lamont, M., Scheffer, M., Österblom, H., Carpenter, S. R., Chapin, F. S., Seto, K. C., Weber, E. U., Crona, B. I., Daily, G. C., Dasgupta, P., Gaffney, O., Gordon, L. J., Hoff, H., Levin, S. A., Lubchenco, J., Steffen, W., & Walker, B. H. (2021). Our future in the Anthropocene biosphere. *Ambio, 50*(4), 834–869. https://doi.org/10.1007/s13280-021-01544-8

Foster, G. D. (1981). Law, morality, and the public servant. *Public Administration Review, 41*(1), 29–34. https://doi.org/10.2307/975721

Frederick, R. E. (1999). An outline of ethical relativism and ethical absolutism. In R. E. Frederick (Ed.), *A companion to business ethics*. Blackwell Publishers Ltd. https://doi.org/10.1002/9780470998397.ch6

Freeman, R. E., & Gilbert, D. R. (1988). *Corporate strategy and the search for ethics*. Prentice-Hall.

Friedman, M. (1962). *Capitalism and freedom*. University of Chicago Press.

Geale, S. (2012). The ethics of disaster management. *Disaster Prevention and Management,, 21*(4), 445–462. https://doi.org/10.1108/09653561211256152

Gergen, K. J. (1999). *An invitation to social construction*. SAGE Publications Ltd.

Gilligan, C. (1977). In a different voice: Women's conceptions of self and morality. *Harvard Educational Review, 47*(4), 481–517. https://psycnet.apa.org/doi/10.17763/haer.47.4.g6167429416hg5l0

Gilligan, C. (1982). *In a different voice: Psychological theory and women's development*. Harvard University Press.

Gilligan, C. (1995). Hearing the difference: Theorizing connection. *Hypatia, 10*(2), 120–127. https://doi.org/10.1111/j.1527-2001.1995.tb01373.x

Gilson, E. (2011). Vulnerability, ignorance, and oppression. *Hypatia, 26*(2), 308–322. https://doi.org/10.1111/j.1527-2001.2010.01158.x

Gilson, E. C. (2014). *The ethics of vulnerability: A feminist analysis of social life and practice*. Routledge. https://doi.org/10.4324/9780203078136

Grint, K. (2005). Problems, problems, problems: The social construction of 'leadership. *Human Relations, 58*(11), 1467–1494. https://psycnet.apa.org/doi/10.1177/0018726705061314

Gorddard, R., Colloff, M. J., Wise, R. M., Ware, D., & Dunlop, M. (2016). Values, rules and knowledge: Adaptation as change in the decision context. *Environmental Science and Policy, 57*, 60–69. https://doi.org/10.1016/j.envsci.2015.12.004

Gyatso, K. (2003). *Universal compassion: Inspiring solutions for difficult times*. Cumbria, England: Tharpa Publications.

Hampshire, S. (1983). *Morality and conflict*. Harvard University Press.

Harris, I. (1995). Buddhist environmental ethics and detraditionalization: The case of EcoBuddhism. *Religion, 25*(3), 199–211. https://doi.org/10.1006/RELI.1995.0019

Harvey, P. (2017). Avoiding unintended harm to the environment and the Buddhist ethic of intention. *The Journal of Buddhist Ethics, 14*, 1–34. http://www.buddhistethics.org/14/harvey-article.pdf

Hawk, T. F. (2011). An ethic of care: A relational ethic for the relational characteristics of organizations. In M. Hamington & M. Sander-Saudt (Eds.), *Applying care ethics to business*. Springer Dordrecht. https://doi.org/10.1007/978-90-481-9307-3

Hawk, T. F., & Lyons, P. R. (2008). Please don't give up on me: When faculty fail to care. *Journal of Management Education, 32*(3), 316–338. https://doi.org/10.1177/1052562908314194

Held, V. (2006). *The ethics of care*. Oxford University Press.

Hoppe, K. (2020). Responding as composing: Towards a post-anthropocentric, feminist ethics for the Anthropocene. *Distinktion: Journal of Social Theory, 21*(2), 125–142. https://doi.org/10.1080/1600910X.2019.1618360

Hosking, D. M. (1988). Organizing, leadership and skilful process. *Journal of Management Studies, 25*(2), 147–166. https://doi.org/10.1111/j.1467-6486.1988.tb00029.x

Hulme, M. (2014). Climate change and virtue: An apologetic. *Humanities, 3*(3), 299–312. https://doi.org/10.3390/h3030299

Humphreys, S. (2014). Climate justice: The claim of the past. *Journal of Human Rights and the Environment, 5*, 134–148. https://doi.org/10.4337/9781784711900.00014

Izraeli, D. (1988). Ethical beliefs and behavior among managers: A cross-cultural perspective. *Journal of Business Ethics, 7*, 263–271. https://doi.org/10.1007/BF00381831

Jenkins, W., Berry, E., & Kreider, L. B. (2018). Religion and climate change. *Annual Review of Environment and Resources, 43*(1), 85–108. https://doi.org/10.1146/annurev-environ-102017-025855

Jordan, K., & Kristjánsson, K. (2017). Sustainability, virtue ethics, and the virtue of harmony with nature. *Environmental Education Research, 23*(9), 1205–1229. https://doi.org/10.1080/13504622.2016.1157681

Jurkiewicz, C. L. (2017). Ethics in crisis management. In A. Farazmand (Ed.), *Global encyclopedia of public administration, public policy, and governance* (pp. 1–5). Routledge. http://dx.doi.org/10.1007/978-3-319-31816-5_2749-1

Kaza, S. (2014). Buddhist contributions to climate response. *Journal of Oriental Studies, 24*, 73–92. https://www.totetu.org/assets/media/paper/j024_073.pdf

Kopnina, H., Washington, H., Taylor, B., & Piccolo, K. (2018). Anthropocentrism: More than just a misunderstood problem. *Journal of Agricultural Environmental Ethics, 31*, 109–127. https://doi.org/10.1007/s10806-018-9711-1

Larios, J. (2019). Levinas and the primacy of the human. *Ethics and the Environment, 24*(2), 1–22. https://doi.org/10.2979/ethicsenviro.24.2.01

Latour, B. (2017). *Facing Gaia: Eight lectures on the new climactic regime* (C. Porter, Trans.). Polity Press.

Levinas, E. (1998). *Entre nous: On thinking-of-the-other* (M. B. Smith & B. Harshav, Trans.). Columbia University Press.

Levy, J., & Pandey, B. (2019). Combining the ethics and science of disaster management: Key issues, policy considerations and best practices. In *3C Tecnología-Glosas De Innovación Aplicadas a La Pyme* (pp. 223–251). https://doi.org/10.17993/3ctecno.2019.specialissue3.233-251

Li, C. (1994). The Confucian concept of Jen and the feminist ethics of care: A comparative study. *Hypatia, 9*(1), 70–89. https://www.jstor.org/stable/3810437

Liden, R. C., & Antonakis, J. (2009). Considering context in psychological leadership research. *Human Relations, 62*(11), 1587–1605. https://doi.org/10.1177/0018726709346374

Lilla, M. T. (1981). Ethos, ethics, and public service, *The Public Interest, 57*, 3–17. https://www.nationalaffairs.com/public_interest/detail/ethos-ethics-and-public-service

Lim, H. (2019). Environmental revolution in contemporary Buddhism: The interbeing of individual and collective consciousness in ecology. *Religions, 10*(2), 120. https://doi.org/10.3390/rel10020120https://doi.org/10.3390/rel10020120

Liu, I. (2018). Ethical pluralism and the appeal to human nature. *European Journal of Philosophy, 26*(3), 1103–1119. https://doi.org/10.1111/ejop.12350

MacIntyre, A. (2007). *After virtue: A study in moral theory* (3rd ed.). University of Notre Dame Press.

Madsen, R., & Strong, T. B. (2003). *The many and the one religious and secular perspectives on ethical pluralism in the modern world.* Princeton University Press.

Martinez, J. M. (1998). Law versus ethics: Reconciling two concepts of public service ethics. *Administration & Society, 29*(6), 690–722. https://doi.org/10.1177/009539979802900609

Mayeroff, M. (1971). *On caring.* Harper & Row.

McDonald, G. (2010). Ethical relativism vs absolutism: Research implications. *European Business Review, 22*(4), 446–464. https://doi.org/10.1108/09555341011056203

McHugh, N. (2007). It's in the meat: Science, fiction, and the politics of ignorance. In M. Grebowicz (Ed.), *SciFi in the mind's eye; Reading Science through Science fiction.* Open Court Press.

Metz, T., & Clark Miller, S. (2016). Relational ethics. In H. Lafollette (Ed.), *The international encyclopedia of ethics.* John Wiley & Sons Ltd.

Moore, S. (2019, March 19). 'Real leaders do exist': Jacinda Ardern uses solace and steel to guide a broken nation. *The Guardian.* https://www.theguardian.com/world/2019/mar/19/real-leaders-do-exist-jacinda-ardern-uses-solace-and-steel-to-guide-a-broken-nation

Morrell, K., & Dahlmann, F. (2022). Aristotle in the Anthropocene: The comparative benefits of Aristotelian virtue ethics over utilitarianism and deontology. *The Anthropocene Review, 10*(3), 615–635. https://doi.org/10.1177/20530196221105093

Noddings, N. (2013). *Caring: A relational approach to ethics and moral education.* University of California Press.

Nussbaum, M. C. (1996). Compassion: The basic social emotion. *Social Philosophy and Policy, 13*(1), 27–58. https://doi.org/10.1017/s0265052500001515

O'Neill, J. (2005). *The philosophy of need.* Cambridge University Press.

Ostrom, E. (1999). Coping with tragedies of the commons: Local lessons, global challenges. *Annual Review of Political Science, 2*, 493–535. http://dx.doi.org/10.1146/annurev.polisci.2.1.493

Ostwald, M. (1990). *Nomos and Phusis in Antiphon's Peri Aletheias.* University of California.

Parkash, S. (2012). Ethics in disaster management. *Annals of Geophysics, 55*(3), 383–387. http://dx.doi.org/10.4401/ag-5633

Pine, T. (2018). *Preparation for the novel crisis: A curriculum and pedagogy for emergent crisis leadership.* UH Research Archive. https://doi.org/10.18745/TH.20539

Prieur, M. (2012). *Ethical principles on disaster risk reduction and people's resilience.* Council of Europe, European and Mediterranean Major Hazards Agreement. https://edoc.coe.int/en/environment/7166-ethical-principles-on-disaster-risk-reduction-and-people-s-resilience.html

Proctor-Thomson, S. B. (2019). Revitalising leadership for a humane world. *Journal of Management & Organisation, 25*(3), 1–4. http://dx.doi.org/10.1017/jmo.2019.18

Putman, D. (1991). Relational ethics and virtue theory. *Metaphilosophy, 22*(3), 231–238. https://www.jstor.org/stable/24437015

Ray, S. (2018). *Relational ethics and environmental concern* (Publication No. 10812963) [Master's dissertation, Purdue University]. ProQuest Dissertations Publishing.

Raz, J. (2005). *The practice of value.* Oxford University Press.

Rios, C. L., Redlener, M., Cioe, E., Roblin, P. M., Kohlhoff, S., Rinnert, S., Lang, W., Powderly, K., & Arquilla, B. (2015). Addressing the need, ethical decision making in disasters, who comes first? *Journal of US-China Medical Science, 12*, 20–26. http://dx.doi.org/10.17265/1548-6648/2015.01.003

Robinson, J. G. (2011). Ethical pluralism, pragmatism, and sustainability in conservation practice. *Biological Conservation, 144*(3), 958–965. https://doi.org/10.1016/j.biocon.2010.04.017

Rockström, J., Gupta, J., Lenton, T. M., Qin, D., Lade, S. J., Abrams, J. F., Jacobson, L., Rocha, J. C., Zimm, C., Bai, X., Bala, G., Bringezu, S., Broadgate, W., Bunn, S. E., Declerck, F., Ebi, K. L., Gong, P., Gordon, C., Kanie, N., Liverman, D. M., Nakicenovic, N., Obura, D., Ramanathan, V., Verburg, P. H., Van Vuuren, D. P., & Winkelmann, R. (2021). Identifying a safe and just corridor for people and the planet. *Earth's Future, 9*(4), 1–7. https://doi.org/10.1029/2020EF001866

Roy, E. R. (2019, March 19). 'Real leaders do exist': Jacinda Ardern uses solace and steel to guide a broken nation. *The Guardian.* https://www.theguardian.com/world/2019/mar/19/real-leaders-do-exist-jacinda-ardern-uses-solace-and-steel-to-guide-a-broken-nation

Schmidt, P. F. (1955). Some criticisms of cultural relativism. *The Journal of Philosophy, 52*(25), 780–791. https://doi.org/10.2307/2022285

Skeggs, B. (2005). The making of class and gender through visualizing moral subject formation. *Sociology, 39*(5), 965–982. http://dx.doi.org/10.1177/0038038505058381

Smith, A. (1937). *The wealth of nations.* Modern Library.

Smith, A. (1976). *The theory of moral sentiments.* Oxford University Press.

Smith, T. (2006). *Ayn Rand's normative ethics: The virtuous egoist.* Cambridge University Press. https://doi.org/10.1017/CBO9781139167352

Steffen, W., Grinevald, J., Crutzen, P., & McNeill, J. (2011). The Anthropocene: Conceptual and historical perspectives, *Philosophical Transactions of the Royal Society of London. Series A: Mathematical, Physical, and Engineering Sciences, 369*(1938), 842–867. https://doi.org/10.1098/rsta.2010.0327

Stivers, C. (2008). *Governance in dark times: Practical philosophy for public service.* Georgetown University Press.

Strauss, C., Taylor, B. L., Gu, J., Kuyken, W., Baer, R., Jones, F., & Cavanagh, K. (2016). What is compassion and how can we measure it? A review of definitions and measures, *Clinical Psychology Review, 47*, 15–27. https://doi.org/10.1016/j.cpr.2016.05.004

Swoyer, D. (2017). *How chief fire officers' transformational leadership influences personnel in life-threatening and routine situations* (Publication No. 10633535) [Doctoral dissertation, Grand Canyon University]. ProQuest Dissertations Publishing.

Thich, N. (1992). *The diamond that cuts though illusion: Commentaries on the prajnaparamita diamond sutra.* Parallax Press.

Thich, N. (1999). *The heart of the Buddha's teaching.* Random House UK.

Tilley, J. J. (2023). On deducing ethical egoism from psychological egoism. *Theoria, 89*(1), 14–30. https://doi.org/10.1111/theo.12440

Treves, A., Santiago-Ávila, F. J., & Lynn, W. S. (2019). Just preservation. *Biological Conservation, 229*, 134–141. https://doi.org/10.1016/j.biocon.2018.11.018

Trevino, L. K., Brown, M., & Hartman, L. P. (2003). A qualitative investigation of perceived executive ethical leadership: Perceptions from inside and outside the executive suite.(sociological research)(Author abstract). *Human Relations, 56*(1), 5–37. https://doi.org/10.1177/0018726703056001448

Tsalikis, J., & Fritzsche, D. J. (1989). Business ethics: A literature review with a focus on marketing ethics. *Journal of Business Ethics, 8*(9), 695–743. https://www.jstor.org/stable/25071957

Tsalikis, J., & Nwachukwu, O. (1988). Cross-cultural business ethics: Ethical beliefs difference between Blacks and Whites. *Journal of Business Ethics, 7*, 745–754. https://doi.org/10.1007/BF00411021

Tschakert, P. (2020). More-than-human solidarity and multispecies justice in the climate crisis. *Environmental Politics, 31*(2), 277–296. https://doi.org/10.1080/09644016.2020.1853448

Tschakert, P., Barnett, J., Ellis, N. R., Lawrence, c, Tuana, N., New, M., Elrick-Barr, C., Pandit, R., & Pannell, D. (2017). Climate change and loss, as if people mattered: Values, places, and experiences. *Wiley Interdisciplinary Reviews: Climate Change, 8,* 476–495. https://doi.org/10.1002/wcc.476

Tschakert, P., Schlosberg, D., Celermajer, D., Rickards, L., Winter, C., Thaler, M., Stewart-Harawira, M., & Verlie, B. (2021). Multispecies justice: Climate-just futures with, for and beyond humans. *Wiley Interdisciplinary Reviews: Climate Change, 12*(2), 1–10. https://doi.org/10.1002/wcc.699

Tsering, G. T. (2005). *The four noble truths: The foundation of Buddhist thought.* Wisdom Publications.

United Nations. (2017). *Transforming our world: The 2030 agenda for sustainable development.*

United Nations Office for Disaster Risk Reduction UNISDR. (2015). *Sendai Framework for disaster risk reduction 2015–2030.* United Nations Office for Disaster Risk Reduction. https://www.undrr.org/publication/sendai-framework-disaster-risk-reduction-2015-2030

Urquhart, C. (2019, March 18). Jacinda Ardern is the type of leader Australia desperately needs. *News.com.au.* https://www.news.com.au/world/pacific/jacinda-ardern-is-the-type-of-leader-australia-desperately-needs/news-story/fb070685d61eeb4e44445b41bdfdfc40

Verchery, L. (2021). *Impersonal intimacy: Reltional ethics and self-cultivation in a transnational Chinese Buddhist monastic network* (Publication No. 37368306) [Doctoral disseration, Harvard University].

Voegtlin, C. (2016). What does it mean to be responsible? Addressing the missing responsibility dimension in ethical leadership research. *Leadership, 12*(5), 581–608. http://dx.doi.org/10.1177/1742715015578936

Wheatley, M. (2017). *Who do we choose to be?: Facing reality, claiming leadership, restoring sanity.* Berrett Koehler Publishers.

Whyte, K. (2020). Too late for indigenous climate justice: Ecological and relational tipping points. *Wiley Interdisciplinary Reviews: Climate Change, 11*(1), 1–7. https://doi.org/10.1002/wcc.603

Williston, B. (2019). *The ethics of climate change: An introduction.* Routledge.

Wilson, S., Cummings, S., Jackson, B., & Proctor-Thomson, S. B. (2018). *Revitalising leadership: Putting theory and practice into context.* Routledge.

Wisner, B., Gaillard, J., & Kelman, I. (2012). *The Routledge handbook of hazards and disaster risk reduction.* Routledge.

PART 2

Suffering and Vulnerability

4

UNDERSTANDING SUFFERING
AS A BASIS FOR RELATIONALITY

> When we begin to see the true nature of our own suffering, we begin to understand how those who we are asked to lead, serve, and protect suffer as well. As our understanding improves, the door to relationality opens.

Central to our roles as leaders is the moral obligation to protect others from suffering, as well as not to unnecessarily cause them suffering. As leaders, what we (consciously or unconsciously) think, say and do can have a significant bearing, directly or indirectly, on the extent to which we may cause ourselves and others to suffer. This is particularly true when we make decisions on behalf of others, and it is especially true when others are not participants in our decision-making processes. A key insight from my research was to reveal that many of the leaders I interviewed did not have a good understanding of suffering and, by their own admission, thought they could do a lot more to understand it and alleviate it. However, despite this, they were still making significant decisions on behalf of others that, while made mostly in good faith, often did not meet the wishes of those experiencing suffering, whom they were called upon to lead and protect (Crosweller, 2022; Crosweller & Tschakert, 2021).

Some scholars contend that, to be virtuous, we must possess the capacity to experience suffering. Virtues such as compassion, courage, vulnerability, love, and wisdom can only be realised and expressed through these experiences. In other words, while suffering is intrinsically bad, it can also be intrinsically good if it motivates a virtuous attitude towards others that aids in reducing their suffering (Brady, 2018; Coplan & Battaly, 2021). Other scholars argue that ethics and morals do their best work in negating, minimising, or managing suffering, rather than only pursuing notions of good, such as flourishing, well-being and

DOI: 10.4324/9781003499510-6

happiness. Their arguments extend to claim that these goods, within the context in which they are being pursued, are not fully attainable while suffering is in existence (Mayerfield, 2002; White, 2012).

But what is suffering? Philosopher A.C Grayling argues that "we know in the most general terms what makes for suffering and what conduces to good; these facts by themselves call on us to act appropriately in response" (Grayling, 2021, p. 55). Nevertheless, we can gain a deeper appreciation by seeking to understand the nature of suffering from a selection of western and eastern philosophers, noting that there are many divergent views within the corpus of moral philosophy. We then reflect on some of the ways in which suffering is experienced, what happens when we do not understand suffering, and explore questions about who has responsibility for minimising suffering.

A western perspective

The etymology of the concept of suffering is derived from its Latin origins *"suffere"* or *"ferre,"* referring to a universal human experience whereby to suffer is to bear, to endure, to shoulder (Milton, 2013). Broadly speaking, suffering may be an experience of unpleasantness and aversion associated with the perception of harm or threat of harm in an individual. The opposite of suffering is pleasure or happiness (Katz, 2016).

Aristotle

Aristotle (2004) was one of the earliest philosophers to explore the tension between pleasure (happiness) and pain (suffering) within a framework of virtue. He argued that human excellence was of two kinds: intellectual and moral. Intellectual was borne, in the most part, from teaching and, as a result, needed time and experience, whereas morality came not from nature—although nature allowed our capacity to receive morality—but from custom. Virtues (morals) were gained through actions working towards excellence that were habituated from early life. All actions were to be done in moderation rather than to excess, and the extent to which they were judged as right or wrong was contingent upon our reason and social custom (right and just). We gained mastery of our virtue (morality) by willingly abstaining from pleasure (happiness) while courage was achieved through our willingness to do what was right without fear of pain (suffering). As such, all actions and feelings induced either pleasure (happiness) or pain (suffering).

For Aristotle (2004), virtues (morals) had for their object–matter pleasures (happiness) and pains (sufferings), because, by reason of pleasure (happiness), we do what is bad and by reason of pain (suffering), we decline doing what is right. Virtue, then, is assumed to be that habit which effects the best results (avoiding excessive pleasure (happiness) and willingly enduring pain (suffering)), and vice (indulging in excessive pleasure (happiness) and avoiding pain (suffering)), the contrary. The honourable, expedient, and pleasant moved us to choice, and the dishonourable, hurtful, and painful moved us to avoidance. Aristotle further argued that, while all individuals were motivated by honour and expediency to achieve pleasure, only the good succeeded through their morality, whereas the bad failed and caused hurt and pain (suffering). For Aristotle, virtuous actions that achieved good results led to happiness, while non-virtuous actions that achieved poor outcomes led to suffering.

Enlightenment philosophers

Following Aristotle, western philosophers of the Enlightenment, such as Jeremy Bentham (1998), Jean-Jacques Rousseau (Jonas, 2010) and Arthur Schopenhauer (1965), named the principle of sufferability as the belief that there is capacity for all living (sentient) beings to suffer. That is, suffering is a common and universal experience (Ricoeur, 2019). For Bentham, all sentient beings, irrespective of species, race, or sexual orientation, wished for happiness and to avoid suffering. This was to be achieved by undertaking actions that brought the greatest benefit (happiness) to the greatest number at the lowest cost (suffering).

For example, Bentham advocated for actions that included the abolition of slavery, the equality of men and women, the decriminalisation of homosexuality, the freedom of the media, and advocacy for animal rights. Importantly, human self-centredness also featured in Bentham's understanding of the causes of suffering (Erdős, 2020; Leroy, 2008). For Rousseau, happiness was to be found, not in pleasure, but in living well and educating oneself in much the same way as Aristotle had advocated for practical wisdom (*phronesis*) and human flourishing (*eudaimonia*). Maintaining our mental, physical and moral capabilities with our desires in equilibrium aided in the avoidance of suffering and the creation of happiness (Mintz, 2012).

For Schopenhauer, the source of suffering was the inability of our human will to cease striving for the satisfaction of being free from deficiency and the dissatisfaction of our own mental and/or physical state or condition in the present. Put simply, rather than accepting that suffering is a part of life, we suffer because we wish present unfortunate circumstances to be other than what they are. When our mind is in this state, happiness can only be found in the past by reflection, or by the desire for future favourable events or circumstances (Ali, 2007). We also suffer when we identify ourselves as individuals within a world of experience and causal relations (subject–object distinction), when we want things to be in certain states and not in other states, when we associate things going well with happiness and things not going well with suffering, all of which create a disjunction in our minds between how we want the world to be and how the world is (Young, 1987).

An eastern perspective

Similar sentiments have also been captured in eastern philosophies, such as Daoism, Confucianism and Buddhism. These philosophies all assert that the acceptance of suffering and adversity is preferred over actively seeking control of its causes, albeit the arguments to support such a proposition vary within each philosophy (Xie & Wong, 2021).

Daoism

Daoism promotes the natural course of suffering that a person should acknowledge and follow as a means of achieving liberation through non-attachment and non-action (Hwang, 2001). Happiness does not arise from psychological dependence or attachment to forms of domination (to avoid suffering), but from our initiatives and actions towards a modest life without attachment. Human pleasures of the senses, human relations, curiosity, and belief are narrow, relative, and temporary. These pleasures lead to conceptions of gains and losses—and therefore happiness and suffering—which inevitably torture both mind and body. Attaining the Dao involves acting non-intentionally—for example, by not holding onto things (material and non-material) that otherwise could be lost. Instead, difficult and easy complement each other, long and short form each other, high and low fill each other out, and front and back follow each other. Such non-attachment to things results in freedom from self-interest, desires, actions, and affairs that would otherwise result in suffering (Feng, 2017).

Confucianism

Confucianism promotes the acceptance of suffering as a matter of destiny while encouraging humans to address the causes of suffering through virtuous character and action (Cheng et al., 2013). Pain and suffering are seen as essential to the existential condition for human greatness (Wei-Ming, 1984), and similar to Daoism, the preoccupation of external factors over which we have little or no control is futile and only brings suffering upon oneself (Ning, 2003).

Buddhism

In Buddhism, the root cause of all human suffering arises from a mind of self-cherishing and self-grasping (Gyatso, 2006; Tsering, 2005). Self-grasping views the "I" as an inherently existent sense of self *(Atta)* that is independent of others *(Atmatantra)* and is permanent, fixed, and unchanging *(Alaya)*. Self-cherishing believes that such an "I" is most precious and more important than others, and its relentless desire *(Abhidhaya)* for pleasure, happiness, and freedom from (and avoidance of) suffering is supremely important over others' happiness and well-being (Gyatso, 2006, 2011). From self-grasping and self-cherishing emerges the three poisons of the human mind variously described as greed, hatred, and delusion (Bodhi, 2000), attachment, anger, and ignorance (Gyatso, 2014), or attachment, aversion, and ignorance (Tsering, 2005). The combination of self-grasping, self-cherishing, attachment, anger, and ignorance establish the basis for the creation of suffering *(Dukkha)* for self and other.

Some of the ways we may experience suffering

While these selected western and eastern perspectives of suffering vary, they all point towards suffering as being part of the human experience and that we should accept this rather than trying to deny, disavow, or ignore suffering while concurrently striving for happiness. They suggest that being virtuous is the basis for happiness, and being non-virtuous is the basis for suffering. They also centre the "I" as ultimately having choice about whether to act with virtue or non-virtue (and therefore accept responsibility for happiness and suffering in our own lives). Finally, they intimate that it takes a lifetime to improve our ability to make right (virtuous) choices through various methods and techniques.

Having established the nature of suffering, we now briefly explore some of the ways in which we may experience suffering.

Loss of sense of self

According to American physician and bioethicist Eric Cassell (2004),

> suffering occurs when an impending destruction of the person is perceived; it continues until the threat of disintegration has passed or until the integrity of the person can be restored in some other manner. It follows, then, that although suffering often occurs in the presence of acute pain, shortness of breath, or other bodily symptoms, suffering extends beyond the physical. Most generally, suffering can be defined as the state of severe distress associated with events that threaten the intactness of person.
>
> *(p. 32)*

Often, when we experience suffering in this way, rather than feel "intact," we feel as though a part of us is missing, has been lost, or is damaged. We perceive that we need to be fixed, healed, or re-established through processes such as psychology or justice so that we can feel complete again.

Loss of engagement

Suffering can also materialise as a loss of engagement with the world together with others, a lack of meaning and purpose, or relatedly the inability to real-ise core life values (Gordijn & Ten Have, 2020). Theologian Henri Nouwen (1996) wrote of his conviction that each of us suffers in a way that no other human being suffers and that each person's pain is so deeply personal that to compare it to another's can scarcely bring any consolation or comfort. Our present inability to truly share with others the totality of the lived experience of suffering may well be the reason that it causes so much distress and harm (Scarry, 1985).

When we experience suffering in this way, we often accompany our thoughts and words with "no one can possibly understand what it is that I am experi-encing." Similarly, if we are witnessing suffering in this context, our thoughts and words are shaped by an internal dialogue that says, "I cannot possibly imagine what others are going through right now." Our suffering feels very personal and unique, and we can easily form the view that others cannot relate to our suffering or that we cannot relate to the suffering of others.

Injustice

Suffering can also materialise through social causes and effects that lead to in-justice. Sociologist Iain Wilkinson suggests that (social) suffering is the mate-rial deprivation, social injustice, and denial of civil liberties shaped by physical, psychological, social, economic, political, and cultural influences. These influ-ences may in turn give rise to negative emotional states, such as depression, anxiety, guilt, humiliation, and distress that, while common to all, can only be known uniquely as our own (Wilkinson, 2005).

Social suffering reveals the lived experiences of those who are without power and who must endure various forms of personal degradation and ob-jectification from those who do hold and exercise power over them. Generally, in these circumstances, while agency is still available to the sufferer, it is often expended on coping and surviving rather than moving towards happiness, well-being, and flourishing (Frost & Hoggett, 2008).

These and other scholars suggest that our experiences of suffering may be expressed in both language and silence. The meaning we bring to our experience of suffering through language becomes inexorably connected to the meaning of our world more broadly and our lives more specifically (Morgan & Wilkinson, 2001; Weber, 1948; Wilkinson, 2005). When our suffering is acknowledged by others, it fortifies our human dignity (Parse, 2013) and can incentivise our individual and collective actions to prevent or minimise future suffering (Harris, 2010). However, we need to be cautious when attempting to translate and make rational sociological sense of such lived and interpretive personal experiences. This is because we may distort the individual's truth and appear ethically offensive if we do not fully comprehend the gravity of their experiences while seeking to impose solutions upon them (Bourdieu, 1999).

Alternatively, in response, some scholars argue that suffering is best acknowledged through silence. For example, Arthur W. Frank, professor of sociology at the University of Calgary, argues that

> suffering is the present or anticipated loss of what is missed and is no longer recoverable, as well as the absence of what we fear will never be. A sense an irreparable wrong with no recourse to a right. No thing nor material resource can bridge that separation, and in the absence of any form of such help, suffering is experienced as the unspeakable, the concealed, the darkness, and the dread, a wound that neither kills nor can it be healed.
>
> *(Frank, 2001)*

Sometimes, our suffering is so intense, complex, pervasive and enduring that all forms, words, sounds, shapes, or colours fail to do justice to what we are feeling.

However, when we relegate suffering to the realm of silence, we risk suppressing, subordinating, perpetuating and compounding the suffering that arises from human rights abuse and social injustice by those who hold power and responsibility to prevent or minimise it (Cohen, 2001; Das, 1997). Silence through ignorance of the suffering of others may also mystify what we dare not understand because of the very fact that, without the silence, we will indeed understand our human complicity (Rose, 1996). Silence may also degrade and trivialise the enormity of our suffering and the suffering of others (Arendt, 1958). Therefore, as leaders, politicians, experts, and citizens, not only do we need to acknowledge the harm and suffering inflicted upon another, but we need to, as part of our collective responsibility, move to action in order to do something about it or to prevent it from happening in the first place (Wilkinson, 2005).

Illness

Seeing suffering principally as an illness can distort our lived experience as something to be explained against functional and adaptive clinically normative standards. That is, suffering is a personal responsibility and ought to be curable. This can all too easily lead to possibilities of the dehumanising objectification of suffering that causes us to experience shame, guilt, and sense of failure for not living up to expectations in situations where suffering was not relieved or alleviated. In these circumstances, those of us who do not heal run the risk of being discarded (Frank, 2001; Milton, 2013).

Conversely, when we honour and affirm the ways in which people connect with others as they experience suffering, human dignity arises with reverence, as does the awe and solemn regard for our inability to adequately explain our human experiences. Therefore, there is an obligation upon us to suspend judgement and surrender any right/wrong response in attempting to "fix" the suffering of others (Parse, 2010, 2013). Who one is can never be fully known and, as such, to be in the presence of someone who is suffering is "holding dear the precious gift of humanness with devout acknowledgment of uniqueness" (Parse, 2010, p. 258).

Virtue

Theological approaches of why we suffer associate the experience of suffering with the development of virtues, such as justice, love, and faith. Non-theological approaches, such as those of Fredrick Nietzsche, stress the importance of suffering in the development of health and strength. Put simply, certain types of suffering (such as physical pain and emotional remorse) can motivate us towards the good through virtuous thought, word, and action. Philosopher Michael Brady (2018) argues that we all suffer because we have cares and concerns for things that we *value*, such as our bodies and minds, loved ones, reputations, the welfare of others, and the state of the world in general. Inevitably, these values will, at times, be threatened, undermined, harmed or unfulfilled— all of which degrade our ability to live a life of happiness, well-being, and flourishing. However, such inevitability and our inability to prevent negative experiences can also motivate us towards developing virtues associated with strength of character, vulnerability, and social virtues related to compassion, justice, and trust, as a means of alleviating suffering (Brady, 2018).

Meaning

Developing virtues through experiences of suffering can also extend to finding meaning through suffering as demonstrated in the work of Viktor Frankl (1959). Frankl wrote the book *Man's search for meaning* after being released from the concentration camps in Germany, where he spent three years, during World War II. The success and attention of his book symbolised the "mass neurosis of modern times." He called it the "unheard cry for meaning." Frankl observed that those prisoners who had oriented themselves towards a meaning of life were more likely to survive.

When they oriented themselves towards a future that may have included waiting to see their families or loved ones or to help other prisoners survive, then, even under the most oppressive conditions of psychic and physical distress, they were able to preserve their spiritual freedom. Frankl wrote "...suffering in and of itself was meaningless; we give our suffering meaning by the way in which we respond to it" and that "forces beyond your control can take away everything you possess except one thing, your freedom to choose how you will respond to the situation. You cannot control what happens to you in life, but you can always control what you will feel and do about what happens to you" (Frankl, 1959).

Suffering as a universal experience

Implicit in these experiences of suffering—whether it be a loss of sense of self, loss of engagement, injustice, perceived illness, the development of virtue, finding meaning, or any other experience—is the suggestion that suffering is individualised and unique to our sense of self, our circumstances, or our perceptions and interpretations. Our own experiences of suffering would, for most of us, validate this suggestion.

Dukkha

The truth of the experience of suffering is not quite so straightforward. Buddhism's definition of *Dukkha* captures the universality of the human experience of suffering. *Dukkha* generally refers to bodily and mentally painful feelings as well as the unsatisfactory nature, dis-ease, and general insecurity of all phenomena that are without exception impermanent in nature and liable to suffering (Thera, 2019). More specifically, *Dukkha* suggests that all living beings suffer from: birth, ageing, sickness and dying; sorrow, grief, pain, unhappiness, and unease; having to experience unpleasant things; loss and separation from pleasant things and people we love; not having wishes fulfilled; and finally, in short, the aggregates of body and mind[1] that give rise to self-grasping ignorance. These attributes of suffering are summarised as the First Noble Truth—the truth of suffering (Gethin, 2014; Harvey, 2013; Tsering, 2005). This Truth can be used to give us greater insight to the claim by many philosophers that all humans suffer.

Universally shared suffering

We are all born into this world through our mothers and, although we do not remember it, our birth is physically painful for both of us. If we can read this book, then we are in the process of growing old and experiencing the effects of an ageing body and mind. Throughout the course of our lives, we experience many kinds of illness—either temporary, permanent, or both. We all die, usually in a manner and at a time not of our choosing. Sorrow, grief, pain (mental and physical), unhappiness, and unease happen countless times throughout our lives for myriad reasons. We have had to experience unpleasant things on an almost daily basis—just watching the nightly news is enough to cause us some distress. Being cut off by another driver in traffic, becoming soaked in a thunderstorm, eating food we do not enjoy—the list is endless.

Losing things that are pleasant to us can be as simple as misplacing our favourite book or, more tragically, having our house burn down in a bushfire or having it washed away in a flood. It may also include the loss of relics, artefacts, and culture. Losing people we love inevitably occurs when they die before we do, but it can also include failed or unrequited relationships, or forced relocations that place vast distances and time between us. Not having our wishes fulfilled also happens multiple times a day in the most subtle of ways. Wishing for someone to acknowledge and answer our emails, checking a lottery ticket to see if we have won the jackpot, hoping that we receive a promotion at work, and yearning for a reconciled relationship with someone who is important to us are just a few simple examples.

Relatable experiences

Some people may argue, "yes this is all fine, but my suffering is immense, and you could not possibly understand how I feel or what I have gone through!" I was once challenged on this very issue about losing a loved one. The circumstances involved the loss of a child, perhaps the greatest loss of all, especially for parents. It is true, so far, I have been blessed not to experience losing a child, although I did share the experience of losing two children through miscarriage. I have also shared, on more than one occasion, the experience of losing a child with the parents of that child. I have witnessed the deaths of both adults and children during the course of my career. I have lost loved ones in tragic and unfortunate circumstances, and I have guided loved ones to and through their last dying breath.

So, while I cannot claim to have had a direct experience of losing a child, I have had many experiences of losing someone I loved, including the sudden and tragic loss of my wife. I have also been in the presence of those who lost someone they loved dearly, including children. In other words, I have some points of reference for relating to the experiences of losing a loved one and for developing understanding, empathy, and compassion.

The same is true of all suffering. We may not have had the exact same experience, but we have all had, to varying degrees, relatable experiences. Put simply, our capacity to relate to others through shared experiences of suffering is not binary. It is neither zero nor one. The universality of our suffering places us, in all circumstances and experiences, somewhere greater than zero and probably less than one. What makes us think of suffering in binary terms—as has been highlighted by the aforementioned moral philosophers—is our insatiable desire to ignore, deny, or disavow suffering and unskilfully seek permanent happiness. This perpetual cycle is what Buddhist philosophy labels "*samsara*"—an endless cycle of suffering without end.

However, it is only by getting in touch with our own suffering can we fully appreciate the suffering of others. Rather than ignoring, denying, disavowing, or avoiding suffering, we should take the time to enquire deeply within our minds about the nature of our suffering. In so doing, we need to learn to cultivate compassion towards ourselves in this process and then extend that compassion to others—a process we will discuss further in Chapter 8.

What happens when we do not understand suffering

One of the tragic consequences of not understanding suffering—or worse, avoiding, disavowing, ignoring, or denying suffering—is that otherwise avoidable suffering flourishes. For example, of the disaster management leaders that I interviewed for my research, over 80% admitted that they did not understand suffering well or at all, while over 90% thought they could do more to alleviate it. For most of these leaders, suffering was a concept they struggled to express or describe. Only about half the leaders interviewed were able to identify attributes of suffering, such as psychological and physical effects, as well as the loss of things material and non-material that were of value. However, many of these leaders could not express their understanding beyond these generalised attributes and some leaders did not offer up any attributes at all (Crosweller, 2022).

A significant factor in not understanding suffering was that of "denial." Some leaders denied their suffering by avoiding being overwhelmed with emotion and feeling vulnerable to deep emotions such as sadness. Other leaders interpreted resilience as denying the suffering being experienced by others, as a means of coping. There were also instances of a lack of leadership authenticity and emotional intelligence. As one political leader noted:

> I think leaders could be humbler about what they see. I think they could also find more wisdom for a response to a particular event or situation from the voice of those who have experienced that pain and suffering directly… rather than just assuming a better system, plan, or statutory framework or so on is the only answer.
>
> *(Crosweller, 2022)*

Distance and privilege were also key factors for several leaders. The further a leader was from the direct experience of suffering, the less likely they were to properly appreciate what others were experiencing. Leaders who were regarded as well-educated and economically prosperous appeared less likely to be empathetic towards others. As one senior operational leader observed:

> But when we have a leadership cadre that is mostly coming from a position of secure upbringing and good education and financial stability then it's hard for most leaders to really feel and to really touch what genuine suffering and grief and loss is.
>
> *(Crosweller, 2022)*

Similarly, some leaders expressed the view that, if a leader did not have compassion or empathy, or unless a leader had experienced suffering at the personal level, then it would be very difficult to relate to the suffering of another person (Crosweller, 2022).

For other leaders, overriding operational objectives, economic and organisational performance-oriented priorities, and numerous bureaucratic needs were more important than the needs of the citizens they were being asked to protect. Similarly, when crises were politicised, there was political competition, or when the need to protect reputation by favouring success and ignoring the nuance of suffering was present, suffering often flourished. As one leader noted:

> I just don't think (suffering) comes into their brains, honestly. I just think they are so focused on the operational task at hand, which is to put the fire out or mitigate the flood or whatever the task is, and people get in the way of that, really.
>
> *(Crosweller, 2022)*

My research showed that, when leaders failed to see the suffering of those they were asked to lead and protect, otherwise avoidable suffering increased.

The challenge for leaders

As leaders, it is critically important that we become familiar with the ways in which we suffer. Rather than denying, ignoring, or disavowing our own suffering, we need to become more conscious of it. By using a philosophical framing such as the First Noble Truth (as an example) to help us understand our suffering, we can begin the process of developing our relationality with those we are called upon to lead, serve and protect. We can begin to see that our experiences of suffering or the experiences of others are not unique. By realising that we sit somewhere on the scale of relatability to suffering that is more than zero but probably less than one, we can enhance our ability to reduce suffering by showing compassion towards ourselves and others—a subject that we will return to in more detail in Chapters 9 and 10. In the meantime, we now turn our thoughts to how the responsibility for minimising suffering is shared between citizens and their governments in disaster management.

Note

1 For example, see extensive commentary on the six primary minds and 51 mental factors in Gyatso (2014).

References

Ali, Z. (2007). Al-Ghazālī and Schopenhauer on knowledge and suffering. *Philosophy East & West*, 57(4), 409–419. https://doi.org/10.1353/pew.2007.0041

Arendt, H. (1958). *The human condition*. University of Chicago Press.

Aristotle (2004). *Selected writings: Selections from Nicomachean ethics and politics.* CRW Publishing Limited.

Bentham, J. (1998). *The principles of morals and legislation.* Prometheus Books.

Bodhi, B. (Ed.). (2000). *Ādittapariyāya Sutta; Dhammacakkappavattana Sutta.* Wisdom Publications.

Bourdieu, P. (1999). *The weight of the world: Social suffering in contemporary society.* Polity Press.

Brady, M. (2018). *Suffering and virtue.* Oxford University Press.

Cassell, E. J. (2004). *The nature of suffering and the goals of medicine.* Oxford University Press.

Cheng, C., Cheung, S., Chio, F., & Chan, J. H.-M. (2013). Cultural meaning of perceived control: A meta-analysis of locus of control and psychological symptoms across 18 cultural regions. *Psychological Bulletin, 139*(1), 152–188. https://doi.org/10.1037/a0028596

Cohen, S. (2001). *State of denial: Knowing about atrocities and suffering.* Polity Press.

Coplan, A., & Battaly, H. (2021). Enough suffering: Thoughts on suffering and virtue, *Journal of Value Inquiry, 55,* 593–610. https://doi.org/10.1007/s10790-021-09860-8

Crosweller, M. (2022). Disaster management leadership and the need for virtue, mindfulness, and practical wisdom. *Progress in Disaster Science, 16*(2002), 100248. https://doi.org/10.1016/j.pdisas.2022.100248

Crosweller, M., & Tschakert, P. (2021). Disaster management and the need for a reinstated social contract of shared responsibility, *International Journal of Disaster Risk Reduction, 63,* 1–13. https://doi.org/10.1016/j.ijdrr.2021.102440

Das, V. (1997). Sufferings, theodicies, disciplinary practices, appropriations. *International Social Science Journal, 49*(154), 563–572. https://doi.org/10.1111/J.1468-2451.1997.TB00045.X

Erdős, L. (2020). Animals are back—The ethics of Jeremy Bantham. *Green heroes: From Buddha to Leonardo DiCaprio* (pp. 19–21). Springer International Publishing.

Feng, C. (2017). The enjoyment of the sage and the common people. *Frontiers of Philosophy in China, 12*(3), 377–392. https://www.jstor.org/stable/26571907

Frank, A. W. (2001). Can we research suffering? *Qualitative Health Research, 11*(3), 353–362. https://doi.org/10.1177/104973201129119154

Frankl, V. E. (1959). *Man's search for meaning.* Beacon Press.

Frost, L., & Hoggett, P. (2008). Human agency and social suffering. *Critical Social Policy, 28*(4), 438–460. https://doi.org/10.1177/0261018308095279

Gethin, R. (2014). *The foundations of Buddhism.* Oxford University Press.

Gordijn, B., & Ten Have, H. (2020). Suffering. *Medicine Health Care and Philosophy, 23*(3), 333–334. https://doi.org/10.1007/s11019-020-09968-x

Grayling, A. C. (2021). The philosophy of compassion. In M. Hawkins & J. Nadel (Eds.), *How compassion can transform our politics, economy, and society* (1st ed.). Routledge. https://doi.org/10.4324/9780429331176

Gyatso, G. K. (2006). *Joyful path of good fortune: The complete Buddhist path to enlightenment.* Tharpa Publications.

Gyatso, G. K. (2011). *Modern Buddhism: The path of compassion and wisdom.* Tharpa Publications.

Gyatso, G. K. (2014). *How to understand the mind: The nature and power of the mind.* Tharpa Publications.

Harris, S. (2010). Antifoundationalism and the commitment to reducing suffering in Rorty and Madhyamaka Buddhism. *Contemporary Pragmatism, 7*(2), 71–89. https://doi.org/10.1163/18758185-90000168

Harvey, P., (2013). Dukkha, non-self, and the teaching on the four "Noble truths". In S.M. Emmanuel (Ed.), *A companion to Buddhist philosophy.* Wiley. https://doi.org/10.1002/9781118324004.ch2

Hwang, K.-K. (2001). The deep structure of Confucianism: A social psychological approach. *Asian Philosophy*, *11*(3), 179–204. https://doi.org/10.1080/09552360120116928

Jonas, M. E. (2010). When teachers must let education hurt: Rousseau and Nietzsche on compassion and the educational value of suffering. *Journal of Philosophy of Education*, *44*(1), 45–60. https://doi.org/10.1111/j.1467-9752.2010.00740.x

Katz, L. D., (2016). Pleasure. In Edward N. Zalta (Ed.), *The Stanford encyclopedia of philosophy* (Winter 2016 Edition). https://plato.stanford.edu/archives/win2016/entries/pleasure/

Leroy, M.-L. (2008). Jeremy Bentham or sympathy for the greatest number. *Revue Du Mauss*, *31*(1), 122–136. https://www.cairn-int.info/journal-revue-du-mauss-2008-1-page-122.htm

Mayerfield, J. (2002). *Suffering and moral responsibility*. Oxford University Press.

Milton, C. L. (2013). Suffering. *Nursing Science Quarterly,*, *26*(3), 226–228. https://doi.org/10.1177/0894318413489184

Mintz, A. I. (2012). The happy and suffering student? Rousseau's Emile and the path not taken in progressive educational thought. *Educational Theory*, *62*(3), 249–265. https://doi.org/10.1111/j.1741-5446.2012.00445.x

Morgan, D., & Wilkinson, I. (2001). The problem of suffering and the sociological task of theodicy. *European Journal of Social Theory*, *4*(2), 199–214. http://dx.doi.org/10.1177/13684310122225073

Ning, C. (2003). Mohist, Daoist, and Confucian explanations of Confucius's suffering in Chen-Cai. *Monumenta Serica*, *51*(1), 37–54. https://doi.org/10.1080/02549948.2003.11731390

Nouwen, H. J. M. (1996). *Can you drink this cup?* Ave Maria Press.

Parse, R. R. (2010). Human dignity: A human becoming ethical phenomenon. *Nursing Science Quarterly*, *23*(3), 257–262. https://doi.org/10.1177/0894318410371841

Parse, R. R. (2013). Living quality: A human becoming phenomenon. *Nursing Science Quarterly*, *26*(2), 111–115. https://doi.org/10.1177/0894318413477145

Ricoeur, P. (2019). Suffering is not pain. *Isegoría*, 93–102. https://isegoria.revistas.csic.es/index.php/isegoria/article/view/1052

Rose, G. (1996). *Mourning becomes the law: Philosophy and representation*. Cambridge University Press.

Scarry, E. (1985). *The body in pain: The making and unmaking of the world*. Oxford University Press.

Schopenhauer, A. (1965). *On the basis of morality*. Bobbs-Merrill.

Thera, N. (2019). *Buddhist dictionary: Manual of Buddhist terms and doctrines*. Buddhist Publication Society.

Tsering, G. T. (2005). *The four noble truths: The foundation of Buddhist thought*. Wisdom Publications.

Weber, M. (1948). Religious rejections of the world and their directions. In H. H. Gerth & C. Wright Mills (Eds.), *From Max Weber: Essays in sociology*. Routledge.

Wei-Ming, T. (1984). Pain and suffering in Confucian self-cultivation. *Philosophy East & West*, *34*(4), 379–388. https://doi.org/10.2307/1399173

White, R. (2012). Levinas, the philosophy of suffering, and the ethics of compassion. *The Heythrop Journal*, *53*(1), 111–123. https://doi.org/10.1111/j.1468-2265.2011.00707.x

Wilkinson, I. (2005). *Suffering: A sociological introduction*. Polity Press.

Xie, Q., & Wong, D. F. K. (2021). Culturally sensitive conceptualization of resilience: A multidimensional model of Chinese resilience. *Transcultural Psychiatry*, *59*(3), 323–334. https://doi.org/10.1177/1363461520951306

Young, J. P. (1987). The standpoint of eternity: Schopenhauer on art. *Kant-Studien*, *78*, 424–441. https://doi.org/10.1515/kant.1987.78.1-4.424

5

RESPONSIBILITY FOR MINIMISING SUFFERING

> As leaders, we have in our possession the equities of power, wealth and resource, and access to senior decision makers. By being more conscious of the nature of suffering and its causes, we can shape policies, decisions and advice that are more aware of and alert to the suffering of those we are called upon to lead, serve, and protect.

Regardless of whether suffering is viewed through the lens of either western or eastern philosophy—expressed or in silence, as an illness, an incentive towards other virtues, as the basis of finding meaning and purpose, or as a universal experience of humanity—it is generally accepted (with some notable exceptions) that suffering reflects a defect, flaw, disorder, or chaos, either in individual character and constitution or within the organisation of society (Michaelis, 2001).

These views also suggest that suffering is an experience from which we need to be liberated (through political, social or cultural actions) or from which we need to liberate ourselves, as soon as possible (Michaelis, 2001). It also suggests that, even though some suffering can bring benefits, the vast majority of suffering has little, if any, value, is destructive of virtue, and robs us of the opportunity to live a life of happiness, well-being, and flourishing (Brady, 2018; Wilkinson, 2013). Therefore, we should do all that we can, both collectively and individually, to alleviate it.

Of course, the extent to which politics should be held responsible for the alleviation of suffering, what kinds of suffering are deemed to be the focus of public recognition and relief, and what kinds of suffering are best left to individuals to endure privately to the best of their ability remain highly contested and central to the politics of modern western liberal democracies (Michaelis, 2001).

DOI: 10.4324/9781003499510-7

In this chapter we take an extensive look at how politics, in the context of the social contract for shared responsibility in disaster management, addresses responsibility for minimising suffering. More specifically, we examine how the socio-cultural influences of neoliberalism and communitarianism influence the effectiveness or ineffectiveness of four core elements that capture the relationship between the primary role of governments (governance and leadership), the role of citizens to exercise their resilience (citizen resilience), and the relationship between leaders and citizens (trust) shapes the social contract of shared responsibility. The evidence used to undertake this examination is drawn from various public inquiries of three catastrophic disasters and includes the witness statements of citizens. This has the effect of gaining perspectives from people outside of the emergency management system.

The role of politics in alleviating suffering

Despite political contestation as to who has responsibility for alleviating suffering, politics still plays an important role and has done so for over 2500 years. Politics, as a category of philosophy, was first considered by Plato and then by Aristotle (Lane, 2018). Both philosophers addressed questions about the origin of political institutions, as well as investigated the concepts used to interpret and organise political life. These included such matters as justice and equality, the association between the intentions of ethics and the nature of politics, and the relative merits of different constitutional arrangements or regimes (Lane, 2018). Many western philosophers, including Thomas Hobbs, John Locke, Adam Smith, Karl Marx, and Max Weber further progressed political philosophy to address human suffering through such matters as liberty, rights, property, justice, and law. These and other philosophers also sought to address what laws are, why they are needed, how they are enforced, and what rights and liberties should be protected (Knowles, 2001; White, 2012).

It is also the role of political philosophy to address the legitimacy of governments, their duties to the citizen, and the duties of the citizen to their government. Enlightenment philosophers, such as Thomas Hobbes, John Locke, Emmanuel Kant, Jean-Jacque Rousseau, and John Rawls, variously used the metaphor of the social contract as a way of understanding this relationship in western liberal democracies (Boucher & Kelly, 1994; O'Brien et al., 2009). One of the key functions of the social contract is to provide the conditions for citizens to act as political subjects with the legitimacy to endorse and comply with the fundamental social rules, laws, institutions, and principles of that society (D'Agostino et al., 2019).

This includes a guarantee by the state that it will provide security, order, and the rule of law as a general duty of care to, among other things, minimise the vulnerability, harm, and suffering of citizens. In return, citizens surrender some of their rights (liberties and freedoms) while obeying the government's dictates. They also take personal responsibility for their choices and the subsequent outcomes of those choices (Quinn, 2017). Constitutions often codify social contracts through the incorporation of basic rights and duties, the parameters of national identity and common values, and obligations to provide political rights and make sound economic decisions (Sobhy, 2021).

The role of the social contract

In disaster management, the social contract of shared responsibility takes shape in the form of resilience and preparedness strategies (Hunt & Eburn, 2018; McLennan & Handmer, 2014). For example, in Australia, the National Strategy for Disaster Resilience specifically refers to shared responsibility as a key element of achieving resilience (Council of Australian Governments, 2011). In the USA, the National Preparedness Goal places the responsibility for achieving reliance on every citizen (Federal Emergency Management Agency, 2015). While this shared obligation may seem appropriate, it becomes more complicated when we consider that resilience is an ambiguous term shaped by a plethora of definitions (Manyena et al., 2019).

Often, due to this ambiguity, resilience is referred to in policy terms as a "boundary object" that encompasses various meanings over time and across locations. This suggests that, rather than limit resilience to a singular definition, we need to consider important questions about how we individually and collectively see ourselves, our governments, and the relationships that exist in between (McLennan & Eburn, 2015). While these questions remain ambiguous, there is the potential to unreasonably transfer risk, cost, and responsibility away from governments and towards citizens.

The elements of an effective social contract

Ideally, an effective social contract can be achieved when certain principles are followed within the areas of governance and leadership along with the ethic of trust that needs to exist with the citizens they serve and protect. Governments need to make provision for structures that facilitate the contestability and negotiation of ideas through participative and representative democratic processes. These processes can then be used to determine the rights and responsibilities of individuals to achieve safety and inform decision-making processes about how to collectively manage emerging risks (Lodge, 2009).

Governments also need to exercise their power to regulate, plan, fund, prioritise, facilitate, and deliver on community needs such as safety. This includes a commitment to fairly distributing the equities of power, wealth, and resources made available to them to minimise risk. This is usually achieved through programs of prevention, mitigation and preparedness to reduce vulnerability and exposure, and includes the need to establish safe locations and sustainable livelihoods for citizens (Wisner et al., 2012).

Finally, governments need to provide economic, scientific and technical knowledge to aid in the calculability of risk (Beck, 1992, 2009). Social and cultural knowledge to address non-commensurable risks—including those things that we value and upon which we cannot place an economic value, such as sense of place, relics, artefacts, memories, and the like—are also important (Barnett et al., 2016; Tschakert et al., 2017), as is the provision of risk knowledge for situational awareness (Handmer & James, 2007).

It is equally important that we, as leaders, convert our agency or department's vision and mission to protect citizens into collective action by recognising diversity, showing mutual respect, and committing to community service (Perruci & Schwartz, 2002; Sotarauta et al., 2012). This collective action needs to be targeted towards ensuring human survival and well-being through relational processes while utilising our political and government institutions to achieve these objectives (Etzioni, 2015).

What establishes the bond with citizens in the social contract of shared responsibility is an ethic of trust (Bishara & Schipani, 2009; Cowden & Singh, 2017; Etzioni, 1998; Quinn, 2017; Skyrms, 2008,), in concert with the democratic processes that help us all to determine our collective understanding of the common good (Ridley-Duff, 2007). Without trust, citizens lack the fundamental means to deal with risk and instead risk being paralysed by existential dread and anxiety (Lupton, 2013).

In order for these leadership practices to establish and sustain trust, we also need to value the processes of social engagement in policy and strategy development and decision-making, understand and appreciate the complexity of human and socio-political behaviour, and treat citizens with dignity. We also need to recognise citizens for their moral worth and innate rights as precious sentient beings (Caro, 2016a, 2016b).

When trust is established and valued, citizens can look to our expertise and expert systems that support our advice for guidance on how they can protect themselves with a sense of confidence, while avoiding unnecessary stress and anxiety (Giddens, 1991, 1994; Krolikowski, 2008). This has the beneficial effect of underwriting the citizen's capacity to exercise their agency by helping them choose courses of action that have beneficial outcomes while still sharing responsibility for managing risk with government (Bickerstaff et al., 2008; Rogers & Frederick, 2000).

Effective resilience

When an effective social contract like the one above is in place, resilience strategies stand a much better chance of success. For example, commitments from governments and their leadership to respect social and cultural values and beliefs, as well as people–place relationships, provide a range of mutually beneficial outcomes (Barnett et al., 2016; Tschakert et al., 2017). These include providing the opportunity for citizens to exercise their agency, accessing social networks that can render additional emotional and physical support, and accessing various forms of risk knowledge to help them make informed decisions. An effective social contract also allows them to engage in local governance and participate in collective decision-making, access community resources to support their safety and well-being, and participate in and benefit from diverse and innovative economies that can assist to sustain their livelihoods during and after the crisis (Berkes & Ross, 2013; Folke et al., 2010; Van Zandt et al., 2020).

Understanding the principles of the social contract is important for disaster management leaders as we operate inside of the systems that give shape to this contract. In idealised conditions, we should always be thinking about how our political, social, environmental, and economic systems, and the decisions we make within them, can best benefit citizens. These benefits include keeping them as reasonably safe and secure as possible, while aiding them in their pursuit of happiness, well-being, and flourishing, without excessively trading off their individual rights, liberties and freedoms. It is important that we, as leaders, recognise the existing embedded and relational capacities of ordinary people to innovate, co-operate, and construct communities of shared interest. Sadly, too often, state-based entities ignore these capacities and instead view citizens only as passive objects of governance (Chandler, 2014).

As one highly experienced political leader observed during the course of my research:

I think (trust in government) is decreasing because people's fundamental needs are not being met. And if governments don't exist so that you can achieve your needs, safety, security, economic opportunity, personal fulfilment, a good life, a happy life, then what is government there for?

(Crosweller & Tschakert, 2021)

In her Nobel Lecture in 2009, American political economist Elinor Ostrom argued:

A core goal of public policy should be to facilitate the development of institutions that bring out the best in humans. It is not the role of the state to embark upon making people happy, altruistic, and wise, but it should provide the most appropriate conditions for people to bring the best of themselves to the surface and allow altruistic and wise people to thrive without being highjacked by selfish, reckless free-riders.

(Legrand, 2021, p. 12)

Of course, this is no small political, operational, or administrative task, but it can be made even more difficult by certain socio-political influences that seek to shift the burden of responsibility to prevent, minimise, or manage suffering too far towards citizens and too far away from governments, as is presently the situation with the social contract of shared responsibility in many modern western liberal democracies.

The political influence of neoliberalism and personal responsibility

Let's look at the example of the social contract. The original concept included a guarantee by the state that it would provide security, order, the rule of law, and space for citizens to operate as political subjects (Quinn, 2017). However, several scholars argue that citizens have been repositioned through resilience and risk reduction policies shaped by neoliberalism (Grove, 2017; Harvey, 2021; Joseph, 2016). These policies seek to reframe the social contract by rewriting the rules of engagement from political debates between governments and citizens to foregrounding and taking advantage of shifting market expectations.

This takes place predominantly through government-controlled policymaking, as well as private-sector influence. In so doing, it places the greater burden of responsibility for minimising suffering upon citizens rather than governments. This has the effect of moving the citizen from a political subject with certain (albeit often limited) rights within a social contract to an economic agent driven by the expectation of individual optimisation—personal responsibility for safety and protection without obligating the state (Collier, 2009; O'Brien et al., 2009).

When the social contract is weighted in this way, in order to satisfy their desires, citizens are expected to function autonomously while simultaneously participating in the marketplace that is governed by buyers, sellers, employers and employees. Instead of finding fulfilment in relationships with others, the citizen is encouraged to find fulfilment in the freedom from unnecessary government intervention in their affairs (Harvey, 2005; Lodge, 2009). Any regulatory intervention by a government, rather than being viewed as a tool to improve the quality of life for all people, is seen as a disruption to a functioning market economy. This has the effect of rendering governments as obsolete or an impediment in the lives of citizens (Lyster, 2019).

Liberalisation policies such as privatisation, fiscal austerity, deregulation, and decreases in government spending aimed at increasing the role of the private sector in the economy and society (Brassett & Vaughan-Williams, 2015; Dean, 1999) then extend the role of the market into almost all human actions, rather than just the production and distribution of goods and services (Adams et al., 2019; Howard & King, 2004). This has the added effect of expecting citizens to make choices that work in their best interests (often at the exclusion of the interests of others), such as enhancing personal safety through the purchase of insurance (Collier, 2009, 2013). In addition, citizens are expected to accept that they live in a dangerous world, rather than a world that aims to be safe and secure in partnership with government (Evans & Reid, 2014).

When a social contract shaped by neoliberalism is in place, resilience strategies and policies tend to reflect the bias towards individualised adaptive capacity over state responsibility by promoting self-reliant, autonomous and entrepreneurial citizens who should (but unreasonably for many people) be responsible for their own safety and protection (Garrett, 2015). These strategies and policies expect citizens to exhibit responsible behaviour, self-reliance, agency, self-efficacy, and adaptive capacity. On this presumption, governments then design and implement programs and strategies of learning, self-reflexivity, awareness and adaptability regarding crises, disasters, and other insecurities. At the same time, governments pull back from their responsibilities, reduce expenditure, or fail to adequately fund programs of risk reduction, mitigation, and preparedness (Evans & Reid, 2013; Hill & Larner, 2017; Joseph, 2016; Taşkale & Sima, 2019).

What happens when a social contract of shared responsibility is ineffective?

When I researched the inquiry reports and transcript evidence from citizens who had experienced catastrophic levels disasters (2005 Hurricane Katrina in the USA,[1] the 2009 Victorian Bushfires in Australia,[2] and the 2011 Queensland Floods in Australia[3]), as well as the resilience, preparedness, and risk reduction policies in Australia and the USA, I found evidence to suggest that the present social contracts of shared responsibility for each country were ineffective in the areas of governance, leadership, trust, and resilience (Crosweller & Tschakert, 2021). What follows is an amalgam of insights that I gleaned from these collective case studies within the areas of governance, leadership, trust, and resilience that demonstrate the effect of the bias towards individual responsibility, as well as inadequate and deficient government support.

Governance

In my research (Crosweller & Tschakert, 2021), there was evidence to suggest that inadequate risk methodologies had been developed by local authorities to inform development consent decisions. Rather than being based upon sound science, decisions appear to have been made by measures such as profitability that allowed development to occur in areas of known risk. This risk was then transferred to citizens and others when developments were sold or leased. This had the effect of placing them in harm's way, often unknowingly, sometimes willingly.

In addition, deficient instruments of power constrained state planning policy, land-use planning schemes, flood plain assessment and management, and development and construction approval processes. This limited the ability of governments to install the necessary controls to avoid or minimise risk and allowed risk to be transferred to developments and subsequent land and property acquisitions. This deficiency also constrained authorisations to act, including environments for local communities. This resulted in confusion, illegitimate self-authorisations, and sub-optimal risk treatment outcomes (Crosweller & Tschakert, 2021).

Some risk control processes were deficient because the knowledge they relied upon to make an informed assessment was either "old," absent, or present but institutions failed to act on it. As a result, some people made inadequate long-term investment decisions such as purchasing/building a dwelling/property as well as short-term welfare decisions to protect themselves and others from impacts and consequences. This had the effect of exposing them to otherwise avoidable risks. Also, inaccurate flood risk information and a poor understanding of previous flooding events resulted in citizens making sub-optimal decisions for their welfare and the welfare of others (Crosweller & Tschakert, 2021).

Likewise, poor situational awareness limited an institution's ability to issue timely warnings and information. This directly attributed towards death, injury, and loss. Despite citizens being encouraged to seek information as a function of being resilient, when individuals sought information, at times it was not available to them, or it was not in a form they could contextualise to their circumstances. A failure of institutions to plan and act in anticipation, even when knowledge was freely available from previous exercises and lived experiences, directly attributed towards deaths, losses, and other sufferings (Crosweller & Tschakert, 2021).

State-level disaster management arrangements were found to be ineffective due to incompatible systems, structures, and processes between agencies. This resulted in the inability of institutions and citizens to make informed and effective decisions to protect life and minimise loss. Also, government agencies did not exercise interoperability to the fullest extent possible. This resulted in paralysed command, control, and co-ordination; a lack of mutual understanding of capability and operating protocols between agencies; poor planning and prepositioning of resources; and inadequate evacuation planning. This, in turn, hampered effectiveness, resulting in many avoidable deaths and injuries (Crosweller & Tschakert, 2021).

There was also a lack of investment and resources in disaster planning, mitigation, and supporting capability—despite risks being well understood—which resulted in risks remaining untreated. Long-term economic constraint and, in some rural areas, decline, prevented landowners from undertaking traditional land management practices that would otherwise help mitigate the effects of natural hazard impacts. There were inadequate investments in outsourced and privatised critical infrastructure even though, for many people, the risks to this infrastructure were foreseeable. Rationalisation of local councils led to declining investments in maintenance, mitigation, and capital upgrades. Citizens felt that, through this process, their communities were forgotten or subordinated by higher priorities within an environment of fiscal constraint. This often resulted in a decrease in trust (Crosweller & Tschakert, 2021).

Leadership

There was evidence from my research (Crosweller & Tschakert, 2021) to suggest that when some citizens and communities sought reasonable information and assistance from local authorities or offered their competencies for the greater good, they were dismissed by political leaders as being troublesome or demanding. Some political leaders failed to visit localities to offer support or appreciate what citizens were experiencing and, at times, were dismissive, defensive and/or combative rather than empathetic and helpful. Many citizens proved they were willing to be resilient while acknowledging their vulnerability. However, when they sought assistance, often it was not forthcoming.

Often, this happened because of a lack of resources, commitment, and appreciation of their circumstances. Other times, it happened because of an overriding priority for political leaders to comply with rules and plans. Relief and recovery efforts were hampered because of political tensions between governments. Also, collaboration and partnership between communities and politicians were constrained by political mandates. At the same time, rigid timeframes for program delivery appeared insensitive to the needs of citizens and local communities. This often resulted in disillusionment and disappointment (Crosweller & Tschakert, 2021).

There was also evidence to suggest that operational leaders sometimes failed to meet what citizens perceived as their core and basic responsibilities, to render reasonable assistance when requested. For example, at times the critical emergency services were uncontactable, and even when assistance was eventually forthcoming, it often arrived too late to be of any help. If citizens were able to make contact, some were told the local authorities could not assist due to other priorities, even when their circumstances were dire. Some operational leaders appeared not to accept local advice nor listen to the needs of citizens and communities. Instead, they were more focused on complying with their command-and-control objectives. Reasonable requests by citizens, albeit not necessarily operationally critical, were often refused. Also, some operational leaders did not sufficiently take the time to understand the needs of victims, preferring instead to maintain strict compliance with procedures, despite a citizen's suffering being clearly on display (Crosweller & Tschakert, 2021).

On several occasions, administrative leaders would not heed calls for assistance. Rather than engender a culture of urgency, some administrative leaders positioned themselves only to the extent their planning required, rather than positioning for the extraordinary needs that severe to catastrophic disasters required. Outside professional assistance was preferred by government agencies to the knowledge and competencies of local communities. Compliance with rules, management processes, risk and liability avoidance, and timeframes took precedence over citizens' needs at local and state levels, as did the desire for efficiency over quality and effectiveness (Crosweller & Tschakert, 2021).

Trust

There was evidence from my research (Crosweller & Tschakert, 2021) to suggest that breaching and compromising trust by government agencies were defined by four aspects: perceptions of incompetence (insensitivity and insufficiency), including failing to appreciate the suffering of others, not listening to local advice and knowledge, and failing to effectively communicate; a lack of timely and accurate warnings and information; not having promises kept or commitments fulfilled, including physical assistance; and feelings of abandonment by government.

Resilience

Many resilience policies established the expectation that all citizens would exercise their agency in all circumstances while at the same time denying the opportunity for the individual to be vulnerable. Resilience strategies consistently called for citizens who chose to live in hazard-prone zones to be aware of their disaster risks and accept responsibility for preparing and managing their own response and recovery. However, those who had been disadvantaged for a long time simply did not have the means to participate in such aspirational activities. Many policies promoted resilience as a strength, irrespective of the hazard or the personal circumstances that citizens found themselves in at the time of the disaster (Crosweller & Tschakert, 2021).

There appeared to be scant regard towards accepting that some citizens could do no more and needed assistance from their respective governments. The absence of any assistance from authorities forced many citizens not only to exercise their agency to the extent to which they were able but also to extend themselves beyond their conscious capacity without any hope of assistance. As one disaster survivor painfully recounted:

> We were abandoned. City officials did nothing to protect us … We never felt so cut off in all our lives. When you feel like this you do one of two things, you either give up or go into survival mode. We chose the latter.

This is how we made it. We slept next to dead bodies, we slept on streets at least four times next to human faeces and urine. There was garbage everywhere in the city. Panic and fear had taken over.

(Crosweller & Tschakert, 2021)

What went wrong with the social contract?

By any measure, reading this evidence raises deep concerns about how sometimes we can get things wrong. All these observations were made by citizens in their transcript evidence to various inquiries. The evidence tends to suggest that we do not fully appreciate the suffering of others for myriad reasons.

For example, there were many instances when private interests were prioritised over public good, such as in land-use planning, urban design, construction standards, and flood plain management that created otherwise avoidable risks that were subsequently transferred to citizens and communities. Despite assurances informed by expert systems and professional expertise that existing risk treatments implemented by governments would be sufficient to afford protection, this was often not the case. Instead, there were underfunded and inadequate commitments to pre-disaster prevention and mitigation. Public safety was usurped by other factors deemed more important, such as profitability and political popularism, which established the basis for numerous breaches of trust. There were also many instances where there was an absence of state-of-the-art disaster risk knowledge and targeted knowledge provision for accurate decision-making in disaster risk reduction (Crosweller & Tschakert, 2021).

Also, some disaster management leaders failed to sufficiently respond and protect citizens and communities, appearing unable or unwilling to meet their duty to protect them. The evidence suggested that sometimes leaders favoured compliance and defence of rules and operating frameworks over their duty to provide protection. There was also evidence to suggest that there were unqualified expectations that citizens should have been resilient in all circumstances, that this was their moral responsibility, and that they should have relied upon their individual agency and fate rather than the state. However, even when citizens did display resilience until they exhausted their capacity, assistance from government agencies was often not forthcoming for reasons that some witnesses deemed hard to understand (Crosweller & Tschakert, 2021).

The political influence of communitarianism and shared responsibility

Fortunately, there are other socio-cultural alternatives to neoliberalism. Communitarianism influences the way governments establish policies based on the idea that "much social conduct is, and that more ought to be, sustained and guided by the informal web of social bonds and by the moral voices of the community" (Etzioni, 1998, p. xii). Communitarianism advocates for governance structures that allow negotiation, conflict and contestation through both participative and representative democracy when determining individual rights and responsibilities between governments and citizens. Governments play a central role in exercising power to minimise vulnerability and exposure to risk, as well as creating safer communities through various government programs, including mitigation and resilience (Lodge, 2009; Ridley-Duff, 2007; Wisner et al., 2012).

Communitarianism challenges classical liberal–individualist conceptions of society by promoting strong communities that help create social stability and cohesion and prevent social ills (Cowden & Singh, 2017; Sage, 2012). Here, the citizen is an inherently social entity created within a broader group identity that has a strong desire for community and from which social goods flow (Sage, 2012). From a communitarian perspective, the citizen "recognises the embeddedness and interdependence of human life and promotes social and civic values above individual ones" (Driver & Martell, 1997, p. 29).

Unlike neoliberalism, governments commit to the equitable distribution of power, wealth and resources to minimise risk through mitigation and prevention systems, as well as other programs that can help reduce vulnerability and exposure to risk. At the same time, they establish safe locations and sustainable livelihoods for citizens (Wisner et al., 2012). Such approaches can also provide them with greater opportunities to exercise agency as part of their "social contract" to protect themselves and their communities through strategies of resilience (Berkes & Ross, 2013).

Communitarian approaches to resilience aim to establish strong foundations for good governance, dependable access to community infrastructure, and diverse and innovative economies (Berkes & Ross, 2013). Against these foundations, access to reliable information, support for individual adaptive capacity (Norris et al., 2008), agency (Brown & Westaway, 2011), functional social networks, and the ability to assist others (Ross & Berkes, 2014) are arguably most important. Equally key is the capacity for citizens and communities to shape and influence local resilience policies and programs (Mackinnon & Derickson, 2013), as well as having their values and beliefs recognised and respected (Tschakert et al., 2017).

My research was able to show that effective resilience was achieved when communities received genuine government support, especially when they were able to create and organise their own events and projects in their own time and in a manner consistent with their history, culture and social processes. In addition, the strong presence of a functional social network—coupled with individual agency and local community capacity—increased the community's proficiency in coping with the disaster's effects. Communities also felt empowered and were more successful in achieving resilience outcomes when alternative funding sources were made available to them, and the community possessed the skills required to communicate and interface with the government over matters including funding and policy (Crosweller & Tschakert, 2021).

In these circumstances, well-functioning knowledge and systems within governance helped citizens in making informed decisions in the best interests of themselves and others. Effective mitigation was achieved when supported by sensible government investments. Leadership was far more effective when utilising institutional resources in tandem with being relatable, committed, venturous, accountable, and compassionate when protecting citizens. Where access to adequate power, wealth and resources was made available, along with accurate and accessible information, citizens did step in, step up, and achieve significant benefits for themselves and others through resilience. In circumstances such as these, trust was largely upheld between themselves and their governments (Crosweller & Tschakert, 2021).

How can leaders help reinstate the social contract to lessen suffering?

The limitations of neoliberalism

The evidence suggests that neoliberalism contributed towards some of the causes of what went wrong during Hurricane Katrina, the Victorian Bushfires, and the Queensland Floods by shifting responsibility for disaster risk management too far away from governments and too far towards citizens (Crosweller & Tschakert, 2021). However, the evidence also suggests that neoliberalism may have further contributed to the problems it tried to solve by revealing the limitations of its approach. Subsequently, this may open up pathways for the social contract to be reinstated.

Contemporary forms of neoliberalism tend to approach disaster management and resilience from a top–down, highly regulatory, and interventionalist perspective. This approach presumes that emerging problems exist within a "closed system" defined by "known knowns" and "known unknowns"— things that can be controlled through the progressive accumulation of expert knowledge, laws, and the regulation of human affairs that favour market interventions and the creation of resilient economic citizens. In an attempt to govern these problems, this approach also presumes that interventions are made from outside of the system (Chandler, 2014). That is to say, "within the limits of risk treatment effectiveness" (governance and control) (see Figure 2.2 in Chapter 2).

However, this approach does not adequately take into account the interdependent complexity of life that also produces "unknown unknowns" (Cilliers, 1998; Toffler, 1984). It fails to consider that some of the causes and effects of problems and solutions cannot be known prior to experience (Folke et al., 2010;

Walker et al., 2006). As a result, these same neoliberal interventions fail in their desire to govern and control. Instead, they contribute towards problems by becoming self-limiting in providing solutions (Chandler, 2014; Schmidt, 2015). That is to say, the consequences of the disaster go "beyond the limits of risk treatment effectiveness" (governance and control) (see Figure 2.2 in Chapter 2) and rend the government and its agents vulnerable in concert with citizens.

Beyond the Neoliberal approach

In these circumstances, interventions to increase resilience and reduce suffering can only be approached through self-reflexivity (the capacity to learn from experience) and responsivity (the capacity to act quickly in protecting oneself and others) (Byrne & Callaghan, 2014). Rather than opposing government intervention and contesting the neoliberal order, self-reflexivity and responsivity open up opportunities for alternative interventions that recognise and support existing and available capabilities of citizens and communities to exercise agency (Schmidt, 2015).

To achieve this, as leaders we can work with our governments to create interventions that remove institutional blockages resulting from unintended and unforeseeable outcomes of markets and state policymaking (Chandler, 2014; Grove & Chandler, 2016). For example, prior to the Victorian fires, firefighters were prohibited from giving specific advice to residents about how to prepare their properties for fire. The legislation made no provision for indemnity from professional liability and residents were expected to seek such advice from the private sector in the form of consultants.

Those who could afford to pay for the advice would receive it, but those who could not had to work it out for themselves. In essence, the system was asking citizens to become fire management experts. After 39 years in this sector, I can assure readers that it takes many years to develop the level of expertise required to prepare for and understand the effects of catastrophic fire activity. Amending legislation to afford protection from liability for firefighters would seem a sensible approach that is easily achievable for a government to enact while increasing the agency of citizens to act in the interests of their own safety.

At the same time, we can work with our governments to address questions of social difference (class, gender, race, religion, etc.), inequality, hierarchy (Joseph, 2002), and injustice (Ziervogel et al., 2017) within communities that increase the otherwise avoidable vulnerability of citizens. Rather than taking a unilateral perspective on resilience (one size fits all), we could accelerate our efforts to work with communities to genuinely understand the different social needs and then work with our governments to address these needs. While some may argue this is already occurring in many communities, we should continue to seek out, exemplify, and expand these approaches in partnership with community.

We could also encourage contestation and ongoing consideration of diverse options and complex trade-offs to address the dynamics of differential power between governments and their citizens (Harris et al., 2017). Put simply, we could be more generous in sharing our decision-making power with those citizens that we aim to serve and protect. We could afford them greater choice rather than forcing them to comply with our policies, systems and processes.

I remember being told a story of some community members who had come together after a major flood to help each other with essential needs, such as food and shelter. Unfortunately, their water storage had become contaminated with floodwater, and they needed a fresh supply. When they contacted the authorities, they were told that they would need to leave their property and register at the relief and evacuation centre. The residents explained their dilemma and that they were more than happy to persist on their properties. All they needed was a delivery of fresh water. The authorities refused, as it was not in accordance with their relief and recovery plans, and they could not spare the resources to fulfil the request. Ironically, this was a case where citizens were prepared to be responsible and innovative, but "the system" would not grant them permission to exercise their agency, as it was perceived by "the system" as a loss of control.

Alternative modes of governance

Such resilience-thinking brings into focus the opportunity for different modes of governance that may help reframe government interventions, rebalance the citizen from an economic agent to a political subject, and reinstate the social contract for shared responsibility in disaster management. Two possible approaches are through "everyday democracy" and "polycentric governance."

British political theorist Marcus Stears (2011) argues that "everyday democracy" involves governing through society by strengthening social relationships and by recognising the existing resilience capacities and capabilities of citizens. Everyday democracy also validates a citizen's ability to co-operate, innovate, and construct communities of shared interest without overlooking indisputable struggles that many people face in everyday life. In other words, effective relationships do not displace the need for government interventions, but rather They "establish structures that enable otherwise disconnected people to... come together to identify shared concerns... and build solidarity" (Stears, 2011, p. 71). As highlighted by Mackinnon and Derickson (2013, p. 255), "if alternative social relations are to be realised democratically and sustainably, and in ways that are wide reaching and inclusive, then uneven access to material resources and the levers of social change must be addressed."

American political scientists Elinor Ostrom and Vincent Ostrom (Ostrom, 1989, 1991, 1999, 2010) proposed a system of "polycentric governance" that could still operate within the contemporary neoliberal political economy.

Their proposed approach involved the establishment of political collectives of variable composition and scale. These collectives would be shaped in response to problems defined by human choices, values, and interests as well as by data, information, and intelligence (knowledge) used by administrations to inform their expert decisions. In this model of governance, governments and their expertise and expert knowledge would still be present; but rather than to establish pure facts and instrumentality in which to govern, they would help the collective understand the size of the problem and potential pathways to solution alongside those whose interests, values, and preferences were being affected at scale (Biggs et al., 2012; Collier, 2017).

To further assist, governments should also be prepared to acknowledge the institutional limitations of their knowledge. This would afford citizens the opportunity to accept government knowledge and the accompanying narratives as contingent and open to change and challenge. In turn, it would allow citizens to better realise their own sense of agency to the extent they are able (Collier, 2017; Rossdale, 2015). The provision of risk knowledge should also be adjusted according to the contextual needs of citizens and their social, cultural, and economic circumstances, and integrated into the design of knowledge management systems (Spiekermann et al., 2015). Such an approach would assist in improving the trust between citizens and their governments.

These modes of governance make provision for processes of deliberation and contestation between citizens and their governments within a democratic political framing to enable just outcomes. They improve the opportunity for the fair distribution of social and material benefits; enable meaningful participation on decision-making processes; acknowledge and respect social, cultural, and political differences; and recognise the right to access minimum levels of capabilities and opportunities to achieve livelihood and well-being aspirations of citizens (Ziervogel et al., 2017). They also open up opportunities for the shared development of resilience policies that are place-based and values-placed (Tschakert et al., 2017) and address multidimensional vulnerabilities that prevent citizens from exercising their willingness and capacity for resilience (Crosweller & Tschakert, 2020; Wisner et al., 2012). In so doing, they make a substantial contribution towards minimising suffering.

The challenge for leaders

Implicit in the definitions of suffering from both the western and eastern philosophers that we have cited in Chapter 4 is the notion of personal responsibility—that our thoughts, words, and actions contribute towards the extent to which we either suffer or find a genuine sense of happiness. However, the political philosophers that I have cited in this chapter, who have given shape to the notion of the social contract of shared responsibility, also recognise that suffering has social causes. That is, we can find ourselves being affected either positively or negatively by the decisions made by other people within political or social institutions and the manner in which they use and distribute the equities of power, wealth and resources made available to them to shape those decisions.

As leaders, we must constantly navigate this tension between individual and social responsibility for suffering. A neoliberal political discourse will want us to place the greater burden of responsibility towards the citizen and away from government. Alternatively, a communitarian political discourse will seek to ensure our political and social institutions take on greater responsibility for providing the conditions for citizens to achieve happiness and well-being, and to flourish. Our capacity to shape the political discourses that emerge from these various critiques of government intervention is extremely difficult but not impossible.

As institutional leaders, we have in our possession, to varying degrees, the equities of power, wealth and resources. We also have varying degrees of access to senior policy and decision-makers, either directly or indirectly. By being more conscious of the nature of suffering and its causes, we can help shape policies, decisions, and advice in a way that is more aware of and alert to the suffering of others whom we lead, serve and protect. The degree of equity and access may seem small depending on where we sit within the institutional framework, but it is not zero. Again, it is somewhere between zero and one, and all thoughts, words, and actions matter.

With this tension in mind, along with the equities made available to us, we can achieve better outcomes for those we seek to lead and protect, by being in action before otherwise avoidable suffering arises. And to achieve this, we must gain a greater appreciation of vulnerability.

Notes

1 Hurricane Katrina made landfall at Buras, on the southeast corner of Louisiana at 6:10 a.m. on Monday 29 August 2005. Loss and damage included the deaths of 1577 people; an area of 90,000 square miles damaged; 300,000 homes destroyed or rendered unliveable; economic losses of USD125–150 billion; 1.7 million people without power; and 118 million cubic yards of debris (United States Bipartisan Committee to Investigate the Preparation for and Response to Hurricane Katrina, 2006).
2 Saturday 7 February 2009, culminated in 316 grass, scrub or forest fires that caused the death of 173 people and destroyed over 2000 homes, thousands of other structures, and over 10,000 kilometres of fencing. Approximately 430,000 hectares of land burned with an estimated economic cost greater than AUD4 billion. According to the Bushfires Royal Commission, at that point, this was one of Australia's worst disasters (Teague et al., 2010). It was only to be exceeded by the more recent catastrophic bushfire events in Australia in 2019/2020.
3 During December 2010 and stretching into January 2011, 33 people died in the floods and three remain missing. More than 78% of the state (an area bigger than France and Germany combined) was declared a disaster zone, with 2.5 million people affected and 29,000 homes and businesses inundated. The estimated cost of flooding was above AUD10 billion (Holmes, 2012).

References

Adams, G., Estrada-Villalta, S., Sullivan, D., & Markus, H. R. (2019). The psychology of neoliberalism and the neoliberalism of psychology. *Journal of Social Issues*, *75*(1), 189–216. https://doi.org/10.1111/josi.12305

Barnett, J., Tschakert, P., Head, L., & Adger, W. N. (2016). A science of loss. *Nature Climate Change*, *6*(11), 976–978. https://doi.org/10.1038/nclimate3140

Beck, U. (1992). *Risk society: Towards a new modernity*. Sage Publications.

Beck, U. (2009). World at risk society and manufactured uncertainties. *Iris. European Journal of Philosophy and Public Debate*, *1*(2), 291–299. https://doi.org/10.1400/181900

Berkes, F., & Ross, H. (2013). Community resilience: Toward an integrated approach. *Society & Natural Resources*, *26*(1), 5–20. https://doi.org/10.1080/08941920.2012.736605

Bickerstaff, K., Simmons, P., & Pidgeon, N. (2008). Constructing responsibilities for risk: Negotiating citizen–state relationships. *Environment and Planning A*, *40*(6), 1312–1330. https://doi.org/10.1068/a39150

Biggs, R., Schlüter, M., Biggs, D., Bohensky, E. L., Burnsilver, S., Cundill, G., Dakos, V., Daw, T. M., Evans, L. S., Kotschy, K., Leitch, A. M., Meek, C., Quinlan, A., Raudsepp-Hearne, C., Robards, M. D., Schoon, M. L., Schultz, L., & West, P. C. (2012). Toward principles for enhancing the resilience of ecosystem services. *Annual Review of Environment and Resources*, *37*, 421–448. https://doi.org/10.1146/annurev-environ-051211-123836

Bishara, N. D., & Schipani, C. A. (2009). Strengthening the ties that bind: Preventing corruption in the executive suite. *Journal of Business Ethics*, *88*(Suppl. 4), 765–780. https://doi.org/10.1007/s10551-009-0325-4

Boucher, D., & Kelly, P. (1994). *The social contract from Hobbes to Rawls*. Routledge.

Brady, M. (2018). *Suffering and virtue*. Oxford University Press.

Brassett, J., & Vaughan-Williams, N. (2015). Security and the performative politics of resilience: Critical infrastructure protection and humanitarian emergency preparedness. *Security Dialogue*, *46*(1), 32–50. https://doi.org/10.1177/0967010614555594

Brown, K., & Westaway, E. (2011). Agency, capacity, and resilience to environmental change: Lessons from human development, well-being, and disasters. *Annual Review of Environment and Resources*, *36*(1), 321–342. https://doi.org/10.1146/annurev-environ-052610-092905

Byrne, D. S., & Callaghan, G. (2014). *Complexity theory and the social sciences: The state of the art*. Routledge.

Caro, D. H. (2016a). The nexus of transformational leadership of emergency services systems: Beyond the Wu-Shi-Ren (WSR)-Li paradigm. *International Journal of Emergency Services*, *5*(1), 18–33. https://doi.org/10.1108/IJES-11-2015-0024

Caro, D. H. (2016b). Towards transformational leadership: The nexus of emergency management systems in Canada. *International Journal of Emergency Management*, *12*(2), 113–135. https://doi.org/http://dx.doi.org/10.20381/ruor-870

Chandler, D. (2014). Beyond neoliberalism: Resilience, the new art of governing complexity. *Resilience: International Policies, Practices and Discourses*, *2*(1), 47–63. https://doi.org/10.1080/21693293.2013.878544

Cilliers, P. (1998). *Complexity and postmodernism: Understanding complex systems*. Routledge.

Collier, S. J. (2009). Topologies of power: Foucault's analysis of political government beyond governmentality. *Theory, Culture & Society*, *26*(6), 78–108. https://doi.org/10.1177/0263276409347694

Collier, S. J. (2013). Neoliberalism and natural disaster: Insurance as political technology of catastrophe. *Journal of Cultural Economy*, *7*(3), 273–290. https://doi.org/10.1080/17530350.2013.858064

Collier, S. J. (2017). *Neoliberalism and rule by experts*. Palgrave Macmillan.
Council of Australian Governments. (2011). *National strategy for disaster resilience*. Australian Institute Disaster Resilience.
Cowden, S., & Singh, G. (2017). Community cohesion, communitarianism and neoliberalism. *Critical Social Policy*, *37*(2), 268–286. https://doi.org/10.1177/0261018316670252
Crosweller, M., & Tschakert, P. (2020). Disaster management leadership and policy making: a critical examination of communitarian and individualistic understandings of resilience and vulnerability. *Climate Policy*, 1–19. https://doi.org/https://doi.org/10.1080/14693062.2020.1833825
Crosweller, M., & Tschakert, P. (2021). Disaster management and the need for a reinstated social contract of shared responsibility. *International Journal of Disaster Risk Reduction*, *63*, 1–13. https://doi.org/10.1016/j.ijdrr.2021.102440
D'Agostino, F., Gaus, G., & Thrasher, J. (2019). Contemporary approaches to the social contract. In E. N. Zalta (Ed.), *The Stanford encyclopedia of philosophy* (Fall 2019 ed.) Metaphysics Research Lab, Stanford University.
Dean, M. (1999). *Governmentality: Power and rule in modern society* (2nd ed.). Sage Publications.
Driver, S., & Martell, L. (1997). New labour's communitarianisms. *Critical Social Policy*, *17*(52), 27–46. https://doi.org/10.1177/026101839701705202
Etzioni, A. (1998). *The essential communitarian reader*. Rowman & Littlefield Publishers.
Etzioni, A. (Ed.). (2015). *Communitarianism*. John Wiley & Sons.
Evans, B., & Reid, J. (2013). Dangerously exposed: The life and death of the resilient subject. *Resilience: International Policies, Practices, and Discourses*, *1*(2), 83–98. https://doi.org/10.1080/21693293.2013.770703
Evans, B., & Reid, J. (2014). *Resilient life: The art of living dangerously*. Polity Press.
Federal Emergency Management Agency. (2015). *National preparedness goal* (2nd ed.). https://www.fema.gov/emergency-managers/national-preparedness/goal
Folke, C., Carpenter, S. R., Walker, B., Scheffer, M., Chapin, T., & Rockström, J. (2010). Resilience thinking: Integrating resilience, adaptability and transformability. *Ecology and Society*, *15*(4), 419. https://doi.org/10.5751/ES-03610-150420
Garrett, P. M. (2015). Questioning tales of 'ordinary magic': 'resilience' and neoliberal reasoning. *British Journal of Social Work*, *46*(7), 1909–1925. https://doi.org/10.1093/bjsw/bcv017
Giddens, A. (1991). *Modernity and self-identity: Self and society in the late modern age*. Polity Press.
Giddens, A. (1994). *Beyond left and right: The future of radical politics*. Polity Press.
Grove, K. (2017). Disaster biopolitics and the crisis economy. In J. Lawrence & S.M. Wiebe (Eds.), *Biopolitical disaster* (pp. 30–46). Routledge. https://doi.org/10.4324/9781315620213-4
Grove, K., & Chandler, D. (2016). Introduction: Resilience and the Anthropocene: The stake of 'renaturalising' politics. *Resilience: International Policies, Practices, and Discourses*, *5*(2), 1–13. https://doi.org/10.1080/21693293.2016.1241476
Handmer, J., & James, P. (2007). Trust us and be scared: The changing nature of contemporary risk. *Global Society*, *21*(1), 119–130. https://doi.org/10.1080/13600820601116609
Harris, L. M., Chu, E. K., & Ziervogel, G. (2017). Negotiated resilience. *Resilience: International Policies, Practices, and Discourses*, *6*(3), 1–19. https://doi.org/10.1080/21693293.2017.1353196
Harvey, D. (2005). *A brief history of neoliberalism*. Oxford University Press. https://doi.org/10.1093/oso/9780199283262.001.0001
Harvey, M. (2021). *Climate emergency: How societies create the crisis*. Emerald Publishing Limited.

Hill, L. J., & Larner, W. (2017). The resilient subject. In L. J. Hill & W. Larner (Eds.), *Assembling neoliberalism* (pp. 263–281). Palgrave Macmillan. https://doi. org/10.1057/978-1-137-58204-1_13

Holmes, C. E. (2012). *Queensland Floods Commission of Inquiry Final Report*. Queensland Floods Commission of Inquiry. http://www.floodcommission.qld.gov.au/__ data/assets/pdf_file/0007/11698/QFCI-Final-Report-March-2012.pdf

Howard, M. C., & King, J. E. (2004). *The rise of neo-liberalism in advanced capitalist economies: Towards a materialist explanation*. In P. Aretsis & M. Sawyer (Eds.), *The rise of the market*. Edward Elgar Publishing. https://doi. org/10.4337/9781845423315.00008

Hunt, S., & Eburn, M. (2018). How can business share responsibility for disaster resilience? *Australian Journal of Public Administration, 77*(2), 482–491. https://doi. org/10.1111/1467-8500.12320

Joseph, J. M. (2016). Governing through failure and denial: The new resilience agenda. *Millennium Journal of International Studies, 44*(3), 370–390. https://doi. org/10.1177/0305829816638166

Joseph, M. (2002). *Against the romance of community*. University of Minnesota Press.

Knowles, D. (2001). *Political philosophy* (1st ed.). Routledge.

Krolikowski, A. (2008). State personhood in ontological security theories of international relations and Chinese nationalism: A sceptical view. *The Chinese Journal of International Politics, 2*(1), 109–133. https://doi.org/10.1093/cjip/pon003

Lane, M. (2018). Ancient political philosophy. In E. N. Zalta (Ed.), *The Stanford encyclopedia of philosophy* (Winter 2018 ed.). https://plato.stanford.edu/archives/win2018/entries/ancient-political

Legrand, T. (2021). *Politics of being: Wisdom and science for a new development paradigm*. Ocean of Wisdom Press.

Lodge, G. C. (2009). Ideology and national competitiveness. *Journal of Managerial Issues, 21*(4), 461–477. https://www.jstor.org/stable/40604664

Lupton, D. (2013). *Risk*. Routledge.

Lyster, R. (2019). The idea of (climate) justice, neoliberalism, and the Talanoa dialogue. *Journal of Human Rights and the Environment, 10*(1), 1–24. http://dx.doi. org/10.4337/jhre.2019.01.03

Mackinnon, D., & Derickson, K. D. (2013). From resilience to resourcefulness. *Progress in Human Geography, 37*(2), 253–270. https://doi.org/10.1177/0309132512454775

Manyena, B., Machingura, F., & O'Keefe, P. (2019). Disaster resilience integrated framework for transformation (drift): A new approach to theorising and operationalising resilience. *World Development, 123*, 104587. https://doi.org/10.1016/j. worlddev.2019.06.011

McLennan, B., & Eburn, M. (2015). Exposing hidden-value trade-offs: Sharing wildfire management responsibility between government and citizens. *International Journal of Wildland Fire, 24*(2), 162. http://dx.doi.org/10.1071/WF12201

McLennan, B., & Handmer, J. (2014). *Sharing responsibility in Australian disaster management: Final report for the sharing responsibility project*. Bushfire CRC. https://www.bushfirecrc.com/sites/default/files/managed/resource/sharingresponsibilityfinal_report.pdf

Michaelis, L. (2001). Politics and the art of suffering in Hölderlin and Nietzsche. *Philosophy & Social Criticism, 27*(5), 89–115. https://doi.org/10.1177/019145370102700504

Norris, F. H., Stevens, S. P., Pfefferbaum, B., Wyche, K. F., & Pfefferbaum, R. L. (2008). Community resilience as a metaphor, theory, set of capacities, and strategy for disaster readiness. *American Journal of Community Psychology, 41*(1–2), 127–150. https://doi.org/10.1007/s10464-007-9156-6

O'Brien, K., Hayward, B., & Berkes, F. (2009). Rethinking social contracts: Building resilience in a changing climate. *Ecology and Society, 14*(2), 12–28. http://dx.doi.org/10.5751/ES-03027-140212

Ostrom, E. (1999). Coping with tragedies of the commons: Local lessons, global challenges. *Annual Review of Political Science, 2,* 493–535. http://dx.doi.org/10.1146/annurev.polisci.2.1.493

Ostrom, E. (2010). Beyond markets and states: Polycentric governance of complex economic systems. *The American Economic Review, 100*(2), 641–672. https://doi.org/10.1080/19186444.2010.11658229

Ostrom, V. (1989). *The intellectual crisis in American public administration, Tuscaloosa.* University of Alabama Press.

Ostrom, V. (1991). *The meaning of American federalism: Constituting a self-governing society.* ICS Press.

Perruci, G., & Schwartz, S. W. (2002, September 3–6). *Leadership for what? A humanistic approach to leadership development* [Paper presentation]. Art of Management and Organisation Conference, King's College, London, UK.

Quinn, M. (2017). Place leadership and the social contract: Re-examining local leadership in the east midlands. *Local Economy, 32*(4), 281–296. https://doi.org/10.1177/0269094217707279

Ridley-Duff, R. (2007). Communitarian perspectives on social enterprise. *Corporate Governance: An International Review, 15*(2), 382–392. https://doi.org/10.1111/j.1467-8683.2007.00568.x

Rogers, B., & Frederick, C. (2000). Beyond "identity. *Theory and Society, 29,* 1–47. https://doi.org/10.1023/A:1007068714468

Ross, H., & Berkes, F. (2014). Research approaches for understanding, enhancing, and monitoring community resilience. *Society & Natural Resources, 27*(8), 787–804. https://doi.org/10.1080/08941920.2014.905668

Rossdale, C. (2015). Enclosing critique: The limits of ontological security. *International Political Sociology, 9*(4), 369–386. http://dx.doi.org/10.1111/ips.12103

Sage, D. (2012). A challenge to liberalism? The communitarianism of the big society and blue labour. *Critical Social Policy, 32*(3), 365–382. https://doi.org/10.1177/0261018312444411

Schmidt, J. (2015). Intuitively neoliberal? Towards a critical understanding of resilience governance. *European Journal of International Relations, 21*(2), 402–426. https://doi.org/10.1177/1354066114537533

Skyrms, B. (2008). Trust, risk, and the social contract. *Synthese, 160*(1), 21–25. http://dx.doi.org/10.1007/s11229-006-9075-3

Sobhy, H. (2021). The lived social contract in schools: From protection to the production of hegemony. *World Development, 137,* 104986.

Sotarauta, M., Horlings, I., & Liddle, J. (2012). *Leadership and change in sustainable regional development.* Routledge.

Spiekermann, R., Kienberger, S., Norton, J., Briones, F., & Weichselgartner, J. (2015). The disaster-knowledge matrix—Reframing and evaluating the knowledge challenges in disaster risk reduction. *International Journal of Disaster Risk Reduction, 13,* 96–108. https://doi.org/10.1016/j.ijdrr.2015.05.002

Stears, M. (2011). *Everyday democracy: Taking centre-left politics beyond the state and the market.* Institute for Public Policy Research. https://www.ippr.org/articles/everyday-democracy-taking-centre-left-politics-beyond-state-and-market

Taşkale, A. R., & Sima, E. H. (2019). In pursuit of the neoliberal subject. *New Political Science, 41*(1), 149–152. https://doi.org/10.1080/07393148.2019.1559130

Teague, B., McLeod, R., & Pascoe, S. (2010). *Final report of the 2009 Victorian Bushfires Royal Commission.* The 2009 Victorian Bushfires Royal Commission. http://royalcommission.vic.gov.au/Commission-Reports/Final-Report.html

Toffler, A. (1984). *Foreword: Science and change.* In I. Prigogine & I. Stengers (Eds.), *Order out of chaos: Man's new dialogue with nature* (pp. xi–xxvi). Bantam Books.

Tschakert, P., Barnett, J., Ellis, N. R., Lawrence, c, Tuana, N., New, M., Elrick-Barr, C., Pandit, R., & Pannell, D. (2017). *Climate change and loss, as if people mattered: Values, places, and experiences. Wiley Interdisciplinary Reviews: Climate Change,* 8(5), 476–495. https://doi.org/10.1002/wcc.476

United States Bipartisan Committee to Investigate the Preparation for and Response to Hurricane Katrina. (2006). *A failure of initiative: Final report of the select bipartisan committee to investigate the preparation for and response to Hurricane Katrina.* U.S. Government Printing Office. https://digital.library.unt.edu/ark:/67531/metadc1259401/

Van Zandt, S., Masterson, J. H., Newman, G. D., & Meyer, M. A. (2020). *Engaged research for community resilience to climate change.* Elsevier. https://doi.org/10.1016/C2017-0-03017-3

Walker, B., Salt, D., & Reid, W. (2006). *Resilience thinking: Sustaining ecosystems and people in a changing world.* Bibliovault OAI Repository, the University of Chicago Press.

White, M. J. (2012). *Political philosophy: A historical introduction.* Oxford University Press.

Wilkinson, I. (2013). The problem of suffering as a driving force of rationalization and social change. *The British Journal of Sociology,* 64(1), 123–141. https://doi.org/10.1111/1468-4446.12009

Wisner, B., Gaillard, J., & Kelman, I. (2012). *The Routledge handbook of hazards and disaster risk reduction.* Routledge.

Ziervogel, G., Pelling, M., Cartwright, A., Chu, E., Deshpande, T., Harris, L., Hyams, K., Kaunda, J., Klaus, B., Michael, K., Pasquini, L., Pharoah, R., Rodina, L., Scott, D., & Zweig, P. (2017). Inserting rights and justice into urban resilience: A focus on everyday risk. *Environment & Urbanization,* 29(1), 123–138. https://doi.org/10.1177/0956247816686905

6

UNDERSTANDING VULNERABILITY AS A BASIS FOR RELATIONALITY

If you show your vulnerabilities in an appropriate way, it doesn't undermine your credibility, instead it shows that you're human like everybody else.

Importantly, if we are to achieve a reduction in the suffering of ourselves and others, it is critical that we address vulnerability as a key element of risk. In this Chapter, we recap our understanding of vulnerability from Chapter 2 as both a positive and negative conception, as well as the potential for us to become invulnerable. We then briefly examine the socio-cultural influences that shape our worldview of vulnerability and examine the effects of vulnerability and invulnerability on our organisational cultures. We conclude with a reflection on how to be vulnerable with wisdom.

Understanding vulnerability

As discussed in Chapter 2, vulnerability is a pervasive and universal feature of the human condition, experience, and identity, rather than only a property of particular marginalised or disadvantaged groups. Irrespective of who we are or the circumstances in which we find ourselves during the course of our lives, we can be susceptible to harm and suffering without the ability to cope and adapt. Even though the causes, extent, duration, intensity, frequency, and specific circumstances in which we become vulnerable can be highly variable and often driven by exposure to unfavourable circumstances, we all have ethical obligations towards each other to ensure we and others are no longer susceptible to the harmfulness and suffering that arises from being vulnerable. This is especially true if we hold power and influence over others. It is also important

DOI: 10.4324/9781003499510-8

that we contextualise vulnerability as both positive and negative in the way it is experienced. Positively, it opens up opportunities for compassion, love, relationality, and support. Negatively, it opens up possibilities of suffering, harmfulness and violence. However, if we only view vulnerability as something to be negated, we run the risk of developing a worldview driven by fear, defensiveness, denial, avoidance, and disavowal of vulnerability—that is, we risk becoming invulnerable.

An important distinction that is implicit in the definition of vulnerability is that 'susceptibility' to suffering is a future state—or in other words, "anticipatory." To be vulnerable is not to suffer in the present moment. Rather, it is the possibility, probability, or likelihood that we will suffer at some time in the future. This distinction is important because it opens up the opportunity for something to be done or actions to be undertaken to avoid, minimise or manage that possibility, probability, or likelihood in the intervening space between when the potential to suffer becomes conscious and when suffering might actually be experienced. This space is a "space of opportunity" where leadership can do some of its best work. However, to do this work, we need to appreciate some of the socio-cultural factors that can lead us off course.

The influence of institutional habitus

The influences that inform our ability to understand and acknowledge our vulnerability or to become invulnerable are likely to come from a range of factors. One example can be found in the research undertaken by Matthew Desmond (2007), in his extensive study of the lives and deaths of USA wildland firefighters. He found that a predominance of masculinity within organisational culture, shaped in part by a rejection of femininity, disavowed vulnerability in favour of an idealised image of a heroic firefighter. Here, a firefighter's character was often shaped by voluntarily undertaking serious challenges to gain social recognition under the guise that risk and any subsequent possibility of death could be tamed through competence and the exercise of control. As sociologist Erving Goffman (1967, p. 268) argued, "where honour is highly valued… men must be prepared to put up their lives in order to save their faces."

Another study involving the response to the 2011 Japan earthquake and tsunami that resulted in the Fukushima nuclear accident showed that a dominant masculinity shaped the attitudes of political and economic elites. Rather than leading through the lens of a feminist ethic of care that many people advocated for the nurturing of nature and community, leaders dismissed these calls and instead attempted to deny the vulnerability of citizens while emphasising normalcy and control (Kimura & Katano, 2014)—akin to saying, "don't worry, nothing to see here, we've got this!"

Often, the taking of such risks, along with the denial or disavowal of vulnerability, does not only find its roots within personal character. Instead, it is often the case that invulnerability manifests within the institutions where the risk takes place, as well as the manner in which our institutions make people deployable through training, education, motivation, and discipline. All of this is done in a vain attempt to manage external risks while denying, disavowing, or ignoring vulnerability altogether (Beck, 1992; Desmond, 2007; Douglas, 1986,). In other words, we can be directed and influenced towards thinking that we are or can be in control of our circumstances, such that we do not need to give much thought to the possibility that we or others might still be vulnerable. Institutional thinking and acting this way in the world constitute what sociologist Pierre Bourdieu (2000) calls a "specific *habitus.*"

For Bourdieu, a specific habitus is a "game" which is never imposed nor explicitly set out. Instead, it occurs insensibly, gradually, progressively, and imperceptibly. As leaders, we do not consciously commit nor voluntarily enter any form of contract about its intentions—in this case, to be consciously invulnerable. Instead, the institutional habitus of invulnerability pervades organisational culture and attitudes as a normal, common sense, logical and rational way of viewing the world, even when any level of legitimate analysis would suggest otherwise.

Similarly, social cognition theories suggest:

> …that people are significantly predisposed and probabilistically more likely to detect, internalise, and over time, conform according to social information that is (1) repeatedly encountered and observed; (2) cognitively, affectively, and behaviourally congruent and contiguous; and (3) institutionally and culturally ubiquitous, valorised, and enforced.
>
> *(Leyva, 2019, p. 255)*

When this happens, we are more likely to derive at least a part of our self-identity from these influences, as well as conform to ways of being and acting that those in power wish us to be and act in. We are also more likely than not to organise and constrain behaviours consistent with the structural conditions that frame these situations and perpetuate them further up and down throughout our institutions (Leyva, 2019). This often results with invulnerability being unconsciously accepted as part of the institutional culture. The pressure to fit in and comply can be so strong as to forge an identity that we may or may not be comfortable with, be overwhelming for some, or for others, lead to psychological numbing that can lead to moral injury, or at least inner moral conflict.

How vulnerability reduces suffering in organisational culture

To alleviate these concerns, we would do well to lead through a lens of vulnerability as it can have beneficial effects on ourselves, our organisations, and our relationships. However, it can also have risks.

The benefits of vulnerability

When I interviewed the 89 disaster management leaders during my research, I asked them if they perceived themselves as personally or professionally vulnerable, 75% of them replied in the affirmative, staring there were many benefits to this. Some leaders argued it showed a leader's humanity: "I think if you show your vulnerabilities in an appropriate way, it doesn't necessarily undermine your credibility. It just shows you're a human like everybody else" (Crosweller & Tschakert, 2020).

Being vulnerable made leaders more accessible to others. Some leaders expressed the view that they needed to come to terms with their own vulnerability, along with that of the people they manage and that, in doing so, it would positively impact on the way in which they related to others and executed their duties as leaders. Showing vulnerability also opened the opportunity for leaders to express and act through virtues such as compassion and trust. Several leaders expressed the view that it significantly enhanced their capacity to relate to the loss and suffering of others (Crosweller & Tschakert, 2020). As one operational leader observed:

> We cry some days because it's pretty overwhelming, and we're honest about that. So, I think that that honesty, even with the community we're honest that sometimes it's too much for us. But again, it's that conversation that you have with people that they know that you're genuine.

It was much easier for many of the leaders to admit mistakes and grow and learn from them when the organisational culture empathised with their vulnerability towards getting things wrong. As one leader astutely reflected, "vulnerability opens up a creative space instead of a space of expertise," suggesting that arrogance could often flow from the notion of being an "expert." Decision-making tended to be more precise and thoughtful, and the cost of doing business appeared to be lower, when there were low levels of bullying and correspondingly higher levels of productivity.

The risk of vulnerability

However, being vulnerable also had its downside. Leaders who considered themselves vulnerable were sometimes exposed to bullying, undermining their ability to lead, and subjecting them to criticism. As one frontline leader noted: "[H]e yelled and screamed at me and basically belittled me to say that I didn't have an understanding of how to move into a recovery phase, without even discussing it. And I felt very vulnerable at that stage" (Crosweller & Tschakert, 2020). Another senior leader also commented that his experiences of being vulnerable taught him to be a better leader but also exposed him to bullying:

> ...over the last year, [I've had an experience] with the diagnosis of cancer and then treatment for six months and then an all clear, which is quite an interesting personal experience in terms of how suddenly it happens and then how suddenly it goes away again. It's not the experience for most people. But equally, looking back to the time when I was put under a lot of pressure and was bullied by a leader, I know that it affected my judgement and my view and my perspectives and how I behaved and how I interacted with other people. And so, I think every person can be vulnerable at any time in their life, depending on the circumstances—either physically or particularly psychologically—that they might be exposed to. And then, if you're not prepared to accept that vulnerability, then you probably have lost that foresight and judgement about the vulnerability of other people.

Also, the stress of leading through crisis made leaders vulnerable to mental health challenges:

> I think they're more likely to be vulnerable in the mental health space because of the pressures and the decisions that you have to make, and sometimes whether [the] decision you make is absolutely the best decision. But it's made on the available information at time.

Importantly, some leaders also understood the limits to being both physically and mentally vulnerable:

> I think, whilst we are inspired in the work we undertake, there are also stresses that come with our positions. And there is a certain tolerance level that, when it's reached, can impact on both your physical and mental well-being. And that has an impact on families. It has an impact on the self. And if it's not managed well, it's like we talked about earlier. You train yourself and you are prepared to push through. But there's a tolerance level. And at some point, you can go too far. There's evidence that suggests that you can snap. Or you need to step out. And I think the skill of us as leaders is to recognise that threshold and tolerance level, and just say, 'no I've got to back off, I'm going too hard here'.

Fortunately, in some organisations, support was readily available to assist those who were vulnerable:

> I think probably up until 10 years ago, and that's probably as a result of our cultural history of an organisation and how our leaders are supposed to be, perform and act, and be brave while everyone else is falling down around you. But I think in the past 10 years, certainly in the past five years, there's been a huge recognition of the vulnerability of leadership. And programs and practices have been put into place to support people, particularly when they are in difficult positions, and pretty much no one else around them is experiencing the same frustrations or issues or level of stress, that there are programs and systems and the culture to be put into place to say, 'look, it's okay not to be okay'.

Showing vulnerability at work

When I asked leaders if they were prepared to show their vulnerability at work, 88% of them replied in the affirmative and for almost half of those (48%), this was unconditional. Showing vulnerability included being prepared to admit mistakes, not having all the answers, reaching their limits, or being overwhelmed (Crosweller & Tschakert, 2020). Being open and accessible to others invited trust and opened opportunities for relatedness:

> But if you show that humanistic side that, actually, I'm struggling through these things as well... If you show your vulnerability and people can then become empathetic to you actually needing to make decisions, and that builds trust in a way... that relatable human instinct.

However, 39% of leaders would only show their vulnerability to people they trusted: "To a select few who I have a level of trust in. At times, we'll go and have a rant or express views openly. Whereas, certainly to the greater population of work... that I'm leading and managing, no." Several leaders (12%) were not prepared to show vulnerability at all, claiming they were not vulnerable, always needed to be in control, accepted they were vulnerable but did not know how to manage it, or feared being exposed (Crosweller & Tschakert, 2020).

The evidence suggests that when a leader is able to acknowledge and express their vulnerability, suffering decreased for everyone who was exposed to the effects of this disposition. It also contributed towards the basis of relationality between the leader and the people they were asked to lead, serve and protect. Table 6.1 captures these effects.

TABLE 6.1 The cultural and organisational benefits of vulnerability.

Accepting vulnerability as inherent to being fully human and the basis of relationality

✓ Shows a leader's humanity	✓ Increases opportunities for virtue (e.g., compassion, trust and integrity)
✓ Helps make leaders accessible to others	✓ Increases opportunities for relatedness between leaders and followers
✓ Reduces the potential for bullying and harassment to occur	✓ Increases opportunities for identifying errors and promoting learning and growth
✓ Helps shape better decisions	✓ Establishes a creative space rather than a space of expertise
✓ Increases the ability to relate to the loss and suffering of others	✓ Reduces cost and improves effectiveness

How invulnerability increases suffering in organisational culture

Whilst leading through vulnerability has both benefits and risks, leading through a lens of invulnerability can have devastating effects on ourselves, our organisations, and our relationships.

Vulnerability as strength or weakness

When I asked leaders whether vulnerability within their organisation was seen as a strength or a weakness, in response, 55% of them perceived that vulnerability was viewed as weakness. For many of them, this perception promoted bias by treating some people better than others, while some leaders failed to recognise the cultural differences of others. Some leaders observed that, if a person's vulnerability became their identity, then doubts would be cast over their competence, and as a result, antagonistic attitudes would emerge. As one operational leader observed: "At its worst, it can lead to bullying or belittling. Dehumanising.... The old ostracising of individuals... unfortunately, we see too much of that" (Crosweller & Tschakert, 2020).

Other leaders had observed individuals being forced out of "the system"—often through resignation or dismissal. Their organisations were not structured or governanced in a way that could cope with someone being vulnerable. Instead, vulnerable individuals would be isolated from activities, declined opportunities to progress, or lose status and income. For some, vulnerability was viewed almost like an illness. Ironically, for some individuals, such treatment did result in them experiencing health problems, even though their vulnerability was not originally associated with their health. The manner in which they were treated exacerbated or compounded their vulnerability. This also had the effect of further entrenching existing vulnerabilities. Seeing vulnerability as weakness also constrained relationships, undermined compassion and trust, and promoted fear and indecision. It also stifled effectiveness while increasing costs. Arrogance and condescension were also a feature of viewing vulnerability as weakness (Crosweller & Tschakert, 2020).

Fortunately, 45% of all leaders considered that strength could be drawn from vulnerability. Organisational cultures that were more accepting of vulnerability tended to see less bullying and harassment in their workplaces. A key protective factor from bullying and harassment was that being vulnerable opened leaders up to being compassionate. In turn, this enhanced relationships between colleagues, supervisors and followers, and improved trust and integrity within these relationships and across cultures. It also provided opportunities for organisational learning and growth, shaped better decisions, and gave people latitude to be human. As one senior administrative leader observed:

> When we see it as a strength, we're prepared to work with our own vulnerability and with others that are vulnerable, to find an appropriate fit for purpose solution to whatever the problem is that presents before us. That's where vulnerability is at its best. It enables creative thinking. It enables us to look beyond the obvious.
>
> *(Crosweller & Tschakert, 2020)*

Denial of vulnerability

When I asked leaders if they had witnessed a denial of vulnerability (invulnerability) within their organisations, 89% responded that they had witnessed denial, both in their leaders and in their organisational culture. For most leaders, such denial had numerous undesirable consequences (Crosweller & Tschakert, 2020).

Some of the leaders who denied their own or others' vulnerability became unnecessarily hardened and insensitive to the suffering of others. This was driven, in part, by not wanting to be perceived as having failed, which was associated with "looking good and not looking bad":

> As a leader in an organisation, you don't want to be saying 'we're not ready for this with staff'. We make sure that we are encouraging people to be ready and reassuring them that they are well equipped, that they are well trained, that we are going to be ready for whatever comes up. So that balance between maintaining and developing competence in our responders to deal with whatever comes next, I think is probably where denial of vulnerability occurs in terms of an organisation. I've used the term organisational egos and most of our organisations have got pretty big egos and it's not to say the individuals in them are egotistical, necessarily. Some are, but

organisationally, there's that pride in the uniform, the pride in your badge, the pride in what we do, and I think that, if we're not careful, that can sometimes lead to us sticking our head into the sand.

Another leader observed that, while it was becoming increasingly acceptable and expected that vulnerability should be freely expressed within organisational cultures, often it was only given scant regard:

I've seen senior leaders who have misunderstood what vulnerability means. And so, they use, almost like fake vulnerability. They know they've got to be vulnerable, but they don't want to let go of their strength... [what they] perceive as their strength, their professionalism. So, they give you give this lip service to it. And in that case, I think it's the worst kind of misuse of vulnerability, they are asking the team to accept that as vulnerability, but it's not. And so, they don't appreciate it, they don't think it's worthwhile. That's why they haven't given truth to their vulnerability.

In much the same way as seeing vulnerability as weakness, denying vulnerability also caused compassion, trust, respect, emotional courage, and effectiveness to be compromised (Crosweller & Tschakert, 2020). As one leader observed:

It's like, for the organisation there are elements where they are compassionate. And then, as the journey goes along, they lose their compassion because it's not the hot topic. And I think that it's the direction of the leadership team as well. As an organisation, it's the personalities involved. And being a male and all, but there's a lot of boys and it's like a bit of a boy's club and I think they're fearful of being compassionate.

Several leaders observed that errors were often denied, and this had the effect of stifling learning and growth, allowing ignorance to flourish. Effectiveness also became stifled, and costs increased. Once again, in a similar manner to seeing vulnerability as weakness, bullying and harassment increased and blame and responsibility shifted to individuals rather than systemic and cultural causes. This often led to the masking of mental health challenges that led to self-harm for some leaders. These effects tended to further entrench rather than minimise vulnerability. Other leaders hardened their attitudes towards vulnerability, resulting in further insensitivity towards the suffering of others (Crosweller & Tschakert, 2020). One operational leader observed:

I'm probably getting close to home here, but what I saw after the [name redacted] fire was an organisation, we lost over 100 houses in the community, two people died, and the [leader] said, 'You shouldn't be blaming us. You should have done more to prepare yourselves'.

TABLE 6.2 The cultural and organisational effects of invulnerability.

Denying, ignoring or disavowing vulnerability

✓ Undermines compassion, trust and other virtues	✓ Compromises respect, emotional courage and effectiveness
✓ Undermines ability to lead effectively and exposes leaders to unreasonable criticism	✓ Exposes leaders and followers to bullying
✓ Increases susceptibility to masking mental health challenges that may lead to self-harm	✓ Further entrenches vulnerability through perceptions of weakness
✓ Promotes fear and indecision	✓ Denies errors, promotes ignorance, stifles learning and growth
✓ Promotes blame and shifts responsibility onto individuals	✓ Hardens the attitudes of leaders resulting in insensitivity to the suffering of others
✓ Constrains relationships	✓ Increases cost and stifles effectiveness

All of this led to a strong suggestion that, when invulnerability was present, suffering increased for everyone who was exposed to the effects of this disposition. Table 6.2 captures these effects.

Vulnerability with wisdom

Based upon the empirical research presented in this chapter, as well as the research and insights from numerous other scholars, it is evident that allowing vulnerability to be present and permitted is beneficial, personally, socially, and institutionally. However, it is also important to remember that, while vulnerability establishes the basis of our relatedness, it is also indicative of future suffering. Therefore, we ought not to embrace vulnerability without qualification, but we do need to renounce our habitual denial of its existence (Gilson, 2014). To do this, we need to develop our wisdom about when, how, who, and why we allow ourselves to be vulnerable.

Such wisdom cannot be derived simply through knowledge. To become wise about vulnerability means that it needs to be "experienced," to be "lived." We need to see, sense, and feel what it is like to be vulnerable in the myriad circumstances of our lives. Therefore, vulnerability requires practice. It is not an automatic given—it must be experientially cultivated over time between two or more people. These experiences will necessarily present us with the reality of our fallibility, mutability (tendency to change), unpredictability, and uncontrollability. Realities whereby the outcome of these experiences cannot be known nor orchestrated beforehand (Gilson, 2014).

To do so would not infer vulnerability, but rather, emotional control and manipulation, and if that were to happen, invulnerability would most likely arise in others along with its negative impacts. We also need to set boundaries as to what we will or will not accept, be clear about our intentions towards others, and proceed sensibly towards relatedness. Moving towards relatedness opens opportunities to change (ourselves and others), experience something new, and move from being to becoming—the ability to become the person that we desire to be that honours our capacity for happiness, well-being, and flourishing (Brown, 2018; Butler, 2005; Gilson, 2014).

The challenge for leaders

As leaders, it is important that we expand our understanding of vulnerability. We need to remember that vulnerability is a fact of the human condition, and our shared experiences form the basis of ethical obligations that can compel ethical responses in others. We can either perceive vulnerability as negative—something to be acknowledged, managed and minimised or denied, disavowed, or ignored.

As leaders who seek to protect others from harm and lead others to offer that protection, how we view vulnerability matters. It is important that we increase our awareness of the institutional and socio-cultural factors that can lead us down a path of invulnerability. In so doing, we must also understand that acknowledging, managing and minimising vulnerability leads to decreases in suffering, whilst denying, ignoring, or disavowing vulnerability leads to increases in suffering.

It is also important to understand that vulnerability can be perceived as positive—a universally shared space of affectivity, openness, trust, compassion, and community, as well as the basis of relatedness and relationship. Finally, we must accept that viewing vulnerability as either negative (denied, ignored or disavowed) or positive (the basis of relationality) establishes a tension that can lead to very different outcomes in response to the susceptibility for suffering, and it is this tension that we now explore in detail in Chapter 7.

References

Beck, U. (1992). *Risk society: Towards a new modernity.* Sage Publications.

Bourdieu, P. (2000). *Pascalian meditations.* Stanford University Press.

Brown, B. (2018). *Dare to lead: Brave work, tough conversations, whole hearts.* Vermilion.

Butler, J. (2005). *Giving an account of oneself.* Fordham University Press.

Crosweller, M., & Tschakert, P. (2020). Disaster management leadership and policy making: A critical examination of communitarian and individualistic understandings of resilience and vulnerability. *Climate Policy, 21*(2), 203–221. https://doi.org/10.1080/14693062.2020.1833825

Desmond, M. (2007). *On the fireline: Living and dying with wildland firefighters.* The University of Chicago Press.

Douglas, M. (1986). *Risk acceptability according to the social sciences.* Routledge & Kegan Paul.

Gilson, E. C. (2014). *The ethics of vulnerability: A feminist analysis of social life and practice.* Routledge. https://doi.org/10.4324/9780203078136

Goffman, E. (1967). *Interaction ritual: Essays in face-to-face behavior* (1st ed.). Routledge.

Kimura, A. H., & Katano, Y. (2014). Farming after the Fukushima accident: A feminist political ecology analysis of organic agriculture. *Journal of Rural Studies, 34,* 108–116. https://doi.org/10.1016/j.jrurstud.2013.12.006

Leyva, R. (2019). Towards a cognitive-sociological theory of subjectivity and habitus formation in neoliberal societies. *European Journal of Social Theory, 22*(2), 250–271. https://doi.org/10.1177/1368431017752909

7

THE INVULNERABLE–RELATIONAL LEADERSHIP CONTINUUM

> If you ask anyone in disaster management why they do what they do, fundamentally every single person will say 'to make a difference'. But when you ask them what that means, it's about people. What drives them is their desire to see people restored to a place of purpose, a place of importance, a place where they can function in society effectively.

In Chapter 6, we explored how certain institutional and socio-cultural influences shaped a disaster management leader's worldview of invulnerability and vulnerability. We also explored how those worldviews impacted upon organisational culture. In this chapter, we explore how those same worldviews have the potential to either increase or decrease the suffering of citizens. We then propose a relational leadership continuum model that can assist us further develop our awareness of the potential causes of suffering and how we might respond more compassionately.

How invulnerability shapes a worldview that *increases* the suffering of citizens

When reviewing the evidence from the inquiries into the 2005 Hurricane Katrina, the 2009 Victorian Bushfires, and the 2011 Queensland Floods, I detected four behaviours that appeared to be driven by invulnerability: insensitivity, insufficiency, compliance and defensiveness. These behaviours were being observed, not by the leaders themselves, but by the citizens they were meant to be protecting (Crosweller & Tschakert, 2021). Having detected them in the evidence given by citizens, I then took these behaviours and coded them based on literature drawn from feminist philosophy and ethics, critical

DOI: 10.4324/9781003499510-9

social theory, and relational leadership ethics. I then applied these codes to the transcripts of the 89 leaders that I interviewed. What I discovered was quite unsettling and is expressed below, firstly as qualitative analysis and then as non-parametric statistical analysis.

Insensitivity

When we become invulnerable, we risk becoming *insensitive* to the needs of others—we can fail to adequately see their susceptibility to suffering (vulnerability) or their present suffering. Often, this failure is driven by ignorance. We wilfully "choose not to know," "know or not know that we do not know but still do not care enough to know," or "do not know because others who hold power over us do not want us to know" (Tuana, 2004). We can hide behind our privilege as a means of protecting ourselves from suffering (McHugh, 2007), while failing to see the suffering of others (Markowitz & Shariff, 2012). We can become overconfident in our ability to avoid our own suffering (Cunliffe & Eriksen, 2011; Sugarman, 2015) while pursuing our own ambitions (Rickards et al., 2014). We can both morally judge and devalue the suffering of others (Layton, 2014), exhibit emotional dissonance (Blumgart, 1964; Fox & Lief, 1963), or fear being exposed as a vulnerable human being (Jeffers, 2007).

The results showed that insensitivity was present in the worldview of 43% of the leaders I interviewed. Some leaders expressed overconfidence in the frameworks and capabilities they used to manage risks and they also discouraged input or feedback to improve them. For other leaders, it was evident that they were making decisions *on behalf of* people rather than *with* people. There was a presumption by some leaders that they had superior unquestionable knowledge, while other leaders judged colleagues or citizens as less than competent. Some leaders predicated success on people following their instructions without question (Crosweller, 2022).

Still other leaders chose not to see the suffering of others for a variety of self-protecting and other reasons. These included a preference for competitiveness, risk aversion, or a desire to achieve objectives rather than seeing the suffering of others. Often, it resulted in them losing touch with those impacted (Crosweller, 2022). One political leader observed:

So, I don't think political leaders think enough about the consequences of… loss… some political leaders I think find it hard to relate to the intimacy of loss and grief and suffering. So, I think they view a response… to a natural disaster event, in very abstract terms, in terms of numbers, and dollars, and fiscal amounts and number of dwellings and so on and so forth. But they don't necessarily always make the connection between that and the personal suffering that people see. And I think they put that at a distance in some way. They might make an attempt to feel that, or to relate to that, but to what extent that is genuine and to what extent it's simply an expression of an attempt to show empathy for the broader public consumption purposes is, I guess, something that you could question at times.

Several leaders failed to see the suffering of others because of their privilege, or because they saw themselves as better (elitism), held power and authority over others, hid behind service uniforms while avoiding scrutiny, were overconfident, or promoted a sense of entitlement. Devaluing others, indifference, overly rational assessments, fear of vulnerability, ambition, or subjective judgements about victims were also present in the views of some leaders (Crosweller, 2022). As another political leader observed:

> I think sometimes it is very hard for political leaders to have a clear understanding of the loss or grief or suffering and show empathy. It's particularly difficult in spaces like justice and policing and the courts and the prisons. But there's so much grief and suffering there. But rarely do you see political leaders, I think, really relate to the grief, suffering and loss that's experienced by people who are in that system. So, I guess there are worthy victims, and there are less worthy victims.

Insufficiency

When we fail to understand that we share in our vulnerability which, in turn, shapes who we are as fully functioning human beings, it results in us becoming less human. As a result, our ethical responses for protection or assistance become *insufficient* (Crosweller, 2022; Gilson, 2014). Instead, we lack any genuine commitment to minimise the suffering of others, we prioritise our commitments towards cost avoidance (Bouckenooghe et al., 2015), or we limit our commitment to the duties and obligations contained within our legislative obligations and their associated power structures (Gilson, 2014).

The results showed that insufficiency was present in the worldview of 27% of the leaders I interviewed. Some of these leaders spoke of compassion but their responses indicated that they had failed to sufficiently act to relieve suffering. Other leaders appeared to lack a commitment to learning and change, did not follow through on intentions and commitments, gave inadequate attention to funding priorities, or prioritised institutional efficiency over the genuine needs of others. As one political leader observed: "I have seen (and) been involved in situations where sometimes economics overrules a compassionate response" (Crosweller, 2022).

A few leaders were observed not sufficiently listening to the culturally diverse needs of their communities, inadequately co-operating and co-ordinating with others or operating within inflexible systems and authorising environments that only supported minimum standard broadscale solutions. As one key informant commented to me:

> My experiences taught me that the bureaucracy that do the day to day, do not do disaster work (well)... They tend to be super cautious... want to be very factual... want a lot of information. They are risk averse and want as much detail as possible before they make decisions. There is a lot of concern about waste, abuse, fraud, and making mistakes.
>
> *(Crosweller, 2022)*

Compliance

Our susceptibility to be insensitive and insufficient may also limit our actions to *compliance* regimes to avoid being vulnerable while imposing regimes of safety upon those we deem as vulnerable (Butler, 2003). The results showed that compliance was significantly present in the worldview of 73% of leaders interviewed. For many leaders, their ability to respond to the needs of others was hampered by prioritising compliance with performance measures, procedures, reporting obligations, data collection, statistics, and command and control objectives. Likewise, staying within the bounds of their prescribed roles and responsibilities also hampered their efforts (Crosweller, 2022).

A poignant example of how compliance may be an impediment can be found in the observation of one local political leader, when having to face a dire set of circumstances involving their community:

> The chain of command in a disaster [frustrates me] so much. It was ridiculous. And I will never put myself in that situation again where I had to wait for State disaster management to give the okay to just send in flood boats to get eight family members off a roof in 23 metres of water... but I tell you what, I will not wait so long next time, I would sooner take the consequences than be facing a coroner's court.

For some leaders, common sense and discretion were overridden by a preference to only meet minimum compliance obligations. Several leaders were observed turning to rules for fear of legal liability and punitive action, while other leaders were constrained by strong political and bureaucratic mandates. Overreliance on compliance permitted strategies for avoiding vulnerability that also overshadowed opportunities to exercise virtues like compassion (Crosweller, 2022).

Defensiveness

Finally, we may become *defensive*, choosing to blame others who are vulnerable or are suffering rather than accept accountability for our own actions (both personally and institutionally) that cause ourselves and others to suffer

(Hamman, 2009; Lewis et al., 2011; Romero & Kemp, 2007). The results showed that defensiveness was present in the worldview of 23% of leaders interviewed. For some leaders, the fear of being blamed or the need to protect their reputation was more important than the suffering of others. When leaders took this view, their organisational cultures tended to be dominated by arrogance and close-mindedness that led to further avoidance (Crosweller, 2022).

A few leaders shifted blame or responsibility away from themselves and onto either citizens or organisations, particularly when things did not go well. Other leaders withdrew from those they were meant to protect and disavowed their own vulnerability resulting in failing to see the suffering of others. As one political leader insightfully commented:

> I think there needs to be someone that says to the leader, just come out of that space you are in, which is all focused on process, procedure, structure, and plan and all that stuff. Just come out here and listen, or sit, and talk, or just immerse yourself in that space. Take enough time to do that… Maybe we need to be reminded to go and sit with people who have lost and factor that in as well.
>
> *(Crosweller, 2022)*

Statistical analysis

To help understand how these behaviours of invulnerability are distributed, the following non-parametric statistical analysis is provided (Figure 7.1) along with the coding table (Table 7.1) that identifies the attributes for each behaviour.

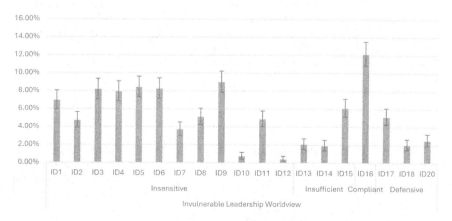

FIGURE 7.1   How the attributes of an invulnerable leadership worldview are distributed (Crosweller, 2022).

TABLE 7.1 Behaviours and attributes that inform an invulnerable leadership worldview.

Behaviours		*Attributes*	*References*
Insensitive	ID1	Others are vulnerable/in need of paternalistic intervention	(Mackenzie, 2014; O'Neill, 2005; Skeggs, 2005)
	ID2	Denial (I do not suffer/I am not vulnerable/suffering does not exist)	(Arendt, 1958; O'Neill, 2005; Rose, 1996; Tuana, 2004)
	ID3	Wilful ignorance (choosing not to know) Knowing that we do not know but do not care enough to know Not knowing we do not know but do not care enough to know Not knowing because privileged others do not want us to know	(Tuana, 2004)
	ID4	Privileged positioning	(McHugh, 2007)
	ID5	Overconfidence	(Cunliffe & Eriksen, 2011; Sugarman, 2015)
	ID6	Devaluation (understating the value or vulnerability of other)	(Layton, 2014)
	ID7	Indifference/choosing or appearing not to care	(Tuana, 2004)
	ID8	Reason only based norms and assumptions/emotional dissonance	(Blumgart, 1964; Fox & Lief, 1963)
	ID9	Fear of being vulnerable or exposed	(Jeffers, 2007)
	ID10	Judgemental	(Layton, 2014)
	ID11	Fails to see the suffering of another	(Markowitz & Shariff, 2012)
	ID12	Ambitious	(Rickards et al., 2014)
Insufficient	ID13	General lack of commitment	N/A
	ID14	Commitment prioritised towards cost avoidance	(Bouckenooghe et al., 2015)
	ID15	Commitment limited to duty/obligation within power structures	(Gilson, 2014)
Compliant	ID16	Following and staying within rules/procedures	(United States Congress, Senate, Committee on Homeland Security and Governmental Affairs, 2006)
	ID17	Withdrawal/avoidance	(Layton, 2014)
Defensive	ID18	Blameworthiness of others	(Hamman, 2009; Lewis et al., 2011; Romero & Kemp, 2007)
	ID19	Blameworthiness of nature	(Wisner et al., 2012)
	ID20	Generally defensive	N/A

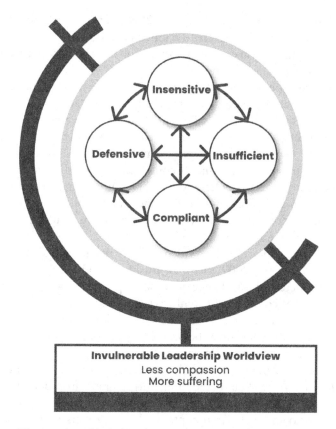

FIGURE 7.2   The invulnerable leadership worldview that perpetuates further suffering (Crosweller, 2022).

To summarise, when we become invulnerable, we establish a non-virtuous cycle that perpetuates further suffering—suffering that could otherwise be lessened through a more compassionate disposition but is unavailable to us due to our insensitivity towards the suffering of others, our insufficient responses, our desire to remain compliant with our own governance regimes, and our propensity to become defensive when criticised. Figure 7.2 depicts this cycle.

Fortunately, there are other behaviours that actively contest the effects of invulnerability through relationality, and it is to these that we now explore in detail.

How vulnerability informs a worldview that *reduces* the suffering of citizens

There are many eastern and western scholars and philosophers who argue that all embedded human experience is "relational," and that this relationality can be seen from the perspective of "selves-in-relation-to-others" grounded in the ethic of compassion (Gregory & Sabra, 2008; Kwee, 2012; Ricœur, 1994; Thich, 1987). Relationality refers to **connectedness**, a view of the world that underlines how no person or thing exists in isolation, because existence necessarily means being "in relationship" (Oxford, 2017). We find connectedness through shared experiences that we and those we are in relationship with can relate to—our shared capacity to suffer and be vulnerable.

Seeing the world in this way allows us to grow and increase our self-worth through connection with others. It can also help us understand that we often suffer when we become isolated from them (Jordan, 2011; Nicholson & Kurucz, 2017). Put simply, an ethic of compassion establishes our relationality (Feenan & Herring, 2017) where we, as the compassionate agent, and those who suffer are in a relationship of care, concern, mutuality, co-operation, and shared intent to prevent, minimise or relieve suffering (Dutton et al., 2014; Goetz et al., 2010; Kanov et al., 2017).

When further reviewing the evidence from the inquiries into the 2005 Hurricane Katrina, the 2009 Victorian Bushfires, and the 2011 Queensland Floods, I also detected four behaviours that appeared to be driven by vulnerability: relatability, commitment, venturousness, and accountability. These behaviours were also being observed, not by the leaders themselves, but again by the citizens they were meant to be protecting and appeared to be contesting the invulnerable behaviours (Crosweller & Tschakert, 2021).

Having detected them in the evidence given by citizens, I then took these behaviours and coded them based on literature drawn from feminist philosophy and ethics, critical social theory, and relational leadership ethics, and then applied these codes to the transcripts of the 89 leaders that I interviewed. What I discovered was quite comforting and is expressed below, firstly as qualitative analysis and then as non-parametric statistical analysis.

Relatability

To be able to *relate* to the suffering and vulnerability of ourselves and others, we must allow ourselves to be open. Open to affectivity (our ability to feel and our ability to evoke feelings in others), to be emotionally engaged (Fisher & Tronto, 1990; Gilligan, 1982; Preston, 2017) and develop a sense of empathic purpose—an intentionality to assist others (Bouckenooghe et al., 2015). We must be open to change within ourselves, cognitively, emotionally, spiritually. We must be open to not knowing about matters concerning people, places and circumstances, rather than holding preconceived notions and ideas about them. We must be open to being tolerant of the differences we find in others—racially, culturally, religiously, politically, sexually, generationally, etc. We must be open to being wrong in our views, perspectives and knowledge. We must also be open to changing ourselves in ways that allow others to connect with us (Gilson, 2011).

It is also important that we have the ability to see, sense, and feel the vulnerability and suffering of ourselves and others (Gilson, 2014; Harris, 2010; Strauss et al., 2016), to show emotional resonance by "walking in their shoes" (Soto-Rubio & Sinclair, 2018), and to develop a level of distress tolerance—the ability to hold space with another who is suffering, while tolerating uncomfortable feelings arising from the experience (Gilbert, 2009).

The results showed that relatedness was present in the worldview of 31% of leaders. Most of these leaders showed a willingness to emotionally engage with the plight of others by taking the time to try and understand what others were going through. Other leaders showed and encouraged vulnerability and collaboration, both within their organisations and with their communities. Some leaders incorporated their lived experiences of loss and suffering into their leadership practice as the essence of their wisdom (Crosweller, 2022). As one senior institutional leader observed:

> There are those leaders [for whom] I would use the term mature leaders, who have had experience and exposure to a variety of different losses, emotions, suffering; who have integrated, and I use that term intentionally, integrated that loss, suffering, grief into their practice as wisdom, and are able to draw on that to make more decisions that incorporate the emotions of their people, their work force or those they are working with.

Several leaders desired to see people return to a place of purpose, importance, and function.

Other leaders valued and incorporated the rational, emotional, ethical, and spiritual intelligence that they had learned from witnessing, as well as experiencing their own loss and suffering, to lead through crisis (Crosweller, 2022).

Many leaders were mindful of the great burden that responsibility for protection placed upon them but remained motivated to do more while tending to their own well-being. Some leaders surrendered to having to be right all the time, or permitted learning, growing, and improving from experiences that aided in understanding their own limitations. Several leaders established safe, adaptable, and flexible environments to create solutions that improved decision-making (Crosweller, 2022).

A few leaders recognised that they and others suffered together, placed the needs of others over their own personal judgements, or recognised that vulnerability was critical to their leadership effectiveness, as was the relatedness of personal experience with the experiences of others. When leaders accepted vulnerability in this way it afforded them the opportunity to show their humanity. They became more accessible to others which increased their ability for relatedness with those whom they were leading (Crosweller, 2022). As one highly experienced fire commissioner, who experienced first-hand the devastating impacts of the 9/11 terrorist attack, argued:

> Well, I believe the most important thing [leaders] can do is to be there for the people that have suffered the loss or suffering in whatever way that you are suffering. I believe that you have to be there for your people. You have to be approachable. You have to understand what they're going through. And you have to understand the stages of grief, anger and all that stuff. But you have to be there for them. You have to have empathy for them.

Commitment

It is equally important that, within this relational construct, we not only feel empathy for those who suffer, but we also *commit* to action to relieve their suffering (Dutton et al., 2002; Sinclair et al., 2017). Feeling without action allows suffering to continue unabated. The results showed that commitment was present in the worldview of 42% of leaders (Crosweller, 2022).

Many leaders committed to a strong ethos to serve and protect others make a difference for the benefit of others, or contribute to the greater good. Being this way was important to them and, for many, a lifetime commitment or a calling:

> ...if you ask anyone in emergency management, for example, why they do what they do, fundamentally every single person will say, 'it's to make a difference'. But when you ask them what that means, and you unpack that a bit more, it's really about people. It's really about making sure people are safe, have an experience of the system that effectively enables those people to get back on with their life in some way, shape or form. So, I think what drives people is humanity, is their desire to see people restored to a place of purpose, a place of importance, a place where they can function in society effectively. And to that end, some people, that motivator will drive them to continue to work even in environments that are toxic and damaging to them personally and professionally. And we've actually seen that.

Several leaders committed to overcoming personal fear and adversity whilst moving beyond self-interest to support and inspire others to make a difference. Often, those experiences were shared with the survivors of the disaster, and sometimes, they were colleagues within the disaster management machinery (Crosweller, 2022).

Other leaders noted that witnessing and experiencing suffering deepened their commitment to doing something about it and specifically motivated them to act to relieve the suffering of others (Crosweller, 2022). As one key informant noted:

> I've had an upper-middle class upbringing, and we haven't really suffered. Although we weren't wealthy, extremely wealthy or anything. I was brought up with an expectation that you have a responsibility to make a contribution, whatever it is. And I think in terms of my early upbringing, that's really important. And then, after that I saw a lot in aid and humanitarian response, seeing people suffering and also not just the suffering, seeing the compassion that others who were also suffering were showing. They have nothing and they're being compassionate. They've lost everything. So, I think you'd have to be a rock for that not to touch you in some way.

For a few leaders, every interaction became an opportunity to exercise their personal leadership ethos to assist others through their access to authority, wealth and resources. Numerous leaders showed empathic purpose and set aside their own emotions and feelings while seeking to appreciate the emotions and feelings of others experiencing difficult circumstances (Crosweller, 2022).

Venturousness

By being in action, sometimes that action means we may need to be *venturous*. We may need to undertake a risky or daring journey or course of action in the face of uncertainty (Frost et al., 2000; Koerner, 2014; Worline et al., 2002). In these circumstances, compassion becomes an exercise in profound vulnerability. We must push against tides of risk, uncertainty, and notions of invulnerability that perpetuate suffering (Dutton et al., 2006; Gilson, 2011). We must actively, intentionally, and effortfully take risks to seek out and alleviate the suffering of others, often in subtle and benign circumstances, while exemplifying extraordinary courage (Kanov et al., 2017).

We must also be venturous in our pursuit in changing the circumstances where suffering is created by organisations but left unaddressed (Caro, 2016b). We must forge our venturousness from our lived experiences in attending to vulnerability and suffering of others, which in turn shapes our sense of self as complete human beings, including our sensitivity to being able to relate to others (Thorup et al., 2012). Such acts become exercises in profound vulnerability due to their emotionally tumultuous nature and their capacity to shape our identity, which are more difficult than we realise (Jinpa, 2015).

The results showed that venturousness was present in the worldview of 39% of leaders. Several leaders developed the courage to genuinely acknowledge the suffering of others; accepted that loss, suffering, and failure are a part of life; and integrated the emerging lessons from these experiences into their leadership approach through reflection (Crosweller, 2022).

Some leaders genuinely accepted responsibility for personal and organisational limitations and sought to improve and make restitution. Other leaders understood the relatedness of suffering between self and other and actively sought to walk in the shoes of another to understand their plight. Numerous leaders exhibited the courage to face up to those things they feared most including navigating unknown futures, actively challenging norms and assumptions, or prioritising their ethics in the interest of others (Crosweller, 2022). As one highly experienced Chief Officer observed:

> Leaders are all human beings and they've got compassion for those who are directly affected, those who are indirectly affected but are still affected, and that includes your own people who, whilst they might not have been standing on the front line, are impacted.

> When it comes to dealing with the community, media and politicians, there needs to be humility. There also needs to be honesty... although, it's fairly difficult as a senior leader because honesty could open the door for litigation against the agency or political issues when we didn't do that right. We got that wrong. So, it becomes a bit of a tightrope to say look, if I'm really upfront and honest with what happened, and I know we made some mistakes along the way, you also have to have, particularly as a senior leader, an eye and an ear to the political discourse, and also where the media might take things, and where the community might take things. And there's loss of the agency's reputation... we live on the trust and goodwill of all our people. Once we lose the trust and confidence of the citizenry and the communities we serve, then we've lost the game. And trying to give a degree of protection to an organisation, but also retaining the trust and confidence of the community, it's a really difficult act.

A few leaders exhibited courage in admitting their limited understanding of compassion and committed to improving through lived experience, education, and relatedness. Numerous leaders understood the limitations of rules and had the courage to go beyond them with wisdom (Crosweller, 2022):

> I like to think that sometimes what we have to do is understand the rules, processes, and procedures, and then understand where they're not going to work in this situation. And so, leadership becomes trying to navigate the path between what's supposed to happen and what's needing to happen. Because sometimes, and particularly so in disasters, the rules and procedures have been developed for an event other than the one they are experiencing, or they've been developed, the parameters have been established by previous disasters.

And if you are in a situation that's worse than what has previously been experienced, it's almost a given that the rules and processes aren't going to fit. Because the disaster's been planned for based on our pre-existing knowledge. We haven't been able to plan beyond the precipice. We haven't been able to plan and predict what this certain experience will be, because we haven't ever been there before. So, we're taking with us a toolbox of rules and processes and regulations that are almost inevitably going to fall short.

Some leaders understood the limits of their personal exposure to mental harm, suffering and stress, and actively sought methods and assistance from others to nurture and protect themselves (Crosweller, 2022). For one highly experienced and respected political leader, the experience was profound:

So, I learned my life experience sort of mirrored my political career, I guess [it] would to be fair to say. And I went through a divorce. I went through depression. I went through a range of other challenges. And I think that's where I've ended up with all these other things we've just been talking about. Because I think that what I wanted in my life and are really important to my life more generally, which is gentleness, compassion, kindness, thoughtfulness and courage, things which I think are important in your own life. And those come from sharing what happens when you forget about your own humanity. When you don't look after yourself very well and you're not kind to yourself, and you don't nurture yourself physically or emotionally.

And I've seen that experience in relationship breakdowns, and I've seen that experience in poor health, and the sadness of depression. And I think what I know at the end of my political career is that I am someone who needs a lot more of all those things I rank over the other things that I thought were important to be successful, to be happy. I thought I was going to be happy if I had a successful political career. There's no doubt that it brings many benefits, no doubt about that. But it also has a cost. And I think the cost to me has been in relationships, and with my partner, with my children, and I'm still working that out, I think. But I'm clearer about it now than I was even 10 years ago.

Accountability

In addition to being relatable, committed, and venturous, we also need to be *accountable* for our actions, including those actions that contribute towards injustices produced by structural processes that cause suffering. That is, if we have access to power, wealth and resources and are therefore privileged, we have an obligation to remedy these injustices (Maak & Pless, 2009). We must be open to the needs and differences of others in everyday interactions, as well as speaking and acting in ways that maintain our integrity and self-constancy (Cunliffe & Eriksen, 2011). Finally, we must also acknowledge our moral responsibility recognising that "I am accountable to others for my actions, and I should conduct myself so that others can count on me" (Ricoeur, 1994, p. 165).

The results showed that accountability was present in the worldview of 44% of leaders. Many leaders took responsibility for their mistakes and sought to rectify them wherever possible while accommodating the needs of others (Crosweller, 2022). As one leader observed about a very senior operational leader:

> …and she was always out in the community listening. Listening to the anger, listening to the sadness. And whenever she found something that didn't seem to be right, she'd go back in, if necessary, go to Cabinet and argue for an exemption or a change. And I think it's very important that leaders recognise the fundamental insensitivity of any kind of formal system, any system of regulations, and therefore the need to build in a feedback loop and a capacity for variation. We have contract variations for making submarines, don't we? We just know we won't get it right the first time. Well, why can't we have that for assistance criteria after a disaster?

For some leaders, a key aspect of accountability was being prepared to have difficult conversations (Crosweller, 2022).

Other leaders proactively sought to do all in their power and control to protect others who had made genuine mistakes by taking responsibility on their behalf (Crosweller, 2022).

Numerous leaders felt an accountability towards others through the importance of relating to and respecting those they served, as well as the need for compassion (Crosweller, 2022). As one operational leader candidly reflected:

> I had to roll through the autocratic bastardisation sort of mentality when I was recruit, from a young firefighter to achieving rank and an aspirational drive to get to the level that I am now and see the change in what people require. And if you haven't got any compassion for what people are dealing with or how they're trying to navigate through life challenges and loss, whether that be through life, or not being able to meet the aspirational objectives that they put themselves in place for. I mean if you haven't got any compassion, I don't think you should even consider leadership at all. And that self-reflection and being able to, on a daily basis, assess and recollect what's gone on through the day… to see if you've missed anything. And you go back and maybe do a one on one, or a group discussion with people,

just to highlight the need… to look after each and everybody's welfare. Compassion is very high on the agenda for that.

Most leaders were driven by their ethics and values and were prepared to be held to account for them (Crosweller, 2022).

Statistical analysis

To help understand how these behaviours of relationality are distributed, the following non-parametric statistical analysis is provided (Figure 7.3) along with the coding table (Table 7.2) that identifies those attributes for each behaviour.

To summarise, when leaders accept their vulnerability and work with it rather than against it (by denying, ignoring, or disavowing it), it affords them the opportunity to show their humanity. They become more accessible to others, which increases their ability for relatedness with others whom they are leading, serving or protecting. Their willingness to be vulnerable increases opportunities for them to exercise virtues, such as compassion, trust, and integrity, as well as their ability to relate to the loss and suffering that others have experienced or are presently experiencing.

Granting themselves permission to be vulnerable has led them to making better decisions. It has also established the opportunity for creative spaces rather than spaces of expertise, reduced overall costs, improved organisational effectiveness, and reduced bullying and harassment. This strongly suggests that, when vulnerability was present and permitted, suffering decreased for everyone who was exposed to the effects of this disposition (Crosweller, 2022; Crosweller & Tschakert, 2021). Figure 7.4 depicts this cycle.

FIGURE 7.3 How the attributes of a relational leadership worldview are distributed (Crosweller, 2022).

TABLE 7.2 Behaviours and attributes that inform a relational leadership worldview.

Behaviours	Codes	Attributes	References
Relatable	RD1	Openness to affectivity/emotional engagement	(Fisher & Tronto, 1990; Gilligan, 1982; Preston, 2017)
	RD2	Openness to change	(Gilson, 2011; McLeod, 2012)
	RD3	Openness to not knowing	(Gilson, 2011)
	RD4	Openness to tolerance	(Gilson, 2011)
	RD5	Openness to being wrong	(Gilson, 2011)
	RD6	Openness to changing oneself	(Gilson, 2011)
	RD7	Suffering is recognised	(Strauss et al., 2016)
	RD8	Leader shows emotional resonance/ fellow feeling/walk in the shoes of another	(Soto-Rubio & Sinclair, 2018)
	RD9	Distress tolerance	(Gilbert, 2009)
	RD10	Common humanity/everyone suffers	(Bentham, 1998)
	RD11	Non-judgement	(Dalai Lama, 2005)
	RD12	Vulnerability is recognised in others	(Gilson, 2011)
	RD13	Personal experiences of loss and suffering inform leadership	(Harris, 2010; Schwartz et al., 2012)
Committed	RD14	Affective sense of purpose and willingness	(Bouckenooghe et al., 2015)
	RD15	Motivated to act and relieve suffering	(Dutton et al., 2014; Kanov et al., 2017; Sinclair et al., 2017)
	RD16	Empathic purpose	(Ruiz-Junco & Morrison, 2019)
Venturous	RD17	Willing to learn from experience	(Gilson, 2011)
	RD18	Willing to take risks/pursue difficult course of action	(Dutton et al., 2006; Gilson, 2011; Jinpa, 2015)
	RD19	Recognising privilege and putting others first	(Kanov et al., 2017)
	RD20	Willingness to engage individuals/ community in decision-making	(Powley, 2009)
	RD21	Willing to express limits	(Gilson, 2011)
Accountable	RD22	Willing to accept responsibility	(Cunliffe & Eriksen, 2011; Voegtlin, 2016)
	RD23	Driven by values/principles/ethics	(Caro, 2016a, 2016b; Cunliffe, 2009)

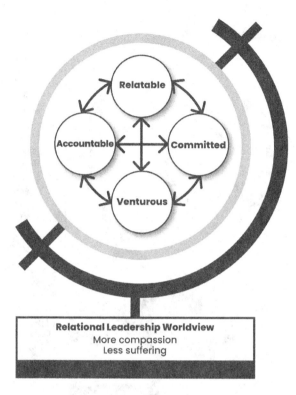

FIGURE 7.4   The relational leadership worldview that promotes more compassion and lessens suffering (Crosweller, 2022).

The challenge for leaders

When we improve our ability to understand that we and others are susceptible for forms of harmfulness and may not be able to cope, we move in the direction of our humanness and our relatedness. We also have the opportunity to fulfil our ethical obligations to minimise or manage the vulnerability of ourselves and others to the best of our ability, with the equities of power, wealth and resource made available to us. We have the opportunity to relate to the suffering of others, commit to minimising suffering and vulnerability, be venturous in that pursuit, and remain accountable for our actions.

However, when we choose to deny, disavow, or ignore our vulnerability and that of others, we perpetuate the very suffering that we wish to free ourselves from and from which we have a duty to protect others. When we view vulnerability in this way, we risk being insensitive to the suffering of others, insufficient in our responses, constrained by our institutionally prescribed compliance regimes, and defensive when criticised.

As leaders, we find ourselves challenged by having to navigate the following continuum (Figure 7.5).

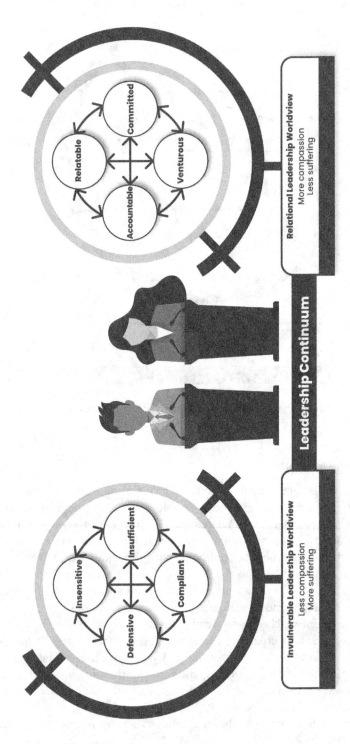

FIGURE 7.5   The Invulnerable–Relational Leadership Continuum that leaders must navigate on a continual basis when seeking to lead, serve and protect others (Crosweller, 2022).

Sometimes our circumstances will pull us in the direction of invulnerability, and at other times, we will be presented with the opportunity to move more towards relationality. Often, we will oscillate along this continuum many times a day in myriad different circumstances. Therefore, the challenge for leaders is to better understand how we can be more consistent in our approach to a relational leadership worldview. To achieve this, we need to deepen our understanding of the ethic of compassion.

References

Arendt, H. (1958). *The human condition.* University of Chicago Press.

Bentham, J. (1998). *The principles of morals and legislation.* Prometheus Books.

Blumgart, H. L. (1964). Caring for the patient. *New England Journal of Medicine, 270*(9), 449–456. https://doi.org/10.1056/NEJM196402272700906

Bouckenooghe, D. M., Schwartz, G., & Minbashian, A. (2015). Herscovitch and Meyer's three-component model of commitment to change: Meta-analytic findings. *European Journal of Work and Organizational Psychology, 24*(4), 578–595. https://doi.org/10.1080/1359432X.2014.963059

Butler, J. (2003). Violence, mourning, politics. *Studies in Gender and Sexuality, 4*(1), 9–37. https://doi.org/10.1080/15240650409349213

Caro, D. H. (2016a). The nexus of transformational leadership of emergency services systems: Beyond the Wu-Shi-Ren (WSR)-Li paradigm. *International Journal of Emergency Services, 5*(1), 18–33. https://doi.org/10.1108/IJES-11-2015-0024

Caro, D. H. (2016b). Towards transformational leadership: The nexus of emergency management systems in Canada. *International Journal of Emergency Management, 12*(2), 113–135. https://doi.org/http://dx.doi.org/10.20381/ruor-870

Crosweller, M. (2022). Disaster management and the need for a relational leadership framework founded upon compassion, care, and justice. *Climate Risk Management, 35*(2002), 100404. https://doi.org/10.1016/j.crm.2022.100404

Crosweller, M., & Tschakert, P. (2021). Disaster management and the need for a reinstated social contract of shared responsibility. *International Journal of Disaster Risk Reduction, 63*, 1–13. https://doi.org/10.1016/j.ijdrr.2021.102440

Cunliffe, A. L. (2009). The philosopher leader: On relationalism, ethics and reflexivity—A critical perspective to teaching leadership. *Management Learning, 40*(1), 87–101. http://dx.doi.org/10.1177/1350507608099315

Cunliffe, A. L., & Eriksen, M. (2011). Relational leadership. *Human Relations, 64*(11), 1425–1449. https://doi.org/10.1177/0018726711418388

Dalai Lama. (2005). *The essence of the heart sutra: The Dalai Lama's heart of wisdom teachings* (T. Jinpa, Ed.). Simon and Schuster.

Dutton, J. E., Frost, P. J., Worline, M. C., Lilius, J. M., & Kanov, J. (2002). Leading in times of trauma. *Harvard Business Review, 80*(1), 54–61. https://hbr.org/2002/01/leading-in-times-of-trauma

Dutton, J. E., Workman, K. M., & Hardin, A. E. (2014). Compassion at work. *Annual Review of Organizational Psychology and Organizational Behavior, 1*, 277–304. https://doi.org/10.1146/annurev-orgpsych-031413-091221

Dutton, J. E., Worline, M. C., Frost, P. J., & Lilius, J. (2006). Explaining compassion organizing. *Administrative Science Quarterly, 51*(1), 59–96. https://doi.org/10.2189/asqu.51.1.59

Feenan, D., & Herring, J. (2017). Compassion, ethics of care and legal rights. *International Journal of Law in Context. 13*(2), 158–171. https://doi.org/10.1017/S174455231700009X

Fisher, B., & Tronto, J. (1990). Towards a feminist theory of caring. In E. K. Abel, & M. K. Nelson (Eds.), *Work and identity in women's lives* (pp. 35–62). Psychology Press.

Fox, R., & Lief, H. (1963). Training for 'detached concern. In H. Lief, V. F. Lief, & N. R. Lief (Eds.), *The psychological basis of medical practice* (pp. 12–35). Harper and Row.

Frost, P. J., Dutton, J. E., Worline, M. C., & Wilson, A. (2000). *Narratives of compassion in organizations.*

Gilbert, P. (2009). *The compassionate mind: A new approach to life challenges.* Constable and Robinson Ltd.

Gilligan, C. (1982). *In a different voice: Psychological theory and women's development.* Harvard University Press.

Gilson, E. (2011). Vulnerability, ignorance, and oppression. *Hypatia, 26*(2), 308–322. https://doi.org/10.1111/j.1527-2001.2010.01158.x

Gilson, E. C. (2014). *The ethics of vulnerability: A feminist analysis of social life and practice.* Routledge. https://doi.org/10.4324/9780203078136

Goetz, J. L., Keltner, D., & Simon-Thomas, E. (2010). Compassion: An evolutionary analysis and empirical review. *Psychological Bulletin, 136*(3), 351–374. https://doi.org/10.12691/rpbs-9-1-4

Gregory, J., & Sabra, S. (2008). Engaged Buddhism and deep ecology: Beyond the science/religion divide. *Human Architecture, 6*(51).

Hamman, T. (2009). Neoliberalism, governmentality, and ethics. *Foucault Studies, 6,* 37–59.

Harman, G. (2009). Skepticism about character traits. *Virtue Ethics and Moral Psychology: The Situationism Debate, 13*(2–3), 235–242. https://www.jstor.org/stable/40345402

Harris, S. (2010). Antifoundationalism and the commitment to reducing suffering in Rorty and Madhyamaka Buddhism. *Contemporary Pragmatism, 7*(2), 71–89. https://doi.org/10.1163/18758185-90000168

Jeffers, S. (2007). *Feel the fear and do it anyway: Dynamic techniques for turning fear, indecision and anger into power, action and love.* Jeffers Press.

Jinpa, T. (2015). *A fearless heart: How the courage to be compassionate can transform our lives.* Hudson Street Press.

Jordan, J. V. (2011). The stone center and relational–cultural theory. In J. C. Norcross, G. R. VandenBos, & D. K. Freedheim (Eds.), *History of psychotherapy: Continuity and change* (pp. 357–362). American Psychological Association. https://doi.org/10.1037/12353-012

Kanov, J., Powley, E. H., & Walshe, N. D. (2017). Is it ok to care? How compassion falters and is courageously accomplished in the midst of uncertainty. *Human Relations, 70*(6), 751–777. http://dx.doi.org/10.1177/0018726716673144

Koerner, M. (2014). Courage as identity work: Accounts of workplace courage. *The Academy of Management Journal, 57*(1), 63–93. https://doi.org/10.5465/amj.2010.0641

Kwee, G. T. M. (2012). Relational Buddhism: Wedding K.J. Gergen's relational being and Buddhism to create harmony in-between-selves. *Psychological Studies, 57*(2), 203–210.

Layton, L. (2014). Some psychic effects of neoliberalism: Narcissism, disavowal, perversion. *Psychoanalysis, 19*(2). http://dx.doi.org/10.1057/pcs.2014.5

Lewis, J., Kelman, I., & Lewis, S. A. V. (2011). Is "fear itself" the only thing we have to fear? Explorations of psychology in perceptions of the vulnerability of others. *Australasian Journal of Disaster and Trauma Studies, 2011*(3), 89–104. http://www.scopus.com/inward/record.url?eid=2-s2.0-84867448035&partnerID=MN8TOARS

Maak, T., & Pless, N. (2009). Business leaders as citizens of the world. Advancing humanism on a global scale. *Journal of Business Ethics, 88*(3), 537–550. https://doi.org/10.1007/s10551-009-0122-0

Mackenzie, C. (2014). The importance of relational autonomy and capabilities for an ethics of vulnerability. In C. Mackenzie, W. Rogers, & S. Dodds (Eds.), *Vulnerability: New essays in ethics and feminist philosophy* (pp. 33–59). Oxford University Press. https://doi.org/10.1093/acprof:oso/9780199316649.003.0002

Markowitz, E. M., & Shariff, A. F. (2012). Climate change and moral judgement. *Nature Climate Change, 2,* 243–247. https://doi.org/10.1038/nclimate1378

McHugh, N. (2007). It's in the meat: Science, fiction, and the politics of ignorance. In M. Grebowicz (Ed.), *SciFi in the mind's eye; Reading Science through Science fiction*. Open Court Press.

McLeod, J. (2012). Vulnerability and the neo-liberal youth citizen: a view from Australia. *Comparative Education, 48*(1), 11–26. https://doi.org/10.1080/0305006 8.2011.637760

Nicholson, J., & Kurucz, E. (2017). Relational leadership for sustainability: Building an ethical framework from the moral theory of 'ethics of care. *Journal of Business Ethics, 156*(1), 25–43. https://doi.org/10.1007/s10551-017-3593-4

O'Neill, J. (2005). *The philosophy of need*. Cambridge University Press.

Oxford. (2017). *English Oxford living dictionaries*. https://www.oed.com/

Powley, E. H. (2009). Reclaiming Resilience and safety: Resilience activation in the critical period crisis. *Human Relations, 62*(9), 1289–1326. https://doi.org/10.1177/0018726709334881

Preston, C. J. (2017). Challenges and opportunities for understanding non-economic loss and damage. *Ethics, Policy & Environment: Loss, Damage, and Harm in Climate Change Policy, 20*(2), 143–155. https://doi.org/10.1080/21550085.2017.1342962

Rickards, L., Wiseman, J., & Kashima, Y. (2014). Barriers to effective climate change mitigation: The case of senior government and business decision makers: Barriers to effective mitigation actions on climate change. *Wiley Interdisciplinary Reviews: Climate Change, 5*(6), 753–773. https://doi.org/10.1002/wcc.305

Ricœur, P. (1994). *Oneself as another*. University of Chicago Press.

Romero, A., & Kemp, S. M. (2007). *Psychology demystified*. McGraw-Hill.

Rose, G. (1996). *Mourning becomes the law: Philosophy and representation*. Cambridge University Press.

Ruiz-Junco, N., & Morrison, D. (2019). Empathy as care: The model of palliative medicine. *Society, 56,* 158–165. https://doi.org/10.1007/s12115-019-00344-x

Schwartz, S. H., Cieciuch, J., Vecchione, M., Davidov, E., Fischer, R., Beierlein, C., Ramos, A., Verkasalo, M., Lönnqvist, J., Demirutku, K., Dirilen-Gumus, O., & Konty, M. (2012). Refining the theory of basic individual values. *Journal of Personality and Social Psychology, 103*(4), 663–688. http://dx.doi.org/10.1037/a0029393

Sinclair, S., Beamer, K., Hack, T. F., McClement, S., Bouchal, S. R., Chochinov, H. M., & Hagen, N. A. (2017). Sympathy, empathy, and compassion: A grounded theory study of palliative care patients' understandings, experiences, and preferences. *Palliative Medicine, 31*(5), 437–447. https://doi.org/10.1177/0269216316663499

Skeggs, B. (2005). The making of class and gender through visualizing moral subject formation. *Sociology, 39*(5), 965–982. http://dx.doi.org/10.1177/0038038505058381

Soto-Rubio, A., & Sinclair, S. (2018). In defense of sympathy, in consideration of empathy, and in praise of compassion: A history of the present. *Journal of Pain and Symptom Management, 55*(5), 1428–1434. https://doi.org/10.1016/j.jpainsymman.2017.12.478

Strauss, C., Taylor, B. L., Gu, J., Kuyken, W., Baer, R., Jones, F., & Cavanagh, K. (2016). What is compassion and how can we measure it? A review of definitions and measures. *Clinical Psychology Review*, *47*, 15–27. https://doi.org/10.1016/j.cpr.2016.05.004

Sugarman, J. (2015). Neoliberalism and psychological ethics. *Journal of Theoretical and Philosophical Psychology*, *35*(2), 103–116. https://doi.org/10.1037/a0038960

Thich, N. (1987). *Interbeing: Commentaries on the Tiep Hien precepts.* Parallax Press.

Thorup, C. B., Rundqvist, E., Roberts, C., & Delmar, C. (2012). Care as a matter of courage: Vulnerability, suffering and ethical formation in nursing care. *Scandinavian Journal of Caring Sciences*, *26*(3), 427–435. https://doi.org/10.1111/j.1471-6712.2011.00944.x

Tuana, N. (2004). Coming to understand: Orgasm and the epistemology of ignorance. *Hypatia*, *19*(1), 194–232. https://doi.org/10.1111/j.1527-2001.2004.tb01275.x

United States Congress, Senate, Committee on Homeland Security and Governmental Affairs. (2006). *Hurricane Katrina: A nation still unprepared: A special report of the Committee on Homeland Security and Governmental Affairs, United States Senate, together with additional views.* U.S. Government Printing Office. http://purl.access.gpo.gov/GPO/LPS77202

Voegtlin, C. (2016). What does it mean to be responsible? Addressing the missing responsibility dimension in ethical leadership research. *Leadership*, *12*(5), 581–608. http://dx.doi.org/10.1177/1742715015578936

Wisner, B., Gaillard, J., & Kelman, I. (2012). *The Routledge handbook of hazards and disaster risk reduction.* Routledge.

Worline, M. C., Wrzesniewski, A., & Rafaeli, A. (2002). Courage and work: Breaking routines to improve performance. In R. G. Lord & R. Kanfer (Eds.), *Emotions in the workplace: Understanding the structure and role of emotions in organizational behaviour.* Jossey-Bass.

PART 3

Compassion and Virtue

8
ESTABLISHING RELATIONALITY THROUGH THE ETHIC OF COMPASSION

> Compassion is an internal driver of desiring to give someone else something that is missing in their world, their life, their psyche, or their environment. To 'suffer with' really means to draw down the depth of your own experience. To feel those feelings really personally and deeply. But yet, at the same time, to walk beside those people in a logical, rational way that enables the capacity for that person to grow and develop and recover well.

Having explored what it means to suffer and be vulnerable in Part 2, we now consider the ethical response to that suffering and vulnerability through compassion. We begin by defining compassion from numerous eastern and western perspectives and explore the ultimate act of compassion—the giving of one's life—through a reflection on the deaths of several firefighters during the tragic fire season of 2019/2020 in Australia. We also explore the tension between the need for compassion and our propensity for blameworthiness of suffering by contrasting the perspectives of Aristotle and the Buddha.

We then reflect on the need for self-compassion and a change of perspective by understanding that (except for involuntary choice) it is often our choices that contribute towards our suffering. We then discuss why our ability to show compassion is constrained by the clinical way in which we view citizens as numbers and statistics and consider how we might move past this constraint by introducing the emotion of affect, moral intuition, and narrative. We also introduce experiential and analytical systems of thought that give rise to the elements of symbolism, sentiment and data to help motivate us towards compassion.

DOI: 10.4324/9781003499510-11

Defining compassion

The word "compassion" derives from Latin "*com*," meaning "together," and "*pati*," meaning "to suffer." Combined, they mean "to suffer with" (Oxford, 2017). Philosopher A.C. Grayling (2021) observes that

> [v]arious philosophical traditions in the great civilisations have promoted compassion at the core of ethics and therefore also of politics—this point according with Aristotle's observation that ethics and politics are seamlessly connected because a good social order is required for the possibility of flourishing individually and in relationships. A survey from Confucius and the Buddha to Hume, Rousseau and Schopenhauer demonstrates this.
>
> *(p. 49)*

Compassion also has a significant influence within the justice, health care, and education sectors across many parts of the world, as well as taking centre place in most of the world's religions.

Compassion and anthropology

Our ability to show compassion extends far back into the history of human development. Charles Darwin stated that "those communities which included the greatest number of the most sympathetic members would flourish best and rear the greatest number of offspring" (Darwin, 1871). An evolutionary analysis and empirical review of the published literature reveals that our compassion arises out of distinct appraisal processes, has distinct display behaviours, distinct experiences, and an approach-related psychological response. This state-like experience of compassion, as well as the trait-like tendency to feel compassion, fall under the purview of three evolutionary arguments: that compassion evolved as part of a care-giving response to vulnerable offspring; that compassionate individuals were preferred in mate selection processes; and that compassion emerged as a desirable trait in co-operative relations between non-kin. These evolutionary arguments give further support to compassion being defined as the feeling that arises in witnessing another's suffering and that motivates a subsequent desire to help. As such, compassion is an affective state defined by a specific subjective feeling (Goetz et al., 2010).

Compassion and psychology

In 2016, Professor of Clinical Psychology Clara Strauss and her colleagues undertook a comprehensive review of the major definitions of compassion.

Their review revealed that compassion is a cognitive (thinking), affective (feeling), and behavioural (acting) process consisting of five elements that refer to both self and other. They are the following:

- We recognise suffering.
- We understand the universality of suffering (all sentient beings suffer).
- We feel empathy for the person suffering and connect with their distress (emotional resonance).
- We tolerate uncomfortable feelings aroused in response to the suffering person (distress tolerance) to remain open to and accepting (non-judgement) of the person suffering.
- We are motivated to act to alleviate suffering (Strauss et al., 2016).

Distress tolerance means we can adequately deal with the difficult emotions that may arise without being overwhelmed by them or feeling the need to desensitise through a reduction of awareness of the other's suffering. Failing to do so renders us potentially too engrossed in self-emotion, desensitises us to the suffering of others, and hinders our ability to help. Non-judgement is our ability to remain accepting and tolerant towards another person even when their condition or response to it gives rise to negative states of mind such as fear, anger, frustration or disgust (Gilbert, 2010; Wispe, 1991). This distinction is important as it is often our perceived enemy that teaches the greatest tolerance, which is a foundational basis of compassion (Dalai Lama, 2002).

The ethical premise of compassion

Professor of neural engineering Richard Reilly (2008) argues that ethics of compassion are grounded in our mindful commitment to our own happiness while recognising that the well-being we wish for ourselves is also wished for by others. This ethic is then extended to incorporate the intention of the Golden Rule to establish two related principles: "One ought not to cause any living being to suffer unnecessarily," and "One ought to protect/relieve living beings from unnecessary suffering." These two principles accord with Arthur Schopenhauer's "supreme principle" of ethics: "Injure no one [(the principle of justice)]; on the contrary, help everyone as much as you can [(principle of compassion)]" (Schopenhauer, 1965). Schopenhauer regarded compassion as the source of all moral values, such as justice and duties of justice, as well as other moral virtues that included loving kindness, generosity, patience, and courage.

The ultimate act of compassion

Schopenhauer (Campbell, 1991) extended his understanding of compassion as the ultimate sacrifice of one life for another. He wrote:

> This is something really mysterious, something for which Reason can provide no explanation, and for which no basis can be found in practical experience. It is nevertheless of common occurrence, and everyone has had the experience. It is not unknown even to the most hard-hearted and self-interested. Examples appear every day before our eyes of instant responses of this kind, without reflection, one person helping another, coming to his aid, even setting his own life in clear danger for someone whom he has seen for the first time, having nothing more in mind than that the other is in need and in peril of his life.
>
> *(Campbell, 1991, p. 53)*

Sadly, Schopenhauer's insights have all too often come to pass within our lived experiences as leaders and citizens alike.

Between the winter of 2019 through to the autumn of 2020, Australia experienced its worst fire season in living memory. 33 people lost their lives across New South Wales, Victoria, and South Australia. Over 2700 homes and over 5200 outbuildings were destroyed across all states and the Northern Territory, with the majority being in New South Wales. Over 5 million hectares of bushland was decimated, and it is estimated that over 1 billion animals perished (Binskin et al., 2020). Importantly, none of these impacts include what also arose simultaneously or soon thereafter from severe cyclone activity in Western Australia, as well as severe thunderstorms, severe flooding, and coastal inundation across many parts of the country.

Amid all of this, countless numbers of people from within and beyond emergency services, as well as the wider community, were stretched beyond their capacity. For the most part, they were doing the very best they could while facing the worst of adversity. They were navigating all of this within the external limitations of the power, wealth and resources available to them. They were also internally navigating the limitations of their minds—limitations such as their knowledge, skills, experience and imaginations of natural hazards and their cascading effects, along with their capacity to act with kindness, compassion, and courage towards others to help alleviate their suffering. All while reconciling with feelings of anger, self-interest, ignorance, and other egotistical aspects of mind that prevent us from acting compassionately (Crosweller, 2016).

When we find ourselves in such situations, we have the opportunity to transform. Disasters take us beyond what is known, comfortable, safe, and predictable. Instead, we are taken to the "edge of the abyss." A space and a place where we are necessarily called to surrender so much of who we thought we were. We are beckoned by the circumstances in which we find ourselves to show ourselves and others who we are truly capable of being. For many, this is the best version of self (Bonanno, 2004). When we extend ourselves beyond our own self-interest and self-importance, internally and externally, we necessarily surrender a part of our identity dominated by our egos. We become selfless, or, in other words, we exhibit less Self. It is the giving up of self that permits our truly compassionate nature to emerge (Gyatso, 2003, 2014). Tragically, for some, the giving up of self for the benefit of others results in tragic outcomes.

What other people's sacrifice teaches us

Over the course of the 2019–2020 fire season in Australia, Ian McBeth, Paul Clyde Hudson, Rick A. DeMorgan, Geoffrey Keaton, Andrew O'Dwyer, Samuel McPaul, Mat Kavanagh, and Bill Slade all perished in the line of duty, paying the ultimate sacrifice while protecting others. There were also 25 other people (citizens) who acted selflessly and who also perished. Sadly, there can be no greater honour or respect for human life than to surrender a life to save another. The comparative mythologist Joseph Campbell so aptly wrote: "How is it that an individual can so participate in the danger and pain of another that, forgetting his own self-protection, he moves spontaneously to the other's rescue, even at the cost of his own life?" (Campbell, 1991).

While Ian, Paul, Rick, Andrew, Samuel, Matt, and Bill sacrificed their physical life for others, they also left us with an example of what it means to be compassionate. The ultimate giving up of self through physical death affords those of us who remain the opportunity to surrender those things that cause us so much grief and suffering. Rampant self-interest and self-importance, anger, jealousy, rage, ignorance, rigid views, closed minds, and subjective judgements are but a few of the sufferings that cause us so much pain and anxiety (Tsering, 2005, 2006). I have no doubt that few if any of these aspects would have been present in the minds of those who were acting selflessly.

Simply put, it is why they were able to do what they did. In those moments, when acting on behalf of others, most if not all of these aspects of mind would have been absent, or at the very least dominated by more virtuous thoughts towards others. And this is how we should remember them. As living, breathing human beings who had the capacity, or balance, to put other before self and to act in ways that reduced their suffering—a capacity that we all possess, exemplified through their actions.

As Schopenhauer wrote:

> My own true inner being actually exists in every living creature as truly and immediately as known to my consciousness only in myself. This realisation,

for which the standard formula is in Sanskrit '*tat tvam asi*' (thou art that), is the ground of compassion upon which all true, that is to say unselfish, virtue rests and whose expression is in every good deed.

(Campbell, 2002, p. 112)

That is, two becomes one. Self and other disappear and we become united in our humanity as selves-in-relation-to-others. Compassion dissolves the separateness and divisions that we create in our minds and affords us the opportunity to surrender suffering.

The legacy that Ian, Paul, Rick, Andrew, Samuel, Matt, and Bill left with us, like countless others who had passed, showed us what we are all capable of within the realm of our knowledge, skills, experience and imaginations. Within our own given contexts, we too can act in the best interests of others. In so doing, we can move our worlds towards the very state of existence that we so desperately desire: to find our happiness and avoid our suffering.

Reconciling compassion with blameworthiness of suffering

However, often the circumstances in which we find ourselves are not so stark or obvious when it comes to showing compassion towards others. While we can accept that our relationality is premised upon self-in-relation-to-others (Cunliffe & Eriksen, 2011; Ricoeur, 1994), this often does not (for most people) extend universally to all sentient beings. In other words, we can be selective in who we show compassion towards and why.

A question of deservedness

There is an ancient Greek belief, based largely upon the philosophy of Aristotle, that the people who deserve compassion are those who do not deserve their suffering (Feldman & Kuyken, 2011). Aristotle argued that the deservedness of suffering was dependent upon three things. Firstly, where the sufferer was not responsible for bringing suffering upon oneself through involuntary choice (such as crimes perpetrated against children). Secondly, where the sufferer was responsible for bringing suffering upon themselves due to their own ignorance and/or absence of will and reason. Thirdly, where the sufferers brought suffering upon themselves due to their voluntary choices (influenced by vice as opposed to virtue) (Aristotle, 2004).

He also argued that where one stood in these three circumstances determined the extent to which blame could be attributed, and to that end, as to whether the blame was proportional to the fault that has been created. Where that blame was out of proportion, the sufferer was seen as undeserving of suffering and thus worthy of compassion. Conversely, when blame was seen as in proportion, the sufferer was considered not worthy of compassion.

The judgement of proportion though, ultimately rested with the compassionate individual, not the sufferer (Nussbaum, 1996). If "*Schadenfreude*" (the experience of pleasure, joy, or self-satisfaction that comes from learning of or witnessing the troubles, failures, or humiliation of another) was present in the mind of the compassionate individual, then compassion would most likely be absent, and suffering would continue to perpetuate and pervade (Berndsen & Feather, 2016).

To view suffering as being deserved in this way is pervasive in the western mind. Our habitual patterns of aversion and self-blame combined with low self-worth, reinforced by western notions of achieving perfection, convince many people that suffering is their own fault and a sign of personal failure or inadequacy. These habitual patterns are reinforced by dominant and pervasive socio-cultural influences such as neoliberalism that reinforce self-judgement and shame and inhibit the emergence of compassion for both ourselves and others (Feldman & Kuyken, 2011; Gilson, 2011; Nussbaum, 1996).

A Buddhist perspective

Notwithstanding, eastern philosophy, and specifically Buddhism, has a definitive position of wishing to bestow compassion upon all sentient beings. That is, to wish for the permanent cessation of suffering. Sentient beings include any living creature that seeks to find happiness and avoid suffering (Tsering, 2005). This wish is worthy of reflection. If we examine our minds, we soon realise that every thought has this wish (premise) as its basis. For example, for most of us, our ritualistic morning cup of coffee is about relieving our suffering of tiredness, boredom, frustration, or lack of energy and so on. We drink it because, for a brief moment, it brings us a level of relief, or in other words, a sense of (temporary) happiness. At an even more basic level, most animals spend their lives seeking food, warmth and shelter while avoiding being eaten by other animals! The difference, of course, is that humans have a consciousness of this wish, whereas animals do not.

The Dalai Lama argues that genuine compassion must have both wisdom and loving kindness. That is to say, we must understand the nature of suffering from which we wish to free ourselves and other sentient beings (this is wisdom), and we must experience deep intimacy and empathy with ourselves and other sentient beings (this is loving kindness) (Dalai Lama, 2005). Buddhism's advocacy for compassion for all sentient beings and the wish for the permanent cessation of suffering is profound. When Buddhists refer to all sentient beings, this includes us. It is not possible to have genuine compassion for any other person or being if we cannot grant it to ourselves (Gyatso, 2006). Therefore, compassion for self, or self-compassion, is important if we wish to become a more compassionate human being.

Compassion includes the self

According to Professor in Human Development Kristin Neff (2003),

> self-compassion entails three fundamental components: (1) extending kind-
> ness and understanding to oneself rather than harsh self-criticism and judg-
> ment; (2) seeing one's experiences as part of a larger humanity rather than
> as separating and isolating; and (3) holding one's painful thoughts and feel-
> ings in balanced awareness rather than over-identifying with them.
>
> *(p. 224)*

The cultivation of self-compassion requires us to re-examine and investigate
our core beliefs of unworthiness, unlovability and imperfection that emerge
from a sense of being undeserving of compassion that in turn fuel perpetual
cycles of inner rejection and condemnation.

Self-compassion involves learning to attend to, approach, investigate and
unpack our negative core belief systems that have been absorbed from others
(such as distorted religious views) or learnt through our personal experiences
of failure and rejection (Birnie et al., 2010). Such harshness and judgement of
ourselves only serve to continually reinforce feelings of inadequacy, helpless-
ness, and anxiety. This, in turn, undermines our natural capacity for acceptance, generosity, and compassion (Leary et al., 2007). To understand suffering
is to understand that it is part of the human condition—what it means to be
human—and is, therefore, a shared experience. This distinction is important.
Compassion, as we have already explored, must necessarily extend to the understanding that everyone suffers (Gyatso, 2006, 2011).

Self-compassion is also concerned with reframing our personal narratives.
Instead of anxiety, depression or obsession being seen as personal failures and
inadequacies, they are seen simply as suffering. Self-compassion permits us
the same compassion that would be extended to anybody else who is suffering. Gradually, with effort, emotional affliction (a shared experience of all of
humanity) can be embraced with kindness, generosity, forgiveness, and acceptance. This profound shift in the relationship with our own suffering helps us
to alter our view of inadequacy and failure that underlies the seemingly endless
stream of negative thoughts that causes us so much grief. Compassion is not
simply a pleasant emotion. It is a radical transformation of our view of suffering and of our view of self and the fundamental way in which we view others
(Feldman & Kuyken, 2011).

Changing perspective

Therefore, rather than seeking to blame ourselves, which is often overused and
the cause of much human suffering, self-compassion allows us to take another
perspective. With the exception of involuntary choice, we can condition our

minds to accept that it is through our choices that we contribute to the causes of our suffering. Those causes arise in part from our ignorance of the full context of the circumstances in which we find ourselves, an absence of our will and reason, and our previous non-virtuous choices (Janaway, 2017). And in this context, we become the authors of our stories and the architects of our lives. That is to say, we often contribute to the causes of our suffering by the way we perceive, act, react, and interact with the world. And the way we do that is by what we do or do not say, think or do, underpinned by the extent to which we operate either through our self-interest and self-importance—as well as our anger, attachments, and ignorance—or through universal compassion for self and other (Gyatso, 2003, 2014).

If our thoughts, words, and actions are contaminated with an over-inflated sense of self to the neglect of others, if our mind is full of anger, if we are too attached to our opinions, beliefs, and worldview, or if we are ignorant of the truth of our circumstances, then we establish the causes for a world of suffering for self and other. However, if our thoughts, words, and actions are shaped by a rebalancing of self with other and our shared experiences of suffering, if our mind is more patient and considered, if it is open to possibilities that may or may not accord with our views (but still speak to our moral conscience), and if we think, speak, and act with a compassionate intention, then we begin moving towards our happiness (Edelglass, 2009; Thich, 2000). If we genuinely stopped and thought about and reflected upon how we spoke to others, what we thought of others, and what we did to others, irrespective of what circumstances had arisen, and whether or not they were within our control, we would soon realise that we are confronted with a powerful choice. A future towards happiness, or a future towards suffering.

Why compassion is constrained

Unfortunately, while we may have an ethical obligation to show compassion in myriad circumstances, there are many reasons why we are constrained. One of those constraints relates to the sheer amount of suffering that, as leaders, we are often called upon to deal with during the course of managing crises and disasters.

The problem with numbers

"If I look at the mass I will never act. If I look at one, I will," observed Mother Theresa, a statement that captures a powerful and deep insight into human nature. It highlights how we can develop compassion for another; however, once "another" becomes "many others," compassion can soon dissolve to indifference and ignorance (Slovic, 2007). Behavioural theories and data confirm that, all too often, numbers represent dry statistics that lack feeling and fail to motivate action (Slovic & Slovic, 2004). Such evidence is exemplified by the actions of several United States presidents who, for example, ignored the genocide in Rwanda (Bill Clinton) and the Nazi Holocaust in Europe (Edward Roosevelt); yet, despite their indifference, still managed to maintain their power and office with little if any reaction from the US public (Power, 2007). Sadly, according to some scholars, the decline for the capacity to be compassionate may begin as low as considering the well-being of two people and further decline to zero once persons are only seen as statistics (Västfjäll et al., 2014). Our compassion may be further limited if it is viewed as "a fragile flower, easily crushed by self-concern" (Batson et al., 1983).

The emotion of affect

Professor of Psychology Paul Slovic and Professor of Cognitive Psychology Daniel Västfjäll (2014) argue that the low numbers are caused, in part, by modern-day risk management approaches that rely on two modes of thought: that of *feeling* (instinctive and intuitive reactions to danger essential to rational thought) and that of *analysis* (logic, reason, quantifications and deliberation). Of the two, feelings are processed much quicker and more easily than analysis and, therefore, tend to be relied upon more when navigating a dangerous, uncertain world. However, both acknowledge that feelings can also be unreliable and hence the need for analysis.

Within the context of feelings is the emotion of "affect"—the capacity to see everything (arising rapidly and automatically, yet without conscious awareness) as either "good–bad" or "like–dislike." The emotion of affect plays a critical role in how we extract meaning from information, as well as motivating our behaviour. Without affect, information lacks meaning, and we will not use it in our judgement and decision-making. This is evidenced when statistics are used as a primary means to convey the extent of loss and suffering. A higher number, rather than increasing compassionate attitude and behaviour, achieves the opposite, as only the analytical aspect of thought is evoked (Slovic & Västfjäll, 2015). That is to say, if we only talk about numbers and statistics without conveying what we think those numbers mean in the context of affect, we can come across as clinical and insensitive.

Therefore, in addition to positive and negative affect, more nuanced *feelings*— such as empathy, sympathy, sadness, compassion and distress—are critical in motivating people to help others (Coke et al., 1978). To give rise to such feelings, *attention* to suffering is also critical, as it gives rise to emotional responses to stimuli that are already emotionally charged (Fenske & Raymond, 2006).

Moral intuition

Professor of Ethical Leadership Jonathan Haidt (2001) refers to the mental phenomenon of attention as "moral intuition," which he defines as the sudden appearance in our consciousness of a moral judgement that includes an affective valence (good–bad, like–dislike). This moral judgement occurs without any conscious awareness of having gone through steps of searching, weighing evidence, or inferring a conclusion (i.e., analysis). When we think in this way, we can often see or hear about a social event and instantly feel approval or disapproval. Such an intuition comes first and usually dominates our moral judgement unless we apply effort and use a process of analysis to critique, and, if necessary, override (or, at least, validate) our original intuitive feelings. According to Buddhist philosophy, it is from our attention to the suffering of another that the spontaneous wish to relieve their suffering arises and from which compassionate actions follow (Gyatso, 2014).

Nevertheless, our propensity to judge through an affective valence (i.e., tone) also creates the propensity for psychic numbing rather than compassion. Psychic numbing is a fundamental psychophysical principle that describes how our ability to detect changes in physical stimulus rapidly decreases as the magnitude of that same stimulus increases (Weber, 1834). This often results in us downplaying and understating the scale and orders of magnitude of suffering that occur during severe to catastrophic disasters, even when the numbers are published and plain to see (Haidt, 2001).

While psychic numbing may prove beneficial (in the short term) for disaster management leaders, when having to deal with such large numbers of casualties as a self-protective factor (Lifton, 1967), it can also lead to apathy and inaction, severely limiting our capacity to feel. Psychic numbing, through moral intuition—unaided by moral judgement—reinforces ignorance, promotes invulnerability, and perpetuates suffering by preventing compassion from arising.

Getting past the numbers

In recognising that, for most people, the ability to maintain a strong commitment to compassion rarely extends beyond a single other, anthropologist Paul Farmer (2010) argues that the solution is through the power of imagination (imagery): through images, narrative, story, and first-person testimony of the individual who suffers as a symbol of the suffering of many. Appealing to the capacity for human relatedness and connectedness through the recognition of the "feeling state" of moral intuition (without a direct correlation with statistics, numbers, facts and figures), allows us to connect and feel what the other is experiencing. Farmer (2010) argues it then motivates us towards an appropriate compassionate response, not only towards that one individual but to the many others they symbolise or represent.

Put simply, *attention* and *imagery* are critical to inducing *feelings* that lead to helping or assisting others (compassion). Compassion is absent when feelings and images are dominated by statistics and numbers (Farmer, 2010; Slovic & Västfjäll, 2015).

The importance of symbolism

In the course of my research, I found that Paul Farmer's insights about symbolism were powerfully reflected mainly in the transcripts of political leaders. My 40 years of working indirectly and directly with politicians would suggest that the reason for this is because the more successful politicians fundamentally understand two things: *sentiment* (the feelings of the constituents) and *symbolism* (the experience of one can represent the experience of many). The following insight from a former US governor gives weight to these observations:

> I don't think governments can be compassionate by how I define it... Then there are the principles that guide your actions. In my case, this was another faith-driven belief that I had. And so, we did make pretty big changes to child welfare systems and to the development of the disabled for that basic reason. I guess my motivation to do it was driven by an understanding of the plight of abandoned and abused children because I took the time to be with families that were struggling with this or foster care families. I wanted to learn and understand, and certainly for programs for the development of the disabled, the countenance for my focus on this was an engagement I had with a person. A woman who came to me front of 300 people very upset. She was a Democrat at the time, and she was very upset, and she just assumed that I didn't care about her child, and she let me know it in front of a bunch of people. So, I told her you know what, you're going to be my teacher and I'll be the student. And if you can calm down here, I promise you I'll give you, in the next few months, I'll give you five days you can fill it anywhere you want. I want to learn, and I want to understand.
>
> And basically, the motivation of this was her emotional belief that I didn't care and that her biggest fear was that she would not outlive her child. And she's now one of my best friends. She's 72 years old. Her child is 33 and she still has that fear. But the programs in the state now are significantly better. And that gives her some comfort. So, I'm proud of what the state... has done. But I wouldn't call that, I'm not sure if I'm being clear, but I don't think governments can be compassionate. They can be effective, responsive, helpful, but the people are compassionate not bureaucracies.

The importance of narrative

This insight is reflected in the writings of philosopher Martha Nussbaum (2014), who argues that compassion is the sentimental basis of a democratic political community and that, without it, we lack the motive to respect others, protect them from harm, and respond to their undeserved sufferings. According to Nussbaum (2014), respect for others' rights or dignity is not sufficient to motivate the kind of care and responsibility integral to democracy. Society's compassion tends to be narrow and polarising, reinforcing the view of philosophers such as Aristotle, who "...only care for [their] own... to the exclusion of others' interests or concerns"—an attitude that gives rise to partiality and partisanship.

Nussbaum (2014) argues that, to address these problems, society needs to educate itself in compassion by following the example of Athenian democracy and its use of tragic narratives to educate citizens to recognise their common human vulnerability. Such education can, in turn, facilitate and support democratic political institutions, practices and norms. These can encourage us to pursue less problematic external goods (love of family, friends and work, perhaps even nation) rather than overvaluing those external goods (money, honour, status and fame) that divide us from others, motivate us to treat them with contempt, and establish the conditions necessary for toxic shame, and with it, serious distortions of our capacity for political compassion (Nussbaum, 2014).

Making systemic change

Professor Paul Slovic (2007) contends that, while imagination of the suffering of another as a symbol of the many may be enough to elicit compassion, it is not enough to make the changes required to alleviate or prevent such occurrences of suffering into the future. Rather, what is needed is the creation and commitment to institutional and political responses based upon reasoned analysis of our moral obligations to stop the suffering of others. To achieve this, he proposes two modes of thinking through experiential and analytic systems as identified in Table 8.1.

System 1 gives rise to moral intuition, allowing affect, relatedness, feelings, images, and attention to give rise to immediate action. However, Slovic (2007) argues that, on its own, System 1 cannot be relied upon for two reasons. Firstly, it has the potential to facilitate a bias towards individual victims

TABLE 8.1 Two modes of thought to elicit compassion.

System 1: Experiential system	System 2: Analytic system
✓ Affective: pleasure–pain oriented	✓ Logical: reason oriented (what is sensible)
✓ Connections by association	✓ Connections by logical assessment
✓ Behaviour mediated by feelings from past experiences	✓ Behaviour mediated by conscious appraisal of events
✓ Encodes reality in images, metaphors and narratives	✓ Encodes reality in abstract symbols, words and numbers
✓ More rapid processing: oriented towards immediate action	✓ Slower processing: oriented towards delayed action
✓ Self-evidently valid: "experiencing is believing"	✓ Requires justification via logic and evidence

with sensational stories that are closer to home and easier to imagine. Secondly, only using System 1 allows self-interest to override concerns for others through psychic numbing. Instead, balancing System 1 with System 2 gives rise to moral judgement and its capacity to monitor the quality of mental operations and overt behaviours produced by System 1. It also establishes the basis for creating laws and institutions that compel appropriate action when information about suffering becomes known. Therefore, according to Slovic (2007), what is required is an appropriate balance between feelings and intuition, and logic and reason.

Slovic's insights were demonstrated in the transcript evidence of my research. As a highly regarded Australian Government minister shared with me:

> I think it gets harder once it goes to scale. Because things become abstract again. And the way you find compassion is through stories of individuals rather than collective groups. So, I think you have to try and relate the stories of individuals to that larger scale to keep it human and not abstract. So that's why finding and hearing stories and relating them in the context of response to a suffering of a group is important. Otherwise, it just becomes abstract numbers. So, when you think about it, say in the context of a prison. I don't think I've really fully appreciated—given my white middle class, white bred background—the circumstances and suffering and the turmoil of the lives of so many people and what they had experienced before they ended up in prison. And I think if I had, I'd probably be better at thinking about how to respond to that.
>
> So, there you've got this whole population, and you know what the stats are. The stats say the economic disadvantage, there's poor levels of completion of secondary schooling, alcoholism, drug addiction, indigenous background and all of the prejudice and discrimination. So, you know what it is in an abstract manner, in a conceptual manner. But you don't necessarily understand the context of, 'what was it really like to live in a household where your mother and father were both alcoholics when you were 6?' You know, what was that really like? So, I think it's relating. A good leader takes the data, takes the evidence, but also hears the human stories and brings them both together to find how they can best impact. I think that took me time to learn. But I think I did ultimately start to learn that and understand that. But I think it doesn't always happen.

Striking the balance between the "head" and the "heart" is a difficult but necessary process for leaders who have to guide others through crises. However, such a balance is further complicated by the extent to which certain political influences shape our views of compassion as leaders of mainly government institutions—a complication we will explore further in Chapter 9.

The challenge for leaders

As leaders, we must be prepared to see, sense, and feel the suffering of others while recognising suffering's universality. We need to connect with their emotional distress while tolerating uncomfortable feelings, remain open and accepting of them, and act in practical ways to alleviate their suffering. In so doing, we must grant ourselves the same obligation. We must develop the courage to look into our own minds, grant ourselves permission to see our own suffering, and commit to looking after ourselves such that we can look after others.

It is important that we develop the wisdom to balance up the sentiments, the symbols, and the data that exposes us to the suffering of others—that signal to us that something is wrong, and something needs fixing. That people are suffering and within the equities of power, wealth, resource, and influence made available to us as leaders, we commit to actions that alleviate their suffering—actions at the individual, organisational, and societal levels. To achieve this, in the following chapter we briefly explore the role of compassion in politics.

References

Aristotle. (2004). *Selected writings: Selections from Nicomachean ethics and politics.* CRW Publishing Limited.

Batson, D. C., O'Quin, K., Fultz, J., Vanderplas, M., & Isen, A. M. (1983). Influence of self-reported distress and empathy on egoistic versus altruistic motivation to help. *Journal of Personality and Social Psychology, 45*(3), 706–718. https://doi.org/10.1037/0022-3514.45.3.706

Berndsen, M., & Feather, N. T. (2016). Reflecting on schadenfreude: Serious consequences of a misfortune for which one is not responsible diminish previously expressed schadenfreude: The role of immorality appraisals and moral emotions. *Motivation and Emotion, 40*, 895–913. https://doi.org/10.1007/s11031-016-9580-8

Binskin, M., Bennett, A., & Mcintosh, A. (2020). *Royal commission into national natural disaster arrangements report.* The Royal Commission into National Natural Disaster Arrangements. https://naturaldisaster.royalcommission.gov.au/publications/royal-commission-national-natural-disaster-arrangements-report

Birnie, K., Speca, M., & Carlson, L. E. (2010). Exploring self-compassion and empathy in the context of mindfulness-based stress reduction (MBSR). *Stress and Health, 26*(5), 359–371. https://doi.org/10.1002/smi.1305

Bonanno, G. A. (2004). Loss, trauma, and human resilience: Have we underestimated the human capacity to thrive after extremely aversive events? *The American Psychologist, 59*(1), 20–28. https://doi.org/10.1037/0003-066X.59.1.20

Campbell, J. (Ed.). (1991). *A Joseph Campbell companion: Reflections on the art of living.* HarperCollins Publishers.

Campbell, J. (2002). *The inner reaches of outer space: Metaphor as myth and as religion* (2nd ed.). New World Library.

Coke, J. S., Batson, D. C., & McDavis, K. (1978). Emphatic meditation of helping: A two-stage model. *Journal of Personality and Social Psychology, 36*(7), 752–766. https://doi.org/10.1037/0022-3514.36.7.752

Crosweller, M. (2016). Thinking differently, leading differently: Lessons from the Canberra fires, 2003. In S. Ellis & K. McCarter (Eds.), *Lessons learnt from emergency responses.* CSIRO Publishing.

Cunliffe, A. L., & Eriksen, M. (2011). Relational leadership. *Human Relations*, *64*(11), 1425–1449. https://doi.org/10.1177/0018726711418388

Dalai Lama. (2002). *How to practice: The way to a meaningful life*. Pocket Books.

Dalai Lama. (2005). *The essence of the heart sutra: The Dalai Lama's heart of wisdom teachings* (T. Jinpa, Ed.). Simon and Schuster.

Darwin, C. R. (1871). *The descent of man, and selection in relation to sex* (1st ed.). John Murray.

Edelglass, W. (Ed.). (2009). *Thich Nhat Hahn's Interbeing: Fourteen guidelines for engaged Buddhism*. Oxford University Press USA – OSO.

Farmer, P. (2010). *Partner to the poor: A Paul farmer reader* (1st ed.). University of California Press.

Feldman, C., & Kuyken, W. (2011). Compassion in the landscape of suffering. *Contemporary Buddhism*, *12*(1), 143–155. https://doi.org/10.1080/14639947.2011.564831

Fenske, M. J., & Raymond, J. E. (2006). Affective influences of selective attention. *Current Directions in Psychological Science*, *15*(6), 312–316. https://doi.org/10.1111/j.1467-8721.2006.00459.x

Gilbert, P. (2010). *The compassionate mind*. Constable & Robinson Ltd.

Gilson, E. (2011). Vulnerability, Ignorance, and Oppression. *Hypatia*, *26*(2), 308–332. https://doi.org/10.1111/j.1527-2001.2010.01158.x

Goetz, J. L., Keltner, D., & Simon-Thomas, E. (2010). Compassion: An Evolutionary Analysis and Empirical Review. *Psychological Bulletin*, *136*(3), 351–374. https://doi.org/10.1037/a0018807

Grayling, A. C. (2021). The philosophy of compassion. In M. Hawkins & J. Nadel (Eds.), *How compassion can transform our politics, economy, and society* (1st ed.). Routledge. https://doi.org/10.4324/9780429331176

Gyatso, G. K. (2003). *Universal compassion: Inspiring solutions for difficult times*. Tharpa Publications.

Gyatso, G. K. (2006). *Joyful path of good fortune: The complete Buddhist path to enlightenment*. Tharpa Publications.

Gyatso, G. K. (2011). *Modern Buddhism: The path of compassion and wisdom*. Tharpa Publications.

Gyatso, G. K. (2014). *How to understand the mind: The nature and power of the mind*. Tharpa Publications.

Haidt, J. (2001). The emotional dog and its rational tail: A social intuitionist approach to moral judgment. *Psychological Review*, *108*(4), 814–834. https://doi.org/10.1037/0033-295X.108.4.814

Janaway, C. (2017). Attitudes to suffering: Parfit and Nietzsche. *Inquiry*, *60*(1–2), 66–95. https://doi.org/10.1080/0020174X.2016.1251165

Leary, M. R., Tate, E. B., Adams, C. E., Allen, A. B., & Hancock, J. (2007). Self-compassion and reactions to unpleasant self-relevant events: The implications of treating oneself kindly. *Journal of Personality and Social Psychology*, *92*(5), 887–904. https://doi.org/10.1037/0022-3514.92.5.887

Lifton, R. J. (1967). *Death in life: Survivors in Hiroshima*. Random House.

Neff, K. D. (2003). Self-compassion: An alternative conceptualisation of a healthy attitude towards oneself. *Self and Identity*, *2*(2), 85–101. https://doi.org/10.1080/15298860309032

Nussbaum, M. C. (1996). Compassion: The basic social emotion. *Social Philosophy and Policy*, *13*(1), 27–58. https://doi.org/10.1017/s0265052500001515

Nussbaum, M. C. (2014). Compassion and terror. In M. Ure & M. Frost (Eds.), *The politics of compassion* (pp. 89–207). Routledge.

Oxford. (2017). English Oxford Living Dictionaries. https://www.oed.com/

Power, S. (2007). *A problem from hell: America and the age of genocide*. Harper Perennial.

Reilly, R. (2008). *Ethics of compassion: Bridging ethical theory and religious moral discourse.* Lexington Books.

Ricoeur, P. (1994). *Oneself as another.* University of Chicago Press.

Schopenhauer, A. (1965). *On the basis of morality.* Bobbs-Merrill.

Slovic, P. (2007). "If I look at the mass I will never act": Psychic numbing and genocide. *Judgment and Decision Making, 2*(2), 79–95. https://psycnet.apa.org/doi/10.1017/S1930297500000061

Slovic, S., & Slovic, P. (2004). Numbers and nerves: Toward an affective apprehension of environmental risk. *Whole Terrain, 13,* 14–18.

Slovic, P., & Västfjäll, D. (2015). The more who die, the less we care: Psychic numbing and genocide. In S. Kaul & D. Kim (Eds.), *Imagining human rights* (pp. 55–68). Oregon State University Press. http://dx.doi.org/10.1515/9783110376616-005

Strauss, C., Taylor, B. L., Gu, J., Kuyken, W., Baer, R., Jones, F., & Cavanagh, K. (2016). What is compassion and how can we measure it? A review of definitions and measures. *Clinical Psychology Review, 47,* 15–27. https://doi.org/10.1016/j.cpr.2016.05.004

Thich, N. (2000). *Interbeing: Fourteen guidelines for engaged Buddhism* (2nd ed.). Full Circle Publishing.

Tsering, G. T. (2005). *The four noble truths: The foundation of Buddhist thought.* Wisdom Publications.

Tsering, G. T. (2006). *Buddhist psychology: The foundation of Buddhist thought* (Vol. 3). Wisdom Publications.

Västfjäll, D., Slovic, P., Mayorga, M., & Peters, E. (2014). Compassion fade: Affect and charity are greatest for a single child in need. *PLOS ONE, 9*(6), e0100115. https://doi.org/10.1371/journal.pone.0100115

Weber, E. H. (1834). *De pulsu, resorptione, auditu et tactu.* C. F. Koehler.

Wispe, L. (1991). *The psychology of sympathy.* Springer. https://doi.org/10.1007/978-1-4757-6779-7

9

THE POLITICS OF COMPASSION

> It takes both courage and wisdom to show true compassion. The courage to step beyond self-interest and self-importance and put the needs of others first, and the wisdom to know how far you can go to alleviate suffering without perpetuating it further.

In this chapter, we turn our attention to political compassion. We begin by exploring how the negative impacts of compassionate conservatism and neoliberalism can desensitise us to the suffering of those less fortunate. We then examine the complexity of universal compassion and its relationship with love, justice and anger and critically analyse the role of anger as a motivator for compassion. We then explore the indigenous concept of Ubuntu as an alternative view of political compassion to contest anger and aggression, as evidenced in the liberation of South Africa from the apartheid regime under the leadership of Nelson Mandela.

Compassionate conservatism and neoliberalism

American author Marvin Olasky (1992) writes that the prevailing definition of compassion, from colonial times through the middle of the 20th century, meant "suffering together with another, participation in suffering." This definition inferred that true compassion meant a personal involvement with the needy, suffering with them, thereby requiring the establishment of a close bond between the sufferer and the person seeking to relieve that suffering. During this time, churches and charities were highly successful in aiding the poor because they adopted close links with them.

DOI: 10.4324/9781003499510-12

However, Olasky (1992) argues that, in recent decades, the meaning of compassion has become corrupted to denote instead a mere feeling or emotion when a person is moved by the suffering or distress of another. Rather than fully engaging with the suffering of another, we become mere spectators of their suffering. This shift in meaning implies that a direct connection or contact with the person who is suffering is no longer required, but rather the only action required is "a willingness to send a check," while leaving it to someone else to do the actual helping.

In the modern age, this someone else usually means the government and the extent to which they are influenced either by socialism or conservatism to determine how suffering may be alleviated. According to Olasky, socialism risks leading to structural and political solutions to remove or reduce suffering while potentially creating "welfare states" of dependency further creating enfeebled civil societies. Conversely, conservatism risks leading to assumptions of social decay through moral deficiencies that lead to a morally superior elite imposition of policies against the morally bereft while denying them the opportunity to develop full agency (Olasky, 1992).

Western governments oriented towards socialism (such as, for example, France) have been influenced by Enlightenment thinkers, such as Diderot and Voltaire, who advocated for the capacity of reason to determine what "good" is (compassion). Governments of such persuasion are susceptible to the arrogant presumption that they know what is in the best interests of all society, as well as attributing causes of suffering to political and structural failures. Conversely, western conservative governments have been influenced by Enlightenment thinkers, such as David Hume and Adam Smith, who viewed compassion as an innate moral virtue directed at individual suffering without requiring such presumption. It is in this latter context that most western conservative governments (e.g., Australia, New Zealand and the USA) have framed their social philosophies. Such framing implies that social problems have moral causes and, by extension, individuals have moral deficiencies. This resulted in marginalisation and depoliticisation of structural causes and the promotion of compassionate conservatism in the early 2000s by US President George W. Bush and British Prime Minister Tony Blair (Himmelfarb, 2004).

Compassionate conservatism views compassion as a "tough minded" rather than "soft hearted" moral virtue as a way of challenging the fundamental precepts of these competing social philosophies. In so doing, compassionate conservatism constructs a paternalistic and inegalitarian doctrine that justifies the authority of the morally superior "compassionate" spectator. It allows them to regulate the lives of those who are viewed as morally deficient and the subjects of their compassion. Such "tough love" demands that citizens be forced to take responsibility for their own lives, and to achieve this, things may need to be taken away, rather than given. This includes such actions as a reduction in welfare payments if the citizen does not comply with the incentives of the state to alleviate their dependency like welfare-to-work programmes (Pilbeam, 2010). This perception of moral deficiency has the effect of further categorising people in need as either those who are worthy of compassion (e.g., willing to work or are truly hungry) or those who are not worthy of compassion (e.g., not willing to work and expect a "free lunch") (Olasky, 1996).

In this context, the compassionate spectator (with a degree of perceived moral superiority) and the sufferer (with a degree of perceived moral deficiency), seen through a lens of neoliberalism, participate in a society that seeks to replace the historical concepts of the welfare state with an inflated narrative of the overtaxed and the underemployed, whose dignity must be restored to them by tax cuts and welfare-to-work programmes. The compassionately conservative state wants to severely limit the mechanisms of laws and programmes that reduce suffering on behalf of the state (through presumptions of knowing what the citizen needs) and shift its economic obligations from redressing poverty to protecting income. It aims to achieve this by taking less from (e.g., taxation) and giving less back (e.g., welfare) to workers and citizens. In so doing, it relocates the template of justice to that of the citizen whose economic sovereignty the state vows to protect. Compassionate conservatism thus advocates a sense of dignity (and a reduction in suffering) to be derived from labour itself (Berlant, 2004).

Neoliberalism extends this logic into the commercialisation of feelings—our emotions take on the properties of a resource, not for the purposes of, for example, creating art or music, or for self-discovery, but to make money. Even our emotional intelligence—rather than being used as a measure of our capacity to engage with self-fulfilment, love, community or the common good—is redirected towards productivity, utility, and self-interest. Also, our sense of personal responsibility is not directed at the welfare of others, but at the values and expectations of the market. More specifically, compassion is seen not as a moral virtue, but as subversive to the achievement of a market society where citizens are expected to be responsible for, and focused upon, themselves in all aspects of their lives for the purposes of achieving economic success (LaMothe, 2019).

These politically conservative judgements, shaped by socio-cultural influences such as neoliberalism and applied either through reason or morality, constrain our capacity for compassion by judging some suffering to be more compelling than other suffering. These judgements force us to make further judgements about which cases deserve attention. While some will argue that justice is the objective response, seeking out the cold, hard facts against the incoherent mess of feeling, we must also be compelled to feel right, and to overcome our aversions to others' suffering by training ourselves in compassionate practice (Berlant, 2004).

The moral elevation of compassion is reversed when we challenge the presumptions of neoliberal compassionate conservativism and raise questions about the scale of suffering, the measures of justice, or the presumed fault of the sufferers. We have the opportunity to choose between a model of compassionate conservatism or a model that honours our capacity to innately express universal compassion for all sentient beings.

Universal compassion and love, justice and anger

Implicit in the understanding of universal compassion is the notion of love. Compassionate love in the literature comprises many definitions. This notwithstanding, it may be commonly defined as an attitude towards others— either close others, strangers, or all of humanity. It contains feelings, cognitions and behaviours that are focused on caring, concern and tenderness. It is also oriented towards supporting, helping, and understanding others, particularly when the others are perceived to be suffering or in need. Compassionate love can therefore be summarised as extending beneficence to another (Fehr et al., 2014). Nevertheless, the concept of love is deemed a politically inappropriate emotion because of its association with feelings and perceptions of irrationality, unreasonable thinking and close one-to-one relationships that seek to operate in a space between people where politics would otherwise operate (Arendt, 1958).

That said, such an understanding of love implies the judgement of *eros*— erotic, romantic, sexual or familial love—rather than in the Christian sense *agape* (Hill et al., 1997) or Buddhism's *affectionate love, wishing love,* and *cherishing love* (Gyatso, 2006). Such a love between individuals is not dependent upon the qualities of each other, nor the need for the other. Instead, it is a love that recognises the other's genuine needs, without judging them, asking anything of them, or thinking of one's own needs. There is no power relationship between the agent and recipient of compassion. Instead, there is a concern for the welfare of all and for justice. These forms of love take the individual into the wider social world, simultaneously allowing recognition and detachment from the self while establishing the basis for political compassion and reasoned judgement (Hill et al., 1997).

Academic theologian Marcus Borg (1997) argues that, by establishing *agape* as the basis for moving beyond individual suffering to the suffering of many, the causes of suffering arising from injustice and inequity become social causes that require political action to address their effects. He further argues that, without justice, compassion risks quietly perpetuating the systems that cause the suffering in the first place, creating even more sufferers. Therefore, for compassion to be effective, injustice must be addressed through justice (judgements) and actions motivated by compassionate anger to ensure that the inadequacies in the systems that create the root causes of social suffering are changed (Borg, 1997).

Some scholars argue that the domestication of anger in politics supports compassionate anger and that, in its absence, compassion is politically silent, being relegated instead to the realm of charity. In so doing, it colludes with the very system that produces the harms that compassion seeks to address. Instead, angry speech gives a voice to the injustices (Lyman, 2004). Other scholars argue that if the foundation of liberal societies lies in a shared sense of human vulnerability, then tracking harm through anger needs to be granted as one of our most important moral sentiments, particularly in any conception of justice (Muldoon, 2008). Therefore, anger needs to arise in conditions where the operations of the political process are the cause of suffering—where governments and their agencies do not listen or hear and likewise do not respond—and suffering or injustice arises, particularly when representing those who are unable to participate in the political process (Whitebrook, 2014).

Nonetheless, two problems emerge from this argument. The first is, who judges, through what lenses are they judging (reason or morality, and if so, whose morality?), and to what extent are those judgements shaped by neoliberal influences that have already been argued above? Clearly, compassion in its political form is not a "soft" virtue but will, in effect, require the dominant political system to both recognise and realise certain principles and values, including a fundamental basis for social justice (Whitebrook, 2014). Secondly, is anger *useful* in this pursuit?

Anger as a motivator of political compassion

By looking beyond the distress of others and towards social and structural causes of suffering, political compassion has an important cognitive function. It establishes the conditions necessary for anger or indignation to arise as a means of alerting states and citizens to sources of harm and suffering that require political redress. It also focuses our compassion on systemic causes. For supporters of such a view, there is no necessary or compelling reason to believe that such compassion-fuelled anger or indignation necessarily leads to violent excess. Nor is there any reason to believe that the risk of anger or indignation might be sufficient to disbar it from politics any more than we think fear should be disbarred because it might generate cowardice or impotence. Therefore, according to some scholars the task at hand is not to dismiss anger, but to regulate and discipline it so that it can fulfil its important political function: identifying and protesting against systemic injustice (Nussbaum, 1996; Whitebrook, 2014).

Controlling anger

However, controlling anger is not so easy. Being consciously aware of feeling angry and of being "physically" motivated by anger is in sharp contrast to the Nietzschean characterisation of anger which manifests itself as a self-righteous worldview that seeks to resolve conflict by assigning blame and exacting revenge.

It is also often used to blame the victim by ignoring the social relationships, and perhaps even the social injustices, that cause an angry response (Lyman, 2004). Therefore, anger warrants special attention when considering judgement and decision making, as its effects often diverge from other negative emotions such as sadness. This is because anger is mostly experienced as a negative, unpleasant and unrewarding experience when reflected upon, but experienced as relatively pleasant when projected forward (Lerner & Tiedens, 2006).

As Aristotle wrote:

> ...anger may be defined as an impulse, accompanied by pain, to a conspicu-ous revenge for a conspicuous slight directed without justification towards what concerns oneself or towards what concerns one's friends. If this is a proper definition of anger, it must always be felt towards some particular individual, e.g., Cleon, and not 'man' in general. It must be felt because the other has done or intended to do something to him or one of his friends. It must always be attended by a certain pleasure that which arises from the expectation of revenge. For since nobody aims at what he thinks he cannot attain, the angry man is aiming at what he can attain, and the belief that you will attain your aim is pleasant. It is also attended by a certain pleasure because the thoughts dwell upon the act of vengeance, and the images then called up cause pleasure, like the images called up in dreams.
>
> *(Aristotle, 1959)*

Accordingly, it is important to give attention to anger for a number of rea-sons. Firstly, anger is one of the most frequently experienced emotions, arising anywhere from several times per day to several times per week (Averill, 1982). Secondly, anger has an unusually strong capacity to capture attention, both of the person perceiving it and the person experiencing it (Solomon, 1990), as evidenced by expressions of anger that are implicitly perceived as threaten-ing, competent, powerful and dominant (Hansen & Hansen, 1988). Thirdly, anger's infusive potential and its common ability to carry over from past situa-tions to unrelated judgements and decisions (Lerner & Tiedens, 2006).

As Aristotle noted in his *Nicomachean ethics*, anyone can become angry— that is easy. But to be angry with the right person, to the right degree, at the right time, for the right purpose, and in the right way—that is not easy (Aristo-tle, 2004). Anger makes us indiscriminately punitive (Goldberg et al., 1999), indiscriminately optimistic about our own chances of success (Fischhoff et al., 2012), careless in our thoughts (Bodenhausen et al., 1994), and eager to act out of ignorance (Harmon-Jones et al., 2003). These outcomes occur be-cause anger seeks to influence any given situation's most basic attributes of judgement and decision making—perceptions of control, responsibility, and certainty—and because anger lingers after the triggering events, aiding its jus-tification (Lerner & Keltner, 2001).

False confidence

Anger is also associated with the sense that we (or someone close and important to us) have been offended or injured. This includes a strong perception of certainty or confidence about what happened and what caused it, as well as a belief that another person is responsible. Anger also convinces us that we still have some control or influence over the situation (Lazarus, 1991). The angrier we feel, the more we feel that others are responsible (blame attribution), and this, in turn, increases our anger further (Quigley & Tedeschi, 1996).

Anger can also act as a precursor to prejudice by limiting our capacity to assign positive attributes to outgroups. At the same time, it accelerates our capacity to assign negative attributes, and when combined with the perception of strength (e.g., righteousness of view or opinion), motivates us (individually or collectively) to act, including the wish to fight, harm or injure those we consider responsible (Frija et al., 1989; Mackie et al., 2000). This is often carried out through motivations of spite, vengeance, contempt, or insolence (Aristotle, 2012).

Ironically, despite anger generally being regarded as a negative emotion, such actions can be viewed as positive (in a destructive sense), as they give rise to exhilaration when planning to enact revenge (Tripp & Bies, 1997) or when witnessing the misfortune of disliked others (*Schadenfreude*) (Leach et al., 2003). Hence, what may be regarded as a positive aspect of anger lays the groundwork for very negative consequences, such as violence and aggression (Lerner & Tiedens, 2006), all of which gives rise to further suffering.

Delusion of the mind

In Buddhist philosophy, anger is considered a significant factor in the creation of human and non-human suffering as it allows the human mind to exaggerate the bad qualities of another, considers them to be undesirable, and wishes to bring harm to them. It is also accredited with the root cause of all human violence in the world. Put simply, if the human mind did not possess anger, then there would be no violence, and it is often the case that the cause of the suffering we are objecting to has arisen from a mind of anger or violence. Anger begets anger, violence begets violence. Additionally, while the human mind allows anger into its consciousness it cannot be simultaneously compassionate. The human mind can only consciously cognise one object in any given moment. We can be angry, or we can be compassionate—we cannot simultaneously be both (Gyatso, 2006, 2014).

When we view anger as a strength and a motivator, it fuels our perceptions of control and certainty, which often lead to high levels of self-optimism. This includes our capacity to de-emphasise the importance and potential impacts of negative events or consequences upon ourselves that, in turn, fuel our arrogance. Thinking in this way often results in our propensity to take more risks, and we tend to assign the confidence for positive outcomes to ourselves rather than the outcomes for others (Lerner & Keltner, 2001).

When we get angry, we also tend to engage in relatively automatic, superficial and heuristic processes. We rely principally on general knowledge structures, rather than processing stimuli through thoughtful and reflective processes that tend to be the norm for those of us who feel sadness rather than anger (Bodenhausen et al., 1994). Also, when we are angry, we do not find sad messages motivating, but rather only angry messages (DeSteno et al., 2004), all of which seek to perpetuate our ignorance.

The need to be cautious

Therefore, while some scholars argue that social suffering is often the result of systemic injustices and that compassion-fuelled-anger can be harnessed to motivate the necessary systemic changes through the pursuit of justice (judgement) to alleviate suffering at its root cause (Borg, 1997), anger has its limitations. It is clear that such an approach can also lead to the hindering of objectivity and rationality. It can also promote the potential for ignorance and arrogance through overconfidence and control, as well as thinking the worst of others that may cascade into undesirable outcomes, such as violence, physical or emotional harm and aggression, unrealistic optimism, and overconfidence (Lerner & Tiedens, 2006). Fire is a well-known analogy for anger. For those of us who have experienced fire firsthand, we know how quickly it can spread uncontrollably under the right conditions. Therefore, we would do well to appreciate how easy it is to lose control of anger and its effects.

The need for respect and for action

In acknowledging the limitations of acting through anger as a motivator for compassion, we must be cautious that we do not, in any way, dismiss the pain and suffering being experienced by those who are impacted by systemic, racial and other social injustices. Their voices matter—whether angry or not. If we are to temper our anger in society, then it is critical that those who hold privilege, along with the equities of power, wealth and resource, open up genuine pathways where voices can still be heard, and actions can be undertaken to relieve suffering wherever and for whomever it arises. Simply seeking order and control (peace and patience) while ignoring the suffering of others is to perpetuate the very same suffering we are seeking to address.

If we are to navigate towards a more peaceful and compassionate world, then we must seek a world that is just for all. We must genuinely listen to and understand the needs of others, and where those needs involve the desire for equitable access to power, wealth and resources to pursue happiness, wellbeing, and flourishing, we should do all that we can within our power to aid them. When we do this, we can accommodate expressions of compassionate anger while being simultaneously taking action to reduce its causes without succumbing to anger and its negative effects.

An alternative view for political compassion—Ubuntu

An example of the power of peaceful and just solutions without anger was exemplified by Nelson Mandela during the period in which he led the dismantling of apartheid in South Africa. During this period, the potential for the devastating effects of uncontrolled anger in response to the many years of social injustice was significant. Fortunately, what ultimately manifested was not an uncontrolled descent into anger, aggression, vengeance, and retribution. Instead, an environment of interdependence, mutuality and compassion emerged, where South Africans found themselves in a position of being embodied and illustrative "border crossers." They were able to come together to construct meaning in the porous spaces between individuals and groups in a dynamically transforming and transformational society (Cilliers, 2008).

Former Archbishop of Cape Town, South Africa and theologian Desmond Tutu argued that harmony, friendliness, compassion, and community are the greatest goods of a society, and anything that undermines these societal goods—such as anger, resentment, lust for revenge, or even success through aggressive competitiveness—are to be avoided. Therefore, to be free of these harmful effects, society needs to forgive, not just as altruism, but as self-interest. As what dehumanises the individual inexorably dehumanises the other, whereas forgiveness gives people resilience, enabling them to survive and emerge still human despite all efforts to dehumanise them (Tutu, 1999).

This approach is captured in African culture through *ubuntu,* which speaks of the essence of being human, through generosity, hospitality, friendliness, care, and compassion. The humanity of one is inextricably bound up in the other. A person is a person through other people. Rather than *cogito, ergo sum* (I think therefore I am') (Encyclopaedia Britannica, 2023a), *ubuntu* says, "I am human because I belong, I participate, I share," being open, available and affirming to others, without feeling threatened that others are able and good. Those with *ubuntu* have proper self-assurance that arises from knowing that they belong in a greater whole and therefore feel diminished when others are humiliated or diminished, tortured or oppressed or treated as lesser (Tutu, 1999).

Ubuntu's origins

Ubuntu's origins extend back to ancient oral traditional belief systems, establishing both a "way of life" and a "universal truth" (Cilliers, 2008). Historically, there is no defined theodical position in African culture that defines reasons for suffering that exist in monotheistic religions (punishment and sin) or karmic based religions (e.g., Buddhism, Hinduism, and Jainism). Instead, suffering of the individual is seen in the context of the community and vice versa. Harmful and negative actions (viewed as evil) and their effects enacted by individuals have a direct impact on communal life (including ancestors) (Du Plooy, 2014).

As a result of the effects of modernity, this ancient system of beliefs has semantically shifted, firstly by industrialisation, urbanisation and the influence of Christianity, followed by a second semantic shift, with the influence of human rights, globalisation and nation building (Keep & Midgley, 2007). Both of these influences have led to a moral ethical theory encompassing values internal to the individual (life, well-being, rights, and self-realisation), and relationship-based values (group solidarity and the production of harmony, promoting shared identify and goodwill) (Metz, 2007). Thus, *ubuntu* has become a contemporary utopian symbol of humanist ideals of peaceable and interconnected human living and a methodology and praxis for a global village (Du Plooy, 2014).

Ubuntu influences through discourses, ethical and moral theory, public policy, and imperative for peace and harmony, as a beneficent power in the relations between individuals and groups in the volatile South African socio-political and ideological climate. The *South African Constitution and Bill of Rights*, *The Ubuntu Pledge* and the *Moral Regeneration Movement* all signify overt and covert codifications of the principles of *ubuntu*, as does former South African President Thabo Mbeki's call for an African Renaissance (Du Plooy, 2014).

Unfortunately, South Africans lost their concept of *ubuntu* during apartheid times, which left the country fractured and with no shared moral discourse while fighting for liberation. Fortunately, *ubuntu* re-emerged and re-invigorated South African discourses after the end of apartheid by attempting to mobilise its peoples to embrace the constitutional values of non-racialism, non-sexism, non-discrimination, and respect for freedom, human rights and dignity (Letseka, 2012; Masango, 2006).

Criticisms of Ubuntu

In much the same way that compassionate conservatism has been criticised, *ubuntu* has also been criticised for inducing denial of past atrocities (Cilliers, 2008). It has also been criticised for being appropriated for all too familiar nationalist purposes through moralising discourses of nation-building and citizenship, glorifying an invented tradition and imagined past, resulting in cultural conformism, implied exclusions, reliance on authoritative practices and ideals, and the stifling of dissent (Marx, 2002). In addition, being "a pastiche of the original idea," a mere remnant of what it was in its original form, "a 'catch-all' term," "one of those protean terms that has been adopted by a variety of institutions and events in their attempt to capture the spirit of *ubuntu* and to give them greater credence" (Hailey, 2008) are also valid criticisms. Also, African social systems, from which *ubuntu* arises, have had to face challenges and transitions as a result of the powerful forces of colonialism and imperialism so dynamic as to almost spiral out of control, and where European culture, rather than African culture, now dominates amidst a sea of other global cultures (Mbiti, 1969).

From self to other as a pathway to compassion

Nevertheless, despite the criticisms, the concept of *ubuntu* remains significantly influential. Characteristic of *ubuntu* is the absence of "Self." *Ubuntu*, as an African epistemology, is often understood as circular, organic, collectivist, interpretive, expressive, understanding, and harmonious, as opposed to what is traditionally conceived as its dichotomous polar opposite: "western" linearity, unitisation, materialism, individualism, verification, rationalism, prediction, and control (Swanson, 2008). In African thought, humanity is a force of energy that imbues individual and communal existence in an integrated and indistinguishable way. Conversely, in western thought, the personal choice to believe and act upon individual reasoning contains in itself a distinctly human transcending energy (Shutte, 1993).

From a western perspective—and drawing upon the principles of *ubuntu*, politically and ethically—the risk of compassion is well worth taking, as the sublime experience can overwhelm rational, self-contained, self-interested people, compelling them to experience their common vulnerability and their openness to others' suffering. Compassion can break down and remove the sharply demarcated boundaries of rational individuals, motivating them to act based on an ethics of generosity of giving, without thought of return, rather than an ethics of exchange and reciprocity (Frost, 2004).

Such experiences can transcend the political, historical and cultural boundaries and distinctions of friend/enemy, insider/outsider, citizen/stranger that divide one from the other. These distinctions prevent individuals from responding to one another first and foremost as mortal, needy suffering creatures, rather than exclusively as agents whose relations are largely regulated by pre-existing legal, economic, cultural, and historical dynamics (Frost, 2004). Thus, the principles of a common humanity and the transcendence of egotism results in a genuine self-love that turns out to be a love of precisely that which is within and most deeply shared with others, and that is, our shared humanity (Shutte, 1993).

South Africa's Truth and Reconciliation Commission was an example of a political practice that afforded citizens the possibility of exercising compassion across deeply entrenched political divisions by bracketing the question of whether those who received their compassion warranted or deserved their assistance and focused instead exclusively on assuaging others' suffering. As Desmond Tutu himself argued:

> ...even the supporters of apartheid were victims of the vicious system which they had implemented and which they supported so enthusiastically. Our humanity was intertwined. The humanity of the perpetrator of apartheid's atrocities was caught up and bound up in that of his victim whether he liked it or not. In the process of dehumanizing another, in inflicting untold harm and suffering, the perpetrator was inexorably being dehumanized as well.
>
> *(Tutu, 1999)*

While South Africa continues to face challenges with social, racial, and other inequalities, there is no doubt that Nelson Mandela, Desmond Tutu, and many others, driven by a deeply embodied understanding of *ubuntu*— the essence of being human, through generosity, hospitality, friendliness, care, and compassion—avoided significant amounts of suffering for their people. Their experiences during this period allow us to find a place in our shared human history where we can draw examples about how to navigate the complex environments of contestation and conflict that we, as leaders, find ourselves.

Even though most of us reading this book will never become national presidents nor prime ministers, we can still draw inspiration and insight from these leaders to help us navigate the political and organisational tensions that we inevitably have to experience. In profound ways, they showed us that relating to the suffering of others, moving to action to alleviate that suffering, exemplifying great courage in the execution of those actions, and being accountable for actions which others can count on yielded significant benefits for many millions of people.

The challenge for leaders

As leaders, we must be mindful of the way that certain social and cultural influences such as neoliberalism can pull us off track from genuinely seeing, sensing, and feeling the suffering of others. We must also be cautious about our anger and righteousness. To be motivated by anger to alleviate suffering is one thing, to harm another and cause suffering through our anger is quite another thing altogether. It is critical that we understand the difference and act accordingly. Our leadership effectiveness would also benefit from bracketing the question of "deservedness of suffering" and instead focusing on the causes of suffering and minimising, managing or negating them wherever possible as a universal principle.

To best equip us for this challenge, it is also critical that we understand compassion in the context of the virtuous nature of our character, and it is to this question that we now turn our minds.

References

Arendt, H. (1958). *The human condition.* University of Chicago Press.
Aristotle (2004). *Selected writings: Selections from Nicomachean ethics and politics.* CRW Publishing Limited.
Aristotle (2012). *Rhetoric* (W. R. Roberts, Trans.). Bibliotech Press.
Aristotle (1959). *Ars rhetorica* (D. Ross, Ed.). Clarendon Press.
Averill, J. R. (1982). *Anger and aggression: An essay on emotion.* Springer-Verlag.
Berlant, L. (2004). Introduction compassion (and withholding). In L. Berlant (Ed.) *Compassion: The culture and politics of an emotion* (1st ed., pp. 1–13). Routledge. https://doi.org/10.4324/9780203871096
Bodenhausen, G. V., Sheppard, L. A., & Kramer, G. P. (1994). Negative affect and social judgment: The differential impact of anger and sadness. *European Journal of Social Psychology, 24*(1), 45–62. https://doi.org/10.1002/ejsp.2420240104
Borg, M. J. (1997). *The God we never knew: Beyond dogmatic religion to a more authentic contemporary faith.* HarperCollins.
Cilliers, J. (2008). *In search of meaning between Ubuntu and into: Perspectives on preaching in Post-Apartheid South Africa* [Paper presentation]. 8th International Conference of Societas Homiletica, Copenhagen, Denmark.
DeSteno, D., Petty, R. E., Rucker, D. D., Wegener, D. T., & Braverman, J. (2004). Discrete emotions and persuasion: The role of emotion-induced expectancies. *Journal of Personality and Social Psychology, 86*(1), 43–56. https://doi.org/10.1037/0022-3514.86.1.43
Du Plooy, B. (2014). Ubuntu and the recent phenomenon of the charter for compassion. *South African Review of Sociology, 45*(1), 83–100. https://doi.org/10.1080/21528586.2014.887916
Encyclopaedia Britannica. (2023a). Cogito, ergo, sum. In *Encyclopedia Britannica.* Retrieved October 3, 2023, from https://www.britannica.com/topic/cogito-ergo-sum
Fehr, B., Harasymchuk, C., & Sprecher, S. (2014). Compassionate love in romantic relationships: A review and some new findings. *Journal of Social and Personal Relationships, 31*(5), 575–600. https://doi.org/10.1177/0265407514533768
Fischhoff, B., Gonzalez, R. M., Lerner, J. S., & Small, D. A. (2012). Evolving judgments of terror risks: Foresight, hindsight, and emotion: A reanalysis. *Journal of Experimental Psychology Applied, 18*(2), e1–16. https://doi.org/10.1037/a0027959
Frija, N. H., Kuipers, P., & Ter Schure, E. (1989). Relations among emotion, appraisal, and emotional action readiness. *Journal of Personality and Social Psychology, 57*(2), 212–228. https://doi.org/10.1037/0022-3514.57.2.212
Frost, L. (2004). Compassion as risk. In M. Ure & M. Frost (Eds.), *The politics of compassion.* Routledge.
Goldberg, J. H., Lerner, J. S., & Tetlock, P. E. (1999). Rage and reason: The psychology of the intuitive prosecutor. *European Journal of Social Psychology, 29*(5–6), 781–785. https://doi.org/10.1002/(SICI)1099-0992(199908/09)29:5/6<781::AID-EJSP960>3.0.CO;2-3
Gyatso, G. K. (2006). *Joyful path of good fortune: The complete Buddhist path to enlightenment.* Tharpa Publications.
Gyatso, G. K. (2014). *How to understand the mind: The nature and power of the mind.* Tharpa Publications.

Hailey, J. (2008). *Ubuntu: A literature review. Tutu Foundation.*

Hansen, C. H., & Hansen, R. D. (1988). Finding the face in the crowd: An anger superiority effect. *Journal of Personality and Social Psychology, 54*(6), 917–924. https://doi.org/10.1037/0022-3514.54.6.917

Harmon-Jones, E., Sigelman, J., Bohlig, A., & Harmon-Jones, C. (2003). Anger, coping, and frontal cortical activity: The effect of coping potential on anger-induced left frontal activity. *Cognition and Emotion, 17*(1), 1–24. https://doi.org/10.1080/02699930302278

Hill, B., Knitter, P. F., & Madges, W. (1997). *Faith, religion & theology: A contemporary introduction.* Twenty-Third Publications.

Himmelfarb, G. (2004). *The roads to modernity: The British, French, and American enlightenments.* Alfred A. Knopf.

Keep, H., & Midgley, R. (2007). *The emerging role of Ubuntu-Botho in developing a consensual South African Legal Culture.* Paper presented at the Annual meeting of the the Law and Society Association, Berlin, Germany.

King, M. L. (1964). *Why we can't wait.* Signet.

LaMothe, R. (2019). Pebbles in the shoe: Acts of compassion as subversion in a market society. *Pastoral Psychology, 68*(3), 285–301. http://dx.doi.org/10.1007/s11089-018-0833-1

Lazarus, R. S. (1991). *Emotion and adaptation.* Oxford University Press.

Leach, C. W., Spears, R., Branscombe, N. R., & Doosje, B. (2003). Malicious pleasure: Schadenfreude at the suffering of another group. *Journal of Personality and Social Psychology, 84*(5), 932–943. https://doi.org/10.1037/0022-3514.84.5.932

Lerner, J. S., & Keltner, D. (2001). Fear, anger, and risk. *Journal of Personality and Social Psychology, 81*(1), 146–159. https://doi.org/10.1037//0022-3514.81.1.146

Lerner, J. S., & Tiedens, L. Z. (2006). Portrait of the angry decision maker: How appraisal tendencies shape anger's influence on cognition. *Journal of Behavioral Decision Making, 19*(2), 115–137. http://dx.doi.org/10.1002/bdm.515

Letseka, M. (2012). In defence of ubuntu. *Studies in Philosophy and Education, 31*, 47–60.

Lyman, P. (2004). The domestication of anger: The use and abuse of anger in politics. *European Journal of Social Theory, 7*(2), 133–147. https://doi.org/10.1177/1368431004041748

Mackie, D. M., Devos, T., & Smith, E. R. (2000). Intergroup emotions: Explaining offensive action tendencies in an intergroup context. *Journal of Personality and Social Psychology, 79*(4), 602–616. http://dx.doi.org/10.1037//0022-3514.79.4.602

Marx, C. (2002). Ubu and ubuntu: On the dialectics of apartheid and nation building. *Politikon: South African Journal of Political Studies, 29*(1), 49–69. https://doi.org/10.1080/02589340220149434

Masango, M. (2006). African spirituality that shapes the concept of ubuntu. *Verbum Et Ecclesia, 27*(3), 930–943. http://dx.doi.org/10.4102/ve.v27i3.195

Mbiti, J. S. (1969). *African Religions and philosophy.* East African Educational Publishers Ltd.

Metz, T. (2007). Toward an African moral theory*. *Journal of Political Philosophy, 15*(3), 321–341. https://doi.org/10.1111/j.1467-9760.2007.00280.x

Muldoon, P. (2008). The moral legitimacy of anger. *European Journal of Social Theory, 11*(3), 299–314. https://doi.org/10.1177/1368431008092564

Nussbaum, M. C. (1996). Compassion: The basic social emotion. *Social Philosophy and Policy, 13*(1), 27–58. https://doi.org/10.1017/s0265052500001515

Olasky, M. (1992). *The tragedy of American compassion* (1st ed.). Regnery Publishing.

Olasky, M. (1996). *Renewing American compassion.* The Free Press.

Pilbeam, B. (2010). The tragedy of compassionate conservatism. *Journal of American Studies, 44*(2), 251–268. https://doi.org/10.1017/s0021875809990697

Quigley, B. M., & Tedeschi, J. T. (1996). Mediating effects of blame attributions on feelings of anger. *Personality and Social Psychology Bulletin, 22*(12), 1280–1288. https://doi.org/10.1177/01461672962212008

Shutte, A. (1993). *Philosophy for Africa*. University of Capetown Press.

Solomon, R. C. (1990). *A passion for justice: Emotions and the origins of the social contract*. Addison-Wesley.

Swanson, D. M. (2008). Ubuntu: An African contribution to (re)search for/with a 'humble togetherness. *Journal of Contemporary Issues in Education, 2*(2), 53–67. http://dx.doi.org/10.20355/C5PP4X

Tripp, T. M., & Bies, R. J. (eds.) (1997). What's good about revenge? The avenger's perspective. In R. J. Lewicki, R. J. Bies, & B. H. Sheppard (Eds.), *Research on negotiation in organizations* (Vol. 6, pp. 145–160). JAI Press.

Tutu, D. (1999). *No future without forgiveness*. Doubleday.

Whitebrook, M. (2014). Love and anger as political virtues. In M. Ure, & M. Frost (Eds.), *The politics of compassion* (pp. 21–36). Routledge.

10

ENHANCING RELATIONALITY THROUGH THE LENS OF VIRTUE ETHICS

> Developing virtue is a life-long process of trial and error, reflection, education, honouring of moral conscience, and forgiveness. Sometimes we succeed, and sometimes we fail. The art of virtue is to know that we can build upon success and learn from failure, moment by moment, day by day, and over the course of a lifetime, honour those virtues that truly define us as thoroughly human beings.

In this chapter, we place the ethic of compassion within the wider context of virtue ethics. We begin by briefly exploring the history of virtue ethics and its focus on character and the rightness of action, followed by a brief examination of virtue, deontology and utilitarianism. We then consider the importance of our ethical premise as disaster management leaders, followed by the importance of character, the common properties of virtues, and the most common virtues across most cultures, doctrines and religions. We briefly examine one of the key criticisms of virtue ethics from situationists and empirical psychologists that virtue ethics are empirically inadequate, which leads us to further examine our human fallibility and moral hypocrisy.

A brief history of virtue ethics

To understand the history of virtue, we must go back in time, prior to the works of the ancient Greek philosophers, and briefly reflect on Homer's *Iliad* and *Odyssey*. These works provided the means by which the ancient Greeks made sense of their moral lives. However, they were works of poetry, not philosophy. Homer articulated an implicit morality intertwined with an explicit history, told through stories and myths. These stories and myths allowed the

DOI: 10.4324/9781003499510-13

audience the opportunity to understand the relationship between the gods, their fate, how they worked, and how they related to their own personal lives (Malik, 2014).

Traditionally, there were five virtues: courage, moderation, piety, wisdom, and justice. However, over time, the dominant influences of scepticism and relativism (as rhetoric and persuasion) of Protagoras and Democritus resulted in the increasing uncertainty of the meaning of each of these virtues. In response, Socrates argued that moral inquiry and the virtues that arose were philosophical, not rhetorical, as they were concerned with truth, not persuasion. Ethics appealed to rational argument, not custom, tradition or authority and relied on principles not derived from natural speculation, but from a rational study of the human condition. From that time on, a virtue-based approach to ethics extended over much of the course of history, from the period of Aristotle through the Mediaeval period and into the Renaissance period of the 15th and 16th centuries (MacIntyre, 2007; McCloskey, 2008).

Between about 400BC to about 1790AD, the moral universe as described by Europe was composed on the seven primary virtues (four being "Pagan" and three being "Christian"): courage, temperance, justice and prudence; and faith, hope and love (McCloskey, 2008). Following the Renaissance, logic, reason and the empiricism of science arising from the Enlightenment period dominated moral reasoning and decision making (MacIntyre, 2007). By the 19th century, virtue and its character-based approach were relegated to imply a life of chastity or abstinence (Solomon, 1992). By the 20th century, virtue had been further relegated by the social sciences due to perceived concerns about maintaining the scientific method and its secular and objective values (Peterson & Seligman, 2004).

Adam Smith's (1976) seminal work, *Theory of moral sentiments* noted, "Of all of the corrupters of moral sentiments… faction and fanaticism have always been by far the greatest" (McCloskey, 2008). In this regard, Smith, Hume, Kant, Bentham, and Locke (all Enlightenment philosophers, from whom deontology and utilitarianism arose, and will be discussed shortly) sought to remove ethics from religion and locate them within the human realm of reason. Aristotelian virtue ethics went into further eclipse during the 17th century, because it lacked a notion of human rights that became politically indispensable during that period when religious wars were raging (Schneewind, 1997).

At the same time, the modern state was emerging as a plural society where prosperity and progress could be assured only if people with deeply held differing views about religion could somehow learn to live together tolerantly and peacefully. Concurrently, the notion that people had rights against each other helped make this all possible. The idea of rights deliberately rejected the idea that political life depended on people having correct moral, religious and political beliefs. The Aristotelian view that individual virtue and just society relied upon a social justice that further depended on (correct) shared virtue or virtues was therefore also rejected. Aristotelianism was also not well adapted to the needs of the emerging world of modern-day societies and the corresponding rise of individualism. It therefore went into disuse in large part for that reason (Slote, 2015).

However, the absence of any notion of strong individualism in eastern societies and their philosophies, and the corresponding continuation of a virtuous ethos, provides an interesting contrast in demonstrating the strong role that individualism has played in the west. Most ethics outside the west have been virtue-ethical in character, and non-virtue-ethical thinking has largely been confined to western philosophy. For example, Buddhism, Daoism and Confucianism are arguably forms of virtue ethics. Likewise, are the various forms of African ethical thought, which are frequently interpreted as either virtue-ethical or as having deep affinity with virtue ethics (Slote, 2015).

Following the Enlightenment period, virtue ethics did not re-emerge until 1958, with the publication of Elizabeth Anscombe's *Modern moral philosophy'* (Anscombe, [1958] 1997), followed by Phillipa Foot's *Virtues and vices* (Foot, 1978), Alastair MacIntyre's *After virtue: A study in moral theory'* (MacIntyre, 2007), Martha Nussbaum's *The fragility of goodness: Luck and ethics in Greek tragedy and philosophy'* (Nussbaum, 1986), Michael Slote's *Agent-based virtue ethics'* (Slote, 1995), and Rosalind Hursthouse's *On virtue ethics* (Hursthouse, 2001). All of these philosophers have built on the work of Aristotle, leading to a contemporary virtue ethics marked by a clear focus not just on character but also on action and the rightness of action (Russell, 2009).

Virtue, deontology and utilitarianism

Importantly, virtue, along with deontology and utilitarianism, establishes three normative ethical frameworks that are utilised extensively in ethical decision making, particularly for businesses and governments (Sison et al., 2012). Virtue ethics focuses on the character of the ethical agent: "Virtuous agents are those that respond at the right time, to the right objects, towards the right people, with the right motive and in the right way" (Carr, 2003, p. 219). (We will discuss virtue ethics in more detail later in this chapter).

Deontological ethics focuses on duties of ethical agents. Emmanuel Kant argued that all moral decisions should be founded upon a "categorical imperative": that we should consider the means by which we should act rather than considering only the end results, and that people should not be used as means to an end, but rather as ends in themselves (Guyer, 2002). The categorical imperative also implied that we should consider the questions, "what would the world look like if everyone confronting this dilemma acted in this way?" and, "how would I feel if the same decision was taken that impacted upon me?," suggesting that a universal solution could be found to any moral dilemma (Bruton, 2004). Utilitarian ethics focuses on the outcomes of actions of ethical agents. John Stuart Mill argued all moral decisions should be taken upon a single criterion: securing the greatest utility for the greatest number, suggesting that decisions should be made in terms of their overall outcomes (Chryssides & Kaler, 1993).

These three normative ethical frameworks can be best summarised as acting in a virtuous way that builds good character and is consistent with a good life (virtue), following prescribed duties that should in turn be for everyone else to follow (deontological), and maximising welfare or minimising harm (utilitarian) (Morrell & Dahlmann, 2022, p. 617). Importantly, both Emmanuel Kant (deontology) and John Stuart Mill (utilitarianism) stressed the importance of moral character and virtue as key elements within their respective normative ethical debates (Crisp, 1996; Korsgaard, 1996).

However, deontological and utilitarian ethics are often criticised for being too abstract to be useful. They are also criticised for being too complex in their language and interpretation which is off-putting for practitioners engaged in organisational life (Monast, 1994; Stark, 1993). More specifically, deontology is often criticised because a "categorical" imperative such as always telling the truth could ultimately interfere with other moral imperatives (Morrell, 2006). Telling a criminal assailant where their victim is hiding is but one such example. Utilitarianism approaches to ethical dilemmas can run into problems, for example, when trying to measure utility (often referred to as happiness) or when overall utility denies an individual certain basic rights (Velasquez, 2001).

Some scholars assert that both deontological and utilitarian approaches to ethics treat ethical dilemmas as a matter of dispassionate calculation (Overman Smith & Thompson, 2002) and, similarly, that they are abstract—we give the same level of consideration to complete strangers as we do to well-known friends, colleagues, community members, and so on (Velasquez, 2001). But perhaps more importantly, neither deontological nor utilitarian ethical frameworks adequately take into consideration the contextual, contingent and relational nature of leadership, which are central to its function. Instead, both approaches seek to achieve a universalised set of principles through differing methods to solve ethical problems (Ladkin, 2006).

Notwithstanding, deontological and utilitarian ethics can be useful in management and decision-making. For example, all disaster survivors should be treated with the same level of fairness, respect and dignity, irrespective of their circumstances (deontological). Likewise, suffering should be minimised for as many humans and non-humans in the most efficient and effective way possible (utilitarian). The abstract principles derived from both deontological and utilitarian normative frameworks can more easily translate into governance mechanisms that can apply across entire sectors or even the global population (Morrell & Dahlmann, 2022).

Deontological and utilitarian approaches to decision-making are clearly useful and necessary at scale, but they can fail to address the specific context and circumstances in which individuals and communities find themselves. For example, they can fail to address what is truly valued and important within the context of place. Conversely, virtue ethics provides the normative foundation for addressing these and other related needs. According to Morrell and Dahlmann (2022), virtue ethics "has comparative benefits that afford greater scope to consider interrelations at different spatial scales, to focus on temporality, culture and norms" (p. 621).

Our ethical premise

Central to a virtue ethics approach to relational leadership is the need for a clear focus on character as well as rightness of action, and this leads us to consider our ethical premise. Our ethical premise, often referred to as our moral compass, is a way of describing those ethics that are important to us and influence how we make sense of the world in which we live. As Clive Hamilton (2008) writes in his book *The freedom paradox*, "in contrast with the prevailing view that being free means being able to do what we please, we cannot be truly free without committing ourselves to a moral life along with its internal constraints" (p. iv). He argues that knowing our constraints—what it is that we will or will not accept—plays a significant role in defining who we are as thinking, sensing, and feeling human beings. The ethics that we consider personally most important help us to define the boundaries that give shape to our morality and our sense of identity (self).

For example, if compassion is important, then either perpetuating or witnessing harmfulness towards others will be unacceptable to us, and if we commit an act of harmfulness, we will have crossed a personal boundary that will inevitably bring feelings such as disappointment, guilt and shame upon ourselves. Our ethical premise also helps us to define "the ground upon which we stand"—those things for which we hold a deep sense of right and wrong, just and unjust, good and bad. Without establishing our ethical premise—when faced with too many choices, coupled with low self-control (desire)—we risk letting ourselves down and losing our deeper sense of Self (Hamilton, 2008).

This erosion of our deeper sense of Self through a lack of ethical clarity and commitment can open us up to suffering from poor mental and physical health (Waring, 2016). It can also erode our relationships with important others (Hart, 2017), undermine our sense of meaning and purpose about our lives (McPherson, 2020), and dilute our sense of what we hold as value and whom and what we place value upon (Chappell, 2006). In short, not having a strong ethical foundation in which we can commit and improve over time leads us to greater and greater levels of suffering. It will also most likely increase the suffering of emotionally or physically close or distant others with whom we interact.

Most people have a "sense" of what their ethical premise might be, but many struggle to define what it is in descriptive terms, or perhaps more importantly, what each of the ethics that are important to them might mean. For example, during the course of my research, many participants, when attempting to describe compassion, often described either sympathy or empathy. While these descriptions have a "goodness" about them, not fully understanding them may lead us to not knowing how and when to use them and in what circumstances. So, a "sense" of what good could look like is a "good start," but it is rarely enough to give us sufficient skill to navigate the complexities of life.

The importance of character

It is this inseparable relationship between our ethos and our identity that leads to the understanding that the virtues inform a significant aspect of our "character." A common view of character is that it refers to "the enduring personal characteristics we value in ourselves and for which we want to be valued by others" (Sennett, 1998, p. 10) that unfolds through our lived experience of time and space over a lifetime. Character forms part of what is called "our wanted identity"—the way we wish to be seen by others and the way in which we define ourselves.

Similarly, character can also be defined as "those inter-penetrable habitual qualities within individuals, and applicable to organisations, that both constrain and lead them to desire and pursue personal and societal good" (Wright & Goodstein, 2007, p. 932). Importantly, moral discipline or self-restraint is emphasised in this definition and is regarded as instrumental in helping monitor the actual behaviour of individuals and their organisations. In other words, and again using compassion as an example, our moral discipline reinforces the will that is needed to be compassionate and not intentionally bring harm to others (Wright & Goodstein, 2007).

Moral philosophers and virtue ethicists have always focused on character as the central point of virtue (Alzola, 2008). Aristotle is regarded as one of the earliest thinkers to explore character through the expression of *arête* (excellence) as a theory of virtue and its relationship to *eudemonia* or "human flourishing" as the means for achieving a person's full potential (Arjoon, 2000). Virtue came to signify moral and intellectual excellence as the highest good that individuals could attain and, through their virtues, they contributed to the creation of a good society (Solomon, 1992). For Aristotle (2004), the virtuous person perceives, feels, and does the right things consistently at the right times, for the right reasons, in the right proportion, neither excessively nor deficiently, all of which leads to human flourishing or happiness. Another way to describe the continuum is to say that ethics are the virtues, the virtues are excellences, and excellences lead to human flourishing and happiness.

Common properties of virtue

Character is also common to all virtue ethical theories. These theories stress how a person's good habits, or virtues, give them the propensity to act in ways that are good. Here, good is defined as fostering the ultimate end for humans (e.g., to be happy and well), satisfying the fundamental nature of being human (e.g., to flourish), or the intrinsic goods of the virtues themselves, such as compassion, care and consideration of others. All of these notions of "good" aim to move us away from suffering and towards achieving genuine happiness, well-being, and flourishing for ourselves and others (Dawson, 2015). Thus, according to many theorists, when virtuous people act with a virtuous intention from virtuous character, they do so for the good of themselves and others, their communities, their country, and society (MacIntyre, 2007).

In addition, most virtue ethicists consistently cite five properties that are found in most virtue theories:

1 Virtue is a deep property within us that defines goodness at the individual level, where habituated thoughts, emotions, motivation, intention, volition, and action develop well-being and are morally excellent.
2 Virtue is a capacity that we can develop through our personality, proclivities, and dispositions so that virtues become second nature.
3 Virtue practices—manifested through substantive virtues, such as compassion—flow from our virtuous character, which is developed through complex forms of socially established co-operative human activity that systematically extends, elevates or amplifies our capacity to achieve excellence.
4 Virtue always includes some degree of attentiveness to context and circumstance and must therefore include practical wisdom or *phronesis*—the virtue of habituated excellence in reasoning (such as between deficiency and excess).
5 Virtue generally produces good outcomes that should encourage "unqualified flourishing" for ourselves and the community where it is practiced (Bright et al., 2014).

According to Aristotle, there are three conditions that must be met if our virtuous actions are to be seen as arising from our virtuous character (McPherson, 2013). Firstly, we must *know* that what we are doing consists of virtuous actions. Secondly, we must *choose* these actions and choose them for their own sake. Thirdly, we must also *do them* from a firm and unchanging state. Performing virtuous actions for their own sake with *integrity* and *constancy* removes the need or desire for us to receive reciprocity or benefit from these actions. Put another way, rather than expecting happiness/pleasure, pain/suffering or recognition from the results of an action (such as achieving or losing money, fame or power), the virtuous person experiences a sense of *eudemonia* (happiness) through the performing of virtuous actions for their own sake as a constitutive part of living a good life—to do good for goodness' sake (MacIntyre, 2007).

Virtue ethics are appealing because they encourage "good works" that are intellectually and morally praiseworthy, discretionary, and positively directed towards high standards of thought, word and action (Stansbury & Sonenshein, 2012). They are also the antithesis of the more mainstream emphasis in ethics, such as deontology and utilitarianism, that seek to avoid or rectify those things considered unethical rather than emphasising those things that are good in their own right (Solomon, 1992). That is, compassion is good in its own right, as is truthfulness, trustworthiness and courage.

However, virtue cannot be defined solely in terms of outcomes or independent of consequences. That is, if a behaviour seen as consistent with a virtue is producing dysfunctional outcomes, it cannot be characterised as virtuous. For example, we might think we are acting with courage when robbing a bank! Thus, virtue is linked but not synonymous with excellence in that "all virtues are excellences but not every excellence is a virtue." A virtue is always oriented towards some greater good, whereas an excellence may arise out of a lesser motivation (Zagzebski, 1996).

Common virtues

Although virtue ethics have their roots in religion or spirituality, they do not derive exclusively from any traditional or cultural background. In one of the most comprehensive studies ever undertaken on virtues, Peterson and Seligman's book *Character strengths and virtues* (2004) listed six broad categories that have consistently emerged from historical surveys. They are wisdom, courage, humanity, justice, temperance and transcendence. These virtues are generally regarded as the core characteristics of moral philosophers and theologians. They argue that these core virtues are universal and are perhaps even grounded in biology, with the survival of the human species through evolutionary processes. From these six categories, there are numerous interrelated attributes that are captured in the following word cloud (Figure 10.1).

In 2004, a group of American researchers undertook a comprehensive study involving 804 individuals representing 18 different organisations from 16 different industries. Their aim was to ascertain a scale to measure organisational virtuousness following a comprehensive literature review on virtues. From their study, a five-factor model emerged that regarded the following virtues as the five highest and most important for any organisation: forgiveness, trust, integrity, optimism, and compassion (Cameron et al., 2004). In 2021, in the comprehensive study I conducted across the United States, New Zealand and Australia, involving 89 disaster management leaders at the most senior levels of politics, operations, and administration, I found that the ethics of integrity, trust, truthfulness, compassion, humility, and courage ranked as the highest virtues (Crosweller, 2022).

FIGURE 10.1 The most common universal virtues as identified by Peterson and Seligman (2004).

Criticism of virtue ethics

However, virtue ethics—like the other normative ethical frameworks, such as deontology and utilitarianism—is not immune from criticism. A key criticism of virtue ethics can be found in empirical psychology. This criticism revolves around the notion that character traits that are often associated with the virtues (such as compassion) do not influence an individual's behaviour in the way that virtue theorists propose, or, in other words, virtue ethics are empirically inadequate (Darr, 2020; Reed, 2016). This criticism is often argued by philosophical situationists who premise their arguments upon a global conception of character supported by two theses.

The first is consistency, where character traits are expected to reliably manifest in the behaviour of an individual across a range of diverse and widely variable conditions with predictability. The second is stability, where character traits are expected to reliably manifest in behaviours over repeated trials of similar conditions (Doris, 2002; Harman, 2009). That is to say, "a global character trait is a trait that shows stability over time and consistency across situations" (Doris, 2002, p. 22). For example, someone who is compassionate is expected to exhibit compassion in a wide variety of relevant situations (such as at work, home, social settings, and when caring for others), as well as repeated instances of the same kind of situation (such as in the workplace).

Philosophical situationists argue that if most people were compassionate, then even simple tasks of helping others could be reliably predicted under a range of similar conditions. The studies that they reference include "The Good Samaritan Experiment," conducted at Princeton University's Theological Seminary (Darley et al., 1973), "The Milgram Shock Experiment"

(Milgram, 1974), the Isen and Levin "dime" study (Isen & Levin, 1972), and the Latané and Darley group effect studies (Latané & Darley, 1968). All these studies were intended to ascertain the extent to which people were compassionate. However, each study revealed that many participants did not help other people in their distress, and predictions about their behaviour were often highly misleading. They argued that the evidence showed that, in a wide variety of situations relevant to the particular virtue (or vice) under scrutiny, most people do not possess the traditional virtues or vices understood as global character traits (such as compassion, courage, and honesty) (Miller, 2017).

However, other scholars have argued that it is a well-known response of many theorists to the criticisms of virtue ethics as being empirically indeterminate that virtue ethics is not committed to high numbers of people having the virtues. Aristotle persistently claimed that virtue was difficult and uncommon. Instead, virtue ethics is much more empirically modest than situationists recognise, and while empirical standards of adequacy are important, virtue ethics does not require comprehensive empirical grounding to have a valid normative ethical foundation (Reed, 2016).

A response to situationism

Many virtue ethicists refute the situationist notion that virtues can be reduced to psychological traits (Darr, 2020). Instead, they argue that virtues are qualities of our socially constituted character derived from our role in our own life narrative. In turn, this narrative is shaped by the social and historical context of social practices, communities of accountability, and moral traditions (MacIntyre, 2007). According to moral philosopher Alasdair MacIntyre (2007, p. 205), "the unity of a virtue in someone's life is intelligible only as a characteristic of a unitary life, a life that can be conceived and evaluated as a whole," and the demands and expectations of, and answerability to, others "is partially constitutive of what it is to be a unified character" (Darr, 2020, p. 15).

In other words, rather than being narrowly defined as psychological traits, virtues originate developmentally and conceptually in practices that must be mastered over time. Continually asking and answering the question what constitutes a good life "sustain[s] us in the relevant kind of quest for the good, by enabling us to overcome the harms, dangers, temptations, and distractions which we encounter, and which furnish us with increasing self-knowledge and increasing knowledge of the good" (MacIntyre, 2007, p. 219).

Cultivating virtue is still an important aspect of living a moral life, and while neither Plato nor Aristotle claimed that most people were naturally virtuous, they had the capacity to be so through *phronesis* or practical wisdom (Miller, 2017). Similarly, when comparing the philosophy of Aristotle with the philosophy of the Buddha, both regarded human nature as intellectually and emotionally complex, and considered that the final good for the individual lay in the full development of their potential in these two dimensions. Both postulated that this was a gradual, cultivated and cumulative process resulting in a state of perfection reached through *eudaimonia* for Aristotle and *nirvana* for the Buddha, both characterised by happiness as the final goal of human endeavour (Keown, 1992).

It is important to stress that virtuous behaviour is achieved through deliberate and conscious attention to virtues, such as compassion, trust, or humility, throughout everyday life. They are not only abstract ideals but motivators that shape our thoughts and attitudes, as well as guiding our actions and behaviour in certain distinct ways (Jordan & Kristjánsson, 2017). Virtue ethics requires an essential development and education focus and is therefore as much about development towards virtue as it is about virtue itself (Jordan & Kristjánsson, 2017). Aristotle (2004) argued that knowing what is good is ethically useless unless it is put into action, and to do so needs training and education. Regarding moral inquiry in general, its purpose is not to know what virtue is, but rather to become good through practical wisdom and lived experience; otherwise, the inquiry alone is of no individual benefit.

While the response to criticisms of situationism provides a defence by recognising the need for the cultivation of virtues over time and through experience, the criticisms of philosophical situationists are useful for us as they raise important questions about human fallibility and moral hypocrisy. We now explore these two questions in more detail.

Traversing human fallibility

Surrendering perfection

As any leader who has committed to an ethical life will tell you, upholding a virtuous disposition of character is one of the most challenging and worthy pursuits we could ever undertake. However, for most of us, historically and contemporaneously, it has been and continues to be impossible to spontaneously achieve the perfection of virtue. In fact, I would argue that it is simply arrogant to contemplate such a proposition.

Except in the rarest of circumstances, the pursuit of virtue is a long, arduous and perilous journey towards becoming a more complete human being. For Aristotle, the journey takes a lifetime. For the Buddha, many lifetimes. According to scholars, such as Carl Jung (1953), Joseph Campbell (2008), and Thomas Moore (2004), pursuing virtue necessarily requires us to journey through a metaphoric "Hell"—a mental space where all our tendencies towards the bad manifest in our consciousness. Avoiding the journey and only aligning with virtue risks us being blind to our own capacity to commit wrongful acts of body, speech and mind and constrains us from seeing our own immorality. And if we cannot see our own immorality, we cannot address its harmfulness towards self and others. Achieving virtue requires us to surrender our innocence and take some authority in and from the darkness of our mind. According to the aforementioned scholars and esteemed mystics such as Therese of Ávila (Myss, 2007), surrendering perfection and instead living with compassion for self and other would seem far more desirable and realistic than pursuing any arrogant notions of pure virtuosity. That is to say, we must come to accept that we suffer and are fallible.

What causes fallibility

Fallibility is a universal feature of the human condition (Besser-Jones, 2008; Bloser, 2019; Kreitmair, 2021). At its most basic level, it is our tendency to make mistakes, err, or be wrong—particularly with our capacity for ethical judgement—and much of it revolves around ignorance. We are often constrained by our own defects of information, sensitivity, maturity, imagination, and coherence. We tend to judge others too quickly without all the available information, or we gather only the information that supports our biased perspective. We can be insensitive to the reasons why others hold alternative views, or why they find themselves in difficult circumstances that we would often judge as immoral or unethical (Besser-Jones, 2008).

We can fail to draw upon our own lived experiences of being fallible to appreciate the circumstances of others, or we can fail to adequately use our imagination to try and appreciate what circumstances others may be facing. We can also have knowledge about individual facts, but be let down by our theories, beliefs, and overall perspectives that are bound to be biased and/or inconsistent when judging the moral and ethical dilemmas of others. Relatedly, our view of the world can never perfectly align with the actual situation that we engage with (Haidt, 2021).

According to philosopher Paul Ricoeur (1965), we also possess infinite desire for the future but finite knowledge (ignorance) of the consequences of acting on that desire. Some of those desires result in good outcomes, but sadly, many do not. Often, what leads us into moral and ethical dilemma is that we do not think enough about the consequences of our actions, both upon self and other. Excessive self-importance and self-interest play a significant role in this harmful mental process. Or if we do think it through to some degree, we often convince ourselves that those consequences will be good, or at least neutral.

Sometimes, but admittedly not always, there will be the "seed of doubt" sitting within our mental peripheral vision, though we often ignore it. That "seed of doubt" emerges from the darkness of our soul, and as Carl Jung reminded us, it is from that darkness that our fate will be determined (Jung & Jaffé, 1963). Left unaddressed, that "seed" will flourish as negative, and often painful, consequences—consequences that could have otherwise been avoided or minimised, if only we had taken the time to reflect more deeply, gather more information, and dispel as much of our ignorance as possible about their potential ramifications.

Finally, another aspect of our fallibility is that we often fail to live up to our own moral and ethical standards under idealised conditions. As noted earlier, philosophical situationists argue that we fail in our *consistency* to reliably manifest our behaviours across a range of diverse and widely variable conditions with predictability, and we fail in our *stability* to reliably manifest our behaviours in similar circumstances (Doris, 1998, 2002).

How to approach fallibility

Despite our human fallibility, cultivating our virtue is still an important aspect of living a moral life. We can achieve this through *phronesis* or practical wisdom over the course of our lifetime (or lifetimes) to attain a state of happiness as the final goal of human endeavour (Keown, 1992, 2017). Philosopher Alasdair MacIntyre argues that our unfolding life story—shaped by our lived experiences and the social practices, communities of accountability, and moral traditions of the societies in which we lived—contributes towards improving our virtuosity (MacIntyre, 2007).

In essence, what these philosophers were trying to tell us is simply to "become a better human being over time," in whatever circumstance we find ourselves. To help achieve this, we would do well to accept that fallibility is part of being human. We should give up trying or pretending to be perfect, listen more intently to the wisdom of our mind as well as the wisdom of the sages, and learn from the successes and mistakes of our lived experiences. As one political leader that I interviewed observed:

> I think it's when we stay very abstract. I think it's when... we sort of lose our sense of humanity and sense of understanding things [and] recognising what things look like at a human level. And we start to think conceptually, and then we think, 'oh we know all the answers, or we know what we're doing is best'. I know I'm guilty of that. Most people are. And yes, it's when we stop feeling and just think about things in a very sort of abstract, conceptual way that often completely ignores people and individual circumstance.

> And at a government level, sometimes you think, 'well, it just has to be done because there is this objective that has to be reached'. And we do have to be a bit impersonal about it. So, there's this sort of judgment about greater good. And sometimes that's alright, but I think even in those circumstances, there's a better way of getting there rather than just doing that to people. Being dismissive and being arrogant or being impersonal. That's something I certainly wish at times I'd been more, like seeing that more

clearly than as I do now, I would hope. I came out of politics… thinking the best thing that I've learned is to recognise that we're all human, we're all flawed, and we're all vulnerable in some way. And that we should judge less and help more. And it took me quite a while to learn that. But I think maybe that's part of life as well. But I think if I was back in politics, those would have been the things that would be the most important.

Finally, we need to be more compassionate towards self and other, and we need to keep going! The road to virtue is long and winding, but then again, so is life—by making virtue our lifelong companion, we will never be isolated from a genuine sense of happiness, meaning, and purpose, irrespective of the external circumstances in which we find ourselves.

Tackling moral hypocrisy

The dilemma of moral pride

Most of us take great pride in being seen as ethical. As noted earlier, ethics and, more specifically, the virtues (such as trust, compassion, kindness, care, and courage) form a large part of our identities—how we view ourselves and how we wish to be viewed by others. Being seen as "on the side of good, right and just" is important for most of us, notwithstanding that good, right and just can be highly subjective and contested between people, communities, religions, politics, philosophies and cultures. We also derive a sense of happiness, contentment or satisfaction when we think, speak and act ethically, and when we are seen by others in the same light. That is the power of virtue. As Aristotle claimed, ethics are virtues and virtues are excellences that lead to a deep sense of human happiness and flourishing over the course of a lifetime. The Buddha said similar things.

For most of us, being seen as ethical or virtuous is important. However, being *seen* as ethical does not necessarily translate into *being* ethical. As Niccolò Machiavelli wrote, "the great majority of [hu]mankind are satisfied with appearances, as if they were realities, and are often more influenced by the things that seem than by those that are" (Machiavelli & Crick, 1970). For some of us, being seen as ethical is so important that we will rigorously defend ourselves if we feel in any way slighted by the criticisms of others. As history has shown, sometimes this defence is taken to extremis—the taking of a life or lives. The Buddha, Jesus of Nazareth, and the Prophet Muhammad are three significant historical examples, and countless other examples have occurred over time (such as the death of Dr. Martin Luther King Jr).

All three men discovered what some might call "inconvenient truths" about the nature of the human condition and proposed pathways to a better future. There were numerous attempts on the life of the Buddha by his cousin Devadatta (Bhikkhu, 1992), several attempts on the life of Muhammad (Conveying Islamic Message Society, 2022), and history records the death of Jesus of Nazareth (Blainey, 2011). Fortunately, most of us do not become so obsessed as to threaten to take the life of another, but we can certainly head in a direction of wanting to punish others when our moral and ethical beliefs are affronted, at least in our minds. But on what basis do we claim the high standards of our ethics or virtues? And what or who determines that those standards are better than others? Well, it turns out that we are afflicted with what is known in philosophy as "moral hypocrisy."

Where does moral hypocrisy come from?

In essence, moral hypocrisy arises when we seek to find the moral faults of others without accepting our own moral faults. In Christianity, there is a biblical passage that says:

> Why do you see the speck in your neighbour's eye, but you do not notice the log in your own eye? ... You hypocrite, first take the log out of your own eye, and then you will see clearly to take the speck out of your neighbour's eye.
>
> *(Matthew 7:3–5)*

Likewise, in Buddhist teaching:

> It is easy to see the faults of others, but difficult to see one's own faults. One shows the faults of others like chaff winnowed in the wind, but one conceals one's own faults as a cunning gambler conceals his dice.
>
> *(Easwaran, 2007)*

This Japanese proverb also captures a similar perspective: "Though you see the seven defects of others, we do not see our own ten defects."

Unfortunately, according to author Jonathan Haidt (2021) and his book *The happiness hypothesis*, stories about the moral failings of others form the basis of most of our gossip. We hear it play out every day in mainstream and social media, and it is often the most popular topic in the workplace, especially when talking about our leaders, or those people who might have contrary views to our own. Ironically, when we condemn another's hypocrisy, we compound our own.

Condemning others usually leads to destructive moralism and divisive self-righteousness. For example, numerous studies have shown that when we overstate our morality, we will only do the right thing if it accords with our self-interest. If doing the right thing appears to be to our detriment, many of us will not do it (Grayling, 2022). Interestingly, when we can see our own image, either in a mirror or on camera, we are far less likely to do the wrong thing (Haidt, 2021).

In seeking to justify our perceived moral actions, many of us deludedly think that we are fundamentally good people, and our actions are always motivated by good reasons. We then attempt to seek out pseudo-evidence to justify our moral decisions and support our preferred belief or action. A metaphor that can be used to describe this phenomenon is to be our own "inner lawyer." That is, we use a part of our minds to find evidence that justifies our position, rather than acting as the "inner judge" that seeks to weigh up all of the available evidence on both sides of the argument before coming to a decision. Relatedly, we see our own virtues as self-perceived strengths and seek evidence to reinforce that same view of ourselves (Haidt, 2021).

Of course, all of this justification, analysis, and defence goes on inside of our minds, whereas when we judge others, we do so by judging their exhibited behaviour. We cannot get inside their head to see what is really going on for them that may be causing them distress—often the very same distress that we suffer, but in which we mentally seek to find the evidence to justify. Also, we can be very open to any information that will predict the behaviour of others, but often refuse to adjust our own behaviour when that same information is presented to us—preferring instead to defend and justify our character rather than change behaviour. All of this can lead to hypocritical indignation (Haidt, 2021).

Lastly, we can also get caught up in mental notions of good versus evil: "I am on the side of good, they are on the side of evil." Much of this affliction emanates from a perception that we can see the world as it really is and that our view is the correct view. This affliction has also been the biggest obstacle to world peace and social harmony: "My group is right because we see things as they really are, whereas those who disagree are afflicted by their religion, ideology or self-interest." This attitude has often galvanised thousands or even millions of people to take a side and pursue a perceived pure good against a perceived pure evil (Bowker, 2015).

History is full of such examples and, without exception, they have resulted in much human misery and suffering, often spanning millennia, as a result of being handed down from generation to generation. Sadly, people usually have reasons for committing violence. Often those reasons involve retaliation for a perceived injustice or in self-defence. However, it is also true that people turn to violence when they are morally affronted, driven by their moral idealism and morally righteous indignation. As the anthropologist Clifford Geertz wrote, "man is an animal suspended in webs of significance that he himself has spun" (Haidt, 2021).

Avoiding moral hypocrisy

So, how do we get out of this potential trap? How do we avoid these pitfalls that are common to all of humanity? Firstly, we should not take ourselves so seriously. Yes, there are atrocities in the world that should be taken very seriously indeed! The war in the Ukraine is but one contemporary example. But, at the same time, most of us will not have to experience such distress. Our distress will be much more mundane, even banal, for most of the time in our day to day lives. Seeing the silliness of our hypocrisy and moral indignation is a great way to ease our distress and access our humility (Chodron, 2019).

Secondly, it helps to see the world as both Hindus and Buddhists view it. That is, we have a role to play in the function of the universe. The god Krishna said:

I love the [hu]man who hates not nor exults, mourns not nor desires... who is the same to friend and foe, [the same] whether [they] be respected or despised, the same in heat and cold, in pleasure and in pain, who has put away attachment and remains unmoved by praise or blame... contented with whatever comes [their] way.

(Easwaran, 2007)

Buddhists further advocate the practice of non-judgement, for judgementalism is indeed a disease of the mind that leads to anger, torment and conflict. Practicing non-judgement through meditation and mindfulness settles the mind, helps us see through delusion, and refines our judgements of what is truly valuable. And for most of us, what is valuable is our virtue and the virtue of others (Chodron, 2001).

Finally, returning to the Christian scriptures, the Buddhist Lam Rim, and the Japanese proverb, we must take the log out of our own eye first before attending to the speck of our colleague or neighbour. Realise that, apart from the rarest and most exceptional of circumstances, our hypocrisy plays a major role in setting up the causes for our own suffering. It contributes towards the very circumstances that we find so unpleasurable. Removing the log will feel unpleasant at first, but it will then be followed with relief. Relief because we come to realise that there is something we can do about our circumstances, something to learn for next time, and something in which we can both seek and offer forgiveness (Haidt, 2021; Tutu & Tutu, 2014).

Right and wrong then becomes only partly right or partly wrong. In so doing, it does not require us to surrender our ethos. Instead, it allows us to become less moralistic, less angry, less aggressive and less righteous. It also makes room for more compassion, patience, kindness, and wisdom about any given circumstance. That is, we become more virtuous, but this time without the hypocrisy. We become more authentically identified with the way we wish to be and to be seen, and a genuine sense of happiness emerges—the very same happiness that liberates us from the bonds of our suffering that we so ardently wish to free ourselves from.

The challenge for leaders

As leaders, we must become intimately familiar with the virtues that are critical to how we define our moral character. We need to accept that our virtues will need nurturing and development over the course of our lifetime and that sometimes, we will not get them right, but we should seek to improve them, nonetheless.

We must also accept that we are all fallible to greater or lesser degrees—that our knowledge of context will almost inevitably be incomplete—and that we should be cautious not to judge others too harshly before we are in possession of all the facts of their circumstances. Similarly, we must accept that we all suffer from moral hypocrisy, preferring to highlight the faults of others instead of our own, and often only doing the right thing if it accords with our own self-interest. In response, we would do well to adopt a set of rules that can help keep us grounded and it is to these rules that we now turn to in the next chapter.

References

Alzola, M. (2008). Character and environment: The status of virtues in organizations. *Journal of Business Ethics*, *78*(3), 343–357. https://doi.org/10.1007/s10551-006-9335-7

Anscombe, E. M. ([1958] 1997). *Modern moral philosophy*. Oxford University Press.

Aristotle (2004). *Selected writings: Selections from Nicomachean ethics and politics*. CRW Publishing Limited.

Arjoon, S. (2000). Virtue theory as a dynamic theory of business, *Journal of Business Ethics*, *28*, 159–178, https://doi.org/10.1023/A:1006339112331

Besser-Jones, L. (2008). Social psychology, moral character, and moral fallibility. *Philosophy and Phenomenological Research*, *76*(2), 310–332. https://doi.org/10.1111/j.1933-1592.2007.00134.x

Bhikkhu, Ñ (1992). *The life of the Buddha according to the Pali Canon*. Buddhist Publication Society Inc.

Blainey, G. (2011). *A short history of Christianity*. Penguin Group.

Blöser, C. (2019). Human fallibility and the need for forgiveness. *Philosophia*, *47*(1), 1–19. https://doi.org/10.1007/s11406-018-9950-4

Bowker, J. W. (2015). *Why religions matter*. Cambridge University Press.

Bright, D., Winn, B., & Kanov, J. (2014). Reconsidering virtue: Differences of perspective in virtue ethics and the positive social sciences. *Journal of Business Ethics*, *119*(4), 445–460. https://doi.org/10.1007/s10551-013-1832-x

Bruton, S. V. (2004). Teaching the golden rule, *Journal of Business Ethics*, *49*, 179–187. https://doi.org/10.1023/B:BUSI.0000015783.98570.a3

Cameron, K. S., Bright, D., & Caza, A. (2004). Exploring the relationships between organizational virtuousness and performance. *American Behavioural Scientist*, *47*(6), 766–790. https://journals.sagepub.com/doi/10.1177/0002764203260209

Campbell, J. (2008). *The hero with a thousand faces*. New World Library.

Carr, D. (2003). Character and moral choice in the cultivation of virtue. *Philosophy (London)*, *78*(2), 219–232. http://dx.doi.org/10.1017/S0031819103000251

Chappell, T. D. (2006). *Values and virtues: Aristotelianism in contemporary ethics*. Clarendon Press.

Chodron, P. (2019). *Welcoming the unwelcome: Wholehearted living in a brokenhearted world*. Shambala Publications Inc.

Chodron, P. (2001). *The wisdom of no escape: How to love yourself and the world.* HarperCollins.

Chryssides, G. D., & Kaler, J. H. (1993). *An introduction to business ethics.* Chapman & Hall.

Conveying Islamic Message Society. (2022, January 13). 8 Attempts on the life of Prophet Muhammad. *Conveying Islamic Message Society.* https://islammessage. org/en/article/15915/8-attempts-on-the-life-of-prophet-muhammad-(pbuh)

Crisp, R. (1996). Mill on virtue as a part of happiness. *British Journal for the History of Philosophy, 4*(2), 367–380.

Crosweller, M. (2022). Disaster management leadership and the need for virtue, mindfulness, and practical wisdom. *Progress in Disaster Science, 16*(2002), 100248. https://doi.org/10.1016/j.pdisas.2022.100248

Darley, J., Batson, C. D., Wells, R., Fisher, B., Shafto, M., Sheras, P. L., Detweiler, R., & Glasser, K. (1973). "From Jerusalem to Jericho": A study of situational and dispositional variables in helping behavior, *Journal of Personality and Social Psychology, 27*, 100–108, https://doi.org/10.1037/h0034449

Darr, R. (2020). Virtues as qualities of character: Alasdair MacIntyre and the situationist critique of virtue ethics. *Journal of Religious Ethics, 48*(1), 7–25. https://doi. org/10.1111/jore.12297

Dawson, D. P. (2015). Two forms of virtue ethics: Two sets of virtuous action in the fire service dispute? *Journal of Business Ethics, 128*(3), 585–601. https://doi. org/10.1007/s10551-014-2121-z

Doris, J. M. (1998). Persons, situations, and virtue ethics. *Noûs, 32*(4), 504–530. https://doi.org/10.1111/0029-4624.00136

Doris, J. M. (2002). *Lack of character: Personality and moral behavior.* Cambridge University Press.

Easwaran, E. (2007). *The Bhagavad Gita: Vol 1* (2nd ed.). Nilgiri Press.

Foot, P. (1978). *Virtues and vices and other essays in moral philosophy.* Oxford University Press.

Grayling, A. C. (2022). *For the good of the world: Is a universal ethics possible?* (1st ed.). Oneworld Publications Ltd.

Guyer, P. (2002). Ends of reason and ends of nature: The place of teleology in Kant's ethics. *The Journal of Value Inquiry, 36*(2), 161–186. https://doi. org/10.1023/A:1016140116768

Haidt, J. (2021). *The happiness hypothesis: Putting ancient wisdom and philosophy to the test of modern science* (2nd ed.). Random House UK.

Hamilton, C. (2008). *The freedom paradox: Towards a post-secular ethics.* Allen & Unwin.

Harman, G. (2009). Skepticism about character traits. *Virtue Ethics and Moral Psychology: The Situationism Debate, 13*(2–3), 235–242. https://www.jstor.org/ stable/40345402

Hart, P. (2017). The reality of relationships with young people in caring professions: A qualitative approach to professional boundaries rooted in virtue ethics, *Children and Youth Services Review, 83*, 248–254. https://doi.org/10.1016/j. childyouth.2017.11.006

Hursthouse, R. (2001). *On virtue ethics.* Oxford University Press.

Isen, A. M., & Levin, P. F. (1972). Effect of feeling good on helping: Cookies and kindness. *Journal of Personality and Social Psychology, 21*(3), 384–388. https://doi. org/10.1037/h0032317

Jordan, K., & Kristjánsson, K. (2017). Sustainability, virtue ethics, and the virtue of harmony with nature. *Environmental Education Research, 23*(9), 1205–1229. https://doi.org/10.1080/13504622.2016.1157681

Jung, C. G. (1953). *Collected works of C. G. Jung, vol. 12: Psychology and alchemy* (R.F.C. Hull, Trans.) (2nd ed.). Routledge & Kegan Paul.

Jung, C. G., & Jaffé, A. (1963). *Memories, dreams, reflections*. Collins and Routledge & K. Paul.

Keown, D. (1992). *The nature of Buddhist ethics*. Palgrave Macmillan.

Keown, D. (2017). On the good in Aristotle and early Buddhism: A response to Abraham Vélez, *Journal of Buddhist Ethics*, 24, 97–115. https://www.academia.edu/53764433/Virtue_Ethics_in_Early_Buddhism

Korsgaard, C. M. (1996). *The sources of normativity*. Cambridge University Press.

Kreitmair, K. V. (2021). Medical ethics, moral courage, and the embrace of fallibility. *Academic Medicine: Journal of the Association of American Medical Colleges*, 96(12), 1630–1633. https://doi.org/10.1097/ACM.0000000000004420

Ladkin, D. (2006). When deontology and utilitarianism aren't enough: How Heidegger's notion of "dwelling" might help organisational leaders resolve ethical issues, *Journal of Business Ethics*, 65, 87–98. https://doi.org/10.1007/s10551-006-0019-0

Latané, B., & Darley, J. M. (1968). Group inhibition of bystander intervention in emergencies. *Journal of Personality and Social Psychology*, 10(3), 215–221. https://doi.org/10.1037/H0026570

Machiavelli, N., & Crick, B. R. (1970). *The discourses*. Penguin Books.

MacIntyre, A. (2007). *After virtue: A study in moral theory* (3rd ed.). University of Notre Dame Press.

Malik, K. (2014). *The quest for a moral compass: A global history of ethics*. Atlantic Books.

McCloskey, D. (2008). Adam Smith, the last of the former virtue ethicists. *History of Political Economy*, 40(1), 43–71. https://doi.org/10.1215/00182702-2007-046

McPherson, D. (2013). Vocational virtue ethics: Prospects for a virtue ethic approach to business, *Journal of Business Ethics*, 116, 283–296. https://doi.org/10.1007/s10551-012-1463-7

McPherson, D. (2020). *Virtue and meaning: A neo-Aristotelian perspective*. Cambridge University Press.

Milgram, S. (1974). *Obedience to authority*. Harper and Row.

Miller, C. (2017). Character and situationism: New directions, *Ethical Theory and Moral Practice*, 20, 459–471. https://doi.org/10.1007/s10677-017-9791-4

Monast, J. H. (1994). What is (and isn't) the matter with "What's the matter. *Business Ehics Quarterly*, 4(4), 499–512. https://doi.org/10.2307/3857346

Moore, T. (2004). *Dark nights of the soul: A guide to finding your way through life's ordeals*. Piatkus Books.

Morrell, K. (2006). Governance, ethics and the national health service. *Public Money & Management*, 26(1), 55–62. doi: 10.1111/j.1467-9302.2005.00501.x.

Morrell, K., & Dahlmann, F. (2022). Aristotle in the Anthropocene: The comparative benefits of Aristotelian virtue ethics over utilitarianism and deontology. *The Anthropocene Review*, 10(3), 615–635. https://doi.org/10.1177/20530196221105093

Myss, C. (2007). *Entering the castle: An inner path to god and your soul*. Free Press.

Nussbaum, M. (1986). *The fragility of goodness: Luck and ethics in Greek tragedy and philosophy*. Cambridge University Press.

Overman Smith, E., & Thompson, I. (2002). Feminist theory in tactical communication: Making knowledge claims visible, *Journal of Business and Technical Communication*, 16, 441. http://doi.org/10.1177/105065102236526

Peterson, C., & Seligman, M. E. P. (2004). *Character strengths and virtues: A handbook and classification*. Oxford University Press.

Reed, P. (2016). Empirical adequacy and virtue ethics. *Ethical Theory and Moral Practice*, 19(2), 343–357. https://doi.org/10.1007/s10677-015-9623-3

Ricoeur, P. (1965). *Fallible man*. Fordham University Press.

Russell, D. C. (2009). *Practical intelligence and the virtues.* Oxford University Press.

Schneewind, J. B. (1997). The misfortunes of virtue. In R. Crisp & M. Slote (Eds.), *Virtue ethics.* Oxford University Press.

Sennett, R. (1998). *The corrosion of character: The personal consequences of work in the new capitalism.* Norton.

Sison, A. J. G., Hartman, E. M., & Fontrodona, J. (2012). Guest editors' introduction: Reviving tradition: Virtue and the common good in business and management. *Business Ethics Quarterly, 22*(2), 207–210. https://www.jstor.org/stable/23223723

Slote, M. (1995). Agent-based virtue ethics. *Midwest Studies in Philosophy, 20*(1), 83–101. https://doi.org/10.1111/j.1475-4975.1995.tb00306.x

Slote, M. (2015). Virtue's turn and return, *Dao: A Journal of Comparative Philosophy, 14*, 319–324. https://doi.org/10.1007/s11712-015-9449-7

Smith, A. (1976). *The theory of moral sentiments.* Oxford University Press.

Solomon, R. C. (1992). Corporate roles, personal virtues: An aristotelean approach to business ethics. *Business Ethics Quarterly, 2*(3), 317–339. https://doi.org/10.2307/3857536

Stansbury, J. M., & Sonenshein, S. (2012). Positive business ethics: Grounding and elaborating a theory of good works. *The Oxford Handbook of Positive Organizational Scholarship.* http://dx.doi.org/10.1093/oxfordhb/9780199734610.013.0026

Stark, A. (1993). What's the matter with business ethics? *Harvard Business Review, 71*(3), 38–48.

Tutu, D., & Tutu, M. (2014). *The book of forgiving: The fourfold path for healing ourselves and the world.* HarperOne.

Velasquez, M. G. (2001). *Business ethics: Concepts and cases.* London: Prentice Hall.

Waring, D. R. (2016). *The healing virtues: Character ethics in psychotherapy.* Oxford University Press. https://doi.org/10.1093/med/9780199689149.001.0001

Wright, T. A., & Goodstein, J. (2007). Character is not "Dead" in management research: A review of individual character and organizational-level virtue. *Journal of Management, 33*(6), 928–958. https://doi.org/10.1177/0149206307307644

Zagzebski, L. T. (1996). *Virtues of the mind: An inquiry into the nature of virtue and the ethical foundations of knowledge.* Cambridge University Press. https://doi.org/10.1017/CBO9781139174763

11

THE SEVEN RULES OF VIRTUE

> You're always being compromised as a political leader. So, there's two words: compromised and compromising. Similar but different in how they are applied. You have to do a lot of *compromising* which is ultimately when you say, 'well, I can compromise up to a point, but I won't compromise those five things'. And then you are always, in your gut, wondering where that line is where you're crossing over or not, and then putting the greater good at the forefront of your mind rather than what you personally want to see as an outcome. That's where you get a compromise. You get an 80% win rather than a 100% win.

Our desire to be and to be seen as ethical or moral agents in the face of our human fallibility and moral hypocrisy leads us to think about a set of rules' or guiding principles that might assist us in avoiding their pitfalls. In this chapter, we propose the Seven Rules of Virtue that can help us maintain an ethical focus without becoming arrogant or righteous.

Rule 1: Leave the cudgel of moral superiority on the ground

The importance of character

For those of us that either work within or with institutions, and particularly those institutions embedded within political systems that are accountable to citizens, the subject and scrutiny of leadership character have never been more pronounced. In Australia, we have heard of significant allegations of bullying and harassment, sexual assault, and intimidation within some of our most important public institutions (Sawer, 2021; Zhuang, 2021).

DOI: 10.4324/9781003499510-14

We have been exposed to evidence of subversive and divisive language that has sought to undermine leadership confidence. All of this and more has resulted in significant and unacceptable harm and suffering towards those who were vulnerable and without recourse to speak and act in their defence. We have shaken our heads in dismay and called for major systemic, institutional and cultural reform. We want and expect better leadership, and, fortunately, at least at the surface, most leaders want and expect to be better leaders (Holmes, 2023).

At the heart of this dilemma rests the question of character. To recap, a common view of character is that it refers to a set of enduring intrinsic characteristics that we value and by which we wish to be valued by others (Sennett, 1998). Our character unfolds both through our lived experiences of time and space as well as a range of socio-cultural factors that extrinsically influence us. Some of this influence is helpful, and some of it is not. Our character is also the central point of our virtue—those ethics that lead us to doing the right things consistently at the right times, for the right reasons, and in the right proportion (Alzola, 2008). We take great pride in being identified by our virtues (such as being kind, compassionate, courageous, considerate and so on) and we feel deeply aggrieved when either we do not live up to our own standards and expectations, or worse, when we are attacked for failing to meet standards set by others.

Avoiding moral superiority

By any measure, many of the criticisms levelled towards leadership character in the face of such allegations and the resulting unacceptable harm and suffering are valid. Nonetheless, one of the great dangers of criticising others is that we can develop what Buddhist's call "moral superiority" or "deluded pride" (Gyatso, 2014). We run the real risk of developing an overinflated sense of importance about our own ethical competencies in comparison to others. We see ourselves as better and develop righteousness about our ethical disposition. This is dangerous territory. From here, we develop anger and aversion towards others while reinforcing our ignorance of their circumstances when casting our judgements. In so doing, we perpetuate further harm and suffering towards those we seek to criticise and hold to account, allowing the cycle of suffering to continue.

This applies to those who hold (ignorant) majority views, as well as those who hold minority views. Often, we see biased and harmful majority views change over time and become wiser, more knowledgeable, tolerant, and accepting. As the majority view follows this path, the minority may take up where the majority leaves off, while operating through the same afflictions. That is to say, the righteousness of the majority transfers to the minority and perpetuates further harm and suffering.

However, we are all far better off leaving "the cudgel of moral superiority" on the ground. Metaphorically, or even physically, beating each other up driven by a sense of righteous indignation is futile. Instead, we need an environment of deep listening, understanding, dignity and patience. This needs to be followed by wise and compassionate thoughts, words and actions to alleviate the suffering of ourselves and others and collectively move us towards happiness, well-being and flourishing.

Avoiding anger

As critics of such unacceptable behaviour, we may well be morally superior, but in so being, we should use this position to develop our wisdom about the plight of others. If, through immoral actions, harm arises, then wise actions will be required to alleviate the distress. Clear, concise, unambiguous, assertive, and forceful actions may be needed to alleviate the arising harm, but none of these require the motivation of anger or the intention to cause further harm. Instead, a compassionate motivation and intention to alleviate harm and suffering with wisdom must necessarily lead to better outcomes (Gyatso, 2006, 2014).

This can be a difficult concept for some of us due to the anger and rage we feel when experiencing or witnessing inappropriate behaviour. Anger is a natural human reaction, is perfectly understandable in some circumstances, and needs to be respected and acknowledged. Nonetheless, the difficulty is that anger and rage are rarely helpful in the long term for several reasons.

Firstly, anger and rage cannot be sustained over time as motivators towards improved actions and outcomes. They are physically and mentally exhausting. Secondly, anger and rage lead to further suffering and, ultimately, it is suffering in all its forms that we so desperately wish to see come to an end (Nussbaum, 2016). There are many contemporary and historic examples of leaders thinking, speaking and acting through virtuous characteristics rather than defaulting to anger and righteousness in the face of great tragedy and suffering. Nelson Mandela and Desmond Tutu's commitment to replace anger with forgiveness, patience and courage in their respective stances against apartheid in South Africa (Tutu, 1999), as well as Dr. Martin Luther King's stance of non-violence against racial discrimination in the USA (King, 1964), are just two of countless examples.

If we genuinely want to see change for the better, then we must not succumb to a deluded sense of moral superiority, along with the anger and rage that often follow. Instead, we need to bring forward the best of our own character and, to the extent in which it is possible, work with others. This includes those leaders who let us down but genuinely wish to make amends. In so doing, we can set course for a safer, happier, more productive world where suffering is lessened and people can continue becoming the very best of themselves for the benefit of all of us.

Rule 2: Virtuous recognition must be bestowed, it cannot be declared

Sometimes we witness self-proclamations of virtue: "'My organisation is compassionate', or 'we have shown immense compassion by...'," can often be heard in public discourses, either from individual leaders, or from broader organisational or societal cultures. As one highly experienced and respected political leader told me:

> There's a lot of false compassion these days. There's a lot of people that feign compassion, who talk about... their own acts of compassion, which is kind of total contradiction in terms if you think about it. The power of compassion isn't having it be explained to people. It's the actual act that matters. And it's better when it's done when no one's watching, I think. And you don't brag about it. It's a total contradiction. We have politicians now that really spent a lot of time describing how compassionate they are.

However, by what standard are those self-proclamations being measured? Often, it is a self-established standard. The individual or group may well consider themselves as "being" virtuous in a certain way, but that may not be the perception of those who are meant to receive the benefit of such proclamations. No virtue can be claimed as a permanent state within an individual or a culture. It may be predominant, frequently on display or prioritised, but it still exists within an environment of change, uncertainty, ambiguity, and complexity (von Eschenbach, 2020). Situations, contexts and circumstances can alter their presence, priority or effectiveness, particularly if leaders are relatively unskilled and/or inconsistent in their application or fall to fallibility or moral hypocrisy.

Ultimately, the measure by which a leader or a culture is deemed to have demonstrated virtue must be socially bestowed by those who have received the benefit of their thoughts, words and actions. Committing to being a certain way and having another receive and recognise the benefits that flow would be a solid measure of success for most people and organisations.

By way of example, in 2012, I was preparing to leave my post as Commissioner of Emergency Services for the Australian Capital Territory by celebrating my promotion to the position of Director General for Emergency Management Australia in a local restaurant. At the end of the evening, I was approached by a middle-aged woman who I had not previously met. She walked up to me as I was leaving and said, "Commissioner, do you have a minute?," to which I replied, "Certainly." She said that she wanted to let me know that she was sad to see me leave as Commissioner and I asked her, "Why is that?" She replied, "Every time you spoke to the community through the media [(print, TV, Radio)], you took the time to explain things to people, you were never patronising or condescending, you often showed compassion and understanding and, perhaps most importantly, you accepted responsibility when things went wrong." She went on to say, "Commissioner, I just want you to know that I trusted you and under your leadership, I felt safe."

Having committed to an ethic of trust for most of my career, I could not have asked for a more powerful validation of that same commitment. I had often spoken publicly and written about the need for leaders (including myself) to commit to an ethic of public trust and confidence (Crosweller, 2015, 2016), but I had never proclaimed my own success. I still regard the validation I received from such a generous citizen, who took the time to acknowledge my commitment, as one of the greatest honours of my career. While it was neither the first nor the last time that I had been acknowledged in that way, I have never felt the need for too many such acknowledgements. Committing to virtuous leadership for its own sake delivered me many moments of happiness, as well as some moments of grief, where I felt that I had not honoured my own standard of virtue due to my own fallibility.

Rule 3: Virtuous commitment must be declared, it cannot be bestowed

While virtuous recognition must be socially bestowed, committing to virtuous action must involve a self-declaration, as it is unreasonable for others to commit us on our behalf. Virtuous commitment is an overt statement of intention to be a certain way towards others. It requires integrity, commitment and perseverance—attributes that cannot be imposed by others.

An overt commitment to virtue opens up the opportunity for leaders to do something for someone or something else (who could be close and known, distant and unknown and human or non-human) and move them away from the potential to experience harm and suffering, instead moving them towards a greater sense of happiness, well-being or flourishing. That is, the chance to act with compassion, care, justice, and generosity. However, unfortunately, a lack of commitment can have the opposite effect.

The experience of COVID-19 during 2020 and 2021 provides a good example. The response to this pandemic was highly varied and complex, and much of its effectiveness was contingent upon two key factors. First, was the extent to which the leaders of a country or state had access to the equities of power, wealth and resource. Second, was the extent to which leaders used these equities for the greatest good and for the greatest number.

The globally disproportionate distribution of these equities has proven to show that, despite our collective capacity to vaccinate all peoples across the world, many suffered due to a lack of access and opportunity, as well as an overarching lack of compassion, care, justice and generosity by those more privileged. Unfortunately—and this has been a constraint in the psyche of humanity for centuries—we have tended to prioritise looking after "people like us" over distant and unknown others. Or, in other words, our compassion, care, justice, and generosity only extend to "known others" that we regard as the same or similar to ourselves, who are in close proximity to us, and for which we feel a sense of responsibility to value and protect (Tschakert, 2020).

This constraint is often reflected in the way we govern ourselves. A predominant feature of nation-state responsibilities are the constitutional, legal, regulatory, and political frameworks that determine rights, duties, and obligations between us, and between ourselves and the state (Lodge, 2009). Across a single continent known as Australia, this plays out in the context of six states, two territories, and the commonwealth (Sawer, 1988). All hold various responsibilities for providing protection to their citizens and all have sought to fulfil those responsibilities within the equities of power, wealth and resources made available to them (Wisner et al., 2012).

However, these same governance arrangements, which seek to make sense of how we collectively move forward as people, also have the potential to divide us. One of the ways they do that is by assigning us a political identity that reinforces our relationship with "people like us." For example, a single citizen may be referred to as a Melburnian, a Victorian, or an Australian. One person, three political identities. These identities are often spoken about in absolute terms: all Melburnians, all Victorians, or all Australians, depending upon the political motivations and desires at the time and the debates that ensue.

These identities can keep us entrapped within a regime of allegiance to and compliance with governance arrangements that pursue the greatest good for the greatest number, while reinforcing division and difference. The phrase "Queensland hospitals are only for Queenslanders" (News.com.au, 2020) was famously quoted during the height of the pandemic, when states tried to stop the spread of the virus across their jurisdictional borders. The statement was reasonable if one only considers the obligation to protect another human as being limited to constitutional, legal or regulatory obligations and political identity. However, if one considers the obligation as a compassionate, caring, just, and generous human being, then the statement is unreasonable. Fortunately, most people viewed the statement as "unreasonable."

Allegiance to and compliance with governance arrangements as the basis in which we seek to increase well-being, provide protection, and reduce suffering produces a suboptimal result. Despite the immense equities of power, wealth and resource contained within a country like Australia and its political jurisdictions, such allegiance and compliance rob us of the opportunity to be more compassionate, caring, just, and generous. They rob us of our humanness, often resulting in us seeing others as less-than-human on some level: not as important, not as worthy, not as valuable. As difficult as it is to say, this is endemic in our inter- and intra-jurisdictional arrangements, as has been witnessed many times during COVID-19.[1]

However, as leaders, we can turn this around. If we hold rank, title, position or authority within a public or private institution, then we have (varying degrees of) access to the equities of power, wealth and resource. We also have the ability to commit to being more virtuous: more compassionate, caring, just and generous. By combining these equities and abilities, rather than seeing them as a binary choice, we can make a significant difference. We can leverage them to bridge the gaps and divisions that governance arrangements so often create between leaders at all levels of the political and bureaucratic systems. We can use them to create solutions that honour the constitutional, legal, regulatory, and political obligations of our public and private institutions AND optimise well-being, provide protection, and reduce the suffering of close and known others, as well as distant and unknown human and non-human others.

Rule 4: Be wary of virtue signalling

When I talk to people about the current state of society, many of them comment on a sense of hopelessness or an inability to instigate changes that, in their opinion, would make the world a better place. For some, it is a failure of leadership, particularly institutional leadership, whether public or private, political or apolitical. For others, it is driven by a sense of injustice, either to themselves or on behalf of others they perceive are being treated unfairly. Still, for others, it is the desire to rebalance power differentials between those who can influence change for the better and those who cannot, and of course, there are myriad other reasons as well.

It is eminently sensible to speak out against those things that are harmful to us and others. However, if we reflect closely on these expressions through most forms of mass media and social media, we will notice that many people attribute such dissatisfaction to a moral or ethical breach of some kind by others, while at the same time implicitly declaring their own ethical standards as more intact or complete. In other words, people often express anger and dissatisfaction through a self-declared virtuosity. Such virtuosity of ethical and moral purity may well be true for some, but I suspect it is not true for most. For example, in politics, both Government and Opposition parties often criticise each other for this phenomenon, levelling criticisms for promoting an imposed morality without offering constructive alternatives or commitment to action.

What is virtue signalling?

Self-declared virtuosity, without humility, self-reflection, and personal commitment to ethical mastery over time of thought, word and action, produces an arrogant moral and ethical superiority that most people find offensive. Such a phenomenon has earned the term "virtue signalling." This term was coined by *The Spectator* journalist James Bartholomew in 2015 about "the way in which many people say or write things to indicate that they are virtuous" (Bartholomew, 2015).

In essence, the criticism centres around the ease in which people can express their views or make statements on social media about their anger and dissatisfaction, whilst simultaneously indicating that they are kind, decent and virtuous, without any intention of following through with commitment, action and sacrifice to improve things. As Bartholomew observes, "one of the crucial aspects of virtue signalling is that it does not require actually doing anything virtuous. It does not involve delivering lunches to elderly neighbours... It takes no effort or sacrifice at all" (Bartholomew, 2015).

One of the effects of virtue signalling is that any genuine notion of virtuosity becomes discredited, and people shy away from moral and ethical considerations all together. In other words, any genuine consideration of morality and ethics becomes shameful and therefore suppressed. An irony then emerges whereby moral and ethical considerations become eroded and further reinforce the causes of virtue signalling, while at the same time undermining a more sensible and sophisticated moral and ethical discourse. In essence, through virtue signalling, we lose our moral and ethical courage.

Avoiding righteousness and moral superiority

To a reasonable person, harm and suffering have no place in a society that aspires to a genuinely prosperous, healthy and happy life. However, unfortunately due to our fallibility, hypocrisy, and delusions of mind, harm and suffering exist. Therefore, speaking out against harm and suffering to ourselves and others through ethics and morality is essential, but it is also important that we become neither righteous nor superior.

For example, in Buddhist philosophy, while it is important to master morality, it is a mistake to allow morality "to get the better of oneself." In other words, the focus should always be on our own faults, not those of others. It is only when our own much larger problems are dealt with, that we can perhaps make commentary about the moral failings of another. Increasing our wisdom through virtuous actions of body, speech and mind has the mutual benefit of improving our own life, as well as helping others by understanding they suffer the same afflictions as us. And through this understanding, we are afforded the opportunity to reduce our anger and dissatisfaction and see the problems that are aggrieving us in a different light (Gyatso, 2006, 2014).

However, speaking out, while essential, is not enough. All ethical and moral considerations need to move to commitment and action otherwise they simply become rhetoric, and that action begins with Self. Too often—and this is what virtue signalling points to—are the words without the actions, along with the implicit assumption of superiority. If we are genuinely concerned about the state of the world, and we certainly should be, then it is not only what we think and say about it that matters, but perhaps more importantly, it is what we do about it. This includes what we do about our own limitations. In short, if we want to improve the quality of our societies, then we need to do it through a personal commitment to our own ethical and moral standards. We should also *exemplify* those standards through how we interact with the world. The adage "be the change you want to see" fits comfortably here.

Being in action

Whether we participate in society through a public or private life, we have an obligation to demonstrate, through virtuous actions of body, speech and mind, an ethic that brings the maximum benefit to ourselves and others. A benefit that moves towards a genuine happiness, well-being and flourishing. To do this, we need to exemplify and express, with courage, confidence and humility, those ethics that speak to the essence of who we are as compassionate human beings. And while we may be unskilful in our ethical discourse and narratives, we will at least have the benefit of following through with our actions, silencing both those who cry out in anger and frustration at the lack of ethics, as well as those who quickly condemn others for pointing out such absences.

Rule 5: Moral courage is greater than physical courage

What is moral courage?

Moral courage can be defined as the fortitude to convert moral intentions into actions despite pressures from either within or beyond organisations to do otherwise (May et al., 2003). In a positive sense, these actions may lead to being lauded by others, whereas, in a negative sense, they may lead to facing adverse consequences and social disapproval (Hannah et al., 2015). Such courage requires incredible strength of character. It involves standing apart from the crowd while simultaneously internalising the aims and objectives towards the good of the collective. Therefore, it needs high moral efficacy—a belief that one can carry out the moral task effectively that can be improved through training, education, and lived experience (May et al., 2013).

Central to this level of courage is the capacity to put aside egotistical self-interest while simultaneously being potentially isolated from others, which is what can make it more difficult to achieve than anything in the physical world. Not only do we have to set aside personal desire, but we may end up lonely in the process through ostracisation, isolation, and perhaps even condemnation (Barsky, 2009). Therefore, to be confident in the exercise of our moral judgements, we must apply as much wisdom as possible. We must necessarily ensure that our intention to act with moral courage is genuinely informed by the well-being, safety, and non-harmfulness towards others, along with as little egotistical self-interest, pride, righteousness, or superiority as possible (Hannah et al., 2015). The purer the intention, along with as much knowledge and insight of the circumstances and causes as possible, the easier it is to navigate the consequences of our actions instigated by others, irrespective of how unpleasant they may be.

Moral courage during COVID-19

During the years of 2020 and 2021, we witnessed many leaders displaying moral courage by committing to minimising exposure and delivering on the needs of those who experienced suffering arising from the COVID-19 global pandemic. Sadly, we also witnessed other leaders failing in their moral courage, as well as their constitutional and political duty to exercise such commitment. In Australia, at least, it appears that leadership efforts were largely appreciated by most people, as reflected in the political opinion polls at the time. This was, in part, a testament to the character of these leaders in times of genuine crisis, and for this, most of us were grateful.

While no leader has nor could claim perfection, many clearly focused their efforts and priorities on the well-being of others to the extent to which they were able. In so doing, they relied upon and increased their efforts to think, speak and act through the virtues of empathy and compassion. Those in receipt of these actions responded with increased levels of trust and gratitude. This is usually a slow, cautious, and progressive process between leaders and followers, and while the reciprocity within this equation seems both simple and obvious (people doing good things by others = increased trust and gratitude), there is a profundity that is worth exploring further.

The impact of fatigue

Unfortunately, in almost all disasters, people (and especially leaders) get tired. They must navigate through tiredness and fatigue irrespective of the complexity and duration of the event. Amid all this, mistakes will be made. And as we witnessed, mistakes were numerous. The extent to which these mistakes are isolated or systemic will be determined by the commissions of inquiry that will follow in the post-event reviews. However, it is almost certain that most of them will be systemic, infused with errors of judgement (Cole et al., 2018).

Ultimately, most systems fail when put under enough pressure. This is especially true when leaders of both public and private institutions insufficiently anticipate, plan, design, and invest in systems for rare but high-consequence events (US Congress, 2006). When this happens, the onus of trust, confidence, safety, and protection falls even more heavily upon the leadership. More specifically, and more importantly, it falls to the ethics that inform the leader's judgements and decisions. The system can no longer aid in supporting the complex processes of good, right and just along with what it means to live well. Instead, the leader's ethos is required to fill the void (Crosweller & Tschakert, 2019).

The revealing of character

Contrary to what many people might think, crises and disasters reveal character, but they do not create it. When a leader's tiredness and fatigue set in, and the systems designed to support them fail or reach their point of limitation, a leader's capacity and moral courage to exercise ethical judgements and decisions supported by the equities of power, wealth and resources available to them become exposed for all to see. Any trust and gratitude that may have been accumulated over a sustained period are brought to the fore and tested. For many leaders, what they do next arises from the strength of their moral character, and the extent to which they utilise these equities makes a substantial contribution to whether trust and gratitude will be sustained or destroyed (Crosweller, 2016). This is irrespective of how tired or fatigued they may feel.

Let me give you an example. In Australia, a young woman living in the nation's capital city of Canberra received news that her father was terminally ill in the northern state of Queensland. When the young woman sought permission to visit her dying father, she was denied entry on the basis she was a "risk" to the state, even though Canberra had not recorded a single case of COVID-19 for more than 60 days. It is important to understand that, for there to be a risk, there must be a hazard, the potential for some exposure to that hazard, and the possibility of being harmed by that hazard. However, there was no risk because there was no possibility of viral transmission (hazard). It was absent from the Canberra community.

Despite this, the system said to the young woman, "No, you cannot come!." Eventually, after some pressure, the state agreed, but only on the condition that she self-quarantine for two weeks before visiting her dying father. She agreed, but sadly, her father died before the quarantine period ended. Unfortunately, it got worse. After he died, the state denied the young woman the ability to go to her father's funeral. Instead, she was permitted a private viewing of her father's body without any support from her family or friends.

In this circumstance, the system clearly failed. It failed in its ability to appreciate how risk is determined. It failed in its ability to respond to the compassionate needs of a young woman desperate to visit her dying father. And it failed in its ability to use the immense equities of power, wealth and resources available to it to make a discerning decision on compassionate grounds while satisfying any residual safety concerns it may have had. The public outcry was significant (Noble & Powell, 2020).

It is often said that ethics such as trust "arrives on foot and leaves on horse-back." It takes a long time to trust a leader and their institution and a very short time to lose trust and confidence in them. I have no doubt that the tiredness and fatigue of the state's institutional leaders played a significant part in the decision. I also have no doubt the system was inadequately prepared to deal with the complexity of such (largely predictable) circumstances that, by any measure, called for a more compassionate response. Nonetheless, "trust left on horseback" for many people and particularly for the young woman. The full effect and resulting consequences may never be known, but there is little doubt they will be detrimental to the reputation of some leaders.

Futility of blame

However, blaming any leader for this is futile. Blame only leads to further suffering. But we can learn from this. Sadly, we live in a society that relies too heavily on "the system" to provide the ethical frameworks for decision-making and not enough on the virtuous ethics of the leadership. If we want to "leave the horse in the stable," then we must make a more conscious effort to design systems to support and develop a leader's strength of moral character and presence of mind to exercise their virtue. Such leaders, supported by the immense equities of power, wealth and resources available to them, have the potential to make a substantial and lasting difference to the lives of many people.

Perhaps, most importantly, circumstances like the example above open the opportunity to allow ethics to do its greatest work. When the system lapses and capabilities reach their limitations, it is ultimately the ethics of the leadership that is called upon to step in, step up, and run towards the needs of those who are genuinely suffering. It is one of the great tests of leadership. Conditioning leaders to understand this while increasing their competence and confidence, combined with putting in place ethical capabilities that can lend support, will significantly reduce the possibility that another person might have to experience such agony in the future. If we learn this lesson from such an unfortunate set of circumstances, then perhaps the horse can retire to pasture!

Rule 6: Exemplify rather than sanctify

The downside of virtue dependency

Most people desire to see more virtue in the world. More integrity, compassion, kindness, patience, and consideration, as examples. That same desire is often aimed towards leaders across most aspects of society, from the global to the local, and even within families and intimate relationships. For the most part, such expectations are reasonable. Clearly, we need leaders to be this way as often as possible. However, when this need tilts towards dependency on others to be a certain way for us to feel happier, the expectation moves towards being unreasonable. It can also be viewed as an abrogation of our own responsibility as moral agents.

Placing the burden of our need for virtue upon another so that we can feel happier about a situation is akin to handing over our power to someone else. We are expecting them to think, speak and act in ways that fulfil our need to feel better about ourselves or a situation. Often, when they fulfil our needs, we sanctify them; when they do not, we demonise them. However, in reality, they are neither a god nor a devil. Instead, they are, in part, an exemplification of what we are capable of (good and bad). A great friend and mentor of mine was a former Australian Army Padre who wore the cloth of a religious minister for over 40 years, and he had some sage advice about sanctification. He said the one thing he spent his professional life avoiding was being sanctified simply because he was a man of religion. He knew the downside. Often, those we sanctify speak to or exemplify truths that we not only desire, but also make some people uncomfortable; and for a select few, very uncomfortable. Uncomfortable enough to kill.

To draw upon the teachings of Lojong practice in Buddhist philosophy (Chodron, 2017; Gyatso, 2014), when a leader acts virtuously, they are exemplifying our own capacity to exhibit similar ethical behaviours. Ethics such as kindness, empathy and well-being are virtues that we *re-cognise*. That is, earlier in our lives, we had an original cognition of, say, kindness that— when exemplified by someone else's kind words and actions—we related to. We recognise (i.e., *re-cognise*) kindness because it sits within our mental continuum. It is already present within our minds. So, yes, leaders can exemplify the ethics we desire to see more of, but no, they cannot be sanctified in the vain hope that they will do even more to appease our desire to see more virtue in the world. If we want more virtue in our world (and let's face it, who doesn't?) then we need to take their lead and think, speak and act with virtue in our own right.

New Zealand prime minister's leadership

Take the leadership of the former New Zealand Prime Minister Jacinda Ardern as an example. The tragic events of the Christchurch shootings on 15 March 2019 (Royal Commission of Inquiry into the terrorist attack on Christchurch masjidain on 15 March 2019) and the way in which the prime minister of New Zealand led the crisis impressed many people across the world (Molloy, 2019). Her commitment to kindness, empathy and well-being was resolute despite the unfolding adversity and was clearly a testament to her ability to lead in such circumstances. Those ethical virtues were fundamental to her government's response to the crisis, as well as the underpinning premise by which the broader community responded.

In short, the New Zealand prime minister, her government, and the community's national response were impressive. In September 2019, I opened a prominent Australian news App (ABC News, 2019) to discover a story that called into question the capacity for ethics, as exemplified by Ms. Ardern, to be effective in delivering on political outcomes. Not an unreasonable question, of course, in the world of a political leader operating within a democratic society. However, there was an undertone. That undertone suggested that the prime minister would need to do more and exhibit further evidence of her ethical premise if she was to be viewed as successful. In other words, the demonising had begun.

The need for personal responsibility

In my view, it is simply both unfair and unreasonable to expect another person to carry the burden of our need for virtue. If we place the entire burden of kindness on one particular person, such as the prime minister, and fail to realise that they are exemplifying what we are capable of, then we will inevitably end up in disappointment. Instead, we are likely to demonise them when they fail to live up to our expectations or stretch us beyond our comfort zone towards a greater truth that we may not be ready to hear. So, rather than view virtue only as an attribute of another person from which we want to see more to increase our sense of happiness, we need to shift the premise of our thoughts to realise that they are simply showing us what we are already capable of, albeit within a different context and circumstances.

So, next time someone inspires us—evoking feelings of joy, inspiration or any other experience that typifies happiness, flourishing or well-being—understand that, while they may well be exhibiting the very ethics that we admire (and should acknowledge), they are also showing us what we are capable of. And, while we may not perceive that we have either the confidence nor the competence to think, speak or act accordingly, we will never get better—and our circumstances will never get better—if we do not at least try.

Leaders such as Ms. Ardern are indeed impressive, and they show great courage in exemplifying the best of who we are capable of being, and to that end maybe to sanctify them is okay. But to demonise them is not okay. To demonise them is to admit our own moral and ethical failure to step up in our own lives and take their lead. If they have the courage and the conviction to be out in front advocating virtue, then the least we can do is not to make them wrong. Instead, we can be grateful and honour their courage by putting into practice those very things we so desire to see more of in the world that they show us through their leadership.

These leaders also give us a chance to be leaders of virtue in our own right and thus inspire others. As I have mentioned in other chapters, if you are in any position of influence over another person—whether it be in formal leadership in politics, organisations or associations, or informal leadership, such as parenting, mentoring or simply having greater agency than those around you—take the opportunity to exemplify what it is you wish to see in others. Be that leader that shows others not only what you are capable of, but what they are capable of too! Perhaps then we may, thought by thought, word by word, and action by action, lead to world to a better place than we currently find ourselves in.

Rule 7: Forgiving self and other for acts and omissions of body, speech and mind

Guilt and shame

Experiencing guilt and shame are a part of being human. Seen positively, guilt and shame can aid us throughout our lives by helping to maintain a close relationship with our ethical premise and our desire to be the best of who we are capable of being and becoming. Put another way, guilt and shame, when properly understood, stop us from getting consumed by our excessive self-importance and self-interest (Gyatso, 2014). However, when they are not properly understood, they can cause us much suffering. Left unchecked or not properly acknowledged and explored, guilt and shame become insidious and permeate into every aspect of our subconscious, closing life down, restricting its flow, and preventing us from living life to our highest potential (Brown, 2018).

In Buddhism, the word most associated with guilt is "regret"—a feeling of remorse for actions carried out in the past. Regret affords us the opportunity to make amends for those non-virtuous actions that we committed towards others, to the best of our ability, and to the extent that our circumstances allow. Of course, sometimes, circumstances dictate that the effects of our past non-virtuous actions have already manifested as negative consequences. When this happens, we must patiently and skilfully navigate through those consequences to the best of our ability (and hopefully without causing further regret for ourselves or suffering to others). Either way, there is no sense in dwelling in misery. If we can make amends, then we should do so. If we cannot, then we must accept the consequences of our actions. Worrying, stressing, and beating ourselves up does not help and lacks wisdom (Gyatso, 2014).

Shame is closely associated with regret insofar as it has an important mental function of ensuring that we avoid our own inappropriate actions of body, speech and mind that could otherwise bring suffering upon ourselves and others. Without a sense of shame, or in other words, if we were shameless, then we would almost certainly commit non-virtuous actions at great personal cost, as well as cost to others. Shame forms the basis of our moral discipline with particular regards to morality's function of restraint. Shame helps us to think more consciously and conscientiously about any thoughts, words or actions that we are about to undertake that could bring suffering to ourselves and others, and encourages us to choose a wiser, more compassionate response (Gyatso, 2014; Tsering, 2006).

Signposts not destinations

It can be helpful to think of guilt and shame as "signposts" rather than "destinations." That is to say, when feelings of guilt or shame arise (the "signposts"), they are usually indicative of a lesson rather than a place in which to dwell or reside ("destinations"). Forgiveness, humility, acceptance, patience, tolerance, atonement, compassion, mindfulness, presence, or understanding, are examples of lessons that eventually we all need to learn, sometimes once, often constantly. For most of us, to unconsciously live with guilt and shame or to consciously wallow in them (by seeing them as "destinations") are an abrogation of responsibility for our own life (Myss, 2009).

If we are living with guilt and shame, on some level we are refusing to accept responsibility for ourselves, and it will be our excessive self-interest and self-importance that are getting in the way. It may be a fear of looking bad; having to admit that we were wrong; that in some way we contributed to the circumstances that caused us or others to suffer; or that we cannot bring ourselves to forgive ourselves or another for something that we had no control over but for which we convince ourselves that we were to blame (such as what happens to children through abuse). Guilt and shame will show us the way to the lesson, but they are never a place in which to reside (Tutu, 1999; Tutu & Tutu, 2014).

Guilt and shame also play a central role in our propensity for harsh self-criticism and, once again, it will arise from excessive self-interest and self-importance. Put simply, if we were to free ourselves of guilt and shame then we would not attack ourselves internally (for those things we did or did not think, say or do) or others externally (for those things we perceived others did or did not think, say or do to us). Guilt and shame often lead to feelings of condemnation, and often form the basis for our anger and aggression, whether towards ourselves or others. According to author and researcher Brené Brown (2018), many people perceive guilt as "I did something bad," while they perceive shame as "I am bad." Both perceptions are unhelpful and are often reinforced as a way of weaponising these aspects of mind in much the same way as virtue signalling.

The need for forgiveness

Our inability to forgive ourselves and others often leads to the judgement that we and they are unworthy of compassion and deserving of punishment. But herein lies the paradox. When we possess a mind that judges, we perceive ourselves as separate from the mind being judged. We believe that, by punishing another, we will escape punishment. But to bring harm or suffering to another through thought, word or action is to bring harm and suffering upon ourselves. Guilt and shame, leading to punishment, either internal or external, informed by an ignorant sense of right and wrong and motivated by right-eousness, cannot be sustained by the mind and will inevitably lead to great mental pain and suffering. Simply put, the capacity to show compassion while wallowing in guilt and shame cannot co-exist, and to accept one is to deny the other, both internally and externally. Without guilt and shame—that is to say, with pure compassion for Self and Others—the ego has no life, and suffering cannot exist (Myss, 2009).

Unfortunately, what I have both witnessed and experienced over the course of my career leads me to believe that, out of all of the lessons disasters provide, forgiveness is the most important one, but it is also the one least often learned. The inability to forgive Self and Other leads us to a mind that becomes flooded with anxieties, burdens us with a sense of injustice, or perhaps even worse, fills us with bitterness and hatred. Unfortunately, these emotions can persist and pervade for many years and, if left unmanaged, become toxic.

We do not have to stop and reflect for too long to see that we carry many burdens through our lack of forgiveness almost daily. Irrespective of how we may justify them, we are the ones that experience the effects of such negative feelings, and they are never pleasant. They also have a negative effect on our health, relationships, leadership ability, career progression, and organisational culture. In short, by thinking, speaking and acting through such feelings, we bring harm to others and in so doing, perpetuate the very cycle of suffering that we are so desperate to release ourselves from.

Viewing people as separate from their behaviour

We should certainly not acquiesce to the destructive behaviours that some people exhibit, and it is indeed true that negative behaviours often become the cause for actions that bring these people to account. However, if we un-derstand that the aggrieving behaviour is separate from the person who is behaving in such a way, and if we further understand that such behaviour is motivated from a mind of unconscious suffering, then such realisations give us a powerful choice. The choice to be righteous and seek vengeance or, the choice to forgive (Tutu & Tutu, 2014).

I have seen many people over the course of my career sit with guilt and shame for far too long and watched them suffer unnecessarily. How many of us have a propensity to take on "too much responsibility" and then be burdened with its weight. Forgiving ourselves is as important as forgiving others. Having enough humility to accept that we make mistakes—and to know that, from them, we can learn and grow—is a sign of a good leader. Not having sufficient humility and maintaining a fixed and righteous view of the world, maintains our arrogance and ignorance. The choice is simple.

The gift of forgiveness

The truth is that forgiveness is a gift that we grant ourselves. It is not just to do with the person we are forgiving. By granting forgiveness through compassion, we initiate an act of transformation in which we release ourselves from the negativity and toxicity that otherwise arises from holding onto the thought, through a mind of anger, that we have been unjustifiably aggrieved and that only righteousness and vengeance will suffice in seeking what our ego would interpret as entitled justice and fairness (Chodron, 2001a). When we truly understand this lesson, forgiveness becomes a daily ritual that contributes significantly to clearing our minds of those past traumas and unfinished business. It also opens space within us to deal with those challenges that, ultimately, we will be called to face as leaders in our chosen field (Myss, 2009; Tutu, 1999: Tutu & Tutu, 2014).

Ask yourself a simple question: can I afford to carry with me any emotional stress caused from lack of forgiveness into the next operation or business venture that I will need to lead and manage? If you are in a position of leadership and you are called upon to lead and manage, you will inevitably come across the very people that caused you grief and you have not yet forgiven. Alternatively, you will come across the very people that you have aggrieved and from whom you have not yet sought forgiveness. Either way, you have taken on a whole load of trouble before you even begin to deal with all the complexities that the circumstances you are about to confront will throw at you.

The reality is that we all make messes. We all aggrieve other people, sometimes consciously, often unconsciously, and other people aggrieve us. No one can ever hold on to the mantle of perfection and claim not to have offended anyone. To even contemplate such a thought would be both arrogant and ignorant.

What forgiveness requires

Forgiveness requires both humility and compassion. The ability to accept wholeheartedly that we are responsible for aggrieving others, and the compassion to understand that most people aggrieve us because of their own internal suffering; suffering to which we too can relate, as it is our own internal suffering that drives us to aggrieve others. We owe it to ourselves, and each other, to reflect upon our own perceived limitations and over time, forgive ourselves for those things that we did or did not think, did or did not say, or did or did not do. Having reached some sense of inner peace about our own perceived limitations, we owe it to others to grant them forgiveness, for they have endured the same internal suffering. For, wherever there is a pure mind of love and compassion for all humanity granted through the power of forgiveness, harm and suffering simply cannot exist.

The challenge for leaders

As leaders, we would do well to remember the Seven Rules of Virtue as a way of keeping ourselves grounded, relatable and accessible to others that we are asked to lead, serve and protect. We should surrender any arrogant sense of moral superiority, rely mainly on the recognition from others of our virtue, commit to virtuous leadership, be wary of virtue signalling, develop our moral courage, lead others by example, and forgive ourselves and others for things done or omitted. We should also commit to understanding what the most important virtues of our leadership are. In Chapters 12 and 13, we explore how we can both develop and sustain our virtue through the practical wisdom of our lived experiences and mindfulness.

Note

1 For example, see the report prepared by the Victorian Ombudsman: "Investigation into decision-making under the Victorian Border Crossing Permit Directions" (7 December 2021).

References

ABC News. (2019, August 16). Alan Jones continues criticism of Jacinda Ardern over climate change comments, despite rebuke from Scott Morrison. *ABC News.* Retrieved September 29, 2023, from https://www.abc.net.au/news/2019-08-16/alan-jones-doubles-down-on-criticism-of-jacinda-ardern/11420102

Alzola, M. (2008). Character and environment: The status of virtues in organizations. *Journal of Business Ethics, 78*(3), 343–357. https://doi.org/10.1007/s10551-006-9335-7.

Barsky, A. (2009). When Right is Not Easy: Social Work and Moral Courage. Retrieved from https://blog.oup.com/2009/12/social-work-moral-courage/

Bartholomew, J. (2015, April 18). The awful rise of 'virtue signalling'. *Spectator.* https://www.spectator.com.au/2015/04/hating-the-daily-mail-is-a-substitute-for-doing-good/

Brown, B. (2018). *Dare To lead: Brave work, tough conversations, whole hearts.* Vermilion.

Chodron, P. (2017). *Start where you are: How to accept yourself and others.* HarperCollins.

Chodron, P. (2001). *The wisdom of no escape: How to love yourself and the world.* HarperCollins.

Cole, L., Eburn, M., Dovers, S., & Gough, M. (2018). Can major post-event inquiries and reviews contribute to lessons management? *Australian Journal of Emergency Management, 33*(2), 34–39.

Crosweller, M. (2015). How a change in thinking might change the inevitability of disasters. *Australian Journal of Emergency Management, 30*(3), 48–55.

Crosweller, M. (2016). Thinking differently, leading differently: Lessons from the Canberra fires, 2003. *Lessons learnt from emergency responses* (S. Ellis & K. McCarter, Eds.). CSIRO Publishing.

Crosweller, M., & Tschakert, P. (2019). Climate change and disasters: The ethics of leadership. *WIREs Climate Change, 11*(2), 1–18. https://doi.org/10.1002/wcc.624

Gyatso, G. K. (2006). *Joyful path of good fortune: The complete Buddhist path to enlightenment.* Tharpa Publications.

Gyatso, G. K. (2014). *How to understand the mind: The nature and power of the mind.* Tharpa Publications.

Hannah, S. T., Avolio, B. J., & Walumbwa, F. O. (2015). Relationships between authentic leadership, moral courage, and ethical and pro-social behaviours. *Business Ethics Quarterly, 21*(4), 555–578. https://doi.org/10.5840/beq201121436

Holmes, C. (2023). *Royal commission into the Robodebt scheme report.* The Royal Commission into the Robodebt Scheme. https://robodebt.royalcommission.gov.au/publications/report

King, M. L. (1964). *Why we can't wait.* Signet.

Lodge, G. C. (2009). Ideology and national competitiveness. *Journal of Managerial Issues, 21*(4), 461–477. https://www.jstor.org/stable/40604664

May, D. R., Chan, A. Y. L., Hodges, T. D., & Avolio, B. J. (2003). Developing the Moral Component of Authentic Leadership. *Organizational Dynamics, 32*(3), 247–260. https://doi.org/10.1016/s0090-2616(03)00032-9

May, D. R., Luth, M. T., & Schwoerer, C. E. (2013). The influence of business ethics education on moral efficacy, moral meaningfulness, and moral courage: A quasi-experimental study, *Journal of Business Ethics, 124,* 67–80. https://doi.org/10.1007/s10551-013-1860-6

Molloy, S. (2019, June 13). 'This is New Zealand's darkest day': Prime Minister Jacinda Ardern responds to Christchurch attacks. *News.com.au.* https://www.news.com.au/world/pacific/this-is-new-zealands-darkest-day-prime-minister-jacinda-ardern-responds-to-christchurch-shootings/news-story/b241bd5d0c51601ce2d963f248366321

Myss, C. (2009). *Defy gravity: Healing beyond the bounds of reason.* Hay House.

News.com.au. (2020, August 28). *Words coming back to haunt Palaszczuk after unborn baby's death* [Video]. News.com.au. https://www.news.com.au/national/words-coming-back-to-haunt-palaszczuk-after-unborn-babys-death/video/231ed16394add615784c605a494b4d8f

Noble, F., & Powell, R. (2020, September 11). Woman forced into full PPE for final lonely goodbye to dad. 9News. https://www.9news.com.au/national/coronavirus-border-restrictions-canberra-woman-sarah-unable-to-see-dying-dad-fighting-queensland-to-attend-funeral/6439f010-02e0-40b8-b507-a5a754c2d076

Nussbaum, M. C. (2016). *Anger and forgiveness: Resentment, generosity, justice.* Oxford University Press.

Sawer, G. (1988). *The Australian constitution.* AGPS Press.

Sawer, M. (2021, December 1). Australia's parliament must not be blighted by bullying and harassment – and the Jenkins report is a vital step forward. *The Guardian.* https://www.theguardian.com/commentisfree/2021/dec/01/australias-parliament-must-not-be-blighted-by-bullying-and-harassment-and-the-jenkins-report-is-a-vital-step-forward

Sennett, R. (1998). *The corrosion of character: The personal consequences of work in the new capitalism.* Norton.

Tschakert, P. (2020). More-than-human solidarity and multispecies justice in the climate crisis. *Environmental Politics, 31*(2), 277–296. https://doi.org/10.1080/09644016.2020.1853448

Tsering, G. T. (2006). *Buddhist psychology: The foundation of Buddhist thought* (Vol. 3). Wisdom Publications.

Tutu, D. (1999). *No future without forgiveness.* Doubleday.

Tutu, D., & Tutu, M. (2014). *The book of forgiving: The fourfold path for healing ourselves and the world.* HarperOne.

von Eschenbach, W. J. (2020). Can public virtues be global. *Journal of Global Ethics, 16*(1), 45–57. https://doi.org/10.1080/17449626.2020.1722728

Wisner, B., Gaillard, J., & Kelman, I. (2012). *The Routledge handbook of hazards and disaster risk reduction.* Routledge.

Zhuang, Y. (2021, November 30). 'Like fresh meat': Detailing rampant sex harassment in Australia's parliament. *The New York Times.* https://www.nytimes.com/2021/11/30/world/australia/parliament-harassment-report.html

PART 4

Practices

12

SUSTAINING RELATIONALITY THROUGH PRACTICAL WISDOM

> I think everybody's life experiences shape them in one way or another. I think mine have shaped me because I've had a passion for learning from life rather than letting life happen to me. I keep trying to let my learning from life shape, finesse, and refine my thinking and skills and my approach to life on an ongoing basis.

The practical wisdom of our lived experience requires us to develop a desire to know the truth and to comprehend the deeper meaning and significance of life events as they relate to our inner selves, as well as between ourselves and others. This necessarily includes accepting the positive and negative aspects of human nature, the inherent limits of knowledge, and the propensity of life to be ambiguous, complex, and uncertain. It also requires us to be reflexive and view all phenomena and events from multiple perspectives through self-awareness and insight, the capacity to self-examine, and the ability to develop compassion for ourselves and others (Ardelt, 2004, 2005).

For Aristotle, critical to the development of virtue is the need to develop "practical wisdom," and at the heart of wisdom, is "knowing how to live well" (Aristotle, 2004). Similarly, Socrates said that "the unexamined life is not worth living" (Brickhouse & Smith, 1994, p. 201). Both philosophers implied that all experiences, good, bad, or indifferent, have value in them in the context of developing a wisdom about the circumstances of our life. Similarly, the Chinese philosopher Confucius said that, by three methods, we may learn wisdom—first, by reflection which is the noblest; second, by imitation which is the easiest; and third, by experience, which is the bitterest (Confucius, 1971). For most of us, wisdom arises from our lived experiences accompanied by our ability to reflect upon those same experiences to find value, purpose and meaning.

DOI: 10.4324/9781003499510-16

In this context, even the most difficult and unpleasant experiences have value embedded within them. For Joseph Campbell, that value extended beyond meaning and purpose:

> People say that what we're all seeking is a meaning for life. I don't think that's what we're really seeking. I think that what we're seeking is an experience of being alive, so that our life experiences on the purely physical plane will have resonances with our own innermost being and reality, so that we actually feel the rapture of being alive.
>
> *(Campbell, 1991)*

In this chapter, we explore the definitions of practical wisdom from western and eastern perspectives and briefly reflect upon what both Aristotle and the Buddha had to say about it. We then explore practical wisdom as transformation, as well as the basis of meaning and purpose through youth, reflection, ageing, and legacy. We also consider how practical wisdom can arise from adversity and inform our resilience, positive adaptation and reshape how we view adversity.

Defining practical wisdom

Western perspectives

Traditionally, wisdom has been categorised in western philosophy as theoretical and practical: *sophia* and *phronesis*. Prior to the middle of the 17th century, philosophy took a profound interest in the understanding of wisdom (*phronesis*) and its relationship with happiness (*eudaimonia*), largely from the writings of Aristotle. However, with the birth of the age of western Enlightenment and modernity, philosophy shifted its focus on wisdom to the pursuit of truth and usefulness (Gaukroger, 2006). Since then, much of modern western thought has tended to presuppose that wisdom is "theoretical" and based principally upon knowledge as justified, true and believable through the scientific method, rather than through lived experience.

Some western scholars argue that wisdom cannot be held by an individual but exists only as an expert knowledge system within culture, doctrine, and other artefacts. This is largely premised upon the argument that these knowledges exist far beyond the human mind's capacity to cognise and retain. They also suggest that people cannot be wiser than these collective works of knowledge (Baltes & Staudinger, 2000; Kunzmann & Baltes, 2003; Staudinger & Baltes, 1996). If this is true, then historical figures, such as Gautama Siddhartha (the Buddha), Jesus of Nazareth, and the prophet Muhammad could not have progressed past what was already known during their time (Ardelt, 2004). But clearly, they did.

The Buddha, Jesus, and Muhammad, as lived examples, all received informal or formal education. They also inquired deeply within the context of their faiths, cultures, traditions, and lived experiences before ultimately moving beyond them to discover "truths" that, some 2500, 2000 and 1500 years later, respectively, many of the world's people still speak of and reflect deeply upon. That is not to suggest that anyone today could achieve such profound insights, but it does suggest that they exemplified pathways to wisdom by studying and learning about, reflecting, musing, meditating upon, drawing inspiration from, and experiencing, life. As Jacob Needleman—American philosopher, author, and religious scholar—argues, all the teachings agree that our capacity to live meaningfully, wisely and compassionately depends entirely on our openness to the higher reaches of the inner world (Applebaum & Needleman, 1990).

Undoubtedly, in a western context, the pursuit of knowledge has resulted in great technological advances that have benefited humanity. However, these same pursuits, with the absence of a more sophisticated understanding of wisdom, have also produced serious existential harms, such as global weaponry, pollution, warming, and the depletion of finite resources that further knowledge alone cannot solve (Beck, 1992; Maxwell, 2013). For example, over the course of the 20th century, the Intelligence Quotient (IQ) of the world rose on average around 0.3 points per year, resulting in a 30-point increase in global intelligence (Flynn, 2016). This has had a profound effect on education standards and our ability to increase our skills to compete within a globalised marketplace, but it has done little to alleviate large scale global challenges, such as income disparity, climate change, poverty, and violence. While intelligence can be viewed as a measure of adaptive capacity, often such capacity is developed at the expense of others rather than for the mutual benefit of oneself along with other individuals, the environment, and entire societies (Sternberg, 2019).

Eastern perspectives

Unlike western Enlightenment thought, eastern thought still regards direct human experience as an equal partner with theoretical knowledge in achieving wisdom. While limitations to knowledge are viewed by the west as troublesome and a frontier to be crossed, the east sees limitations as the realisation of a truth (Baggani, 2018). One of India's greatest poets, Rabindranath Tagore (2016), once wrote that "truth loves its limits, for there it meets the beautiful." For Tagore, sitting with limitation was to sit with our humanness—our capacity to love, be vulnerable, feel, make meaning, and find purpose. Rather than something to be conquered, limitation was something to experience in all its beauty.

Similarly, other scholars argue that intellectual or theoretical knowledge is just that—knowledge. It can only become wisdom when it has been "experienced" by "realising" the truth of that profound knowledge. It is only when the individual is moved, changed or transformed that she becomes wise (Ardelt, 2004). Thus, wisdom transcends the intellect and the cognitive mechanics and pragmatics of our minds that, in themselves, while allowing us to have "knowledge," cannot grant "wisdom' without us "being" wise through transformational experience (Holliday & Chandler, 1986; Moody, 1986; Naranjo, 1972).

As the Chinese scholar, professor and philosopher Wing-Tsit Chan says, "Knowledge is also one's own adventure" (Wing-Tsit, 1967, p. 144), and it can occur even in the most adverse of circumstance. "Situations like death, illness, aging, irremediable oppression or loss, extreme poverty, rightful resistance or rebellion, guilt, absolute failure, danger, and uncontrollable fear, lead to the natural emergence of a transcendental self, if they do not destroy the person first. In the spiritual traditions, this is often regarded as "the ascetic way" to enlightenment" (Pascual-Leone, 2000, p. 247).

However, mere experience or practice alone is unlikely to lead to wisdom. Practice generally requires a deliberative effort to improve, reflect, seek feedback and mentoring, and sustain effort over time (Ericsson et al., 2006, 2007). Further still, such deliberative effort requires a life-long commitment to learning from our experiences. As stated in Judaism, "the wise man learns from every phrase he hears, from every event he observes, and from every experience he shares" (Hoffman, 1985, p. 94). Therefore, lived experience, seen as phenomenological metaphysics or the study of the structure of the world of experience, is existential not scientific, and forms an integral part of developing wisdom. And while Enlightenment philosophers such as Immanuel Kant argued that, while metaphysics was no longer a valid way of understanding the world "as it really is," it was still a valid way of explaining how the world appears to us (Baggani, 2018). "There will always be metaphysics in the world, and what is more, in every human being, and especially the reflective ones" (Kant & Hatfield, 1997, p. 118).

In short, knowledge and experience and the metaphysics that help us interpret those experiences cannot be independent. Intellect alone leads us to extreme limitations. Collapsing the distinction between knowing and doing is critical to eastern philosophy. Our innermost experiences extend far beyond our intellect, which wants to see everything physical or psychological analysed, determined, and defined. However, our innermost experiences cannot be dealt with in this way (Suzuki, 1971). In other words, true and complete awareness is not merely intellectual but actively *experiential* (Carter, 2013, p. 28). That said, to rely solely upon our own knowledge and life experiences without reference points of timeless wisdom, as taught, for example, by the sages, is to perpetuate our own ignorance. While many philosophers have reinforced the need for both theoretical and practical wisdom, two prominent advocates, one western and one eastern, were Aristotle and the Buddha.

Aristotle and *phronesis*

Aristotle is regarded as one of the earliest thinkers to explore and express *arête* (excellence) as a theory of virtue and its relationship to *eudemonia* or "human flourishing" as the means for achieving our full potential as human beings (Arjoon, 2000). Achieving *arête* or excellence was obtained through *phronesis*—the intellectual virtue translated as "practical wisdom," "prudence" or simply "good sense." *Phronesis* allowed an individual to determine the "golden mean" when faced with difficult or complex dilemmas, such as the tension between compassion and justice, which was developed over time and with lived experience (Aristotle, 2004).

For Aristotle, all experiences in life, fortunate or unfortunate, gave rise to the opportunity to practice and express virtue. The more a virtue was practiced with wisdom, the more expertise was developed in the individual and collective conduct and meaning of life (Baltes & Staudinger, 2000). *Phronesis* also provided an alternative wisdom to theoretical wisdom (*sophia*), proposed by Socrates and Plato, that sought to define universal truth. For Aristotle, while theoretical wisdom enabled practical wisdom to distinguish true insight from self-conceit and reasonable deliberation from fantasy (Jonkers, 2020), it was too abstract and context-independent to meet context-dependent choices (Kemmis, 2012; Schwartz & Sharpe, 2010). In other words, and this is a criticism often levelled at philosophy more broadly, it could be too theoretical to be of any practical use.

Aristotelian *phronesis* re-emerged in western scholarship approximately 70 years ago across a wide array of fields outside of philosophy and religion, including political science, geography, and planning theory (Xiang, 2016). As a categorisation of knowledge, *phronesis* (phronetic knowledge) can be described as "the practical wisdom that emerge(s) from having an intimate familiarity of what would work in particular settings and circumstances" (Schram et al., 2013, p. 369). That is to say, a wise person uses theoretical knowledge of the common good and moral principles that follow, knowing that they cannot adequately address all moral decisions in contingent situations.

They combine this knowledge with their own lived experience as a thoroughly human being, someone who remains within the bounds of a human life, to help determine the common good for themselves and others within a given context (Jonkers, 2020; Nussbaum, 1986). The practical wisdom of our lived experience requires us to develop a desire to know the truth and to comprehend the deeper meaning and significance of life events as they relate to our inner selves, as well as between ourselves and others. This necessarily includes accepting the positive and negative aspects of human nature, the inherent limits of knowledge, and the propensity of life to be ambiguous, complex and uncertain. It also requires us to be reflexive and view all phenomena and events from multiple perspectives through self-awareness and insight, the capacity to self-examine, and the ability to develop compassion for others (Ardelt, 2004, 2005).

The Buddha and *prajñā*

In Buddhism, wisdom is defined as a virtuous, intelligent mind that realises what is meaningful to achieve genuine happiness, and includes virtues such as faith, compassion, patience, kindness, and tolerance. The Buddha placed great emphasis on lived experience and reflection as the ultimate teacher of what it meant to be happy and what it meant to suffer (Bhikkhu, 2000). By checking our minds through meditative practice and mindfulness applied to our lived experience, we could distinguish between objects of virtue that led to happiness and objects of non-virtue that led to suffering (Gyatso, 2014). A simple example would be the distinction between patience (virtue) and anger (non-virtue).

The distinction between virtue and non-virtue was to be found in the Dharma (theoretical wisdom) taught by the Buddha as encapsulated in the Four Noble Truths: The truth of suffering (First Noble Truth); The truth of the origin of suffering (Second Noble Truth); The truth of the cessation of suffering and the origin of suffering (Third Noble Truth); and the truth of the path that leads to the cessation of suffering and the origin of suffering (Fourth Noble Truth). The Fourth Noble Truth outlined the Eightfold Path that was constituted by ethics (right speech, right action and right livelihood); concentration (right effort, right mindfulness, right concentration); and wisdom (right view, right thought) (Gyatso, 2006; Tsering, 2005).

From a Buddhist perspective, achieving genuine happiness is achieved through the cessation of suffering, which principally relies upon the ethics of compassion and wisdom. The more we come to understand compassion, the more ethical we become as people, and the more ethical we become as people, the happier we become. This form of happiness is not to be found in a fleeting pause of the pervasive sufferings within our lives, but in a genuine happiness that displaces suffering altogether so that it does not return (Thich, 1999, 2014).

Compassion by its very definition includes being able to see (including sensing and feeling) clearly the suffering of another sentient being and taking whatever action is available to us, with wisdom, to prevent or alleviate that suffering. As such, we must necessarily consider our capacity to genuinely understand, with wisdom, what either helps or harms others and commit to building that capacity over time through lived experience guided by Dharma (theoretical wisdom). Importantly, our compassionate ethic cannot be imposed by others from the outside but must be realised from the inside as a transformational process (Tsering, 2005). Buddhist philosophy simply understood as an intellectual exercise without lived experience (including meditation and mindfulness) is of little, if any, benefit to our genuine sense of wisdom (Gyatso, 2014).

Deriving practical wisdom from meaning and purpose

The capacity to either create or derive meaning and purpose from our lived experiences is uniquely human (Gilbert, 2022). Having meaning in life is about making sense of and seeing the significance of our lived experiences, as well as having a life purpose. Numerous studies have shown that meaning and purpose are protective factors when facing adversity by demonstrating links with lower levels of depression, anxiety and stress, as well as greater life satisfaction (Fullerton et al., 2021). As living, thinking, feeling, intellectual beings, we cannot tolerate a meaningless life. To live properly, we need meaning to navigate our pleasures and pains as well as our joys and our sufferings. As the German philosopher Fredrick Nietzsche wrote, "He who has a why to live for can bear with almost any how" (Nietzsche, 1997). For Nietzsche, understanding profoundly the meaning and purpose of our life allowed us to develop our wisdom about how to overcome life's difficulties, but without meaning and purpose, we risked descending into the abyss.

Nietzsche also introduced the Latin term "*amor fati*," translated as "love of fate." On this insight from Nietzsche, Joseph Campbell (1991) argued that whatever our fate is, we should view it as an experience that will be beneficial to us, even if it looks disastrous. Rather than only viewing it as a negative, we reframe it as an opportunity or challenge by bringing love—not discouragement—for Self and Other into the experience. If we can survive it, it will help shape our character and improve our life. And to Kant's earlier point, if we are reflective, we will see that these events have helped shape our lives in positive, often profound ways that we could not have envisaged prior to experience. We may perceive these events as only negative at the time in which we experience them, but over time, we discern the positive benefits that help us to realise who we are as compassionate sentient beings.

Similarly, for the German psychoanalyst Carl Jung, meaning was to be found not only within the light of our lived experiences (joys and pleasures), but also in the darkness (pains and sufferings). It was in the dark recesses of our minds that we discovered what truly shined (Jung, 1967). Jung argued that, to find meaning in our life, we needed to make the darkness of our minds conscious, integrate the shadow of our personality, go through dark places, and walk to the light at the end: "No tree, it is said, can grow to heaven unless its roots reach down to hell" (Jung & Hull, 2014). According to Jung, this was uncomfortable for those influenced by western traditions, and this is still true today. Modern western liberal democracies continue to "chase the light" and "ignore the shadow." If we only seek meaning and purpose from those things that we think bring happiness, we risk falling into a relentless pursuit to find meaning that is ultimately futile, as it is in the shadows of our minds that our suffering arises as well as where the greatest meaning resides.

As we touched on in Chapter 4, eastern philosophy views suffering as inherent in life and something that needs to be accepted before something can be done about it, including how it is perceived. Finding strength and deriving meaning and purpose from our lived experiences helps us to find our power to create a world that works for us—a world where happiness arises despite seemingly adverse circumstances.

We derive our practical wisdom from meaning and purpose in myriad ways throughout the course of our life, and while it is not possible to capture all of these ways, there are four examples that various philosophers and scholars advocated that might help guide us in this understanding:

- Reflecting upon our youth (Sir Ken Robinson)
- Looking backward while living forward (Soren Kierkegaard)
- Growing old (Simone De Beauvoir and Yuval Harari)
- Leaving legacy (Ralf Waldo Emerson)

Reflecting upon our youth

For many people, meaning and purpose can exhibit itself at a young age, whether or not it is realised by us or others. In his best-selling book, *The element: How finding your passion changes everything,* Ken Robinson (2009) tells the story of a young girl who simply did not fit into society in the way that most of us are expected to fit in. In school, she was unable to settle, constantly chatted, and fidgeted, and often disrupted the class. The school decided that she must have had what we would refer to today as ADHD and sent her off to a psychologist. In short, the school was hoping that she would be referred to a "special school" to remove her as a distracting influence. The young girl went to the psychologist with her parents. He asked her and her parents lots of questions while concentrating on everything she said and did. This made her feel uncomfortable but, on some level, she knew this man was important to her.

After about 20 minutes, the psychologist put on some music and asked the young girl to wait while he and her parents went out of the room to talk in private. The young girl, thinking that her parents and the psychologist were unable to see her (when in fact they could through a small window in the door of the office), began to dance with grace and expression of pleasure. The psychologist turned to her parents and said, "She isn't sick, she's a dancer. Take her to a dance school!" This young girl was Gillian Lynne who went on to dance for the Royal Ballet Company and eventually choreographed the Andrew Lloyd Webber musicals *Cats* and *The Phantom of the Opera.*

Old ways of thinking and being

I have always been touched by this story (and many others like it) because it says something about our society. A society that continues to insist, albeit more subtly than the days prior to the Enlightenment, that we be, think and do things a certain way. According to Ken Robinson, this occurs for many reasons. Some of those reasons include the need to comply with a narrow set of expectations built around an industrialised and capitalised society, under-pinned by a sense of duty to follow rules, and the need to live a life of "thou shalt/I should" (Campbell, 2001).

Much of this influence is reinforced by an education system that is designed to meet the economic interests of our modern western societies that pref-erences, for example, STEM subjects (Science, Technology, English, Maths) while pushing aside "any sort of activity that involves the heart, the body, the senses, and a good proportion of our brains" (Robinson, 2009). In so doing, we tend to maintain a narrow view of intelligence while overvaluing certain "rational" talents and abilities. This narrow approach has the effect of margin-alising all of those who are not adept at learning in this way.

One of the great privileges of being in senior executive leadership and management for so many years is that I have the opportunity to mentor peo-ple, sometimes through formal university Executive Master programmes, but more often than not, through chance meetings and unfolding conversations that lead to requests for mentoring. Without exception, all those that I men-tor are incredibly talented people who are genuinely not only trying, but making a difference to the world in which they live. While all of them are uniquely following their life path and the talents that they bring, they also share a common ethic of caring about what they do, seeking to ensure that they are effective in the world, and perhaps most importantly, having a genu-ine concern for others.

They also share a common story—a story that very few people ever get to hear. Each one of these great people brought a gift to the world as a young child, but for most of them, the world could not see it. The world was too caught up in "thou shalt/I should!" As a result, often they were told that they were "too sensitive." One of my dear friends recalls that she took this so seri-ously that she thought she "should" join the army to toughen up! She went on to become a successful social worker with a penchant for working in pallia-tive care. Another, as a young boy without the skills to master his sensitivity, became bullied and had to fight his way out of his childhood. Fortunately, he was able to combine his sensitivity to the suffering of others with his ability to fight and became a professional firefighter.

Don't give up on realising and sharing your gift

The comparative mythologist Joseph Campbell (1991, 2001) often said that if we did not follow our "bliss," that thing that makes our heart sing, the thing that brings meaning and purpose to our world, then we were living in the wasteland of "thou shalt/I should." He also said that we should "follow our bliss and the universe will open doors where there were only walls," and the money would come. That the pursuit of wealth at the expense of meaning and purpose was the wrong path, but that living in accordance with the gift(s) that we brought to this world would eventually lead either to a fulfilling vocation or career, or our vocation or career would support us in achieving our purpose.

In Hinduism, such a gift is referred to as one's Dharma or purpose in life. The need for, the effect of, and the essence of service and interconnectedness of all life. That is, our capacity, through our unique gifts, to participate meaningfully through everything we think, say or do in the world that presents before us to discover truth (Hacker, 2006; Lipner, 2019). This is a deeply held truth that some have had the opportunity to realise, while, due to a range of circumstances, others have not. Life is not always fair and for some, while they brought a gift, they feel as though they have not had the opportunity to bring it to the world in a way that would benefit themselves and others.

If this is you, I would say this: Have another look. I think you will find that, despite your external circumstances, your gift is still available to the world, although you may not realise it. These external circumstances, including a world that cannot see your gift due to the need for "thou shalt," cannot constrain it. If you are not sure what it is, ask a trusted person who knew you well as a child. If that is not available to you, reflect on your childhood with wisdom, patience and kindness, and you will see it. Except this time, rather than denying it or living through "thou shalt/I should," use your wisdom or find a trusted person who can help you to bring it into the world. It is a gift the world desperately needs. It is never too late, trust me.

Looking backward while living forward

Soren Kierkegaard was a Danish philosopher who lived in the 19th century and is widely acclaimed to be the first existential philosopher. He was also a theologian, poet, social critic, and religious author who had a fondness for metaphor, irony, and parables (myths). Much of his philosophical work addressed issues of how we live as a single individual in a world that fundamentally lacks any inherent meaning. A world that, ironically, without meaning, appears absurd and evokes within us a sense of disorientation, confusion or dread. Kierkegaard's point was that we each had the privilege of personal choice about how we interpreted the world and brought meaning to our experiences with wisdom, as well as the opportunity to be committed to those things in life that were important to us passionately, sincerely and authentically (Hannay, 2018).

Choosing our experiences

One of the great privileges of being human is our capacity to choose what we think, although for many, this is an unconscious insight. Through societal and cultural conditioning, we are taught to think and act in certain ways in response to some sort of stimulus, whether it be mental, physical or both. For many people, the response to that stimulus appears in their mind to be almost automatic. That is, without choice. Of course, if that stimulus was real or perceived as life threatening, then an automatic response would be essential. In these circumstances, it is often referred to as either the fight or flight response (Haidt, 2021). We all possess it, and it is fundamental to our physical survival.

However, leaving aside real or perceived life-threatening situations, we often respond automatically to other "metaphorical" life-threatening situations in a similar manner, except in these circumstances the life under threat is not our physical life, but the life of our ego. To put it another way, we often personalise the circumstances in which we find ourselves, making everything mean something about us. Something happens in the external world, and we instantaneously make it mean something about us in the internal world of our minds. Notwithstanding, according to existential philosophers such as Soren Kierkegaard, external circumstances have no independent meaning separate from the meaning we bring to them.

To demonstrate, I have a good friend who, back in 1983, lost their family home in the Ash Wednesday bushfires in Victoria, Australia. His family consisted of himself, his sister and his father. The meaning my friend brought to the loss of the house was to be reflective, sentimental and philosophical. The meaning his sister brought to the loss was to be devastated, deeply scarred and forever fearful of future fires. His father brought a stoic pragmatism to the loss and simply started designing a new house—one that he always wanted to build. So, one fire, one house lost, three very different meaning making experiences.

The same can be said of all experiences. We bring an array of influences to our thoughts, including our feelings, discriminations, values, beliefs, knowledge, experiences, faith, and morality. And while some of these influences maybe deeply ingrained, they are nonetheless lacking any independent reality. They are created by our minds, and so, to Kierkegaard's point, we can utilise these influences to help us choose, with wisdom, what presenting circumstances mean to us.

Similarly, the Buddha said that all adversities were opportunities to exhibit virtue, such as patience in the face of anger, kindness in the face of disservice, generosity in the face of greed, and so on. It was our perspective of our circumstances that made the difference between them feel pleasant, neutral, or unpleasant. Aristotle said similar things. Each advocated that the development of our virtue was contingent upon the learning that we took from the collective experiences of our lives. Aristotle called it *phronesis*. The Buddha called it *prajñā*. Both words essentially mean "wisdom" (Keown, 1992).

Power in reflection

Kierkegaard advocated that all experiences evoke feelings, and they too need to be honoured. The point of deriving insight from our experiences was not to rationalise away our feelings, but rather to honour them fully and, over time—sometimes a long time—come to understand what it is they taught us from a deeper sense of self through reflection. Over time, the meaning that we bring to those experiences would change, sometimes radically, often subtly (Hannay, 2018). This is a good thing. It means that we are finding the deeper purpose to the experience and the opportunity to find the "gold amongst the dust."

Among the complexity of adversity lies a blessing that only a mind of wisdom can come to realise. By reflecting upon the previous experiences of our lives over time, we come to understand what those experiences have meant to us, how they have shaped who we perceive ourselves to be, and with wisdom, to take from those valuable experiences a deeper understanding of what is important to us passionately, sincerely, and authentically. It also allows us the opportunity to claim back our power, particularly when the experiences were adverse and painful (Frankl, 1959).

The things that shape us

The past, however, is not a place to dwell nor reside. It is the place from which to learn so that we can move forward into the future with greater confidence and competence that we have gained the skills we need to continue navigating our lives in a way that honours and further nurtures those things we are most passionate, sincere, and authentic about. If we look back upon our lives with wisdom, we will come to realise that not a minute has been wasted. Every experience, whether good, bad, or indifferent, has shaped us, crafted our life, and allowed us the opportunity, not to try and solve problems, but to live and experience life fully. These experiences have allowed us to develop our wisdom, and to take back our power to choose. To choose what we genuinely believe to be both wise and beneficial for the greater good of ourselves and others, and to discard the rest. In so doing, we have the opportunity to liberate ourselves from any unnecessary suffering. Suffering that, through the unskilful bringing of meaning to experience, we inadvertently inherited.

Growing old

Does older mean wiser?

There is an old Gaelic proverb that says: "You cannot put a wise head on young shoulders." It suggests that it is only with age that we can develop a wisdom about our life's circumstances. But how true is this? To extend the proverb to our intergenerational experiences over the course of millennia, the question must be asked, "Are we any wiser?" According to historian Yuval Noah Harari (2011), within the span of 70,000 years, we have advanced from an insignificant animal minding our own business in a corner of Africa to viewing ourselves as the master of the entire planet (and sub-consciously the terror of the entire planetary ecosystem). In so doing, he argues we stand on the verge of becoming a god, poised to acquire eternal youth, as well as the divine abilities of creation and destruction. We are actively pursuing genetic and other technologies that in theory, at least, may be able to extend our lives in ways never previously imagined (Harari, 2011).

At the same time, Harari argues that our collective actions are causing the extinction of many non-human species at rates not previously experienced, and these rates are increasing. Even more concerning, despite all our human progress, we remain unsure of our goals, our sense of meaning and purpose, and we appear as discontented as ever. Even as nations compete to inhabit the planet Mars, we still have no collective sense of where we are heading. Despite being more powerful than ever before in our 70,000-year history, we still do not know how to channel our power in ways that are mutually beneficial and sustainable for our fragile planetary ecosystem. Harari concludes by asking, "Is there anything more dangerous than dissatisfied and irresponsible gods who don't know what they want?" (Harari, 2011).

Harari's insight suggests there is a contradiction in our dominant collective thinking. Some of us appear to want to live endlessly in this realm of existence and in our current bodily form driven by our fear of death and insatiable desire for life, but we do not know where we are heading and why. It all sounds very dissatisfying to me. It certainly seems to suggest the eternal perpetuation of suffering and discomfort. It also suggests no ability to translate that suffering into a genuine sense of meaning and purpose that would otherwise lead us to a sense of wisdom and happiness.

Is old age a problem?

When it comes to the pursuit of eternal youth, one could be forgiven for thinking that old age is a problem, a disease, something to be fixed, or even a state to be avoided. Our current age of disruptive technological innovation and advances in medical science operating within a globalised marketplace has convinced us to spend literally trillions of dollars annually on anti-aging remedies, procedures, and lifestyles to delay our mortality. The drivers for this are numerous and include vanity, excessive self-esteem, and inflated perceptions of self-image. All this stems from a subtle but powerful subconscious thought process that says (and to Harari's key point), "I am very important, I exist independently of everyone else, I will not die today, and the world is there to meet my every desire."

However, rather than seeing aging only as a problem to be avoided, fixed or solved, the inevitability of our mortality invites us to contemplate the distinction between living and existing. We are the only species on the planet that consciously knows that we will die, even though our (deluded) thought process is "I will not die today" (and of which there is no guarantee). All other sentient beings understand death as something to be avoided when threatened, but they are otherwise unaware of their own mortality (Gilbert, 2022). As such, they do not plan the future, nor do they anticipate its potential joys and sorrows. They simply live in the moment and address whatever arises, seeking to avoid their own suffering and find their own happiness.

We on the other hand, do contemplate our mortality. We actively engage in thought processes to create futures driven not only by our desire to avoid suffering and achieve happiness (which we share with all other living beings), but to create and contemplate a life of meaning and purpose (which is unique to us as human beings). Put another way, while we are alive at all ages—young, middle-aged, elderly, for example—we derive our existence only through those meaningful experiences, relations and activities that absorb us, that belong to our sense of being. It is our understanding of the inevitability of our death that, over time and with age, facilitates a transformation of our being-in-the-world through our capacity to interpret and reinterpret the history of our lived experiences (Gilbert, 2022).

Growing older as a great adventure

As existentialist philosopher and social theorist Simone de Beauvoir pointed out, old age involves a changed relation with the world and with an individual's own history (Beauvoir, 1972). In other words, as soon as we have an experience, it moves immediately into our past and into our memory. Along the way, the space between something happening and our interpretation of that same something happening (as small as it may seem) allows us to bring meaning and purpose to that experience.

It becomes part of our "unfolding story," our very own mythology—rich in symbolism and insight that can only be appreciated over time as we grow older. This was eloquently described by David Attenborough, in his Netflix documentary *A Life on Our Planet*, when he said, "I am 93 years old. I had the most extraordinary life, but it is only now that I appreciate how extraordinary." Attenborough's insight helps us to understand that we can only know these experiences and how important they are after having lived through them, and as such, aging is necessary for existence and should not be treated as a problem.

My studies in philosophy and mythology, as well as my own lived experiences, taught me profoundly that the two greatest journeys we will ever take in life are coming here and leaving. Being present at the births of my children and being present at the passing of loved ones (and many others throughout my life and career) helped me to realise the "alpha" and the "omega" of the lived experience we call life. It also taught me that the finitude of life in this realm of physical form was indeed a great adventure. That every experience, good, bad, or indifferent, was a chance to develop wisdom about the fundamentals that define the best of our human experience: to live compassionately, to love, and to be loved.

Knowing that we will inevitably pass from this life, and depending upon the basis of our faith, to the next life in whatever form (or not), affords us the opportunity to bring profound meaning and purpose to every experience. It is often said that the greatest teacher of life is death. It demands that we crystalise our thoughts, words and actions towards those things that are truly important and valuable to us (Chodron, 2001b). When things are stable, when we place ourselves above others and at the centre of the world, and when we think we will live forever, what we regard as important and valuable varies widely (Tschakert et al., 2017).

It is also often relatively amorphous and mundane, and perhaps arrogant. But when the potential of death comes knocking, we soon re-channel our focus towards those things that are important to us, and for most of us, ultimately, we arrive at the realisation of the need to love and be loved. As Sebastian Junger observes in his book *War*:

> ...the willingness to die for another person is a form of love that even religions fail to inspire, and the experience of it changes a person profoundly. What the Army sociologists, with their clipboards and their questions and their endless metanalyses, slowly came to understand was that courage was love.
>
> *(Junger, 2010)*

So, if we really want to live endlessly in this realm of existence in our current bodily form and as a god, then we need to discover profoundly and realise fully the power of love towards ourselves, other humans and non-humans, and the entire planetary ecosystem, simultaneously and eternally. However, in the meantime (and I suspect we have eons to go), let us agree that, for most of us, we will die at a time and in a manner not of our choosing, and that before we do, we take away from every lived experience, relationship, and activity, the opportunity to derive a sense of meaning and purpose that adds to the richness of our capacity to show compassion towards ourself and others.

Leaving legacy

Passing on wisdom

While growing old is a privilege, it is also an opportunity to pass on our wisdom to others through the leaving of legacy. The movie *The Best Exotic Marigold Hotel* and its sequel *The Second-Best Exotic Marigold Hotel* both provide poignant imagery and narrative about the uncertainty of life, the timing of our mortality, and the chance to leave a meaningful legacy from which others may benefit.

We often make assumptions in our minds about how long we expect to live, or how long we expect to be healthy, and so on. But there is no guarantee. On one level we know this, but on another level, a deeper level—and as I mentioned in the previous section—we ignore the inevitability of our mortality in favour of "I will not die today." Our minds have a habit of deluding us in ways that may appear helpful but, in reality, work against us.

Assuming, for example, that we will not die today often leads us to putting effort into unimportant, even mundane, or destructive things. It may cause us to treat ourselves and others with indifference, even disrespect and harm. It may also involve putting off until tomorrow those things that are important but can wait because we think we have time (Gyatso, 2006). For most of us, this will end up being true, but for some, the opposite is true. We are all intimately aware of this through witnessing the experiences of others less fortunate. And for those who do end up living a long life, to Kierkegaard's earlier point, we can only know this by looking backwards, not forwards.

Both movies are very much about an older generation that struggles to come to terms with impending mortality along with unmet expectations, missed opportunities, late change in lived experiences and, perhaps more positively, realisations of truth about the meaning and purpose of their lives. In one particular scene, the character played by the esteemed actor Maggie Smith is approached by a gentleman who, in observing her commitment to the younger generation, tells her that he admires her for "planting the seeds of trees under who's shadow one may never sit." I was really captured by this metaphor because of its profound truth about how to approach the "sunset of our lives," whether that is perceived to be long, short, or uncertain.

Important questions

In other words, as we gain more and more a sense of our mortality and its relationship with the uncertainty of its timing and the certainty of its arrival, there are questions which inevitably arise: What legacy do we wish to leave? How would we like to be remembered? What would ease our minds as we move towards the finality of this life? Hopefully, that legacy is oriented, at least in part, towards the benefit of others, whether or not we live to witness that benefit, or perhaps more importantly, whether or not we are ever acknowledged for it.

For those of us who lead formally or informally, tacitly or explicitly, I think these questions are important. As leaders, what we think, say and do matters. And it often matters much more than we give ourselves credit for. So much of what we think, say and do shapes the quality of not only our own lives, but of the lives of those we lead. Today's society is so geared towards efficiency, effectiveness and outcome that the means by which we lead others to achieve these things can either leave a legacy of hope, inspiration and good will, or it can leave a wake of hopelessness, devastation and ill will, not so much by what is trying to be achieved, but the manner in which those achievements are pursued.

Learning from others

A very senior operational leader confided in me about how important it was to hear from those leaders who had gone before him, whom he considered wise. He said that what was important to him was:

> the time spent listening and talking with other leaders and thinking about, not just watching what they have done, but asking them and talking to them about what they've done to understand how and why they've done things and what they would have done differently if they had a second go at anything. I read a lot of biography. I probably read more biographies than any other type of book these days. And not just the biographies of leaders or perceived leadership roles but understanding how people thought about the challenges that they faced and how they tackled them. I think that's really been the other big influence on my leadership.

So, if you hold any position of influence over someone else or a group of others, I will say three things. *Firstly*, your leadership tenure is as uncertain as the tenure of your life. This alone is worthy of great contemplation. *Secondly*, make every thought, word, and action count for the better. Really understand the level of trust and faith people put in you to lead them through an increasingly ambiguous, complex, and uncertain world. Genuinely understand what legacy you leave in every moment of interaction with others. However, imperfect you may be, keep going and develop the courage and confidence to just get better. *Thirdly*, come to understand that the only moment in life you ever have is the one you are in. It is the only moment you have ever had, and it is the only moment you will ever need. For it is only in the present moment, not the past nor the future, do you get the chance to make the difference, leave the legacy, and honour the greatest purpose and meaning of your life.

Deriving practical wisdom from adversity

Implicit in the wisdom of our lived experiences is the inevitable experience of adversity, and with it, the question: how do we respond to it? For example, do we become a victims of circumstance, or do we seek to derive something valuable out of a set of circumstances that would seem anything but pleasant or deserved? This is a difficult question to answer as, in part, it speaks to the tension between personal responsibility and the reasonable expectation of a safer world facilitated by our social institutions. This includes our governments along with the structural, economic, social and other supports that they are obliged to provide through a social contract of shared responsibility.

Without in anyway wishing to diminish the social contract obligations of governments or other social institutions that we have discussed earlier, this section concentrates on how we might respond personally from a position of personal power. How we might take a set of unfortunate circumstances not of our choosing and not deserved and make them mean something that can be regarded as beneficial—a way of helping us maintain a sense of dignity and self-respect while developing our wisdom and compassion in the process.

Many of the leaders that I interviewed expressed the view that much of their own wisdom had been derived from the adverse experiences of their life, rather than seeing themselves as a victim of circumstance. For example, most of these leaders had come to understand the suffering of others through their own experiences of suffering and from those experiences developed their wisdom:

.... As I said with the head injury, I took quite a beating in my life. I had a brilliant director that valued me as a person and my work ethic. So, I was fully supported at getting back to work with my rehab. So that was brilliant. That has been quite integral to my understanding about people's vulnerabilities to some extent. Because before that I didn't. Also valuing life, I've always valued life but also when I came close to dying or being severely disabled, I think that puts another slant on things. I've been a single mom for a long while, so I've always had to be independent and very resilient. Also, I've done some mission work. So, that care for others as well. I've seen horrific circumstances. So, I think all of that, just knowing that I'm so blessed and fortunate, and I can give out to others. I've been blessed with skill sets and wisdom and knowledge so that I can bless others. So, [my lived experiences] really affected how I outlook on life.

Another leader reflected:

I've given you the example of my upbringing with my sisters, but one of them passed away, [and] my experiences with having to deal with cancer on two occasions now, has very much shaped my thinking and that I understand the true vulnerability of the human condition. But I think your life experience is meant to shape you, and if you ignore the lessons that are in there, because we all face adversity in one shape or form, you do so at your peril. We all face suffering in our lives, whether it's us personally or our loved ones or our colleagues. And if you don't heed those lessons, I think you've missed the boat. I'll finish that by saying that wisdom derives from your cognitive intelligence and your life experiences and learning from those life experiences. In my view, wisdom should increase with the amount of life experiences that you have. Sometimes it equates and sometimes it doesn't.

While these reflections are only a small sample of how leaders have viewed adversity, the data showed that there were three recurring and interrelated factors: resilience, adversity, and positive adaptation. Interestingly, these three interrelated factors are also identified in the literature on psychological resilience.

Resilience, adversity, and positive adaptation

Resilience

During the past three decades, over a dozen theories of resilience have been proposed by various researchers (including the debate as to whether resilience is a trait, process, or outcome); and, although there are many differences, a number of common features emerge. These include that resilience is a dynamic process that changes over time; within the process itself the interaction of a wide range of factors determines whether we are able to demonstrate resilience; and, perhaps most importantly, there is a need for lucidity in defining two pivotal concepts related to resilience being "adversity" and "positive adaptation" (Fletcher & Sarkar, 2013).

These two concepts are reflected in a number of proposed definitions (implicit and/or explicit) for individual resilience. These definitions include: our ability as adults in otherwise normal situations who are exposed to an isolated and highly disruptive event, such as death or a violent situation, to maintain relatively stable and healthy levels of psychological and physical functioning (Bonanno, 2004); our capacity to rebound from adversity, misfortune, trauma, or other transitional crises strengthened and more resourceful (McCubbin et al., 1997); a dynamic process encompassing positive adaptation despite challenging or threatening circumstances (Masten et al., 1990); a dynamic process encompassing positive adaptation within the context of significant adversity (Luthar et al., 2000); or our ability to resist the negative effects of adversity and instead seek to attain positive adaptation, rather than resist the adversity itself (Windle, 2011).

Adversity

A general definition of adversity includes any hardship and suffering that we may experience that is linked to difficulty, misfortune, or trauma (Jackson et al., 2007). This could include such things as major health impacts, poverty and economic disadvantage, divorce, depression, exposure to natural disasters and terrorist attacks, and major loss and bereavement (Fletcher & Sarkar, 2013; Windle, 2011). Often, we can experience psychological trauma from traumatic experiences. However, importantly, not all experiences are traumatic. Trauma involves the threat or perceived threat to our life (APA, 2001) and may also involve a negative experience outside the usual realm of human experience, such as losing loved ones, losing our possessions, or not having our hopeful futures fulfilled. These experiences can often leave us feeling helpless, afraid, and/or out of control. In the more severe cases, these experiences may negatively affect our mental health to the extent that we suffer from Post-Traumatic Stress Disorder. This includes re-experiencing the trauma through flashbacks, avoiding or withdrawing from people and situations reminiscent of the trauma, and hyper-arousal (Smith, 2004).

However, while traditionally it has been argued that adversity (negative life circumstances) impedes positive adaptation, research now suggests that people with a history of some lifetime adversity reported better mental health and well-being outcomes than people with no history of adversity (Seery et al., 2010). In some circumstances, in moderation, exposure to adversity can mobilise previously untapped resources, help engage social support networks, and create a sense of mastery for future adversities (Meichenbaum, 1985).

Adversity and trauma can also be understood as an essentially spiritual experience because it forces us to re-examine previously held values and worldviews whether or not we subscribe to certain religious beliefs (Decker, 1993). What we believe about why things happen and why they happen in the larger scheme of things is the essence of our spirituality (Angell et al., 1998). One operational leader reflected:

> I think (lived experience) influences (wisdom) a lot. But, at some point, you also have to recognise that you can change and break free of previously held assumptions and beliefs. For example, I grew up in a very religious sort of household. Sort of right-wing Christian sort of thing. And I was indoctrinated in that. But I now have a much more laissez faire view of religion of faith today. I've probably even gone more sort of the other way. I probably sit in the more agnostic space. Again that's because of my own education. Not because I've necessarily been influenced by others. But I've learned myself based on facts, science and other exposures. And it is nothing to do with a religious debate, it's more to do with the fact that you can change

your point of view and your preferences in your deeply held beliefs through education, through exposures, to fact, to seeing how changes can happen with people.

Positive adaptation

Positive adaptation is concerned with understanding the developmental processes that help us to favourably adjust our cognitive and behavioural patterns when having to experience adversity (Mahoney & Bergman, 2002). Positive adaptation also concerns our ability to behaviourally manifest a level of social competence or success at meeting the required tasks to manage through adversity (Luthar et al., 2000). This includes our capacity to manifest features related to internal well-being and happiness (Masten & Obradović, 2006), providing these features align with the intensity of adversity in terms of competence from mastery at lower levels to average levels for higher intensities (Fletcher & Sarkar, 2013). Put simply, positive adaptation is the ability to positively adjust our thoughts, behaviours, and emotions to sustain our mental and physical health and well-being in response to changing or uncertain circumstances (Fullerton et al., 2021).

For example, in his study of holocaust survivors, Israeli American sociologist Professor Aaron Antonovsky discovered that, for those who had remained well despite having gone through horrible experiences, their resilience emerged from a pervasive, enduring though dynamic feeling of confidence. This feeling of confidence stemmed from being able to view the world as *comprehensible* (rational, understandable, consistent and predictable), *manageable* (albeit challenging) and *meaningful* (things are worth making commitments for). In addition, it was this individual resilience that was responsible for the post traumatic growth that was encountered in people who had managed to survive a crisis, disaster or trauma (Eachus, 2014). These findings were extended to the analysis of the aftermath of Hurricane Katrina. In this case study, it was found that resilience was the capacity of people to anticipate, withstand, and judiciously engage with catastrophic experiences, and actively make positive meaning out of adversity while maintaining "normal" function without fundamental loss of identity (Almedom, 2013).

From these findings three distinctions arose: *anticipation, meaning making*, and *identity*. When unfolding realities posed threats to a person's anticipated future of survival, many people used their cognitive capacity to imagine and change their realities by conceiving new possibilities that in turn created new anticipations for a hopeful and positive future (Bennett, 1996). For many, they were able to deduce positive meaning from the experiences that helped shape their identity through a sense of duty or obligation to come to the assistance of others during times of crisis and in anticipation of adversity (Flynn, 2008). That is to say, when they acted with compassion, their sense of meaning and purpose positively increased towards happiness.

Seeing the suffering and trauma of another human or non-human being can often motivate us to act in such a way as to alleviate their distress. In so doing, we alleviate our own. By thinking, speaking and acting in ways that benefit others, we discover a sense of meaning and purpose that extends beyond self-interest. By moving past self-interest towards interest in others, we find ourselves feeling more positive, alive, and purposeful.

Choosing how we see adversity

Some scholars argue that trauma is not what happens to us but the way we (choose to) see what happens. In this context, trauma is not in itself a pathological event but a pathologised image within our mind that has become intolerable. Therefore, they argue that if these images cause illness and trauma, then wellness and recovery arise from imagination, or in other words, mentally constructed positive meaning and purpose (Hillman, 1983). Put another way, we could reframe our thought process from "life happens *to* us" to "life happens *for* us." Here, narrative theory provides the basis for alternative views and positive meaning by connecting actions with intentions in a manner that gives meaning to personally experienced events. Our intentions become goals or ideals that are future oriented signposts and are altered only when here-and-now behaviours and thoughts are changed, and often it is adversity that motivates such change.

The narrative that we put to an adverse experience becomes a constantly revised account of the event that collapses the past, present, and future into a moment of reflection. The shifting of the story over time as greater meaning is brought to the experience, based upon reflection and learning, provides access to new solutions. This assists in alleviating the trauma and opens up new possibilities for the future which can be experienced individually and collectively (Parry & Doan, 1994). For example, significant losses often serve as turning points in the lives of individuals and communities. These turning points can lead to new perspectives on the meaning of what is important in life and the crisis of loss may be viewed as a potential opportunity to reshape what and who we perceive as valued and valuable (Bull, 1992; Tschakert et al., 2017).

As the German philosopher Fredrich Nietzsche said, "that which does not kill you makes you stronger" (Nietzsche & Hollingdale, 1990). This is not to say that adversity and the resulting harms are okay, deserved, or to be legitimated in some overly rationalistic way. As a basic human principle, intentionally harming oneself or another sentient being is not acceptable, but due to constraints such as human fallibility and moral hypocrisy, harm does exist and must be navigated. But leaving this argument aside, it is important for us to know and understand that the transformational nature of adversity can be a spiritual process of discovery of the true nature of our identities.

When reflecting upon all my own experiences with personal adversity, I came to understand something which I believe to be fundamental to our human experience. The *specific circumstances* in which I found myself were *unique to the world* in time and space: the world had not previously witnessed nor experienced them at the time and place in which they occurred. Those same specific circumstances were *unique in my experience*: they had not occurred previously in my life. However, paradoxically, *the world profoundly understood my experience of the unique circumstances* in which the world and I found ourselves.

Our lived experiences of unique and often very private circumstances are genuinely understood by our mythologies, philosophies, and theologies, as well as our art, music, poetry, theatre, and literature. These and other great bodies of knowledge are critical to helping us understand who we are becoming and what we are capable of as wise and compassionate people.

From my own experiences of loss and suffering I would say this: Our circumstances show us something about ourselves that we may not yet be conscious of or comfortable with. That something will inevitably be about our capacity to feel and the ability to think, speak and act with virtue towards self and others. To feel love. To be compassionate. To show kindness. To be considerate. To be patient. To suspend judgement. To be truthful. To be trusted. To have integrity. And the list goes on.

Such transformations are not easy. They are physically, emotionally and spiritually challenging and confronting and they need kindness, care and understanding. They also need compassion. So, if you know someone going through a transformation, do the best you can to hold space with them and, to the extent to which you are able, offer them any help you can. If you are the one navigating transformation, be kind to yourself. Understand profoundly that many have walked this path before you, that you are genuinely not alone, and that help is never too far away.

Seek out the great bodies of knowledge that speak to your experience. Learn to trust their insights. Get to know them in a way that eases your anxieties and inspires your journey. Seek those who can speak to them with wisdom. Surrender any notion of fixed ideas or beliefs that no longer serve you well but seek wise insights beyond your own limited beliefs. As time progresses, you will genuinely discover that the original circumstances and the related experience taught you something. Something you needed to know. Something that helped you find your truth.

The challenge for leaders

As leaders, we might think about what gifts we brought with us as a child, what life has taught us so far in relation to the development of our virtues, how we have changed as we have grown older, and what legacy we wish to leave for others as a way of accessing the practical wisdom of our lived experience. We may also want to think about how we have positively adapted from our experiences of adversity, transformed over time, shaped our narratives about those experiences, and how our experiences have redefined our lives towards being more relational, compassionate and virtuous.

These are all existential questions that may take us a long time to contemplate and answer. And those answers will almost certainly change over time as we reflect, have more experiences, and develop greater wisdom as a result. This process of regularly asking ourselves these questions and reflecting upon our answers will add a richness to our life and significantly contribute towards our capacity to show self-compassion, as well as compassion towards others who have directly or indirectly shared in our experiences. It will also contribute substantially towards our relatedness with those we lead, serve and protect.

To help find the depth of our wisdom derived from our lived experiences in order to answer these and other questions, we would do well to deepen our understanding and practice of mindfulness, and it is to this practice that we now turn to in the next chapter.

References

Almedom, A. M. (2013). Resilience: Outcome, process, emergence, narrative (OPEN) theory. *On the Horizon, 21*(1), 15–23. https://doi.org/10.1108/10748121311297030

Angell, G., Dennis, B., & Dumain, L. (1998). Spirituality, resilience, and narrative: Coping with parental death. *Families in Society, 79*(6), 615–630. https://doi.org/10.1606/1044-3894.865

APA. (2001). *Diagnostic and Statistical Manual, Version IV-TR*. Washington DC.

Applebaum, D., & Needleman, J. (1990). *Real philosophy: An anthology of the universal search for meaning*. Arkana.

Ardelt, M. (2004). Wisdom as expert knowledge system: A critical review of a contemporary operationalization of an ancient concept. *Human Development, 47*(5), 257–285. https://www.sciencegate.app/document/10.1159/000079154

Ardelt, M. (2005). How wise people cope with crises and obstacles in life. *ReVision, 28*(1), 7–19. https://doi.org/10.3200/REVN.28.1.7-19.

Aristotle (2004). *Selected writings: Selections from Nicomachean ethics and politics*. CRW Publishing Limited.

Arjoon, S. (2000). Virtue theory as a dynamic theory of business, *Journal of Business Ethics, 28*, 159–178. https://doi.org/10.1023/A:1006339112331

Baggani, J. (2018). *How the world thinks: A global history of philosophy.* Granta Books.

Baltes, P. B., & Staudinger, U. M. (2000). Wisdom: A metaheuristic (pragmatic) to orchestrate mind and virtue toward excellence. *The American Psychologist, 55*(1), 122–36. https://doi.org/10.1037//0003-066X.55.1.122

Beauvoir, S. D. (1972). *The coming of age* (1st ed.). Putnam.

Beck, U. (1992). *Risk society: Towards a new modernity.* Sage Publications.

Bennett, J. W. (1996). *Human ecology as human behavior: Essays in environmental and developmental anthropology* (2nd ed.). Routledge.

Bhikkhu, M. (2000). Buddhism and interfaith dialogue. *Global Dialogue (Nicosia, Cyprus), 2*(1), 74–81. https://bcu.idm.oclc.org/login?url=https://www.proquest.com/docview/211515979?pq-origsite=primo

Bonanno, G. A. (2004). Loss, trauma, and human resilience: Have we underestimated the human capacity to thrive after extremely aversive events? *The American Psychologist, 59*(1), 20–28. https://doi.org/10.1037/0003-066X.59.1.20

Brickhouse, T. C., & Smith, N. D. (1994). *Plato's Socrates.* Oxford University Press.

Bull, M. (Ed.). (1992). *Lifetime losses: Seeking a balance.* Baywood Publishing Co., Inc.

Campbell, J. (Ed.). (1991). *A Joseph Campbell companion: Reflections on the art of living.* HarperCollins Publishers.

Campbell, J. (2001). *Thou art that: Transforming religious metaphor.* New World Library.

Carter, R. E. (2013). *The Kyoto school: An introduction.* University of New York Press.

Chodron, P. (2001b). *The wisdom of no escape: How to love yourself and the world.* HarperCollins.

Confucius (1971). *Confucian analects, the great learning & the doctrine of the mean* (J. Legge, Trans.). Dover Publications.

Decker, L. R. (1993). The role of trauma in spiritual development. *Journal of Humanistic Psychology, 33*(4), 33–46. https://doi.org/10.1177/00221678930 334004

Eachus, P. (2014). Community resilience: Is it greater than the sum of the parts of individual resilience? *Procedia Economics and Finance, 18,* 345–351. https://doi.org/10.1016/S2212-5671(14)00949-6

Ericsson, K. A., Charness, N., Feltovich, P. J., & Hoffman, R. R. (2006). *The Cambridge handbook of expertise and expert performance.* Cambridge University Press.

Ericsson, K. A., Prietula, M. J., & Cokely, E. T. (2007). The making of an expert. *Harvard Business Review, 85*(7-8), 114–121. https://hbr.org/2007/07/the-making-of-an-expert

Fletcher, D., & Sarkar, M. (2013). Psychological resilience: A review and critique of definitions, concepts, and theory. *European Psychologist, 18*(1), 12–23.

Flynn, J. R. (2016). *Does your family make you smarter? Nature, nurture, and human anatomy.* Cambridge University Press.

Flynn, S. E. (2008). America the resilient: Defying terrorism and mitigating natural disasters. *Foreign Affairs, 87*(2), 2–8.

Frankl, V. E. (1959). *Man's search for meaning.* Beacon Press.

Fullerton, D. J., Zhang, L. M., & Kleitman, S. (2021). An integrative process model of resilience in an academic context: Resilience resources, coping strategies, and positive adaptation. *PLoS ONE, 16*(2). https://doi.org/10.1371/journal.pone.0246000

Gaukroger, S. (2006). *The emergence of a scientific culture: Science and the shaping of modernity, 1210-1685.* Oxford University Press.

Gilbert, P. (Ed.). (2022). *The science of compassion.* Routledge.

Gyatso, G. K. (2006). *Joyful path of good fortune: The complete Buddhist path to enlightenment.* Tharpa Publications.

Gyatso, G. K. (2014). *How to understand the mind: The nature and power of the mind.* Tharpa Publications.

Hacker, P. (2006). Dharma in Hinduism. *Journal of Indian Philosophy, 34,* 479–496. https://doi.org/10.1007/s10781-006-9002-4

Haidt, J. (2021). *The happiness hypothesis: Putting ancient wisdom and philosophy to the test of modern science* (2nd ed.). Random House UK.

Hannay, A. (2018). *Søren Kierkegaard.* Reaktion Books.

Harari, Y. N. (2011). *Sapiens: A brief history of humankind.* Vintage.

Hillman, J. (1983). *Healing fiction.* Station Hill Press.

Hoffman, E. (1985). *The heavenly ladder: A Jewish guide to inner growth.* Harper & Row, p. 94.

Holliday, S. G., & Chandler, M. J. (1986). *Wisdom: Explorations in adult competence* (J. A. Meacham, Ed.). Karger.

Jackson, D., Firtko, A., & Edenborough, M. A. (2007). Personal resilience as a strategy for surviving and thriving in the face of workplace adversity: A literature review. *Journal of Advanced Nursing, 60*(1), 1–9. https://doi.org/10.1111/j.1365-2648.2007.04412.x

Jonkers, P. (2020). Philosophy and wisdom. *Algemeen Nederlands Tijdschrift Voor Wijsbegeerte, 112*(3), 261–277. https://doi.org/10.5117/ANTW2020.3.002.JONK

Jung, C. G. (1967). *Collected works of C. G. Jung, vol. 13: Alchemical studies* (G. Adler & R.F.C. Hull, Trans.). Princeton University Press.

Jung, C. G., & Hull, R. F. C. (2014). *Aion : Researches into the phenomenology of the self* (2nd ed.). Routledge.

Junger, S. (2010). *War.* Fourth Estate.

Kant, I., & Hatfield, G. (1997). *Prolegomena to any future metaphysics : With selections from the critique of pure reason.* Cambridge University Press, p. 118. https://doi.org/10.1017/CBO9781139164061

Kemmis, S. (2012). Phronesis, experience, and the primacy of praxis. In E.A. Kinsella & A. Pitman (Eds.). *Phronesis as professional knowledge. Professional practice and education: A diversity of voices,* vol 1. SensePublishers, Rotterdam. https://doi.org/10.1007/978-94-6091-731-8_11

Keown, D. (1992). *The nature of Buddhist ethics.* Palgrave Macmillan.

Kunzmann, U., & Baltes, P. B. (Eds.). (2003). *Beyond the traditional scope of intelligence: Wisdom in action.* American Psychological Association.

Lipner, J. (2019). The truth of dharma and the dharma of truth: Reflections on Hinduism as a dharmic faith. *International Journal of Hindu Studies, 23*(10), 213–237. https://link.springer.com/article/10.1007/s11407-019-09262-3

Luthar, S. S., Cicchetti, D., & Becker, B. (2000). The construct of resilience: A critical evaluation and guidelines for future work. *Child Development, 71*(3), 543–562. https://doi.org/10.1111/1467-8624.00164

Mahoney, J. L., & Bergman, L. R. (2002). Conceptual and methodological considerations in a developmental approach to the study of positive adaptation. *Journal of Applied Developmental Psychology, 23*(2), 195–217. https://doi.org/10.1016/S0193-3973(02)00104-1

Masten, A. S., Best, K. M., & Garmezy, N. (1990). Resilience and development: Contributions from the study of children who overcome adversity. *Development and Psychopathology, 2*(4), 425–444. https://doi.org/10.1017/S0954579400005812

Masten, A. S., & Obradović, J. (2006). Competence and resilience in development, *Annals of the New York Academy of Sciences, 1094,* 13–27. https://doi.org/10.1196/annals.1376.003

McCubbin, H. I., McCubbin, M. A., Thompson, A. I., Han, S., & Allen, Y. (1997). Families under stress: What makes them resilient. *Journal of Family and Consumer Sciences, 89*(3), 2–11.

Meichenbaum, D. (1985). *Stress inoculation training.* Pergamon Press.

Moody, H. R. (1986). Late life learning in the information society. In D. A. Peterson, J. E. Thornton, & J. E. Birren (Eds.), *Education and aging* (pp. 122–143). Prentice-Hall.

Naranjo, C. (1972). *The one quest.* Viking Press.

Nietzsche, F. W. (1997). *Twilight of the idols: How to philosophize with a hammer* (R. Polt. Trans.). Hackett Publishing Company, Inc.

Nietzsche, F. W., & Hollingdale, R. J. (1990). *Twilight of the idols/Anti-Christ* (R. J. Hollingdale, Trans.). Penguin Classics.

Nussbaum, M. (1986). *The fragility of goodness: Luck and ethics in Greek tragedy and philosophy.* Cambridge University Press.

Parry, A., & Doan, R. E. (1994). *Story revisions: Narrative therapy in the post-modern world.* The Guilford Press.

Pascual-Leone, J. (2000). Mental attention, consciousness, and the progressive emergence of wisdom, *Journal of Adult Development, 7,* 241–254. https://doi.org/10.1023/A:1009563428260

Robinson, K. (2009). *The element: How finding your passion changes everything.* Penguin UK.

Schram, S. F., Flyvbjerg, B., & Landman, T. (2013). Political science: A phronetic approach. *New Political Science, 35*(3), 35–372. http://dx.doi.org/10.1080/07393148.2013.813687

Schwartz, B., & Sharpe, K. (2010). *Practical wisdom: The right way to do the right thing.* Riverhead Books.

Seery, M. D., Holman, E. A., & Silver, R. C. (2010). Whatever does not kill us: Cumulative lifetime adversity, vulnerability, and resilience. *Journal of Personality and Social Psychology, 99*(6), 1025–1041. http://dx.doi.org/10.1037/a0021344

Smith, S. (2004). Exploring the interaction of trauma and spirituality. *Traumatology, 10*(4), 231–243. https://psycnet.apa.org/doi/10.1177/153476560401000403

Staudinger, U. M., & Baltes, P. B. (1996). Interactive minds: A facilitative setting for wisdom-related performance? *Journal of Personality and Social Psychology, 71*(4), 746–762. http://dx.doi.org/10.1037/0022-3514.71.4.746

Sternberg, R. J. (2019). *Race to Samarra:* The critical importance of wisdom in the world today. In R. J. Sternberg & J. Glück (Eds.), *The Cambridge handbook of wisdom* (pp. 3–9). https://doi.org/10.1017/9781108568272.002

Suzuki, D. (1971). What is the "I"?. *The Eastern Buddhist, 4*(1), 13–27. http://www.jstor.org/stable/44361263

Tagore, R. (2016). *Truth loves its limits.* TagoreWeb. Retrieved October 11, 2023, from https://www.tagoreweb.in/verses/fireflies-200/truth-loves-its-limits-7805

Thich, N. (1999). *The heart of the Buddha's teaching.* Random House UK.

Thich, N. (2014). Healing ourselves, healing the earth. *The mindfulness bell. Autumn, 2014*(67), 4–11. https://www.parallax.org/product/the-mindfulness-bell-autumn-2014-issue-67/

Tschakert, P., Barnett, J., Ellis, N. R., Lawrence, c., Tuana, N., New, M., Elrick-Barr, C., Pandit, R., & Pannell, D. (2017). Climate change and loss, as if people mattered: Values, places, and experiences, *Wiley Interdisciplinary Reviews: Climate Change, 8,* 476–495. https://doi.org/10.1002/wcc.476

Tsering, G. T. (2005). *The four noble truths: The foundation of Buddhist thought.* Wisdom Publications.

Windle, G. (2011). What is resilience? A review and concept analysis. *Reviews in Clinical Gerontology, 21*(2), 152–169. http://dx.doi.org/10.1017/S0959259810000420

Wing-Tsit, C. (1967). Syntheses in Chinese metaphysics. In C. A. Moore (Ed.), *The Chinese mind.* University of Hawaii Press. https://doi.org/10.1515/9780824844912-007

Xiang, W.-N. (2016). Ecophronesis: The ecological practical wisdom for and from ecological practice. *Landscape and Urban Planning, 155*, 53–60. https://doi.org/10.1016/j.landurbplan.2016.07.005

13

SUSTAINING RELATIONALITY THROUGH THE PRACTICE OF MINDFULNESS

> Mindfulness taught me profoundly that when I was fully present in the moment without distraction, I had the power to choose my thoughts, words, and actions in wiser ways that brought benefits to myself and those around me. Mindfulness helped me realise how much power I had in any given moment, despite the circumstances in which I found myself.

At its most fundamental level, mindfulness helps us to realise that the only moment we ever have in life is the one we are in. It is the only moment we have ever had, and it is the only moment we will ever need. Everything that happens to us happens in the present moment—in the Now. Even when we reminisce about the past or dream of the future, it only happens in the present moment. Therefore, what happens in the present moment, or more precisely, how we perceive the present moment, matters enormously. This is because our thoughts, words and actions in response to mental and physical stimuli create our world, and the quality of our world is determined by the quality of our minds and the words and actions that follow.

Importantly, mindfulness is both a practice and a state of mind. As such, it can make a significant difference to the quality of our minds and to do this, mindfulness relies on two principal functions: *attention* and *intention*. The principal function of *attention* is to help focus our minds on a particular object and to remain focused without distraction or forgetfulness, while the principal function of *intention* is to plan for the actions that we wish to undertake towards a specific goal (Gyatso, 2014).

For example, as relational leaders committed to preventing, minimising, or managing the suffering and vulnerability of ourselves and others, it is

DOI: 10.4324/9781003499510-17

important that we focus our *attention* with wisdom on those things that cause suffering and vulnerability, and remain focused, without distraction and without forgetting. While our *intention* is shaped by many mental factors of virtue and non-virtue (such as patience and anger or love and hate, as examples), we should always be aiming, with virtue, to prevent, minimise, or manage the vulnerability and suffering of ourselves and others wherever and whenever we can, with wisdom.

Mindfulness also helps us shift our minds from acting in the interest-of-self to acting in the interest-of-self-and-other. It helps us to rebalance our concerns from excessive self-interest and self-importance to being, at least, just as interested if not more so in the happiness, well-being and flourishing of others.

In this chapter, we explore the practice of mindfulness, commencing with eastern and western definitions, followed by how mindfulness can reduce suffering. We then explore the importance of creating a sacred space to allow mindfulness to flourish.

Eastern perspectives

Mindfulness has its origins in Buddhist philosophy and psychology. Its primary function is to recognise when the root causes of human suffering—being excessive self-interest and self-importance, greed, anger, and ignorance—are present, as well as absent, in our minds (Bodhi, 2000; Gethin, 2014; Gyatso, 2014; Harvey, 2007). It is only when our minds are temporarily free from these negative mental factors that we can develop the capacity to think, speak and act with virtues such as compassion when responding to human and non-human suffering (Anālayo, 2019; Thich, 1992, 1999). When we practice mindfulness, we become consciously aware of the presence of these negative mental factors and their potential to bring universal suffering upon self and other. We also become consciously aware of the need to replace them with a virtuous intention to act with wisdom when negating or minimising the suffering of other humans and non-humans (Kwee, 2012; Lim, 2019; Thich, 1999).

According to numerous scholars researching in the philosophies of engaged and environmental Buddhism, these negative mental factors are the root cause of the suffering emerging from climate change (Anālayo, 2019; Daniels, 2010; Gregory & Sabra, 2008; Kaza, 2014; Lim, 2019). Revered Buddhist monk Ogyen Trinley Dorje observes that:

> Ignorance of the empty nature of self and the rejection of compassion is the root cause of egotism, anger, attachment, and greed. Ignorance is why human beings have degraded the environment and are driving so many species to extinction. Ignorance causes us to place an excessive worth upon the self and anything related to it—*my* family, *my* possessions, *my* country, and even *my* race. Perceiving the diversity of the world through the limited

lens of self means we can impose grave harm upon Earth without concern, because Earth has become 'other'.

(Dorje, 2011, pp. 1094–1095)

This perspective has certain parallels with neoliberalism's insistence of individualism (self-interest and self-importance), the free market, and the emphasis on economic growth as the basis of moral choices and ends (Gregson, 2020; Raco, 2015; Wilson & Swyngedouw, 2015). Or, put another way, while neoliberalism is not the origin of the causes of human and non-human suffering, it does both exemplify and amplify some of these causes, particularly with regard to self-interest and self-importance, greed, anger, and ignorance.

Western perspectives

Mindfulness was introduced into western science approximately 40 years ago and is commonly viewed as an inherent, accessible, and empirically assessable quality of human consciousness that is independent of religious or spiritual beliefs (Baer, 2003). In cognitive psychology, mindfulness is defined as intentional, non-judgemental attentiveness to the present moment grounded in human consciousness that gives rise to increased levels of attention, awareness, and emotional intelligence (Kabat-Zinn, 2005; Wamsler & Brink, 2018). Mindfulness allows us to take "an open, non-judgemental, reflective, self-regulatory, and sometimes transcendent stance toward life" that might help make us more inquisitive, caring, and/or capable of self-control (Verhaeghen, 2021, p. 2). Mindfulness is also generally considered as a dispositional characteristic, a state of mind, and a practice, and is essential in helping us to develop compassion towards humans and non-humans (Condon et al., 2013).

Mindfulness can also facilitate a significant shift in the way we, as humans, think about and act upon economic, social, and ecological crisis at local through to global scales (Ericson et al., 2014; Wamsler, 2018; Wamsler & Brink, 2018). For example, it achieves this by helping us to generate greater sensitivity towards our environment as well as accepting new information and increasing our awareness of multiple problem-solving perspectives (Weick & Putnam, 2006). Mindfulness also enhances our well-being, self-awareness and self-transcendence (Verhaeghen, 2021), as well as "increasing human potential through improved leadership, organisational learning, and compassion for others within and outside of the organisation" (Wamsler, 2018, p. 7).

How mindfulness reduces suffering

As we have discussed in earlier chapters, excessive self-interest and self-importance can lead to significant levels of suffering for ourselves and others. Being only interested in ourselves and our needs and thinking that we are more important than others—or, in other words, neglecting the needs of others—is a significant source of suffering, from individuals to a global scale.

How we feel about ourselves matters

However, while we need to be cautious about these two aspects of mind, there are other aspects about ourselves that are worthy of our *attention*. For example, it is important that we develop our self-confidence, self-esteem, self-respect, self-regard, and self-care. All of these factors are an important element in how we show compassion towards ourselves, how we construct our leadership character, and how we derive a sense of happiness, well-being and flourishing for ourselves and others. As the eminent Buddhist Nun Pema Chodron observes, "Whether distraction or aggression proliferate globally or peacefulness and harmony grow stronger depends on how we as citizens of the world feel about ourselves" (Chodron, 2019, p. 118). If we see ourselves as fundamentally bad, imperfect, or morally messed up and broken, then we are most likely to see others in a similar light. This is likely to be especially true for those who may not look like us or may not agree with our point of view.

In this context and in general terms, a western mind will tend to see self or other as a bad person that requires fixing or salvation. Alternatively, an eastern mind will tend to see self and other as fundamentally good but deluded by bad habits, harmful intentions, and selfish motivations which are temporary and removable habits of mind. In addition, these habits of mind can be improved upon through practices of meditation and mindfulness focused on virtues such as compassion, wisdom, courage and kindness (Chodron, 2019).

Why we suffer

Unfortunately for many of us, and especially high performers, these aspects of our mind are often neglected due to an internal dialogue of harsh self-criticism that demands we should do more and that our present efforts are not good enough. Ironically, this is the voice of self-interest and self-importance arising from our egos. Our egotistical inner voice is only interested in its own survival while seeking to affirm itself with supreme attributes that fuel our moral hypocrisy and fallibility. When we fail to meet its demands for perfection, we suffer (Thich, 2014).

In Buddhist philosophy, it is this aspect of mind—a mind that sees itself as inherently existent and supremely important, to the neglect of others—that is the root cause of all suffering and the mind we need to abandon. It is this aspect of mind or what we call our "Self" that we cling to, and we attempt to solidify our identity while centring our world around "me," "myself," and "I." From this "I," we become attached to and strive for myriad mental and physical phenomena for our happiness, while trying to avoid our suffering. Our anger emerges from

TABLE 13.1 This table represents the delusions of mind that lead to non-virtuous actions and perpetuate further suffering (Gyatso, 2014)

Deluded forgetfulness	Laziness	Resentment
Non-conscientiousness	Concealment	Inconsideration
Shamelessness	Aggression	Harmfulness
Miserliness	Pretension	Non-alertness
Mental excitement	Spite	Jealousy
Distraction	Dullness	Denial

this "I" that exaggerates (sentient/non-sentient and physical/mental) others' bad qualities, sees them as undesirable, and wishes to harm them. Also, our ignorance of the truth of ourselves, our circumstances, our knowledge, and our environments emerges from this "I" (Gyatso, 2011, 2014).

From this root cause, many non-virtuous minds, often referred to as delusions, arise. Table 13.1 lists them for us.

Alleviating our suffering

It is this sense of "I" and the delusions that emerge that we need to become curious, to become mindful. With a virtuous and intelligent mind of non-judgement, patience, generosity, compassion, and wisdom, we need to quietly observe, through meditative practice, how this "I" and its delusions form the basis of our suffering and the suffering of others. Rather than avoiding how it makes us feel, we engage with the mental and bodily feelings that arise and look deeply into them. In doing so, we begin to discover that they have no independent nor fixed reality. They are generated by our mind. They are like "clouds in a clear blue sky." They come and they go (Kornfield, 2008).

When we ask ourselves, "How true are the thoughts that are creating these feelings?," we begin to see that they, in themselves, are not "true." We begin to see that our mind of "I" has made up a story or formed an opinion about a set of circumstances that we may have experienced or imagined but in which we do not have full knowledge (i.e., of which we have ignorance). In other words, our thoughts are often one-sided and untrue. We then "cling" to this story or opinion as though it is true, real and solid. However, with mindfulness practice, we begin to see that our thoughts are neither solid, firm, fixed, nor completely true. Rather, they are translucent, temporary, and founded on partial or full ignorance, opinion, and speculation. We can begin to see through them, and we simply label them as "thinking" (Chodron, 2017).

Harsh judgements may still arise, but we see them as suffering—we do not morally judge our non-virtuous thoughts as bad or wrong. Instead, by seeing non-virtuous or deluded thoughts as suffering, we have the chance to bring a mind of compassion to them. We begin the long process of healing ourselves.

This is the basis of self-compassion and our pathway to happiness, wellness and flourishing (Tsering, 2008).

By bringing attention to our thinking, we start to realise what it is within our minds that we need to abandon (non-virtue) and what it is we need to nourish or attain (virtue). Being mindful ensures that we not only maintain our *attention* on those things (virtues) that bring both us and others happiness, well-being, and flourishing, but it also serves to make sure we do not forget them. We then develop an *intention* to move from a non-virtuous mind to a virtuous mind as often as our mindfulness practice will allow (Gyatso, 2014).

As this process unfolds, we begin to discover another aspect of our minds that is not grounded in self-importance and self-interest. Instead, we begin to discover our wisdom mind—a mind that increasingly understands the source of suffering for ourselves and others. This aspect of mind also comes to realise our shared suffering and wish to be free from suffering are the bases of our shared humanity and relationality. We begin to understand that the suffering we experience and wish to be free of is the same suffering that others also experience and wish to be free from (Kornfield, 2008; Thich, 2000, 2014).

Benefiting our leadership potential

It is this realisation of shared suffering through the practice of mindfulness that provides the foundation for our leadership as relational leaders. By focusing our attention on the causes of suffering and vulnerability and developing an intention to alleviate those causes, we establish the predicates of thought that can drive our words and actions to prevent, minimise or manage suffering and vulnerability for the benefit of ourselves and others in myriad contexts.

For example, we can be more mindful of the distortions in our resilience policy frameworks influenced by neoliberalism that place unreasonable expectations on citizens to be resilient. We can be more conscious of alternative framings of resilience that involve greater levels of partnership, participation, co-operation, and access that communitarianism advocates for in resilience policy. We can be more mindful of sharing the equities of power, wealth, and resources afforded to our institutions with the citizens we are asked to lead, serve, and protect to collectively reduce suffering and vulnerability. These are but a small sample of what is possible when we refocus our *attention* and *intention* towards reducing suffering and vulnerability of self and other, instead of pursuing self-interested and self-important pursuits that neglect the needs of others.

Making time for mindfulness—the need for a sacred space

However, being more mindful is not something that we can achieve in a moment, a day, a month, or even a year. It has to form a regular practice that spans the remainder of our lifetime—in other words, it is a lifetime skill. Therefore, we need to make time to nurture its development, and to achieve this we need a sacred space.

Joseph Campbell's advice

For years, I have read the works of Joseph Campbell—a comparative mythologist who introduced me to the intersections of philosophy, theology and mythology. Campbell was one of those great original thinkers of history. Early in his life, he studied intensely to gain his doctoral degree. However, upon realising that he could not publish what he had learnt and what he thought but could only publish what others thought he should publish, he quit his degree and commenced his own lifetime of research, reflection, study, and publication (Campbell, 1991). While his work may not necessarily be easy to read, it is nonetheless a rich and rewarding experience, offering profound insights into these great branches of knowledge.

He spoke often of the need for a sacred space. A space where one could go that had nothing to do with secular society and its desire for facts, figures, numbers, data, reports, evidence, efficiency, effectiveness, and opinions. Rather, it was a space, any space, where we could simply be ourselves in the most essential way. Sacred spaces can be places that we most connect with. Usually, but not always, they involve some connection with nature, aesthetics or a place that evokes fond memories. It can also be a place of great simplicity. Campbell said that his sacred space was anywhere where he could lay out his books, gather his thoughts, reflect, and write. Wherever we define our sacred space, it will be characterised by the evocation of a deep sense of happiness and joy. A place that lets us experience our own will, our own intentions, our deepest wishes, and for many, a connection with divinity. Campbell said that everyone needed such a place, whether or not we realised this (Campbell, 1991). I think this is true.

Enter the juggernaut

Life places so many demands upon us to be a certain way, to think a certain way, to live a certain way. Anthony Giddens, a prominent sociologist and leading thinker on modernity (the period of history extending from the emergence of the Enlightenment period through to today), describes modern-day life as like being caught up in a juggernaut. Most people would have heard of this metaphor. A "juggernaut" is the anglicised name for the Hindu god Jagannath, the "Lord of the Universe." In the western context, it is used as a metaphor to describe a runaway engine of enormous power which, collectively as human beings, we can drive to some extent, but which also threatens to rush out of our control, crushing those who resist it (Giddens & Pierson, 1998).

The ride is not wholly unpleasant of course, as we place much hope and anticipation in modern society and all that it has to offer us in terms of meaning, purpose, identify and security. But in short, we are not in control of the juggernaut, it is in control of us. If we dare step in its way, it will consume us, as the ground over which it runs is full of high risk and high consequence. Of course, for many of us, fulfilling our life purpose is important. Participating in society is a big part of life and, I would contend, a necessary part. But when the juggernaut takes over, it is time to seek refuge. Hence the need for sacred spaces.

Visiting not residing

Sacred spaces are not generally places in which to reside, but rather spaces that allow us to take refuge, to refresh, recover and re-inspire. I am reminded of a Buddhist story of the monk who spent years separated from his community, meditating constantly with the single desire to become enlightened as soon as he possibly could. To do this, he disconnected from everything and everyone. After about five years or so, he thought he had reached his goal and so he returned to his village. As he entered the village, a dog crossed his path unexpectedly, causing him to experience anger and frustration, the very aversions of mind he had tried so hard to eradicate. In short, he had not really progressed at all because he had ignored all the (pleasant, neutral and unpleasant) realities of life.

While both Aristotle and the Buddha advocated that life's experiences teach us about the virtues, the basis of a good life, and the opportunity to develop wisdom from those experiences, unfortunately in today's modern society, with all its pressures and complexities, we seldom take any time out to reflect or contemplate those experiences. We rarely, if ever, take time out to just be ourselves in a truly authentic way. Sacred spaces give you that opportunity.

The power of myth and ritual

A sacred space is also an opportunity to discover for ourselves the power of our myths and rituals. It is important to understand that a myth is not a lie, as many in the modern western world would have us believe. Joseph Campbell aptly defined myths as "the organisation of symbolic images and narratives, metaphorical of the possibilities of human experience and the fulfilment of a given culture at a given time" (Campbell, 2008).

Myths afford us the opportunity of bringing forward the *meaning* that emerges from our individual and collective lived experiences that further inspire our *purpose*—two things that arise from our wisdom mind and contribute significantly to the quality of our lives. Those collective experiences, interpreted through our great bodies of knowledge such as our art, music, poetry, literature, film, theatre, theologies, and philosophies, create collective meaning that establishes our living myths.

From our myths come our rituals. A ritual is the enactment of a myth. When we participate in a ritual, we are participating in the wisdom of the myth. A wisdom that is inherent within us. The myth, along with its images and narratives and the rituals we enact, reminds our consciousness of the wisdom of our own life.

So, in a quiet moment of reflection, ask yourself this: What is the myth of my life? What has my life story so far taught me about the wisdom that is inherent within my mind? What rituals do I initiate or participate in, both privately and collectively, that honour that wisdom and bring it to life? Our myths and their attendant rituals exemplify the power of the human spirit, a power that exists within each of us. We owe it to ourselves and each other to honour it above all else.

Persistence

I am as guilty as anyone for not taking enough time to sit in a sacred space and just be. And when I leave it too long, I suffer. And if you leave it too long, so will you. I know for some, the mere thought of being by themselves is terrifying, usually because they fear what may arise in that moment of silence without distraction. My advice would be "keep trying." Slowly and briefly, at first, but try extending it over time. Be compassionate with yourself and, if necessary, forgive yourself for any of the things that you either have or have not thought, said or done that cause you angst or grief. In so doing, grant those who have in some way aggrieved you the same forgiveness, for they too suffer in a similar way to you.

As Joseph Campbell rightly asserted, everyone needs a sacred space. Bless yourself with the opportunity of finding that "corner of the world" where you can just be. Sit in the presence of blissful silence of mind and just absorb whatever it is you sense that brings you happiness and joy.

The challenge for leaders

By realising that the only moment we ever have is the one we are in and that the quality of that moment is significantly shaped by our attention and intention to think, speak and act with virtue, as leaders we can progress towards greater levels of awareness about our shared suffering and vulnerability. We can also gain greater awareness about how to minimise them for the benefit of ourselves and others.

Cultivating eastern and western perspectives of mindfulness affords us the opportunity to generate cognitive insights into the nature and causes of suffering in ourselves and others. This includes the social, cultural and political environments in which they exist. It also affords us the opportunity to deepen our cognitive capacity to solve complex problems, make better decisions, develop greater compassion towards others, and minimise suffering. We would also do well to commit time and space for mindfulness practice, along with the rituals that have importance to our spiritual, mental and physical well-being.

References

Anālayo, B. (2019). A task for mindfulness: Facing climate change. *Mindfulness, 10,* 1926–1935. https://doi.org/10.1007/s12671-019-01187-7

Baer, R. A. (2003). Mindfulness training as a clinical intervention: A conceptual and empirical review. *Clinical Psychology: Science and Practice, 10*(2), 125–143.

Bodhi, B. (Ed.). (2000). *Ādittapariyāya Sutta; Dhammacakkappavattana Sutta.* Wisdom Publications.

Campbell, J. (Ed.). (1991). *A Joseph Campbell companion: Reflections on the art of living.* HarperCollins Publishers.

Campbell, J. (2008). *The hero with a thousand faces.* New World Library.

Chodron, P. (2017). *Start where you are: How to accept yourself and others.* HarperCollins.

Chodron, P. (2019). *Welcoming the unwelcome: Wholehearted living in a broken hearted world.* Shambala Publications Inc.

Condon, P., Desbordes, G., Miller, W. B., & DeSteno, D. (2013). Meditation increases compassionate responses to suffering. *Psychological Science, 24*(10), 2125–2127. https://journals.sagepub.com/doi/10.1177/0956797613485603

Daniels, P. L. (2010). Climate change, economics and Buddhism—Part 2: New views and practices for sustainable world economies. *Ecological Economics, 69*(5), 962–972. https://doi.org/10.1016/j.ecolecon.2010.01.012

Dorje, O. T. (2011). Walking the path of environmental Buddhism through compassion and emptiness. *Conservation Biology, 25*(6), 1094–1097. https://doi.org/10.1111/j.1523-1739.2011.01765.x

Ericson, T., Kjønstad, B. G., & Anders, B. (2014). Mindfulness and sustainability. *Ecological Economics, 104,* 73–79. https://doi.org/10.1016/j.ecolecon.2014.04.007

Gethin, R. (2014). *The foundations of Buddhism.* Oxford University Press.

Giddens, A., & Pierson, C. (1998). *Conversations with Anthony Giddens: Making sense of modernity.* Stanford University Press.

Gregory, J., & Sabra, S. (2008). Engaged Buddhism and deep ecology: Beyond the science/religion divide. *Human Architecture, 6*(51), 51–65.

Gregson, J. (2020). The consequences of liberal modernity: Explaining and resisting neoliberalism through Alasdair MacIntyre. *Contemporary Political Theory, 20*(8), 591–613. https://doi.org/10.1057/s41296-020-00434-0

Gyatso, G. K. (2011). *Modern Buddhism: The path of compassion and wisdom.* Tharpa Publications.

Gyatso, G. K. (2014). *How to understand the mind: The nature and power of the mind.* Tharpa Publications.

Harvey, P. (2007). Avoiding unintended harm to the environment and the Buddhist ethic of intention. *The Journal of Buddhist Ethics, 14,* 1–34. https://go-gale-com.virtual.anu.edu.au/ps/i.do?p=AONE&u=anu&id=GALE|A177859639&v=2.1&it=r

Kabat-Zinn, J. (2005). *Full catastrophe living: Using the wisdom of your body and mind to face stress, pain, and illness* (15th anniversary ed.). Delta Trade Paperback/Bantam Dell.

Kaza, S. (2014). Buddhist contributions to climate response. *Journal of Oriental Studies, 24,* 73–92. https://www.totetu.org/assets/media/paper/j024_073.pdf

Kornfield, J. (2008). *The wise heart: Buddhist psychology for the west.* Ebury Publishing.

Kwee, G. T. M. (2012). Relational Buddhism: Wedding K. J. Gergen's relational being and Buddhism to create harmony in-between-selves. *Psychological Studies, 57*(2), 203–210.

Lim, H. (2019). Environmental revolution in contemporary Buddhism: The interbeing of individual and collective consciousness in ecology. *Religions, 10*(2), 120. https://doi.org/10.3390/rel10020120

Raco, M. 2015. Conflict management, democratic demands, and the post politics of privatization. In J. Metzger, P. Allmendinger, & S. Oosterlynck (Eds.), *Planning against the political: Democratic deficits in European territorial governance* (1st ed.). Routledge.

Thich, N. (1992). *The diamond that cuts though illusion: Commentaries on the prajna-paramita diamond sutra.* Parallax Press.

Thich, N. (1999). *The heart of the Buddha's teaching.* Random House UK.

Thich, N. (2000). *Interbeing: Fourteen guidelines for engaged Buddhism* (2nd ed.). Full Circle Publishing.

Thich, N. (2014). Healing ourselves, healing the earth. *The mindfulness bell. Autumn, 2014*(67), 4–11. https://www.parallax.org/product/the-mindfulness-bell-autumn-2014-issue-67/

Tsering, G. T. (2008). *The awakening mind: The foundation of Buddhist thought* (Vol. 4). Wisdom Publications.

Verhaeghen, P. (2021). There is virtue in mindfulness: The relationship between the mindfulness manifold, virtues, and eudemonic wellbeing. *Personality and Individual Differences, 176*, 1–8. https://doi.org/10.1016/j.paid.2021.110767

Wamsler, C. (2018). Mind the gap: The role of mindfulness in adapting to increasing risk and climate change. *Sustainability Science, 13*(4), 1121–1135. https://doi.org/10.1007/s11625-017-0524-3

Wamsler, C., & Brink, E. (2018). Mindsets for sustainability: Exploring the link between mindfulness and sustainable climate adaptation. *Ecological Economics, 151*, 55–61. https://doi.org/10.1016/j.ecolecon.2018.04.029

Weick, K., & Putnam, T. (2006). Organizing for mindfulness: Eastern Wisdom and Western knowledge. *Journal of Management Inquiry, 15*(3), 275–287. https://doi.org/10.1177/1056492606291202

Wilson, J., & Swyngedouw, E. (2015). *The post-political and its discontents: Spaces of depoliticisation, spectres of radical politics.* Edinburgh University Press. https://doi.org/10.3366/edinburgh/9780748682973.001.0001

CONCLUSION

Summing up the challenges for leaders

As we have seen throughout the previous chapters, the interrelated socio-cultural influences of modernity, the risk society, neoliberalism and govern-mentality have played a significant role in how we, as disaster management leaders, give advice and make decisions that can significantly affect the extent to which communities strengthen their adaptive capacities and enhance resilience, or become vulnerable to the effects of existential threats, such as climate change. Relatedly, these influences also contribute towards determining whether we, as leaders, either deny or accept our own vulnerability while seeking to master the effects of disasters and protect citizens.

We have also seen how this tension sits at the heart of disaster management leadership. At one end lies the invulnerable nature of disaster management leadership and culture that positions itself as being able to cope in all situations but then tends to either blame citizens or pose additional obligations upon them when disasters reach thresholds that are beyond a government or agency's ability to cope.

Such insensitivity is also pervasive within our organisational cultures. We appear to be becoming desensitised to the impacts that disasters are having on our own people while demanding more and more from them to cope with their effects. However, fortunately, we have also seen how disaster management leaders are prepared to establish relationality with those they seek to lead, serve and protect by accepting their mutual experience of suffering and vulnerability.

Therefore, our overarching challenge as disaster management leaders is to bring greater awareness to the causes and experiences of suffering and

DOI: 10.4324/9781003499510-18

vulnerability for ourselves and others. Along with the equities of power, wealth, resources and influence available to us, we need to be in action wherever and whenever possible to negate, minimise or manage suffering and vulnerability. We need to do this in relationship with those we seek to lead, serve and protect without in any way denying, disavowing or ignoring vulnerability's and suffering's existence and effects.

Suffering

We all have a personal responsibility to negate, minimise or manage our own suffering wherever and whenever possible, while recognising that our thoughts, words and actions often contribute towards the extent to which we either suffer or achieve a genuine sense of happiness. However, we must also accept that suffering has social causes that must be managed through the notion of the social contract of shared responsibility. That is, we can find ourselves being affected either positively or negatively by the decisions made by us or other people within political or social institutions and the manner in which the equities of power, wealth and resources are used and distributed to shape those decisions in our best interests and in the interests of others.

As leaders, we must constantly navigate this tension between individual and social responsibility for suffering. Certain political discourses, such as neoliberalism, will want us to place the greater burden of responsibility towards the individual and away from government. Alternatively, other political discourses, such as communitarianism, will seek to ensure our political and social institutions take on greater responsibility for providing the conditions for people to achieve happiness, well-being and to flourish. Our capacity to shape the political discourses that emerge from these various critiques of government intervention can be extremely difficult but not impossible.

In addition to the varying degrees of the equities of power, wealth and resources available to us as leaders, we also have varying degrees of access to senior policymakers and decision-makers, either directly or indirectly. By being more conscious of the nature of suffering and its causes, we can help shape policies, decisions, and advice in a way that is more aware of and alert to the suffering of others whom we lead, serve and protect. The degree of equity and access may seem small depending on where we sit within the institutional framework, but it is not zero—it is somewhere between zero and one, and all thoughts, words and actions matter.

Vulnerability

The shared space of vulnerability between governments, leaders and the citizens they aim to protect opens up new possibilities for how we navigate, manage and ultimately transform from the effects of disasters. When we hit the limits of our collective ability to treat risk, when our individual and collective capacity for resilience is exceeded, and when the capacity of our governments to protect their citizens is no longer effective, we are left with a stark choice. We can either seek to blame others and/or become defensive, or we can come together in the spirit of relationality underpinned by an ethic of compassion and forge a better world for all.

This choice is largely shaped either by the extent in which we deny, disavow or ignore our own vulnerability and that of others or, alternatively, by the extent in which we understand and accept our shared vulnerability and seek to collectively execute our moral duty to prevent, minimise and manage it. This choice also determines the extent to which otherwise avoidable suffering is either lessened or increased.

As leaders who seek to protect others from harm and lead others to offer that protection, how we view vulnerability matters. When we improve our ability to understand that we and others are susceptible to forms of harmfulness and may not be able to cope, we move in the direction of our humanness and our relatedness. We also have the opportunity to fulfil our ethical obligations to minimise or manage the vulnerability of ourselves and others to the best of our ability with the equities of power, wealth and resource made available to us. Through a shared understanding of our mutual vulnerability, we can establish our relatability with those we seek to lead, serve and protect, commit to the reduction of our own and their suffering, be venturous in that pursuit, and remain accountable for our actions.

However, when we choose to deny, disavow or ignore our own and others' vulnerability, we perpetuate the very suffering from which we wish to free ourselves and from which we have a duty to protect others. When we view vulnerability in this way, we risk being insensitive to the suffering of others, insufficient in our responses, constrained by our institutionally prescribed compliance regimes, and defensive when criticised. As leaders, we find ourselves challenged by having to navigate the Invulnerable–Relational Leadership Continuum (Figure 7.5).

Sometimes, our circumstances will pull us in the direction of invulnerability and, at other times, we will be presented with the opportunity to move more towards relationality. Often, we will oscillate along this continuum many times a day in myriad circumstances. Therefore, the challenge for leaders is to better understand how we can be more consistent in our approach to a relational leadership worldview with the intention of reducing suffering.

Compassion

To achieve this, we must continue to develop our understanding of compassion. We must be prepared to see, sense and feel the suffering of others while recognising suffering's universality. We need to connect with their emotional

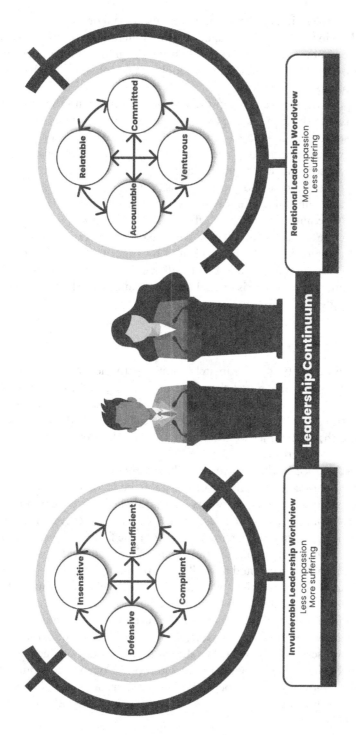

FIGURE 7.5 The Invulnerable–Relational Leadership Continuum.

distress while tolerating uncomfortable feelings, remain open and accepting of them, and act in practical ways to alleviate their suffering. In so doing, we must develop the courage to look into our own minds, grant ourselves permission to see our own suffering, and commit to looking after ourselves so that we can look after others.

It is important that we develop the wisdom to balance up the sentiments, the symbols, and the data that expose us to the suffering of others—that signal to us that something is wrong and something needs fixing. People are suffering and within the equities of power, wealth and resource made available to us as leaders, we commit to actions that alleviate their suffering—actions at the individual, organisational and societal levels.

We must be mindful of the way that certain social and cultural influences such as neoliberalism can pull us off track from genuinely seeing, sensing and feeling the suffering of others. We must also be cautious about our anger and righteousness. To be motivated by anger to alleviate suffering is one thing, to harm another and cause suffering through our anger is quite another thing altogether. It is critical that we understand the difference and act accordingly.

Virtue

As leaders, we must become intimately familiar with the virtues that are critical to how we define our moral character, and once again, be cognisant of the social and cultural influences that can pull us off course. We need to accept that our virtues will need nurturing and development over the course of our lifetime and that sometimes we will not get them right, but we should seek to improve them, nonetheless.

We must also accept that we are all fallible to greater or lesser degrees—that our knowledge of context will almost inevitably be incomplete—and that we should be cautious not to judge others too harshly before we are in possession of all the facts of their circumstances. Similarly, we must accept that we all suffer from moral hypocrisy, preferring to highlight the faults of others instead of our own and often only doing the right thing if it accords with our own self-interest. In response, we would do well to deeply understand non-judgement, humility and forgiveness—the ability to accept with grace our own fallibility and hypocrisy, and the ability to forgive others for theirs.

We would also do well to remember the seven rules of virtue as a way of keeping ourselves grounded, relatable, and accessible to others that we are asked to lead, serve and protect. We should surrender any arrogant sense of moral superiority, rely mainly on the recognition of our virtue from others, commit to virtuous leadership, be wary of virtue signalling, develop our moral courage, lead others by example, and forgive ourselves and others for things done or omitted.

Practical wisdom and mindfulness

With the benefit of the practical wisdom of our lived experience we can examine what gifts we brought with us as a child, what life has taught us so far in relation to the development of our virtues, how we have changed as we have grown older, and what legacy we wish to leave for others. We may also want to explore how we have positively adapted from our experiences of adversity, transformed over time, shaped our narratives about those experiences, and thought about how our experiences have redefined our lives towards being more relational, compassionate and virtuous—to be happier, healthier and flourishing.

These are all existential questions that may take us a long time to contemplate and answer. And those answers will almost certainly change over time, as we reflect, have more experiences, and develop greater wisdom as a result. This process of regularly asking ourselves these questions and reflecting upon our answers will add a richness to our lives and significantly contribute towards our capacity to show self-compassion, as well as compassion towards others who have directly or indirectly shared in our experiences. It will also contribute substantially towards our relatedness with those we lead, serve and protect.

To help find the depth of our wisdom derived from our lived experiences and, in order to answer these and other questions, we would do well to deepen our understanding and practice of mindfulness. By realising that the only moment we ever have is the one we are in, and that the quality of that moment is significantly shaped by our attention and intention to think, speak and act with virtue, we can progress towards greater levels of awareness about our shared suffering and vulnerability. We can also gain greater awareness about how to minimise them for the benefit of ourselves and others. We would also do well to commit time and space for mindfulness practice, along with the rituals that have importance to our spiritual, mental and physical well-being.

Returning to the questions that help shape a relational leadership philosophy

Having navigated our way through suffering, vulnerability, compassion, virtue, practical wisdom, and mindfulness, we now return to think about the questions that we must answer in order to be relational leaders. To help us answer these questions, we bring together some of the threads from all four parts of this book as a way of guiding us to our own unique answers.

Are we willing and able to relate to the lived experiences of others, along with their joys and sorrows?

When we come to appreciate the universal nature of human suffering and vulnerability, albeit in myriad contexts and circumstances, we open the door to relatedness. We begin to see that, despite what looks like the uniqueness of an unfolding event in space and time, there is still a relatedness about the experience of that same event. Our own experiences of birth, ageing, sickness and dying, sorrow, grief, pain, unhappiness, and unease; having to experience unpleasant things; loss and separation from pleasant things and people we love; and not having our wishes fulfilled, unite us. So, too, do the sufferings of our minds—excessive self-interest and self-importance, anger, attachment, and ignorance. These experiences of suffering help us relate to others somewhere greater than zero and probably less than one. We may not be able to completely relate, but often we can relate more than we realise and it is our capacity to reflect upon our own lived experiences over time that affords us that opportunity.

To achieve this, we must allow ourselves to feel and evoke feelings in others. We must be emotionally engaged and develop a sense of empathic purpose—an intentionality to assist others. We must be open to change within ourselves, cognitively, emotionally, spiritually. We must be open to both knowing and not knowing about matters concerning people, places and circumstances, rather than holding preconceived notions and ideas about them. We must be open to being tolerant of the differences we find in others—racially, culturally, religiously, politically, sexually, generationally, and so on. We must be open to being wrong in our views, perspectives and knowledge. We must also be open to changing ourselves in ways that allow others to connect with us.

It is also important that we have the ability to see, sense, and feel the vulnerability and suffering of ourselves and others, show emotional resonance by "walking in their shoes," and develop a level of distress tolerance. We can achieve this by holding space with another who is suffering while tolerating uncomfortable feelings arising from the experience. We can also achieve this by incorporating our lived experiences of loss and suffering into our leadership practice as the essence of our wisdom—our rational, emotional, ethical, and spiritual intelligence that we have learned from witnessing, as well as experiencing our own loss and suffering in order to lead through crisis.

When we realise that we and others suffer together, place the needs of others over our own personal judgements, and recognise that vulnerability is critical to our leadership effectiveness, as is the relatedness of individual experiences with the experiences of others, we are afforded the opportunity to show our humanity. We become more accessible to others, which increases our ability for relatedness with those whom we are leading.

Are we committed to working with ourselves and others to alleviate suffering and vulnerability wherever possible to be happier, healthier and flourishing?

No reasonable person wishes to suffer. Despite the fact that suffering and vulnerability are a part of living, deep down inside our wisdom mind, none of us

wish them for ourselves, and if we delve deeper, we do not wish them for others. This is the universal truth of most eastern moral philosophies. Even if we
are not comfortable with this premise, especially for those people we do not
like, we can trust in this truth as a way of progressing towards a commitment
to practical solutions.

Because of the universality of suffering, we all have ethical obligations towards each other for protection or to prevent, minimise or manage it so that
we and others are no longer susceptible to harm and suffering. This is especially true if we hold power and influence over others. The more we commit
to alleviating the suffering and vulnerability of ourselves and others, over time,
the happier we and they will become. And whilst the capacity to effect change
and improvement may seem miniscule in the context of the enormity of the
task at hand, every thought, word and action that moves in the direction of
alleviating suffering and vulnerability makes a difference, even if that difference
appears unnoticeable.

It is therefore important that, within this relational construct, we not only
feel empathy for those that suffer, but we also commit to action to relieve
their suffering, as feeling without action allows suffering to continue unabated. We must also recognise that certain political discourses will want us
to devalue or dismiss the agency, knowledge and resilience of disempowered
others who, under more favourable personal, social or economic circumstances, would be capable of exercising their agency while pursuing individual and collective priorities and capacities to achieve genuine happiness,
well-being and flourishing. Therefore, it is important that we, as leaders,
recognise the existing embedded and relational capacities of ordinary people to innovate, co-operate, and construct communities of shared interest,
rather than ignore these capacities and instead view citizens only as passive
objects of governance.

This is an immense challenge for disaster management leaders, some of
whom have significant levels of power and authority such as governors, ministers, mayors, departmental secretaries, and chief executive officers, as examples. Some of us have access to or have our hands on the levers of government
control to varying but influential degrees and can therefore begin to make the
difference by targeting the root causes of vulnerability and suffering. While for
other leaders, our power and authority are not so obvious. Nevertheless, we
still have influence. We still shape narratives within our organisational cultures,
brief our superiors, lead our people, and have access to senior political and bureaucratic decision-makers that most citizens do not. Therefore, our advocacy
for change in these circumstances is also critically important.

To assist, we can commit to a strong ethos to serve and protect others,
make a difference for the benefit of others, and contribute to the greater good,
either as a lifelong commitment, or in recognition of a calling. We can also
commit to overcoming personal fear and adversity whilst moving beyond

self-interest to support and inspire others to make a difference. We can do this by sharing our experiences with the survivors of disasters or with colleagues within the disaster management machinery.

In turn, this can deepen our commitment to doing something about suffering and specifically motivate us to act to relieve the suffering of others. We can view every interaction with others as an opportunity to exercise our personal leadership ethos to assist others through our access to power, wealth and resources. We can also show empathic purpose and set aside our own emotions and feelings while seeking to appreciate the emotions and feelings of others experiencing difficult circumstances.

Are we prepared to be venturous with our thoughts, words and actions in this pursuit, and how might we do this?

By being in action, sometimes that action means we may need to be venturous. We may need to undertake a risky or daring journey or course of action in the face of uncertainty, and in these circumstances, compassion becomes an exercise in profound vulnerability. We must push against tides of risk, uncertainty, and notions of invulnerability that perpetuate suffering. We must actively, intentionally, and effortfully take risks to seek out and alleviate the suffering of others, often in subtle and benign circumstances, while exemplifying extraordinary courage. This includes being venturous in our pursuit of changing the circumstances where suffering is created by organisations but left unaddressed, such as the uneven access to material resources and levers for social change.

We must forge our venturousness from our lived experiences in attending to vulnerability and suffering of others, which in turn shapes our sense of self as complete human beings, including our sensitivity to being able to relate to others. In so doing, we should accept suffering as being part of the human experience rather than trying to deny, disavow, or ignore suffering while concurrently striving for happiness. Such acts become exercises in profound vulnerability due to their emotionally tumultuous nature and their capacity to shape our identity, which are more difficult than we realise.

As leaders, it is critical that we have the courage to become intimately familiar with the toxicity of anger and the destructive role it plays in our leadership and choose a wiser path. We need to develop our patience, tolerance and consideration of others, genuinely understand the views of others, and be in action to find mutually acceptable and beneficial outcomes wherever possible. We need to surrender our tightly held worldviews of what we think we ought to be and instead be open to the views of others, without sacrificing what is truly important to us. If we need to be forceful, then we need to develop wisdom about our assertiveness and learn the very clear distinctions between this approach and toxic anger.

We need to exhibit the courage to face up to those things we fear most, including navigating unknown futures, actively challenging norms and assumptions, or prioritising our ethics in the interest of others. We also need the courage to admit our limited understanding of compassion and commit to improving through lived experience, education and relatedness, as well as understanding the limitations of rules and the importance of going beyond them with wisdom. We must also understand the limits of our personal exposure to mental harm, suffering and stress, and actively seek methods and assistance from others to nurture and protect ourselves.

Are we prepared to be accountable for our thoughts, words and actions in this pursuit, and how might we show this?

We need to be accountable for our actions, including those actions that contribute towards injustices produced by structural processes that cause suffering. That is, if we have access to power, wealth and resources and are therefore privileged, we have an obligation to remedy these injustices. To do this, we must be open to the needs and differences of others in our everyday interactions, as well as speaking and acting in ways that maintain our integrity and self-constancy. We must also acknowledge our moral responsibility, recognising that we are accountable to others for our actions, and we should conduct ourselves in a manner such that others can count on us.

Also, as a measure of accountability, if we are to navigate towards a more peaceful and compassionate world, then we must seek a world that is just for all. We must genuinely listen and understand the needs of others, and where those needs involve the desire for equitable access to power, wealth and resources to pursue happiness, well-being and flourishing, we should do all that we can within our power to aid them. We also need to value the processes of social engagement in policy and strategy development and decision-making, understand and appreciate the complexity of human and socio-political behaviour, treat citizens with dignity, and recognise them for their moral worth and innate rights as precious sentient beings.

At the same time, we can work with our governments to address questions of social difference (class, gender, race, religion, etc.), inequality, hierarchy, and injustice within communities that increase the otherwise avoidable vulnerability of citizens. Rather than taking a unilateral perspective on resilience (one size fits all), we could accelerate our efforts to work with communities to genuinely understand the different social needs and then work with our governments to address those needs. We could also be more generous in sharing our decision-making power with those citizens that we aim to serve and protect, affording them greater choice rather than forcing them to comply with our systems and processes.

We can also take responsibility for our own mistakes and seek to rectify them wherever possible, while accommodating the needs of others. We can proactively seek to do all within our power and control to protect others who have made genuine mistakes by taking responsibility on their behalf, or by being prepared to have difficult conversations regarding expectations.

Are we able to identify the ethics that are most important to us in shaping our identities as relational leaders and by which we would like to be known by?

It is critical that we recognise the ethics that we regard as most important in shaping our moral compass as a key aspect of our character. We need to gain insight and understanding into what it is that we will or will not accept—to understand not only what liberates us towards happiness, but what constrains us, in order to prevent bringing harm and suffering upon ourselves and others. The ethics that we consider personally most important help us to define the boundaries that give shape to our morality. If we fail to honour our moral compass, we suffer through self-betrayal and our sense of identity deteriorates. In short, when we move away from our moral compass, we have a weaker sense of who we truly are, and we suffer accordingly.

It is also important that we know that what we are doing are virtuous actions, that we choose these actions and choose them for their own sake (doing good for goodness' sake), and we do them from a firm and unchanging state by practicing integrity and constancy. In so doing, we avoid the need for reciprocity or recognition. We derive deep personal satisfaction from knowing we have done all in our power to do the right thing in the circumstances that have been presented to us.

Having identified the ethics most important to us, we need to dedicate ourselves to getting to know them, their complexity and sophistication, intimately. We must accept that upholding a virtuous disposition of character is one of the most challenging and worthy pursuits we could ever undertake and, at the same time, accepting that it is impossible to spontaneously achieve the perfection of virtue. Rather, it is a long and perilous journey that takes a lifetime in which to excel.

Are we able to draw from the wisdom of our lived experiences, as well as a wisdom that is beyond our own opinions?

The practical wisdom of our lived experience requires us to develop a desire to know the truth of our lives. This means that we need to comprehend the deeper meaning and significance of life events as they relate to our inner selves, as well as between ourselves and others. This requires us to accept the positive and negative aspects of human nature, the inherent limits of knowledge, and the propensity of life to be ambiguous, complex and uncertain. It also requires us to be reflexive and view all phenomena and events from multiple perspectives through self-awareness and insight, the capacity to self-examine, and the ability to develop compassion for ourselves and others.

Importantly, our knowledge about our lived experiences can only become wisdom by "realizing" the truth of that profound knowledge. It is only when we are moved, changed or transformed that we become wise. We also need to make strident efforts to improve, reflect, seek feedback and mentoring, and sustain effort as part of a life-long commitment to learning from our experiences.

Also, collapsing the distinction between knowing and doing is critical. Our innermost experiences extend far beyond our intellect, which wants to see everything physical or psychological analysed, determined and defined—but our innermost experiences cannot be dealt with in this way. In addition, we need to rely not only upon our own knowledge and life experiences, but also on reference points of timeless wisdom as taught by the sages that can be found in our art, music, poetry, literature, philosophy, theology, mythology, and other great bodies of knowledge.

More specifically, our lived experiences of vulnerability and suffering will be instructive in our relationality with others. However, while vulnerability establishes the basis of our relatedness, it is also indicative of future suffering. Therefore, we ought not to embrace vulnerability without qualification, but we do need to renounce our habitual denial of its existence. To do this, we need to develop our wisdom about when, how, who, where, and why we allow ourselves to be vulnerable.

Again, such wisdom cannot be derived simply through knowledge. To become wise about vulnerability means that it needs to be "experienced," to be "lived." We need to see, sense and feel what it is like to be vulnerable in the myriad circumstances of our lives. Therefore, vulnerability requires practice. It is not an automatic given, but it must be experientially cultivated over time between two or more people. These experiences will necessarily present us with the reality of our fallibility, mutability (tendency to change), unpredictability, and uncontrollability. There are realities whereby the outcome of these experiences cannot be known or orchestrated beforehand.

These experiences will also help us to set boundaries as to what we will or will not accept. They will help us be clear about our intentions towards others and proceed sensibly towards relatedness. They will open opportunities to change (ourselves and others), experience something new, and move from being to becoming—the ability to become the person that we desire to be, which honours our capacity for happiness, well-being and flourishing.

Are we clear about what it is we need to be most mindful of in our leadership?

The practice of mindfulness affords us the opportunity to deeply understand what causes us and others to become vulnerable and to suffer—and, just as importantly, to develop our wisdom about how to alleviate them. It allows us to bring attention to both the personal and institutional causes of suffering and ensures that we do not forget them. Mindfulness also allows us to become clear about our intentions towards ourselves and others—to think, speak and act with virtue with the intention of alleviating vulnerability and suffering.

When we are mindful about the vulnerability and suffering of others, it affords us the opportunity to address more skilfully some of the causes of that same vulnerability and suffering that may arise from our decisions. For example, we could be more mindful of the limitation of the ability of some citizens to exercise their agency as a factor of resilience, not because they are unwilling, but because they are locked into a set of structural, social, and/or economic circumstances from which they are unable to free themselves without proper institutional support. By better understanding this, we can begin to make better decisions and influence others in power more positively towards better decisions as well.

We could be more mindful of the need to ensure that citizens are fully consulted and engaged in our policy decision-making processes, including the need to better understand the suffering that exists within marginalised groups in our communities. We could be more mindful of the need to ensure that there is free and full information available to citizens when they make their choices about how to best protect themselves. We could be more mindful of what it is that citizens truly value rather than making assumptions on their behalf. In short, by being more mindful of the individual and social causes of suffering and vulnerability that we have discussed throughout this book, we begin the long road towards a better future for ourselves and those we seek to lead, serve and protect.

In summary

While all these questions are fundamental to relational leadership and deeply philosophical, by continuously answering and, over time, re-answering them founded upon the truth of our ethical premise, the validity of our arguments, the depth of our lived experiences, the exemplification of our thoughts, words and actions, and from the inspiration of others, then we are likely to have succeeded as a relational leader in alleviating the vulnerability and suffering of ourselves and others.

EPILOGUE

As I concluded the research for this book, I was asked to facilitate a discussion for a national forum of disaster management leaders. This forum had been tasked to give prioritisation to the recommendations of the Royal Commission into National Natural Disaster Arrangements that followed the devastating winter/spring/summer of 2019/2020 in Australia. As I facilitated the discussion and recorded the insights from the leaders, all of the burning questions that prompted me to begin this research emerged in my mind. However, this time, I had some empirically, epistemologically, and ontologically valid insights with which to answer these questions.

I was able to listen and observe with clarity the various discourses, shaped by influences such as neoliberalism, that forced these leaders to deny their own, their agencies, and their governments' vulnerability when having to face future crises such as those influenced by climate change. Despite the devastating and significant losses that were experienced during 2019/2020, many of these disaster management leaders appeared unmoved by them in their deliberations. Instead, the long-term practice of protecting the sovereign interests of their jurisdictions, including their financial interests, appeared to be more important than improving the well-being of citizens and reducing their suffering.

In addition, I observed decisions being made that prioritised cost-benefit analyses over citizen protection and shifted responsibilities for that protection towards citizens through calls for more education, awareness and compliance with government directives and warnings. At the same time, there was no discussion about the need for governments and their agencies to do better, increase their effectiveness, and reduce the excessive burden placed upon citizens (and non-human others) to provide protection and adapt against such overwhelming odds.

DOI: 10.4324/9781003499510-19

On the surface, nothing of significance appeared to have changed in the leadership discourse between pre- and post-catastrophic disasters. But something *had* changed; and that something was me. Despite the discourse that I witnessed in this forum, I could now see that these disaster management leaders, whom I would regard as "good people," were without an alternative view. Like me, they had been institutionalised by the strategies, policies, politics, and cultures within governments and disaster management that I had been exposed to prior to undertaking this research. However, unlike me, many were not conscious of how influential these factors could be when shaping their advice, as well as formulating and implementing policies and programmes to preserve or improve the well-being of human and non-human others.

The evidence they provided in their interviews, as presented in this book, is a testament to their potential to consciously think, speak and act differently in order to actively contest these influences when seeking to improve well-being, provide protection, and minimise suffering. The function of the research for this book has been to help turn that potentiality into reality.

In answering my "burning questions," my research was able to show that the greatest measure of success begins with the upholding of public trust and confidence, and the greatest mission, the reduction of suffering. However, my research has also shown that these are not enough. The upholding of public trust and confidence can only be achieved when all humans and non-humans have been afforded the opportunity to have accessed the fair distribution of social and material advantages, and meaningfully participated in or have been faithfully represented in decision-making processes. They must also have had their social, cultural and political differences recognised and respected, and achieved their livelihood and well-being goals. The greatest mission can only be achieved when it is universally recognised that the root causes of all human and non-human suffering (being excessive self-interest and self-importance, greed, anger, and ignorance) are present in the minds of all humans, and it is only when these causes of suffering are replaced with a virtuous intention to act with wisdom through the ethic of compassion that the suffering of humans and non-humans can be truly minimised.

INDEX

Note: Pages in *italics* represent figures and **bold** indicates tables in the text.

Printed in the United States
by Baker & Taylor Publisher Services